ID0878970

Defending Constantine

The Twilight of an Empire
and the Dawn of Christendom

Peter J. Leithart

IVP Academic
An imprint of InterVarsity Press
Downers Grove, Illinois

InterVarsity Press
P.O. Box 1400, Downers Grove, IL 60515-1426
World Wide Web: www.ivpress.com
E-mail: email@ivpress.com

InterVarsity Press® is the book-publishing division of InterVarsity Christian Fellowship/USA®, a movement of students and faculty active on campus at hundreds of universities, colleges and schools of nursing in the United States of America, and a member movement of the International Fellowship of Evangelical Students. For information about local and regional activities, write Public Relations Dept., InterVarsity Christian Fellowship/USA, 6400 Schroeder Rd., P.O. Box 7895, Madison, WI 53707-7895, or visit the IVCF website at <www.intervarsity.org>.

All Scripture quotations, unless otherwise indicated, are taken from the New American Standard Bible®, *copyright 1960, 1962, 1963, 1968, 1971, 1972, 1973, 1975, 1977, 1995 by The Lockman Foundation. Used by permission.*

Design: Cindy Kiple

Images: Polyptych of the Cross by Cristoforo Scacco at Museo Provinciale Campano, Capua, Italy. Scala/Art Resource, NY.

ISBN 978-0-8308-2722-0

Printed in the United States of America

Library of Congress Cataloging-in-Publication Data

Leithart, Peter J.
  Defending Constantine: the twilight of an empire and the dawn of
Christendom / Peter J. Leithart.
    p. cm.
  Includes bibliographical references (p.   ) and indexes.
  ISBN 978-0-8308-2722-0 (pbk.: alk. paper)
  1. Constantine I, Emperor of Rome, d. 337—Influence. 2. Church
history—Primitive and early church, ca. 30-600. 3.
Rome—History—Constantine I, the Great, 307-337. I. Title.
  BR180.L45 2010
  270.1092—dc22

                                                                    2010019863

P	19	18	17	16	15	14	13	12	11	10	9	8	7	6	5	4	3	2	1
Y	26	25	24	23	22	21	20	19	18	17	16	15	14	13	12	11	10			

To Dr. Paul W. Leithart

Beloved Physician, Father, Patriot, Friend

Above all, Follower of Jesus

Contents

Preface

Constantine has been a whipping boy for a long time, and still is today. In popular culture (Dan Brown, *Da Vinci Code*), among bestselling historians (James Carroll, *Constantine's Sword*), and among theologians (Stanley Hauerwas, John Howard Yoder and their followers), his name is identified with tyranny, anti-Semitism, hypocrisy, apostasy and heresy. He was a hardened power-politician who never really became Christian, a hypocrite who harnessed the energy of the church for his own political ends, a murderer, a usurper, an egotist.

Defending Constantine is a rather old-fashioned book. I am asking the traditional "Constantinian questions" that historians have long since tired of answering: Did he *really* convert? Did he control the church? Did he determine orthodoxy at the Council of Nicaea? Did he mandate that every Roman citizen become a Christian? How did he treat pagans and Jews and heretics? At least since Norman Baynes delivered a groundbreaking lecture,[1] there has been a growing consensus among English-speaking scholars on some central questions about the first Christian emperor. From an examination of Constantine's own writings, Baynes argued, against the critics of his day, that Constantine was a sincere Christian gripped with a

---

[1] Norman H. Baynes, *Constantine the Great and the Christian Church*, Raleigh Lecture on History (London: Humphrey Milford, 1929).

profound confidence that God had anointed and appointed him to ensure the expansion of the gospel to the Roman world and beyond. Today, few specialists in the period question the fact that Constantine was a "real" Christian, and those who want to dispute the accounts of his conversion do so because they think he grew up a Christian. Yet, though 1930 is a long time ago, Baynes's thesis has barely penetrated popular consciousness, or even the consciousness of scholars who are not fourth-century specialists. In this book, I summarize some results of the newer scholarship for a wider audience to provide a fairly detailed, fairly popular, and fairly fair account of Constantine's life and work.

It was a dramatic life, full of vivid scenes: his questionable origins, conceived, so one legend has it, in a one-night stand; his nighttime escape from Nicomedia across Europe to Bologne to reach his father; the vision of the cross that preceded his victory at Rome; his entry into the Council of Nicaea; the death of the heretic Arius in a Greek water closet in Alexandria; disguised bishop Athanasius confronting the emperor as he rode into Constantinople; Constantine's baptism and death and his burial as the "thirteenth apostle" in the Church of the Apostles. It is one of the epic lives in Western history, full of firsts and foundings. Constantine was the first overtly Christian Roman emperor, the first emperor to support the church, the first emperor to call and participate in a church council, the founder of Constantinople and thereby the founder of the Byzantine Empire, which lasted for the next millennium. Without sacrificing accuracy, I have attempted to capture some of the drama, some of the epic scope, of Constantine.

Writing a life of Constantine, though, is only one of the four aims I have in this book. Readers who enjoy a fight will be happy that here biography serves the interests of polemic, and as the book progresses biography recedes as polemic comes to the forefront. By the final chapter I have abandoned biography almost completely. Nearly everything about Constantine is disputed, from the date of his birth to the sincerity of his conversion to his exact role in the Council of Nicaea. Again, I summarize the results of recent scholarship to take sides in those debates and to rebut the popular caricatures that are still widespread.

My main polemical target, though, is a theological one, and this theological polemic opens up the third aim of the book. *Constantinianism* is the name given by Yoder,[2] Hauerwas, and their increasing tribe to what they consider a heretical mindset and set of habits that have distorted Christian faith since (at least) the fourth century. Most of my argument is directed at Yoder, who provided the most sophisticated and systematic treatment of the concept. In part my argument is historical; Yoder gets the fourth century wrong in many particulars, and this distorts his entire reading of church history, which is a hinge of his theological project. The heart of my polemic against Yoder, though, is theological. In Yoder's telling, the church "fell" in the fourth century (or thereabouts) and has not yet recovered from that fall. This misconstrues the theological significance of Constantine, and in the final chapter I offer an alternative account. I will not give away that secret now, but I can tell you it has something to do with sacrifice. As always, one aim in this book is to contribute to the formation of a theology that does not simply *inform* but *is* a social science.[3]

My final aim is a practical one. I have found that, far from representing a fall for the church, Constantine provides in many respects a model for Christian political practice. At the very least, his reign provides rich material for reflection on a whole series of perennial political-theological questions: about religious toleration and coercion, about the legitimacy of Christian involvement in political life, about a Christian ruler's relationship to the church, about how Christianity should influence civil law, about the propriety of violent coercion, about the legitimacy of empire.

In that respect, it is a propitious time to be writing a book on Constantine. Never before have American Christians been so exercised by the question of American empire. In the back of my mind I have been asking,

---

[2]The Mennonite theologian and ethicist John Howard Yoder (1927-1997) was for many years the world's most prominent theological proponent of pacifism and was probably the most influential Mennonite theologian who ever lived. He studied at the University of Basel, Switzerland, under Karl Barth, Oscar Cullman, and other prominent theologians and philosophers, then taught at the Goshen Biblical Seminary (now called Associated Mennonite Biblical Seminary) and later at the University of Notre Dame. He influenced theologians from many different traditions (most prominently Stanley Hauerwas of Duke University) and is responsible, more than any other American theologian, for the antirealist direction of contemporary Christian thought about politics. His most important book, *The Politics of Jesus* (1972), included an assault on the theological and ethical inconsistencies in the work of realist Reinhold Niebuhr.

[3]The notion of theology as a social science comes from John Milbank, *Theology and Social Theory: Beyond Secular Reason*, 2nd ed. (Oxford: Blackwell, 2006). In contrast to many modern theologians who consider social science to be foundational for theology, Milbank argues that classical orthodoxy contains its own account of social and political life.

What, if anything, can we learn about the proper Christian response to the wars in Iraq and Afghanistan from examining the church's relation to Constantine Caesar? I offer only incomplete answers to those questions here, but this book will, I hope, be followed by another where I can give more thorough and direct attention to imperialism.

These political issues are of interest to Christians throughout the world, not only in the U.S. What Philip Jenkins calls the "Southern churches" look to be forming the "next Christendom." Given that prospect, root-and-branch rejection of "Constantinianism" or "Christendom" is doubly wrong-headed. First, insofar as Northern churches still set trends for the Southern churches, our hostility to our own heritage of Christian politics encourages the Global South to ignore the history we ignore. If the South is forming into a new Christendom, it is important that it learn from both the successes and the failures of the first Christendom. Northern Christians will be irresponsible if we have nothing more to say than "Don't try it. It went badly last time."

Second, the Northern churches cannot presume to be a "teaching church" to the Southern "listening church." We are, I trust, long past that kind of paternalism. But if the Southern churches think that a new Christendom, Christian nations, Christian legal systems, Christian international alliances are worth pursuing, it is condescending for us to dismiss their efforts with a world-weary shrug and a knowing shake of the head. By listening to the Southern churches, we Northern Christians may be able to examine our own history of Christian civilization with deeper sympathy. And that could only benefit all of us.

Acknowledgments

I have many people to thank for help on this project. Aaron Rench, my literary agent, convinced me to do the book when I was lukewarm. I am very glad he persisted.

I had lively and beneficial conversations with several students, colleagues, and friends over the course of my research. My biweekly coffee meetings with Brad Littlejohn were always challenging. I had fewer opportunities to discuss the themes of this book with Justin Hughes, Davey Henreckson and Josh Davis, but they all contributed and kept me honest. Lisa Beyeler guided me to a better understanding of Constantine's architecture. In conversations with Joshua Appel, Toby Sumpter, Doug Jones and Brendan O'Donnell my ideas have been clarified.

During the spring of 2009 I taught a course on Constantine and Constantinianism, which gave me a chance to coalesce my research; several students provided research help on issues that I could not investigate myself. Colleagues at New St. Andrews College were generous with their time. Tim Griffith assisted with several Latin questions, and Chris Schlect helped me see the complexity of church finances in the medieval period. I presented a version of the final chapter at the Graduate Forum in fall 2009, and I benefited from questions from Roy Atwood and others.

I also had help from scholars who know what they are talking about: Robert Louis Wilken was generous in answering questions and providing bibliographic and other advice; Timothy Barnes graciously responded to emails out of the blue and provided me with an essay of his that I had no access to; David Rankin guided me on some details of Tertullian; Eric Enlow gave me bibliographical help on Roman law; exchanges with Charlie Collier about Yoder helped me, I trust, read him more accurately and charitably, and Charlie also provided a copy of his stimulating recent Ph.D. thesis; Andrew Motyl kindly provided me with an electronic copy of an article I had trouble locating; Bill Cavanaugh read portions of the book and pointed out sizable weak spots in my argument; and Steven Wedgeworth read through the first four chapters and suggested several improvements. Two of my graduate students, Justin Hughes and Stephen Long, helped me revise the original manuscript by proofreading and correcting my Latin, saving me much embarrassment on both scores. My editor at IVP, Dan Reid, was encouragingly excited about this book and offered helpful suggestions to make it more accessible for readers; Dan also forwarded me enthusiastic comments and suggestions from an outside reader.

My family assisted in various ways. My son Woelke provided invaluable research aid. My sons Jordan, Sheffield and Christian each had the misfortune to catch me on a day when I was charged up about things Constantinian, and they listened to my rantings with patient good cheer. They will receive their reward. My wife, Noel, also had to listen as I droned on; she seemed to be as interested as I try to be when she talks about midwifery.

Early on, I had several lengthy conversations with my father, Dr. Paul Leithart, which convinced me that I had done enough research to begin writing. Dad has always been deeply interested in my writing, and I suspect, given his long engagement in politics, that he will find this book of particular interest. I owe more of my interest in political questions to him than I realize, and while he may differ with or be baffled by some parts of this book, I could not have written it without his lifelong example of faithful service to the city of God, a service that does not forget the city of man. With great love and deep gratitude, I dedicate this book to him.

1

Sanguinary Edicts

*Amongst our other regulations for the permanent advantage of the
common weal, we have hitherto studied to reduce all things to a conformity
with the ancient laws and public discipline of the Romans.*

EDICT OF GALERIUS, 311

Hardened by a lifetime of military and civil service, the emperor Diocletian (285-305) was no coward. According to the *Historia Augusta*, he
was "an outstanding man and wise, devoted to the commonwealth, devoted to his kindred, duly prepared to face whatever the occasion demanded, forming plans that were always deep though sometimes over-
bold, and one who could by prudence and exceeding firmness hold in
check the impulses of a restless spirit."[1] Eutropius casts him as a man of
"crafty disposition, with much sagacity, and keen penetration" who "was
willing to gratify his own disposition to cruelty in such a way as to throw
the odium upon others"—in all, "a very active and able prince."[2]

Contemporaries described him as an "investigator of things to come," a

---

[1] *Historia Augusta*, selections available at <http://penelope.uchicago.edu/Thayer/E/Roman/
Texts/Historia_Augusta/home.html>. The *Historia Augusta* is unreliable, often fictional, but
it does reflect a prevailing view of Diocletian's character. The Latin reads, "Virum insignem,
callidum, amantem rei publicae, amantem suorum et ad omnia quae tempus quaesiverat tem-
peratum, consilii semper alti, nonnumquam tamen effrontis sed prudentia et nimia pervicacia
motus inquieti pectoris comprimentis."

[2] *Abridgement of Roman History*, trans. John Selby Watson, available at <www.forumromanum.
org/literature/eutropius>. The Latin reads, "Diocletianus moratus callide fuit, sagax praeterea
et admodum subtilis ingenii, et qui severitatem suam aliena invidia vellet explere."

man "devoted to holy usages." Surrounded by priests and soothsayers, he examined entrails for clues to the future and started at lightning bolts. Diocletian believed his rise to the imperial purple had been foretold by a Druid priestess. He elevated Maximian to the position of second Augustus because the two shared a birthday, and when Galerius was later given the position of Caesar he took the name Maximianus "in order to effect a magic bond with the proven loyalty of the elder Maximian."[3]

Diocletian was no coward, but the incident in 299 was alarming. Visiting Antioch, he had participated in a sacrifice that failed. Priests slaughtered the animal, and the *haruspex*, a soothsayer who foretold the future by reading entrails, stepped forward to take the liver from the hands of the servant. Planting his left foot on the ground, he raised his right foot on a stone and bent low to examine the liver.[4] He found none of the usual indicators. They slaughtered another animal, and another. Nothing. Plutarch had written centuries before about the silencing of the oracles, and the same was happening to Diocletian. His recovery of the Pax Romana was, Diocletian firmly believed, the product of a *pax deorum,* the peace of the gods. Roman sacrifice was at the center of that peace. It was the chief religious act, the act by which Romans communicated and communed with the gods, keeping the gods happy so Romans could be happy.[5] If the gods stopped talking with the emperor, what would happen to Rome? Did the failed sacrifice in Antioch foretell the end of sacrifice? Did it foretell the end of Rome?

---

[3]The information in the foregoing paragraph is from Jacob Burckhardt, *The Age of Constantine the Great,* trans. Moses Hadas (Berkeley: University of California Press, 1983).

[4]For this stance, see David S. Potter, "Roman Religion," in *Life, Death and Entertainment,* ed. David S. Potter and D. J. Mattingly (Ann Arbor: University of Michigan Press, 1999), pp. 148-49.

[5]Paula Fredricksen, *Augustine and the Jews: A Christian Defense of Jews and Judaism* (New York: Doubleday, 2008), p. 89: "Cult, the ancients assumed, made gods happy; and when gods were happy, humans flourished. Conversely, not receiving cult made gods unhappy; and when gods were unhappy, they made people unhappy." Sacrifice was the central religious act in all ancient religions, and that includes the religions of the Greco-Roman classical world. On sacrifice in the Greek world, see Maria-Zoe Petroupoulou, *Animal Sacrifice in Ancient Greek Religion, Judaism and Christianity, 100 BC to AD 200* (Oxford: Oxford University Press, 2008) and Marcel Detienne and Jean-Pierre Vernant, *The Cuisine of Sacrifice Among the Greeks* (Chicago: University of Chicago Press, 1998); on Roman sacrifice, see George Heyman, *The Power of Sacrifice: Roman and Christian Discourses in Conflict* (Washington, D.C.: Catholic University of America Press, 2007), and John Scheid, *Quand faire, c'est croire: Les rites sacrificiels des Romains* (Paris: Aubier, 2005).

What had gone wrong? The presiding diviner investigated and concluded that "profane persons" had interrupted the rites, and attention focused on Christians in Diocletian's court who had made the sign of the cross to ward off demons during the proceedings. Diocletian was outraged and demanded that all members of his court offer sacrifice, a test designed to weed out Christians. Soldiers were required to sacrifice or leave the sacred Roman army.[6] At least at the heart of the empire, in the court and in the army, sacrifices would continue without being polluted by Christians. At the heart of the empire, where it really mattered, gods and men would remain in communion. With the purge of Christians, the problem seemed solved. The miasma was expelled and the gods were satisfied. Diocletian was secure.

The problem, however, had not been solved. An imperial letter probably issued in March 302[7] to the proconsul of Africa confronted another threat to the empire, the dualistic religion of Manichaeanism. Mani was a Persian teacher whose religion, along with other Eastern religions, had been seeping into the Roman Empire and undermining traditional Roman pieties. Diocletian's letter was filled with encouragement of "Roman virtue" and condemnation of "Persian vice," and ended with an exhortation to preserve the *tranquillitas* of the empire by suppressing dangerous Oriental innovations.[8] Diocletian insisted that "it is wrong to . . . desert the ancient religion for some new one, for it is the height of criminality to try and revive doctrines that were settled once for all by the ancients."[9] This "superstitious doctrine of a most worthless and depraved kind" must be stopped.[10] Manichaean leaders were to be burned along with their books, their dis-

---

[6]Lactantius *Death* 10; Timothy D. Barnes, *Constantine and Eusebius* (Cambridge, Mass.: Harvard University Press, 1981). Timothy D. Barnes ("Sossianus Hierocles and the Antecedents of the 'Great Persecution,' " *Harvard Studies in Classical Philology* 80 [1976]: 245) says that this likely occurred in Antioch. A. H. M. Jones (*Constantine and the Conversion of Europe* [Toronto: University of Toronto Press, 1978], p. 49) dates this incident to the previous year, 298.

[7]The date 297 is sometimes given, but Barnes ("Sossianus," pp. 247-50) argues in detail for the later date.

[8]Simon Corcoran, *The Empire of the Tetrarchs: Imperial Pronouncements and Government, AD 284-324,* rev. ed., Oxford Classical Monographs (Oxford: Oxford University Press, 2000), pp. 135-36.

[9]Quoted in Charles Matson Odahl, *Constantine and the Christian Empire* (London: Routledge 2004), p. 66.

[10]Quoted in Ramsay MacMullen, *Constantine* (London: Croom Helm, 1987), p. 22.

ciples decapitated or sent to the mines.[11]

The parallels with Christianity were not lost on Diocletian. Like Manichaeanism, Christianity had come from the East and was non- and perhaps anti-Roman; its unpatriotic teachings undermined civic virtue. As the protector of the empire, Diocletian felt as bound to fight off an invasion of Christians and Manichaeans as he did to turn back attacks from Persians and Goths.[12]

Still the problem was not solved. Several years after the failed sacrifice, Diocletian was back in Antioch when a Christian deacon, Romanus, burst in on another imperial sacrifice loudly denouncing the worship of demons. Diocletian ordered that his tongue be cut out and sentenced him to prison, where he was executed,[13] but the emperor knew something more needed to be done. Wintering in Nicomedia the following year, Diocletian consulted with his Caesar Galerius about the problem. "Arrogant and ambitious" and a "fanatical pagan,"[14] Galerius urged Diocletian to issue a general order against the Christians. Diocletian hesitated. He needed divine guidance, but when he consulted Apollo's oracle at Didyma it informed him that "just ones" had silenced the prophecy.[15] Years later Constantine recalled the incident, which he witnessed while serving in Diocletian's court. Calling on God as a witness, Constantine remembered how the "unhappy, truly unhappy" Diocletian, "laboring under mental delusion, made earnest enquiry of his attendants as to who these righteous ones were" and learned that "they were doubtless the Christians." Diocletian lost no time in issuing "those sanguinary edicts," which Constantine said were "traced, if I may so express myself, with a sword's point dipped in blood."[16]

For the Latin Christian rhetorician Lactantius and Eusebius, bishop of Caesarea, the Caesar Galerius—who was, to refined Romans like Lactantius, a brutal, pagan, barely Romanized barbarian[17]—was the evil genius

---

[11]Barnes, "Sossianus," p. 247.

[12]The notion that Christianity was unpatriotic is found in pagan apologists like Celsus and Porphyry. See Odahl, *Constantine and the Christian Empire*, p. 33.

[13]Barnes, *Constantine and Eusebius*, pp. 20-21.

[14]Ibid., p. 19.

[15]Ibid., p. 21.

[16]Eusebius *Life* 2.51.

[17]Lactantius's description of Galerius's character is found in *Death* 9, and in 11 he attributes Galerius's anti-Christian bias to the influence of his mother.

behind the edict. Many modern historians discount the tale,[18] but there is evidence that the more tolerantly pagan Diocletian was persuaded by his junior colleague to initiate the general persecution. Galerius had never quite sung in harmony with the other rulers of the empire, as Julian the Apostate was later to say. His triumphal arch that still stands in Thessaloniki highlights his personal exploits in his war with the Persians. One panel shows him "defeating the Persian king in direct hand-to-hand combat."[19]

In 303, Galerius was at the height of his power. It had been a long recovery. Seven years earlier, in 296, he had lost a battle to the Sassinid Persian king Narseh, and Diocletian had added to his humiliation by forcing him to walk for a mile in front of Diocletian's carriage, vested in his imperial robes.[20] Two years later, Galerius recovered his honor by defeating the Persians in another campaign. His victory gave him considerable weight, and Diocletian, though senior emperor, had come to fear his junior colleague. The gods must be with Galerius, Diocletian thought. Galerius decided to capitalize on his recovery of *ethos* by jockeying for advantage. When the persecution began, Galerius held the second position in the Eastern empire. In the West, Maximian was the chief, with Constantius, Constantine's father, his imperial lieutenant. If Diocletian died before Maximian, Galerius reasoned, Galerius would be marginalized; it would be the two Western emperors against him. He needed to protect his power, and he discerned that the Christian problem could be turned to his advantage. He hated Christians, while Constantius was sympathetic to them. If he could

---

[18]The most thorough study is P. S. Davies, "The Origin and Purpose of the Persecution of AD 303," *Journal of Theological Studies* 40, no. 1 (1989), which systematically eliminates all possible sources of Lactantius's information. H. A. Drake (*Constantine and the Bishops: The Politics of Intolerance* [Baltimore: Johns Hopkins University Press, 2000], pp. 142-44) suggests that Lactantius is employing a technique of ancient history writing by which writers "convey their own analyses through fictional speeches." Drake concludes that Diocletian was manipulated into beginning the persecution and that the failed sacrifice was "rigged." That may be, but first, Lactantius may have had access to court gossip, and second, even if he made up the specifics of the conference, he presumably had some grounds for describing the interplay of Augustus and Caesar in the way he did. David S. Potter (*The Roman Empire at Bay, AD 180-395*, Routledge History of the Ancient World [London: Routledge, 2004], p. 338) wisely notes, however, that "conversations between important men, even in camera, have a way of becoming public knowledge."

[19]Raymond Van Dam, *The Roman Revolution of Constantine* (Cambridge: Cambridge University Press, 2008), p. 244.

[20]Ibid., p. 243; Potter, *Roman Empire*, pp. 292-93.

persuade Diocletian to attack the church, Galerius would be on the majority side of imperial religious policy and his rival Constantius would be marginalized.[21] So at that private conference in 302, the vigorous Galerius had
firmly nudged the vacillating Diocletian toward persecution.[22]

Diocletian himself believed he had plenty of reason to mount his offensive. Not only did Christians silence the oracles, but they, along with
eunuch sympathizers in court, seemed to have been behind the fire that
roared through Diocletian's palace in Nicomedia several days after the
first edict was issued. More deeply, Diocletian shared with many Romans
the deepening suspicion that Christians were not quite Roman; their refusal to sacrifice could mean nothing else.[23]

He began on February 23, 303. Dates meant everything to Diocletian.
February 23 was the festival of Terminalia (Limits). Established by Numa
in the distant Roman past, Terminalia was a festival of boundaries. Neighbors would gather at border stones consecrated to Jupiter, offer sacrifice,
and share a meal to maintain friendly relations across property boundaries.
Good fences make good neighbors, and good fences, to the Romans, were
best secured by sacrifice. Rome had been founded when Romulus traced
the *pomerium* and killed his brother to protect the sacred space of the city
from violation. Roman homes were sacred, and as the *pater patriae*, the
emperor was the guarantor of the sanctity of the great house that was the
city and empire.[24] Terminalia was also part of the public cult, an annual
reconsecration of the boundaries that separated the sacred Roman from
the profane non-Roman world.[25] As Jupiter's incarnation on earth, Diocletian was especially charged with guarding the frontiers, maintaining the
sacredness of Rome and its empire, and expelling any pollution that might
infect it and bring down the wrath of the gods. As the high priest of the
empire, he had purged the Manichaean contagion. Now he needed to deal
with the Christians, who posed an even more serious threat. The sect of
Christianity had grown out of Judaism, but Diocletian was perfectly tolerant of Jewish citizens. They had their own traditions and had the emperor's

---

[21]Ibid., 338.

[22]Barnes, *Constantine and Eusebius*, p. 19; Odahl, *Constantine and the Christian Empire*; Van
Dam, *Roman Revolution*, 164.

[23]Van Dam, *Roman Revolution*, 146.

[24]Heyman, *Power of Sacrifice*, pp. 13, 47.

[25]Details in Dioysius of Halicarnassus, *Roman Antiquities*, 2.74.

permission to check out of the imperial cult. But at least they had the sense to keep to themselves. These Christians were everywhere. They mixed with other Romans in the markets and even at the court and in the army. Jews could be kept in place, but it would take some fine-grained surgery to remove the cancer of Christianity.[26] Rome would be saved by a baptism in blood, a sacrifice of Christian blood.

On Terminalia in A.D. 303, Diocletian issued the first of what would become four decrees of persecution.[27] The first edict prohibited Christian assemblies and required that churches be razed, Scriptures seized and burned, and Christians expelled from high positions in government and the army. Christians had no recourse. Christians with legal rights lost them, and Christians who were imperial freedpersons reverted to enslavement.[28] Over the next year, three further edicts expanded the scope of the persecution. During the summer of 303, Diocletian ordered the arrest of Christian clergymen, and in November of that year, with prisons bursting with arrested Christians, he issued a constitution at the celebration of his *vicennalia*, the twentieth anniversary of his rule, offering clergy freedom for the price of sacrifice. Early in 304, the emperor demanded that all citizens of the empire sacrifice on pain of imprisonment or death.[29] Over the year this turned into a general persecution, as the bloodshed spread from the emperor's capital at Nicomedia, modern Izmit, on the Sea of Marmara, to Egypt, Phrygia and Palestine. Instead of focusing on the emperor's court, it included, at least theoretically, every resident of the empire. The edicts, particularly the fourth, were unevenly enforced. Even

---

[26]G. W. Bowersock, *Martyrdom and Rome* (Cambridge: Cambridge University Press, 1995). This is a crucial point, since it demonstrates the continuity between the church of the martyrs and the church under Constantine. Neither was an isolated ghetto community; if Christians had been isolated, they would have been left alone.

[27]Johannes Roldanus, *The Church in the Age of Constantine: The Theological Challenges* (London: Ashgate, 2006), p. 30; Barnes, *Constantine and Eusebius*, p. 21.

[28]G. E. M. de Ste. Croix, "Aspects of the 'Great' Persecution," in *Harvard Theological Review* 47, no. 2 (1954): 75-76, and Potter, *Roman Empire*, p. 337, both summarize the contents of the first decree.

[29]Corcoran, *Empire of the Tetrarchs*, 179-82; Simon Corcoran, "Before Constantine," in *The Cambridge Companion to the Age of Constantine*, ed. Noel Lenski (Cambridge: Cambridge University Press, 2006), p. 52; Roldanus, *Church in the Age of Constantine*, p. 30; Odahl, *Constantine and the Christian Empire*, p. 69; Jones, *Constantine and the Conversion of Europe*, pp. 50-51; Drake, *Constantine and the Bishops*, p. 164. Eusebius (*Church History*, 8.14.9) mentions a fifth edict of 309, issued by Maximinus in the East, to revitalize paganism by rebuilding temples, appointing priests, and requiring sacrifice (cf. Corcoran, *Empire of the Tetrarchs*, pp. 185-86).

a single emperor was always dependent on the reliability and energy of provincial rulers, and by 303, four emperors split the empire among themselves; not all of them were as eager to persecute Christians as Diocletian was. Still, sporadic as it may have been in many places, the persecution created an "atmosphere of constant menace."[30]

There had been general persecutions before. Fifty years earlier, Decius had been the first emperor to require universal sacrifice,[31] and a few years later Valerian had launched a general persecution. After Valerian's capture and humiliating execution by the Persians, though, his son Gallienus recognized the church as a legal corporation, and thereafter emperors refrained from attacking the church for nearly a half century.[32] The year 303 was different. Diocletian returned to persecution, with unprecedented ferocity. When the Romans put their minds to it, their tortures could be exquisite.

After the palace fire, Christians in Nicomedia "perished wholesale and in heaps, some butchered with the sword, other fulfilled by fire." Some Christians were so eager to share in martyrdom that they leaped into the flames. Some were tied up, placed in boats, and thrust out from the beach. A Christian named Peter refused to comply with the order to sacrifice. Soldiers stripped him, hoisted him naked, and whipped him until his body was a bloody pulp, his bones sticking through the flesh and skin. Still he refused to sacrifice. The soldiers brought vinegar and salt from the mess and poured it over his wounds. Finding raw meat unappetizing, even when spiced up, they decided to cook him, slowly roasting parts of his body while trying to keep him alive. He was still refusing to sacrifice when he died.[33]

In the Thebais, Christians were "torn to bits from head to foot with potsherds like claws." In the same place, a woman was hung upside down, completely naked. Others were torn in two: each leg was tied to a bent tree, and then the soldiers would let the boughs "fly back to their normal position; thus they managed to tear apart the limbs of their victims in a moment." A Christian woman in Antioch convinced her daughters that

---

[30]The phrase is from de Ste. Croix, "Aspects," p. 105.
[31]Corcoran, "Before Constantine," p. 36.
[32]Drake (*Constantine and the Bishops*, p. 114) links Valerian's defeat and the cessation of persecution, as does Barnes ("Sossianus," p. 241).
[33]Eusebius, *Church History*, 8.6.4.

they should preempt the persecutors by seeking safety in death, and they threw themselves into a river.[34]

Sharp reeds were pounded into the fingers and under the nails of Christians in Pontus; molten lead was poured down their backs, "roasting the vital parts of the body"; their bowels were sliced open and sexual organs cut off. It was almost a "prize competition." Eventually the authorities determined that shedding the blood of citizens was in poor taste, a pollution of the city, and resorted to more humane methods. Eusebius's description drips with irony: "The beneficence of the humane imperial authority [ought] to be extended to everybody, no one henceforth being punished with death; they had already ceased to impose this penalty on us, thanks to the emperor's humanity." Yet imperial humanity left something to be desired: "orders were then issued that the eyes should be gouged out and one leg maimed," so that "as a result of this 'humanity' shown by God's enemies, it is no longer possible to count the enormous number of people who first had the right eye hacked out with a sword and cauterized with fire, and the left foot rendered useless by branding-irons applied to the joints."[35] Eusebius's catalog of maimings at Pontus seems morbid to many today, but for him it was the Christian equivalent to Coriolanus's displaying the scars he suffered for the sake of Mother Rome. Even the apostle Paul had boasted to the Galatians that he bore the stigmata of Christ.

To individual martyrs were added towns of Christians. Roman soldiers attacked a village of Christians in Phrygia, killing every citizen and burning houses along with women and children. The city was razed, Eusebius claimed, because "all those who inhabited the town without exception, the curator himself and the magistrates and everyone else in office and the whole people, professed themselves Christians."[36]

The total number of martyrs is impossible to determine.[37] In the West, the persecution ran out of energy a few years after it began, as Constantius refused to comply and then Constantine overturned the persecution edict in 306-7. In the East, things were different. In the Thebaid, years went by

---

[34]Ibid.

[35]Ibid., 8.12.9.

[36]Quoted in MacMullen, *Constantine,* p. 27.

[37]Assuming that Eusebius records every martyr in Syria Palaestina, de Ste. Croix concludes that ninety were executed in that province ("Aspects," p. 101) and generally estimates that "dozens or scores rather than hundreds" were put to death (p. 102).

when Christians were regularly put to death in groups of ten, twenty, or thirty. "At other times a hundred men would be slain in a single day."[38] Despite the warnings of their bishops and priests, many actively sought martyrdom by offering themselves to provincial governors, ostentatiously tearing up imperial decrees, or otherwise calling attention to themselves. Few were chased down and arrested, and many complied quietly to protect themselves.[39] Because Christianity had expanded to the countryside, however, it was no longer possible to arrest its growth. Christians in villages resisted valiantly, and the church had simply become too scattered to suppress.[40]

Romans could be cruel, but there is something more than cruelty behind these tortures. Romans thought long and hard about not only the pain of their modes of punishment but the rhetoric of punishment. Punishments were humiliating but not, the Romans thought, inequitable. Romans believed criminals got exactly what they deserved. Roman punishments were often enactments of the crimes committed. Sometime in the first century B.C., one Selurus, calling himself "son of Etna," gathered an army and overran the region around Mount Etna. In Rome Strabo saw Selurus "torn to pieces by wild beasts at an organized gladiatorial fight." He was raised on "a tall contraption, as though on Etna," and then the "contraption suddenly broke up and collapsed, and he went down with it into the fragile cages of wild-beasts." His death reenacted the *superbia* of his rise and then his sudden and shameful fall.[41] According to John's Gospel, Jesus' death was a parodic coronation and enthronement, but for the Romans every cross was a mocking throne for rebels, especially slaves who had "lifted themselves up" above their station.[42] Martyrdoms were similar. Peter of Nicomedia's martyrdom was a meal—the Roman soldiers were symbolically cannibalizing him. More commonly, the tortures resemble sacrificial procedures: human beings were flayed and dismembered and

---

[38]*Church History*, 8.9.3.

[39]On voluntary martyrdom, see Bowersock, *Martyrdom and Rome*; de Ste. Croix, "Aspects."

[40]W. H. C. Frend ("The Failure of Persecutions in the Roman Empire," *Past and Present* 16 [1959]: 20, 26) emphasizes the importance of the demographic shift.

[41]K. M. Coleman, "Fatal Charades: Roman Executions Staged as Mythological Enactments," *Journal of Roman Studies* 80 (1990): 53. Bowersock (*Martyrdom and Rome*, p. 18) makes the same connection, also citing Coleman's article.

[42]Joel Marcus, "Crucifixion as Parodic Exaltation," *Journal of Biblical Literature* 125, no. 1 (1996).

burned like animals offered to the gods. One way or another, the Romans said, Christians would offer to the gods. Timid Christians could be compelled, and the bolder ones could be made into living sacrifices. Occasionally the logic of execution was more overt. Perpetua refused to die in the garb of a priestess of Ceres, but her executioners forced it on her to show that Christian criminals fulfilled the double significance of the term "the condemned" (*damnati* [masc.] and *damnatae* [fem.]), which referred to both the offering priest(ess) and the offered sacrifice.[43]

PERSECUTION, POLITICAL AND RELIGIOUS

"Such was the mild spirit of antiquity that the nations were less attentive to the difference than to the resemblance of their religious worship," Edward Gibbon wrote from the comfort of his study. He avowed that Roman magistrates who persecuted Christians did so reluctantly, "strangers" as they were to the "inflexible obstinacy" and "furious zeal" of bigoted Christians. If Christians were persecuted, they had only themselves to blame: "as they were actuated, not by the furious zeal of bigots, but by the temperate policy of legislators, [the officials'] contempt must often have relaxed, and humanity must frequently have suspended, the execution of those laws which they enacted against the humble and obscure followers of Christ."[44] Ever creative, Jacob Burckhardt found hints that Christians were plotting to convert the emperor and take over the empire, and argued that Diocletian persecuted in defense of his fragile empire; his actions are those of a man "on track of a plot."[45]

Gibbon, Burckhardt and other modern historians draw a delicate veil across the horrors of the Roman persecution. Well they might. Some Roman magistrates were reluctant to force a showdown with the Christians, fearing that the Christians might make them look foolish. Officials did not want to risk giving the martyrs a victory.[46] Still, it is hard to make the Romans look noble and businesslike when they are flaying Christians

---

[43]Coleman, "Fatal Charades," p. 66. The point can be made from the other direction as well: Christians applied the category of sacrifice to the martyr (Heyman, *Power of Sacrifice*, chap. 4).

[44]Edward Gibbon, *The Decline and Fall of the Roman Empire*, 3 vols. (New York: Modern Library, 1982), 1:31, 33; 2:87; quoted in Drake, *Constantine and the Bishops*, pp. 21-23.

[45]Burckhardt, *Age of Constantine the Great*, pp. 252-55.

[46]David S. Potter, "Martyrdom as Spectacle," in *Theater and Society in the Classical World*, ed. Ruth Scodel (Ann Arbor: University of Michigan Press, 1993), pp. 61-65.

alive, and it is even more difficult to make Christians look like ignorant zealots when they are treated with such intense hatred.

Faced with the actual practice of Roman torture and execution, it is also difficult to maintain the common distinction between theologically motivated persecution and secular, political persecution. Voltaire hinted at this distinction. From Romulus to the Christians, he argued, Romans persecuted no one. Even Nero persecuted no one for religious belief but because Christians, carried away by their own passions, set fire to Rome. When the Romans did finally get around to persecuting Christians, it was not on religious grounds but for reasons of state, and in any case, the persecutions were not as bad as Christian apologists say. Simply being a Christian was not enough to get one condemned. "St. Gregory Thaumaturgus and St. Denis, bishop of Alexandria, . . . were not put to death," even though they "lived at the same time as St. Cyprian." It must be that Cyprian "fell a victim to personal and powerful enemies, under the pretext of calumny or reasons of State, which are so often associated with religion, and that the former were fortunate enough to escape the malice of men."[47]

In 1882, Frederick Pollock gave the distinction its classical form in his essay "Theory of Persecution."[48] Though Pollock ultimately concluded that modern states have outgrown persecution, he regarded "modern persecution for the sake of public welfare" as more rational, because more testable, than the "theological persecution" of the church and state during the Middle Ages. No one can prove that heresy endangers the soul, and persecution founded on the desire to protect people from perdition cannot be proved useful. On the contrary, modern societies, which tolerate heresy, have proven that heresy is *not* socially destructive, and so modern states have ceased persecuting even while laws permitting persecution remain on the books.

Even Roman persecution is more defensible than Christian. Romans had no "distinctively theological incitement to persecution." Believing they had a corner on the truth, however, medieval Christians became intolerant of error out of love for the wandering soul of human beings. Roman persecution of Christians was "tribal." True, the gods figured into the

---

[47]Voltaire, *On Toleration*, available at classicliberal.tripod.com/voltaire/toleration.html, accessed June 10, 2009.

[48]Frederick Pollock, *Essays in Jurisprudence and Ethics* (London: Macmillan, 1882), pp. 144-75.

picture, but they figured into a *political* picture. Regarding the gods as "the most exalted officers of the state," Romans naturally saw Christians as either "a standing insult to the gods" or "a standing menace to the Government," but in either case "bad citizens." Christians who refused to honor the gods who are guarantors of Roman *imperium* were more than a nuisance; they endangered the prosperity and existence of Rome itself. Roman persecution was thus "essentially a measure of public safety." For Roman emperors, "the removal of the danger . . . is not merely justifiable, but a plain duty of self-preservation."[49] Romans did not persecute from bigotry and zeal, as Christians later did, but out of political necessity.

But then we are brought back to the accounts of the church historians, and the Romans hardly look like practitioners of rational politics. They look bloodthirsty, as Eusebius and others intend, but they also look like practitioners of a form of political theology. Pollock notwithstanding, the Romans did not conceive of an irreligious politics or apolitical religion. Christians were a threat to peace and security because they were a pollution that aroused the wrath of the gods. Romans sacrificed Christians to protect Rome by fending off the unthinkable prospect of the end of sacrifice.[50]

The closest thing we have to a rationale for the Great Persecution itself comes from Galerius, putatively the architect of the edict, who in his obese, worm-ridden, decaying old age revoked the persecution edict in 311 and asked the Christians to pray for him. In an effort to secure "the permanent advantage of the commonweal," the emperors "studied to reduce all things to a conformity with the ancient laws and public discipline of the Romans." The aim was to get Christians, who had "abandoned the religion of their forefathers" and whose "willful folly" had led them to reject "ancient institutions" and make their own laws, to "return to right opinions." It did not work. "Because great numbers still persist in their opinions, and because we have perceived that at present they neither pay reverence and due adoration to the gods, nor yet worship their own God," Galerius wrote, "we, from our wonted clemency in bestowing pardon on all, have judged it fit to extend our indulgence to those men, and to permit

---

[49]Ibid., pp. 145-51.
[50]Potter, "Martyrdom as Spectacle," explores the theatrical and "spectacular" dimensions of martyrdom.

them again to be Christians, and to establish the places of their religious assemblies." The only demand was that they not offend "against good order."[51] This might be read as a purely political justification for persecution, but the "ancient laws" and "public discipline" to which Christians failed to conform included religious laws and disciplines.[52] The persecutions were not conflicts of church and state but conflicts between different visions of political theology, Roman versus Christian. Galerius saw the refusal of Christians to sacrifice as a dangerous "cult vacuum" that could undermine the welfare of the empire.[53]

Theological critics of Constantine have surprisingly little to say about the historical context in which Constantine rose to the purple.[54] They occasionally acknowledge, with gratitude, that Constantine brought a final end to persecution, but they are as squeamish about details of the persecution as are Gibbon and Burckhardt. This has several results. Because they are reluctant to emphasize the religious motivations behind the persecution, they make Constantine seem far more innovative than he was. Constantine was very much a fourth-century Roman soldier and politician, whose thinking about the empire was thoroughly infused with religious concerns. By giving minimal attention to the persecutions, theological critics of Constantine make it difficult to sympathize with the sometimes fawning response of Christian leaders. Eusebius exaggerated Constantine's virtues and ignored his vices, but his attitude toward a Christian empire makes more sense once we realize that he had personally witnessed

---

[51]Lactantius, *Death*, p. 34. Burckhardt (*Age of Constantine*, p. 250) suggests that Galerius is rebuking Christians for abandoning their own ancestral practices, but that seems highly unlikely.

[52]On the integration of religious and political life in Rome, see Jorg Rupke, *Religion of the Romans*, trans. Richard Gordon (Cambridge: Polity, 2007); Mary Beard, John North and Simon Price, *Religions of Rome*, vol. 1, *A History* (Cambridge: University of Cambridge Press, 1998).

[53]The phrase is from Roldanus, *Church in the Age of Constantine*, p. 32.

[54]Craig Carter, *Rethinking Christ and Culture: A Post-Christendom Perspective* (Grand Rapids: Brazos, 2006), provides little more than a page covering the period between Christ and Constantine (pp. 78-79). John Howard Yoder regularly speaks glowingly of the martyr church but rarely acknowledges this as the context for Constantine. J. Alexander Sider ("'To See History Doxologically': History and Holiness in John Howard Yoder's Ecclesiology," Ph.D. diss., Duke University, 2004, p. 154) is correct that from Yoder one could get the impression that the Galerian and Diocletian persecution were not all that significant in the formation of "Christian consciousness" in the early fourth century. Robert L. Wilken (*The Myth of Christian Beginnings* [Notre Dame, Ind.: University of Notre Dame Press, 1970], p. 55) says that the "trauma" of persecution marked Eusebius for life.

some of the horrors of persecution in Palestine. Christians delivered from persecution would regard Constantine the way Poles or Czechs regard Ronald Reagan or John Paul II. These early Christians had survived through the gulag, and they were profoundly grateful to the skilled ruler who led them out.

Persecution also had the unfortunate but obvious consequence of weeding out some of the most determined leaders from the church. Persecutors targeted bishops and priests, and bishops who capitulated survived to rule the church once the persecution ended. Those who did not cooperate often died. It is hardly surprising that, with a few exceptions like Athanasius, the church leaders of the early fourth century were not men of the strongest character.

Finally, critics who ignore Constantine's setting are doing bad political theology. If anything should characterize Christian political thought, it is attention to the gritty realities of history. Creation, incarnation, cross, resurrection—all the cardinal doctrines of Christian faith reveal a God who acts in history. To do political theology without attention to historical context and circumstance is to replace a Christian political theology with a Platonic one. Without detailed attention to the details of history, political theology becomes perfectionistic. Relative judgments—Constantine was *better* than Diocletian or Galerius—give way to absolute, global, often ill-informed polemics against a Constantine who has become more an idea than a man.

Persecution reveals one dimension of the complex situation in the Roman Empire in the early fourth century. To do justice to Constantine, we must attempt to make some sense of that period, and to do that we need to reach back to the previous century.

2

Jupiter on the Throne

The immortal gods will be . . . well-disposed and favourable
to the name of Rome, if we scrutinize thoroughly everyone under
our rule and see they properly cultivate in every way
a pious, observant, peaceful, and chaste life.

EMPEROR DIOCLETIAN

Mother Rome was not well when Diocletian assumed the imperial throne in 285.[1] Over the previous decades, Rome had been shaken by multiple crises: "a constant and rapid turnover of emperors between A.D. 235 and 284 . . . near-continuous warfare, internal and external, combined with the total collapse of the silver currency and the state's recourse to exactions in kind."[2]

Trouble lay at the heart of the imperial system. From its beginning, the empire rested on a delicate political dance, the emperor's ability to balance

---

[1]For summaries of the crisis, see Jakob Burckhardt, *The Age of Constantine the Great*, trans. Moses Hadas (Berkeley: University of California Press, 1983), chap. 1, and A. H. M. Jones, *Constantine and the Conversion of Europe* (Toronto: University of Toronto Press, 1978), pp. 14-19. David S. Potter, *The Roman Empire at Bay*, Routledge History of the Ancient World (London: Routledge, 2004), pts. 2-3, is a richly detailed account. Simon Corcoran, "Before Constantine," in *The Cambridge Companion to the Age of Constantine*, ed. Noel Lenski (Cambridge: Cambridge University Press, 2006), p. 37, offers the more modest view that eschews universal explanations, is more skeptical of contemporary anxieties, and argues that a genuine crisis, brought on by invasions, is most evident in the imperial court and the army.

[2]Averil Cameron, *The Later Roman Empire* (Cambridge, Mass.: Harvard University Press, 1993), p. 3.

the interests and cultural assumptions of the Senate with the brute force of the military, which he commanded. Octavius[3] was a consummate player of the imperial game, ostentatiously humble in relation to the Senate, careful to keep up republican appearances by avoiding threat and intimidation. Imperial power was founded on modesty, on a combination of kingship and citizenship that expressed itself in the ritual of *recusatio*, the emperor's ritual reluctance to assume the imperial post.[4] In theory, the emperor under the Augustan system was no more than a *princeps*, the "first man" of the Senate, a first among equals.

Augustus's system, known as the Principate, had several centuries of relative success, but even before the end of the first century, there were ominous signs of internal fragility. The Year of the Four Emperors, A.D. 69, was a period of chaos that, Tacitus observed, revealed the imperial secret that "emperors could be made elsewhere than Rome."[5] With the Roman Senate's role reduced and the military's increased, imperial power was a reward for the most ambitious and skilled—and sometimes the most ruthless—military commander.

Succession brought the clash of interests to a boiling point. The problem of succession was endemic to the imperial system. Early on, emperors created a pseudo-dynasty by adoption, as Julius Caesar did with Octavius, but by the middle of the fourth century that system was no longer viable. During the "Year of the Four Emperors" and again in the crisis that followed the murder of Commodus (193-97), the succession system, such as it was, broke down. After the murder of Alexander Severus in 235, things became even more tumultuous. Many of the emperors between Alexander and Diocletian ruled for only a few months, and only Gallienus (253-68) ruled more than a decade.[6] Political turmoil at the center encouraged ad-

---

[3]The first Roman emperor has many names. Octavius was his given name, but he is also known by the variant Octavian during parts of his life. Augustus (revered one) was a title given to him in 27 B.C. The protocols of proper usage being unnecessary for my purposes, I refer to him indiscriminately either as Octavius or as Augustus.

[4]Andrew Wallace-Hadrill, "*Civilis princeps:* Between Citizen and King," *Journal of Roman Studies* 72 (1982).

[5]Quoted in H. A. Drake, *Constantine and the Bishops: The Politics of Intolerance* (Baltimore: Johns Hopkins University Press, 2000), p. 52. This summary of the constitutional system of the Principate comes from ibid., pp. 35-53.

[6]Cameron, *Later Roman Empire*, pp. 3-4; Charles Matson Odahl, *Constantine and the Christian Empire* (London: Routledge, 2004), pp. 17-19; Burckhardt, *Age of Constantine*, pp. 18-19; Drake, *Constantine and the Bishops*, pp. 158-62.

venturism in the provinces. Between 257 and 273 five emperors battled over Gaul.[7]

By the third century, the vulnerability at the center of the empire was exacerbated by external threats. The Principate was functional so long as borders were secure. Under Augustus they were; by the third century they were not.[8] Persia threatened as never before, mainly because the dilatory Arsacid dynasty was replaced by the vigorous and ambitious Sassanids.[9] Valerian's reign was comparatively long (253-260), but his name was tarnished by the shame of defeat at the hands of the Persian king Shapur I, commemorated on a monument that can still be found in Naqsh-i-Rustam, Iran. Relief carvings show Shapur seated resplendently on horseback holding the wrist of Valerian and receiving the obeisance of the Roman emperor, Philip the Arab. Valerian died in captivity, and afterward the Persian king stripped his skin off his corpse, dyed it, and kept as a trophy. Nearly forty years later, the Romans were still smarting from the humiliation. After he defeated Shapur's successor Narseh, Galerius, trembling with anger, chided the Persians not only for holding Valerian prisoner but for preserving his skin after his death.[10] Persia was not the only threat. Goths, Franks, and other Germanic and Slavic tribes repeatedly crossed the Rhine and Danube and threatened the empire. Everywhere, and for the first time in its history, the empire was on the defensive. Rome's enemies no longer considered it invincible, and Romans were inclined to agree.[11]

Rome was on the defensive because enemies attacked simultaneously from various directions. Sarmatians, Alemanni, Burgundians, Franks, and Saxons, a group known to the Romans as Skythai, all pressed in together, and this created conditions for rivalry among the leaders of Rome. When a local Roman commander repelled a Gothic invasion along the frontier, he naturally believed he had won some right to rule.[12] He was, after all, the savior of the empire. Because of the pressures from outside,

---

[7]Jones, *Constantine and the Conversion of Europe*, p. 14.
[8]Drake, *Constantine and the Bishops*, p. 54.
[9]Corcoran, "Before Constantine," p. 38.
[10]Ibid., p. 35; Odahl, *Constantine and the Christian Empire*, p. 24; Potter, *Roman Empire*, pp. 294-95. A picture of the relief is found in *The Cambridge Companion to the Age of Constantine*, ed. Noel Lenski (Cambridge: Cambridge University Press, 2006), figure 6.
[11]Corcoran, "Before Constantine," p. 38; Odahl, *Constantine and the Christian Empire*, p. 36.
[12]Ramsay MacMullen, *Constantine* (London: Croom Helm, 1987), pp. 5-6.

the boundaries of the empire weakened and in places broke altogether. In 281, a civil war broke out in Egypt, in which "the inhabitants of one part of the province, the Thebais, assault[ed] the region around Toptos with the aid of nomadic Blemmyes, who dominated what is now the northern Sudan." That is to say, "one portion of a [Roman] province" allied itself with a group from outside the empire to attack another part of the same province.[13]

A SINGLE POLIS

The Roman Empire was a military and political superpower, but Romans believed that their success depended on the gods. Roman emperors had always been deeply religious. Augustus publicized the horoscope that predicted his rise to power, and he surrounded his reign with religiopolitical symbols of rebirth and renewal.[14] Even a philosophical emperor like Marcus Aurelius claimed to have broken a siege with prayer in 172 and attributed his victory over the people Dio Cassius calls the Quadi to the influence of Anuphis, "an Egyptian magician, who was a companion of Marcus" and who called down a powerful rain by invoking "various deities and in particular Mercury, the god of the air."[15] During the third century, the Severans were devoted to the sun god.

Unlike Eastern rulers like Alexander, Augustus did not accept divine honors during his lifetime, and his position as emperor was not underwritten by an explicit theory of divine right. During the reign of Augustus, the eastern provinces did homage to the emperor, but in the capital he was only a man. Sacrifices were performed *for* the emperor but not necessarily offered *to* him.[16] Though power was concentrated in a single man, the empire respected local autonomy and local variations in religion and even in law. Jews in Palestine were not forced to adopt polytheism and were permitted to live by their own cultural and legal traditions. Augustus was

---

[13]Potter, *Roman Empire*, pp. 277-78.

[14]On the horoscope, see ibid., p. 107; on Augustus's iconography and religious claims, see S. R. F. Price, *Rituals and Power: The Roman Imperial Cult in Asia Minor* (Cambridge: University of Cambridge Press, 1984); Paul Zanker, *The Power of Images in the Age of Augustus*, trans. Alan Shapiro (Ann Arbor: University of Michigan Press, 1990); Ethelbert Stauffer, *Christ and the Caesars: Historical Sketches*, trans. K. and R. Gregor Smith (Philadelphia: Westminster Press, 1955).

[15]Dio Cassius, *Roman History*, 71.8; cf. Potter, *Roman Empire*, p. 30.

[16]See Price, *Rituals and Power*, pp. 207-20.

able to balance Senate and military, old and new, religion and power, in a system that maintained the Roman Empire for two centuries.[17] This was the religiopolitical system of the Principate, and, despite bumps and hiccoughs, it worked fairly well for a long time.

By the end of the second century, this system was fracturing. The Senate was losing its ability to check imperial power, and the Severans of the third century began to draw their administrators from the lower equestrian class rather than the senatorial class that was originally essential to the Principate. Within the military, a meritocracy had replaced the old senatorial elite.[18] Led by the youthful and bizarre Elagabalus (218-222), the Severans began to adopt some of the trappings of Eastern kingship. Xenophon captured the Hellenistic notion of kingship in the life of Cyrus, who wore high heels, makeup, and dazzling clothing to enhance his power by overawing his subjects: he intended to "cast a sort of spell upon them."[19] Virgil had implicitly castigated Aeneas for the splendor of his Carthaginian attire; to dress like an African prince was a temptation to be resisted, and we know Aeneas is recovering his sense of destiny when he sheds his exotic attire for the simplicity of a toga. The marks of Roman imperial power were modesty, simplicity of dress, and self-restraint personally and, it was implied, militarily.[20] Over time, the luxurious ways of the East—of Persia and North Africa, of Egypt and the Middle East—eroded Roman simplicity. By the time of Diocletian, emperors went about in purple robes, their golden shoes studded with jewels, accepting the prostrations of their subjects. Only the most intimate of the emperor's court could kiss his garment or enter behind the veil that screened the emperor from lesser men and see his *Dominus* face to face.[21] In place of a Principate (the rule of the "first man") the empire of the early fourth century was a Dominate—the rule of a *Dominus*, a god on earth. Elagabalus had been assassinated for his excesses and his flouting of custom, but by the early fourth century a style similar to his had taken over the court.

---

[17]Elizabeth DePalma Digeser, *Making of a Christian Empire: Lactantius and Rome* (Ithaca, N.Y.: Cornell University Press, 2000), pp. 20-23.

[18]Drake, *Constantine and the Bishops*, p. 118.

[19]Xenophon, quoted in ibid., 47.

[20]Ibid., 48.

[21]Corcoran, "Before Constantine," p. 43; see also Cameron, *Later Roman Empire*, p. 42; Burckhardt, *Age of Constantine the Great*, pp. 51-52; MacMullen, *Constantine*; Raymond Van Dam, *The Roman Revolution of Constantine* (Cambridge: Cambridge University Press, 2008), p. 17.

Just as important was the revision of citizenship that took place with the Antonine Constitution of 212. Promulgated by Caracalla, this edict granted citizenship to all free residents of the empire. It was an act more of economic desperation than of political generosity. A declining population and increasing military expenditures had created a serious financial crisis. Heavier taxes were laid on a smaller tax base, and in response many peasants abandoned the countryside, where they could no longer make a living in agriculture. Invaders meanwhile seized crops and animals from farmers, and when the invaders were expelled, the army seized them too.[22] Agricultural production declined, and with it the base of taxation. Desperate for funds, Caracalla extended citizenship to every resident of the empire, and in doing so imposed the inheritance tax of Augustus on all.[23]

Though fiscally motivated, the constitution had a profound effect on the character of the empire. The empire was transformed from a patchwork of cities with their own local cults, customs and laws into a single *civitas*, all its residents *cives*. Around the same time (223), Ulpian's treatise *De officiis proconsulis* was distributed to provincial governors as "the first standard collection of laws and their underlying principles that provincial governors had ever received."[24] By the middle of the third century, the empire was theoretically a single city, with one law and one worship uniting its citizens. In such a situation, deviation from Roman religion was by definition treason.

Such were the constitutional arrangements when Decius issued the first empire-wide edict of persecution in 249-250. According to this decree, all inhabitants of the empire, considered citizens since 212, had to sacrifice to unspecified "ancestral gods," taste sacrificial flesh, and take an oath to the effect that they had *always* sacrificed. *Libelli* from Egypt indicate that there was also a procedure for local confirmation that the sacrifice had taken place. Those who refused to sacrifice were exiled, lost property, or put to death. Though the edict applied to everyone, Decius may have had

---

[22]Jones, *Constantine and the Conversion of Europe*, p. 17.

[23]Ibid., p. 15. Later emperors imposed taxes on the cities of Italy and eventually on Rome itself. Fees piled on top of fees: tax collectors often charged taxpayers for the privilege of receiving a receipt (ibid., p. 17). Among other effects, the Antonine Constitution arguably devalued citizenship in the eyes of Romans (Corcoran, "Before Constantine").

[24]Digeser, *Making of a Christian Empire*, pp. 4-5, 24-25.

Christians particularly in view.[25] If it was not wholly unprecedented, the theory behind Decius's edict represented a "substantial reversal of the ordinary practice of religion in the classical world" in its union of "local cult to the imperial government, on the imperial government's own terms."[26] Valerian's persecution edict of 258 was explicitly aimed at Christians. He attempted to force Christians into normalcy by arresting leaders and demanding that they sacrifice, prohibiting Christian meetings, and forcing Christians out of the cemeteries where they honored the dead.[27] By treating the whole empire as a religiously as well as politically united *polis*, Decius and Valerian were setting the foundations for Diocletian's later, more vicious, persecution.

ROME MILITARIZED

Another inevitable result of the external threats was an increase in the political importance of the army. Even before the third-century crisis, the army had spread throughout the empire, patrolling distant borderlands and suppressing rebellion. A single emperor could not be in all the places he was needed, and a single emperor had his hands full suppressing rivals who might take control of territory along the empire's frontier. As a result, the army was not always under imperial control. Quite the contrary: the emperor was beholden to the army for his power, and the army knew it. Rome's government became "militarized."[28] As is often the case, iconography tells the story best. Octavius depicted himself on coins and statuary as a clean-shaven youth, serene and even luxuriating contemplatively in the peace he had established. Augustus was the eternally youthful one through whom the republic was reborn. During the third and into the fourth centuries, by contrast, emperors frequently had themselves depicted in mili-

---

[25]The summary of the decree comes from J. B. Rives, "The Decree of Decius and the Religion of Empire," *Journal of Roman Studies* 89 (1999): 137; Rives assembles the contents of the decree, which is no longer extant, from the fragmentary existing evidence. For the *libelli*, see John R. Knipfing, "The Libelli of the Decian Persecution," *Harvard Theological Review* 16, no. 4 (1923): 345-90. A brief summary is available in Potter, *Roman Empire*, pp. 241-45; Potter believes that the edict may have partly been Decius's effort to distance himself from his predecessor, Philip the Arab, who was sympathetic to Christianity and rumored to have been a Christian. On Philip, see also Warwick Ball, *Rome in the East: The Transformation of an Empire* (London: Routledge, 2000), pp. 417-18.
[26]Potter, *Roman Empire*, p. 243.
[27]Ibid., p. 255.
[28]Jones, *Constantine and the Conversion of Europe*, p. 14.

tary gear, their expressions energetic, their grizzled faces testimony to their Spartan life on the front and their ceaseless labors to protect the empire.[29]

With the militarization of the empire went a shift in the social location of power.[30] The first Roman emperors had risen from ancient aristocratic families, some of the oldest and most established of the capital. As successive emperors expanded citizenship, Roman emperors began to emerge from throughout the empire, yet they were still from the aristocratic classes. Macrinus, who became emperor in 217, was the first Roman emperor who had never been a Roman senator. Through the third century, the emperor's physical distance from the original centers of Roman power increased. After 268, many of the emperors rose through the ranks of the military and had little contact with the traditional Roman aristocracy. Diocletian and Constantine both hailed from the Danubian provinces, regions known less for honorable ancestry than for banditry, barbarians, beasts and beer.[31] The age of "soldier-emperors" had dawned.[32] The effects of the erosion of power among traditional elites spread far beyond the ranks of those elites. Gone were the days when a Caesar could gain a following by sheer virtue of his august name. Disentangled from the networks of the capital, emperors of the late empire depended less and less on personal connections, social influence or family heritage and leaned more and more heavily on the sheer military power they could threaten or wield. The Dominate simply brought into the open a secret more chilling than the one Tacitus had already seen behind the facade of legitimation during the Principate—there was in fact nothing to stop an emperor from ruling by sheer terror.[33]

The political and military challenges facing the empire had further interconnected cultural, economic, social and political consequences. Sol-

---

[29]See R. R. R. Smith, "The Public Image of Licinius I: Portrait Sculpture and Imperial Ideology in the Fourth Century," *Journal of Roman Studies* 87 (1997): 179.

[30]For a summary of the changes in the administration of the empire that accompanied these military and social shifts, see Corcoran, "Before Constantine," pp. 45-47. Drake, *Constantine and the Bishops*, p. 121, describes the order of the Tetrarchy itself as another expression of the militarization of the empire, the adoption of military models of order.

[31]Van Dam, *Roman Revolution*, p. 43.

[32]On the disruption of traditional Roman social order, see Jones, *Constantine and the Conversion of Europe*, pp. 18-19. See also Corcoran, "Before Constantine," p. 42.

[33]Peter Brown, *Power and Persuasion in Late Antiquity: Toward a Christian Empire* (Madison: University of Wisconsin Press, 1992), chap. 1.

diers liked to be paid, and there were more to pay and they were more threatening. Taxation was increasingly levied directly by the state, not farmed out to semi-independent collectors; this new practice created both the impression and the reality of an increasingly intrusive government. In the provinces, locals grumbled about big government, as people do in Alabama and Idaho today. Eventually, the Roman government did what governments do—they debased the currency, reducing the silver content of denarii so low that in the 270s Aurelian issued "silver" coins that were only 5 percent silver.[34] That was not the most disastrous of Aurelian's fiscal policies. For decades, inflation was held in check because the debased silver denarius was kept in a fixed ratio (1:25) to the gold *aureus*; even though the silver coins were not so silver anymore, they could always buy the same number of gold coins. Aurelian broke the link. Prices shot up eightfold in Egypt almost overnight, and no doubt his policies had similar effects throughout the empire.[35]

Given the need to patrol the borders of a far-flung empire and the need to lead the army personally, emperors were often far from home, and as a result Rome and Italy declined in strategic and functional importance.[36] Some emperors rarely visited the city at all, apart from ceremonial occasions. Of the emperors and pretenders with whom Constantine contended for power, only Maxentius made Rome his base of operations. A generation later, Constantine's son Constantius was overwhelmed by the beauty of the city when he first visited, long after he had become emperor.[37] Increasingly, eastern cities, closer to the Persian and barbarian enemies, replaced Rome as centers of imperial power. Wherever the emperor stayed, a court developed, with buildings, baths, courtiers and probably courtesans aplenty. Milan in Italy, Trier and Arles in Gaul, Serdica, Sirmium, and Thessalonica in the Balkans became every bit as much capitals as

---

[34]Potter, *Roman Empire*, p. 273.

[35]Ibid., pp. 273-74. See also Corcoran, "Before Constantine," pp. 48-49; Jones, *Constantine and the Conversion of Europe*, pp. 16-17.

[36]On the declining importance of Italy, see Van Dam, *Roman Revolution*, pp. 23-27. One sign of the collapsing privilege of Italian cities, long favored by the emperors, was the decision of Diocletian and Galerius to tax both the cities of northern Italy and Rome itself. In spite of its declining actual importance, emperors still used association with Rome for their political ends. Diocletian may have visited Rome as early as 285 and certainly did in 303, and his victory over Carinus was hailed as a liberation of "the Republic" from "most savage domination" (Van Dam, *Roman Revolution*, pp. 40-41).

[37]According to Van Dam, Constantius had actually visited once before, as a boy.

Rome itself. Nicomedia was Diocletian's first city, and Constantine transformed the ancient backwater of Byzantium into mystical Constantinople.[38] Rome was not the only city in decline. Populations were ravaged by periodic plagues,[39] and taxes and other financial pressures limited the ability of civic elites to build on the extravagant scale of previous generations. Local leaders were responsible for funding local building, and they had no funds. Many tried to escape the responsibility of rule because of the financial burden. Cities were losing financial independence and were less autonomous in other ways, as power became concentrated in the emperor. It was a sign of the times when Diocletian executed the entire city council of Antioch because they presumed to raise an army for their own defense.[40]

Religious invasions were equally a threat, especially strange sects from the direction of Persia, Rome's perennial enemy. Given the porosity of the political boundaries of the empire during the period, it is no surprise that the emperors felt the need to reassert traditional Roman religious standards.[41] Most notably, there was Christianity. During the period of peace after Valerian's death in Persia, the church grew rapidly. Cities and city cults grew less popular, and Christianity was displaying impressive intellectual leadership, organizational strength, and, in persecution, courage. Christians were increasingly integrated into all aspects of imperial society, and despite disputes over lapsed bishops and monarchianism, the church was resilient. Though only 10 percent of the empire was Christian, by the end of the third century the church was too big and well organized to be safely ignored.[42] The problem was not merely that the church was a growing and well-organized religion; it was the kind of religion that the church was. It is surely an overstatement to say that Roman religion had nothing to do with belief,[43]

---

[38]Corcoran, "Before Constantine," pp. 43-45.

[39]Cameron, *Later Roman Empire*, p. 10; Odahl, *Constantine and the Christian Empire*, p. 26.

[40]Corcoran, "Before Constantine," pp. 47-50. Cameron (*Later Roman Empire*, p. 8) questions the direction of cause and effect for many of these crises.

[41]Burckhardt, *Age of Constantine*, chaps. 5-6, offers what is still the most vivid portrait of the religious ferment of the period; also E. R. Dodds, *Pagan and Christian in an Age of Anxiety: Some Aspects of Religious Experience from Marcus Aurelius to Constantine* (New York: W. W. Norton, 1965).

[42]See W. H. C. Frend, *The Rise of Christianity* (Philadelphia: Fortress, 1984), pp. 272-437, for the church's history from the early third century up to Diocletian; Henry Chadwick. *The Early Church*, The Pelican History of the Church 1 (New York: Penguin, 1967), chaps. 5-7, covers the same ground.

[43]Cf. Clifford Ando, *The Matter of the Gods: Religion and the Roman Empire* (Berkeley: Univer-

but Roman religion had never confronted anything like Christianity.

The issue was not monotheism. Monotheism, even exclusivist monotheism, was a well-known feature of Judaism, and paganism of the third and fourth century was increasingly monotheistic, or at least henotheistic (believing in a chief, though not exclusive, high God).[44] The challenge was more radical than the question of numbering God/gods. It had to do with the very nature of religion. Celsus, like many, was a pagan monotheist, but he could not fathom what Christians were about. For Celsus, religion had to do with cultural and political tradition, with support of the city or the state, and this support was expressed primarily in the act of offering sacrifice. According to Origen, religion was a matter of truth, and the one true sacrifice was the unbloody sacrifice of the Eucharist. For paganism, sacrality was altogether a public matter. "Sacred things are those that have been consecrated publicly, not in private," Marcian wrote in his *Institutiones,* and he added that if anyone attempted to make something sacred for himself, then "it is not sacred but profane" (*sacrum non est, sed profanum*).[45] Christianity was certainly a communal religion, but not a civic religion in the Roman sense. It was a religion without sacrifice. Were the church to gain ascendancy, it would be the realization of Diocletian's worst fears. Christianity could not be assimilated into the Roman system without cracking the system wide open. It could not be ignored. Something had to be done. Perhaps, Galerius told Diocletian, Decius and Valerius had not been severe enough. If Christians would not accommodate to the Roman way of life, which is the way of sacrifice, Christianity must be stamped out.

The succession problem, the border problem, and the Christian problem: these were the challenges that faced Diocles when he became emperor, around the age of forty, on November 20, 284, and took the throne name Gaius Aurelius Valerius Diocletianus.

---

sity of California Press, 2008).

[44]R. P. C. Hanson, "The Christian Attitude to Pagan Religions up to the Time of Constantine the Great," *ANRW* 23 (1980): 959. Drake, *Constantine and the Bishops,* pp. 136-39, argues that the similarity of Christianity and monotheistic paganism, not their radical differences, was what made Christianity threatening. T. D. Barnes. "Monotheists All?" *Phoenix* 55, nos. 1/2 (2001), reviews some recent work on the subject, concluding that "even if they worshipped a multiplicity of gods, most thinking men in late antiquity who reflected at all on what this worship meant were in a very real sense monotheists" (p. 143).

[45]Guy G. Stroumsa, *The End of Sacrifice: Religious Transformations in Late Antiquity,* trans. Susan Emanuel (Chicago: University of Chicago Press, 2009), pp. 90-91, including n. 12. The contrast of Origen and Celsus is found on p. 103.

THE NEW AENEAS AND THE BOAR

He was born Diocles, probably around 244, in the city of Salonae in Dalmatia; otherwise the emperor's early life is almost completely unknown. He first appears in the historical record as commander of the bodyguard of the emperor Numerian,[46] and he must have been a courageous, shrewd and competent soldier and commander to rise to that height.

It is appropriate the Diocles first comes to our attention during a succession crisis. Stopping in Sirmium on his way to fight the Persians in 282, the emperor Probus received news that Carus had been proclaimed emperor back in Rome. The army killed Probus as soon as he got the message, and during the following summer the new emperor Carus continued the Persian campaign accompanied by his younger son Numerian. The unreliable *Historia Augusta* records that Carus captured Ctesiphon, but other sources say he died when his tent was struck by lightning that "may have come in the form of torches hurled into his tent."[47] That left Numerian in charge, and timid, pleasure-loving Numerian was no general. The army withdrew from Persia and retreated to Nicomedia. Along the way, Numerian was carried in a closed litter, and the story went out that he suffered from eye strain that made it impossible for him to be in sunlight. When the army got to Nicomedia, Numerian failed to appear for several days, and on investigation was found to be dead.

Suspicion was cast on everyone close to the emperor, and in a dramatic move Diocles appeared before the army to swear that he had not killed Numerian. He went on to accuse the emperor's father-in-law, the praetorian prefect Aper, of conspiring to assassinate Numerian and, according to the *Historia Augusta*, topped off the scene by stabbing Aper to death. "My grandfather reported he was among the assembly," the writer claims, "when Aper was killed by Diocletian's hand. He used to say Diocletian said, when he struck Aper, 'Boast, Aper, "you fall by great Aeneas's hand!"'"[48]

---

[46]D. G. Kousoulas, *The Life and Times of Constantine the Great: The First Christian Emperor*, 2nd ed. (author, 2007), pp. 14-16.

[47]Potter, *Roman Empire*, p. 279.

[48]*Historia Augusta*, trans. Jacqueline Long, selections available at <orion.it.luc.edu/~jlong1/carussel.htm>, 13.3. The sequence of events is summarized in Timothy D. Barnes, *Constantine and Eusebius* (Cambridge, Mass.: Harvard University Press, 1981), pp. 4-5; Corcoran, "Before Constantine," p. 39; Cameron, *Later Roman Empire*, p. 31.

The quotation from the tenth book of Virgil's *Aeneid* is multiply significant. In the poem, Aeneas has wounded Mezentius, and the latter's brash young son Lausus springs to his father's defense. Aeneas is impressed with the young man's filial *pietas* but warns him that he has no chance to win. As he deals the inevitable death blow, Aeneas says that the young warrior can find some comfort in the fact that he was felled by Aeneas. It would be surprising if Diocles intended to compliment Aper, whom he had just accused of both regicide and filicide, but perhaps he was mocking Aper as a young upstart with no chance against the new Aeneas. More to the point, Diocles was putting himself in the place of Virgil's protagonist, the founding hero behind all Roman heroes. Diocles named himself a new founder of Rome, and since Virgil's praise of Aeneas is always also praise of Augustus, Diocles named himself a new founder of the empire. He agreed with his panegyrists: he was reviving the golden age. Aper's one dying boast was that he was stabbed to death by a great man.

Aeneas's final act in Virgil's epic is to run his spear through the defeated Turnus, revenge for Turnus's killing of Aeneas's protégé Pallas. Generations later, Romulus established the boundary of Rome by a Cain-like foundation murder of his brother Remus, and the empire of Augustus emerged from an ocean of blood—the blood of Pompey, of Julius, of Brutus and Cassius, the blood finally of Mark Antony, defeated by Augustus at Actium in 31 B.C. Diocles proved himself capable of using imperial power, the power of the sword, and his action foretold the character of his empire, an empire defended in war and in sacrificial purgation of Christianity. For Diocles, the event had a further significance. Years before, a Druid priestess had predicted that he would become emperor only after killing a boar, and from that time he had searched for a boar on every hunt. Finally, at Nicomedia on November 20, 284, Diocles found his prey, for the name Aper means "wild boar."[49]

GOLDEN AGE

Poets viewed the reign of Augustus as the renewal of the long-lost golden age of human history. Ovid's *Metamorphoses* ends with the apotheosis of

---

[49]Burckhardt, *Age of Constantine*, pp. 41, 48; Kousoulas, *Life and Times*, p. 14. One wonders whether Diocles thought, too, of the *Odyssey*, whose hero is identified by a scar won in a boar hunt.

Julius Caesar and the hope that Augustus will also ascend to receive prayers. Virgil's *Fourth Eclogue,* on which Constantine later mused, foretold a child whose birth would bring in a new age of prosperity, and Virgil no doubt intended to refer to Lord Augustus, not (as Christians later supposed) the Lord Jesus. After the vicious civil wars that had followed the assassination of Julius Caesar, such sentiments were not surprising.

Panegyrists dipped into the rhetoric of the early empire to express their delight in the results of Diocletian's reign. By contrast with the third-century age of defeat, poverty, malaise, and decay, it was morning in Diocletian's Rome.

> Peace ruled everywhere. The Rhine, the Danube, and the Euphrates again formed secure frontiers guarded by Roman troops. Defeated barbarians had been assigned to recover deserted farmland for cultivation. Plowed fields replaced forest, the granaries were filled, there was almost too much produce to harvest. Cities long overgrown with vegetation or abandoned to wild animals were being rebuilt, restored, and repopulated. Men lived long and reared more children. . . . The credit for all this could be assigned to the rulers: forgetful of their own comfort, they surveyed the world to see what needed their attention; they passed their days and nights in incessant concern for the safety of all.[50]

Diocletian was not, in his own mind, doing anything new. He was the *re*storer, the *re*builder, the *re*former of the ancient order of Rome.[51] He was, to Burckhardt, "one of the last and most beneficent" of the Roman emperors.[52]

Diocles' boast was not wholly unfounded. Changing his name to the more patrician and Roman Diocletian, he quickly got to work restoring the empire's stability. During the early months of his reign, he defeated the remaining Caesar, Numerian's brother Carinus, when the latter was assassinated by one of his own soldiers before a battle at the Margus River in the Balkan province of Moesia.[53]

Diocletian was not primarily a soldier, but he knew his limitations and delegated military concerns to more skilled men. His genius was for orga-

---

[50]Barnes, *Constantine and Eusebius,* p. 12.

[51]MacMullen, *Constantine,* p. 8, on the prominence of the prefix *re-* in the rhetoric of Diocletian's empire.

[52]Burckhardt, *Age of Constantine,* p. 68.

[53]Corcoran, "Before Constantine," p. 39; Barnes, *Constantine and Eusebius,* p. 5.

nizing, and that was where he left his mark.[54] For all the traditionalism of
Diocletian's rhetoric, his reign was innovative on many fronts. In taxation,
in religious policy, in administration, he presided over an "activist" government that swept away earlier restraints and inserted state power into
the details of daily life.[55] He reorganized the empire into nearly ninety
provinces—much smaller than earlier provincial regions—and these
ninety provinces he grouped into twelve dioceses. At the top of this system
was the praetorian prefect, no longer a military figure but now a bureau-
crat and judge. With the reorganization came an exponential increase in
the personnel of the empire. During the second century, there had been
some 150 major provincial administrators, but under Diocletian there were
several thousand in the eastern empire alone. Latin inscriptions throughout the east testify to the spread of Roman power.[56] Not only did this result in a more intrusive Roman government, but it created a new class of
bureaucrats whom Lactantius condemned as "rude and illiterate men" who
had none of the eloquence of traditional Roman elites.[57]

Diocletian was wise enough to know that he could not rule the far-
flung empire alone, and late in 285 he appointed his friend Maximian as
Caesar, a second-rank emperor.[58] After putting down a revolt, Maximian
was elevated to the position of a second Augustus on April 1, 286. Two
emperors, however, proved insufficient. A crisis had broken out in Gaul,
and Maximian was not able to handle it. Carausius had been placed over
the province, but he took more than his share of the trade across the English Channel and eventually got himself proclaimed emperor in Britain. In
290, Maximian lost a fleet of ships in an attempted invasion across the
Channel. With the crisis deepening, Maximian crossed the Alps to meet
Diocletian in Milan during the winter of 290. There they decided to expand the imperial college. On March 1, 293, Maximian made Constantius
his Caesar. Diocletian was not present, but he must have approved of the
move, since he took no steps to stop in. A few months later, on May 21, he
appointed his own Caesar, Galerius. Diocletian and Maximian took the
title Augusti, with Diocletian firmly if unofficially in the position of se-

---

[54]Jones, *Constantine and the Conversion of Europe,* p. 21.
[55]Potter, *Roman Empire,* p. 336.
[56]Van Dam, *Roman Revolution,* p. 145 n. 2.
[57]Drake, *Constantine and the Bishops,* pp. 116-17.
[58]Barnes, *Constantine and Eusebius,* p. 6.

nior Augustus. It was the first Tetrarchy, a "rule of four." Two did not quite work; four would do the trick.

The four rulers were known as "tetrarchs," and in some portraits from the period, the Tetrarchs' faces exude stern moral discipline: their wild "burning gaze" communicates their passion for restoring Roman order. In an edict concerning incestuous marriage, Diocletian expresses the hope that the "immortal gods will be . . . well-disposed and favourable to the name of Rome, if we scrutinize thoroughly everyone under our rule and see they properly cultivate in every way a pious, observant, peaceful, and chaste life."[59] The scrutinizing eyes of the Tetrarchs are the eyes of the tribal fathers, the gods of the past, who ensure conformity with Rome's founding traditions.

More important, Tetrarchan art communicates the union of the four. A corner of St. Mark's, Venice, is now the site of a statuary group in porphyry showing the four original Tetrarchs in groups of two, embracing. The faces are indistinguishable, apart from the fact that two—presumably senior—members are bearded. A porphyry bust of a tetrarch in the Egyptian Museum, Cairo, is even more stylized. Large eyes bug out from the stone, staring intensely; the hair and beard are stippled in regular rows; the forehead is furrowed and wrinkled with an imperious intensity. Who is it? No one knows. The point is not to depict a person but a power. The portraits offer a political message: individual tetrarchs are not important but absorbed into the fourfold expression of power. *Harmonia* and *concordia* were the mottos of the new order.

At the same time, Diocletian remained the senior figure in the arrangement. According to the emperor Julian's later account, Diocletian "clasped hands" with his colleagues but they "did not walk beside him; instead, they surrounded him like a chorus," a "perfectly harmonious chorus of four."[60] As Jupiter's nod determined the course of all things, so Diocletian's. On the arch of Galerius in Thessaloniki, constructed after the Caesar's victory over the Persians, the four Tetrarchs wear the same clothes and are the same size. Yet one—Diocletian—holds a scepter.[61]

---

[59]Van Dam, *Roman Revolution*, p. 237. On the iconography of the Tetrarchy, see Smith, "Public Image," pp. 179-83; quotation from the decree is in Smith, "Public Image," p. 182.
[60]Quoted in Van Dam, *Roman Revolution*, p. 359.
[61]Ibid., pp. 239-40.

Between them, the two Augusti and the two Caesars divided up the empire and got to work. Constantius organized the subjugation of Britain. Before Constantius could cross the Channel, Carausius was dead, but Constantius successfully defeated his assassin, Allectus, restoring Britain to the Roman orbit. The Western Augustus, Maximian, put down a rebellion in North Africa, while Diocletian, the Eastern Augustus, secured Egypt. After one unsuccessful attempt, Galerius defeated the Persians and secured the eastern border of the empire. Suppressing the threat from Persia and from Eastern Europe was Diocletian's greatest and most lasting achievement. The panegyrist Eumenius referred to a world map painted on a wall at the hall of Autun, where youth could "see how Diocletian's clemency pacifies the wild insurrection of Egypt; how Maximian shatters the Moors; how under your hands, Lord Constantius, Batavians and Britons again raise their sorrowful countenances from their jungles and floods; or how you, Caesar Galerius, tread Persian bows and quivers down to earth." On the whole "painted earth" there was "naught that is not ours."[62] By the turn of the century, the Roman Empire was at peace, and the age was described with some justice in the infamous Price Edict of 301 as a "peaceful state of the world seated in the lap of a most profound calm."[63]

The Tetrarchy solved the immediate threat to the empire's periphery and was also intended to solve the problem at the core of the empire, the problem of succession. Diocletian had no sons, and he constructed the Tetrarchy to ensure a peaceful transition of power to the next generation. The Tetrarchs were joined as kin: Constantius put away his concubine Helena, mother of Constantine, in favor of Maximian's daughter Theodora, and Galerius married Diocletian's daughter Valeria.[64] More radically, Diocletian envisioned term limits for emperors. In May 305, some twenty years after he assumed the purple, Diocletian did what no other emperor had ever done: he voluntarily retired and induced Maximian to retire as well. Constantius was elevated to the position of Western Augus-

---

[62]Quoted in Burckhardt, *Age of Constantine*, p. 612. Van Dam, *Roman Revolution*, p. 35, notes that the map highlights areas where the Tetrarchs had recently defeated enemies of the empire: "Egypt, where Diocletian had suppressed a rebellion; Africa, where Maximian had defeated the Moors; Batavia and Britain, where Constantius had overthrown a usurper; and the eastern frontier, where Galerius had triumphed over the Persians."

[63]Quoted in Corcoran, "Before Constantine," p. 41.

[64]Barnes, *Constantine and Eusebius*, pp. 8-9.

tus, assuming the senior position, while Galerius took over Diocletian's position as the Augustus of the East. Two Caesars were appointed to replace them—Severus and Maximian Daia. The succession problem seemed to have been solved.

SON OF JUPITER

Diocletian also had to solve the Christian problem; this, he knew, was integral to solving the crises of the previous century. Building on the constitution of 212 and the Decian and Valerian conceptions of a religiously united empire, he deliberately secured the Tetrarchy with a religious ideology. The rhetor Eumenius found the numerical symbolism of the Tetrarchy fruitful ground for cosmological speculation. "He sees the number four as the fundamental principle in the cosmic order, expressed in the four elements, the four seasons, even the four continents. It is not for naught that a lustrum follows upon the passing of four years; in the heavens a four-horse team flies before the chariot of the sun; and the two great luminaries of heaven, sun and moon, are attended by the two lesser lights, the morning star and the evening star."[65] No wonder the tarnished old world had been restored to gold: the political system of the empire was, at long last, in harmony with the nature of things.

The notion that the Tetrarchy matched the structure of the cosmos was reinforced by the associations of the Tetrarchs with traditional Roman gods, an association that arose from religious as well as political motivations and, in the eyes of Christian observers like Lactantius, represented a dangerous innovation. Without the Senate to provide support for his rule, and recognizing that military rule was the cause and not the solution for the political crisis, Diocletian went over the Senate's head and reached for a direct theological legitimation of the empire.[66] Diocletian took the honorific title Iovius and named Maximian the head of the "Heraculian" branch of the imperial college. Coins depicted Maximian in his divine patron's characteristic lion skin.[67] As Heracles in his might carried out the orders of his father Ju-

---

[65]Burckhardt, *Age of Constantine*, p. 61.
[66]Van Dam, *Roman Revolution*, p. 231; he adds, "In theory their standing as gods allowed [the Tetrarchs] to transcend dependence on the affirmation of the senate at Rome or the acclamation of the troops. Now any opposition to their rule could be represented as not just seditious, but also sacrilegious, impious, even unbelief."
[67]Burckhardt, *Age of Constantine*, p. 49.

piter, so Maximian did for Diocletian. This was no idle playacting. Depictions of the Tetrarchs show them not only joined in a fond embrace but also standing at an altar offering a single sacrifice.[68] What buttressed Diocletian's empire was an "elaborate political theology."[69]

At the same time, Diocletian heightened the Eastern trappings of the imperial protocol that had been developing over the previous century. He required that members of his court address him as *dominus* and that they prostrate themselves in his presence and kiss the hem of his purple robe. According to Eutropius, Diocletian "was the first that introduced into the Roman empire a ceremony suited rather to royal usages than to Roman liberty," demanding "that he should be adored" and wearing "ornaments of precious stones on his dress and shoes."[70] Isolated and exalted like a Hellenistic king, glittering with jewels and gold-encrusted robes, the king was no longer the *princeps* of Augustan political theory. He was a god, albeit one whose *potestas* came by the point of a sword.[71] The ceremony and fashions of the Tetrarchy indicate that the emperor was "now a figure for all to adore and venerate."

Even posture and physiognomy had to conform. Dio had described the "ugly and forbidding scowl" of Lady Tyranny, so haughty that she would not "glance at those who came into her presence but looked over their heads disdainfully." Now this haughty gaze became the mark of imperial majesty. The emperor was expected to remain stock still, face fixed in the serene, unsurprised gaze of the gods.[72] He had become a colossus:

Entrance into a city, the *adventus*, offered men a rare glimpse of their ruler. In the world that Constantine was born into it had become a sort of act of

---

[68]Corcoran, "Before Constantine," pp. 40, 51.

[69]The phrase is from Digeser, *Making*, p. 3. See the similar conclusions of Corcoran, "Before Constantine," p. 40; MacMullen, *Constantine*, p. 23; Odahl, *Constantine and the Christian Empire*, 43. Burckhardt points out that Diocles' name includes "Dio," equivalent to "Zeus" (*Age of Constantine*, p. 43).

[70]Eutropius *Brevarium* 9.26. The Latin reads, "Diligentissimus tamen et sollertissimus princeps et qui imperio Romano primus regiae consuetudinis formam magis quam Romanae libertatis invexerit adorarique se iussit, cum ante eum cuncti salutarentur. Ornamenta gemmarum vestibus calciamentisque indidit. Nam prius imperii insigne in chlamyde purpurea tantum erat, reliqua communia."

[71]Drake, *Constantine and the Bishops*, pp. 54-56. Ibid., pp. 58-59, notes that the Senate retained a certain degree of power, especially as "the institutional springboard for the expression of elite concerns."

[72]Ibid., pp. 125-26.

state in itself. As the emperor approached, the senators, Roman or municipal, came out to meet him, accompanied by priests, magistrates, workers'
guilds, constables, brass bands, and a crowd of lesser folk. He appeared
borne on a litter or in a carriage; guards in gilt or silver armor flanked him,
bearing silk banners designed to float inflated in the air, in the shape of
dragons. The soldiers' shields were painted, the chariot painted and jeweled, the rider jeweled and robed in purple down to his shoes. Etiquette
demanded that he make no response to the throng. He sat still and tried to
look enormous. When Constantine's son visited the capital, he aroused
everybody's admiration by playing the giant—ducking his head slightly as
he passed through the gates of Rome![73]

The emperor was also a sacral figure, surrounded by an impenetrable
glow of holiness.[74] When he became emperor, Constantine maintained
aspects of this ceremony but treated it lightly. According to Eusebius,
Constantine displayed the best of both worlds: he dutifully wore his "rai-
ment, interwoven with gold, finished with intricate blossoms," for the sake
of his "subjects' sense of proper style," but he "laughed" at it and had himself depicted in a traditional toga, distributing coins to senators, on the
final panel in the frieze of his arch.[75]

Jupiter was more than the emperor's distant patron. Diocletian fancied
himself virtually an incarnation of the chief god of the Roman pantheon.
A panegyrist honoring the emperor in 291 called him a "visible and present Jupiter, near at hand."[76] Jupiter was the "creator of Diocletian,"[77] and
Diocletian the only begotten son of father Jupiter. Other panegyrists drew
on the mythologies of Jupiter to add a mystical glow to Diocletian's political accomplishments:

> Jupiter Optimus Maximus was the preserve of the Roman community, the
> god who had defeated the old race of the Titans and founded a new Olym-
> pian race. . . . In selecting Jupiter as his divine father, Diocletian claimed
> responsibility for defeating the usurpers, asserted his right to command the
> empire, and identified himself as the source of the other emperors' author-
> ity and the founder of a new golden age. In choosing to call Maximian

---

[73]MacMullen, *Constantine,* p. 11.
[74]Odahl, *Constantine and the Christian Empire,* p. 49; Burckhardt, *Age of Constantine,* p. 52.
[75]Eusebius *Life* 5.4.6-7; on the frieze, see Van Dam, *Roman Revolution,* p. 47.
[76]Digeser, *Making of a Christian Empire,* pp. 3, 27-28.
[77]Van Dam, *Roman Revolution,* p. 230; the Latin from a panegyric is *Diocletiani auctor.*

"Heraculius," Diocletian conveyed similarly important information about his partner. Hercules was Jupiter's son by the mortal woman Alcmene and, as Jupiter's helper, a hero for whom nothing was too difficult. . . . Consequently, Maximian's new name symbolically asserted that he owed his power and divinity to Diocletian. It further confirmed his subordinate role by suggesting that, like Jupiter, Diocletian initiated action and, like Hercules, Maximian carried it out.[78]

The two Caesars likewise adopted divine patrons—Galerius, appropriately, worked under the oversight of Mars, while Constantius was under the patronage of Apollo, the sun god so often linked with his son.[79]

Lactantius took Diocletian's political theology seriously. Like other pagan and Christian writers, Lactantius adopted the euhemerist theory, which taught that the gods were mere men whose reputations had inflated after death, and from this angle he criticized the political theology of the Tetrarchy. To Lactantius, Diocletian's association with Jupiter was no compliment: Jove was "a traitor from his early youth since he drove his father from his reign and chased him away. Nor did he wait for the death of the broken old man in his desire for rule."[80] Jupiter, further, did not preside over the golden age; Saturn did, and the reason for the prosperity of Saturn's tenure was that he permitted the worship of the true God. By now excluding that worship, Diocletian was undermining the aspirations of his own political program. Further, the Tetrarchy did not adhere to the structure of the world. Since there was only one God, there should be a single *princeps*, and Lactantius attempted to convince pagan monotheists as well as Christians of the point.[81]

Diocletian ruled for nearly two decades without persecuting Christians, so it would be a mistake to say that persecution was a deliberate part of his program for Roman renewal.[82] Yet persecution of Manichaeans and Christians was not some strange aberration of imperial policy but consistent with Diocletian's entire political theology. For Diocletian, the Tetrarchy was rooted in traditional Roman religion, and loyalty to the former had to

---

[78]Digeser, *Making of a Christian Empire*, pp. 28-29.
[79]Johannes Roldanus, *The Church in the Age of Constantine: The Theological Challenges* (London: Ashgate, 2006), p. 29.
[80]Quoted in Digeser, *Making of a Christian Empire*, pp. 36-37.
[81]Ibid.
[82]Van Dam, *Roman Revolution*, p. 164.

be expressed by participation in the latter. The peace that Diocletian aimed to preserve was not a secular peace. It was the "peace of the gods," a *pax deorum*.[83]

CONCLUSION

On Roman terms, Diocletian's reign was a success. The empire was safe and free of internal strife. He stayed in power twenty years, a reign long enough to provide some measure of stability. His reorganization of the empire outlasted him. Together with Constantine, he could be considered a savior of the Roman Empire.

On the three crises of the day—the border, the succession, and the Christians—Diocletian achieved midterm success only with the first. As we will see in the next chapter, his solution to the succession problem barely outlasted his retirement. His economic policies were a disaster. He attempted to arrest inflation by issuing a Price Edict that set maximum prices on many goods, which had the expected effect of driving goods and services to the black market. Lactantius complained loudly of the brutality of Diocletian's tax policies, and he was not the only one who did so.

When things went badly, Diocletian adopted the time-tested policy of finding someone to blame. He blamed the Christians for failing to honor the gods, just as later pagans would blame Christians for the evils suffered at the hands of barbarians. Once Diocletian got started persecuting, however, he had no chance of success. Too many Christians stood their ground, and the church was clearly not going anywhere. Pagans had grown in their admiration of Christian fortitude, and some pagans even offered sanctuary to Christians fleeing from the authorities. Diocletian had forced the issue and was faced down by a vigorous and growing minority within the empire, a minority who by the Antonine Constitution were citizens of Rome but who consistently and courageously refused to take part in sacrifice, one of the central defining acts of Roman citizenship. Something would have to budge, either the demands of Roman citizenship or the church, and the church showed no signs of budging.

---

[83]Odahl, *Constantine and the Christian Empire*, pp. 55, 62.

3

Instinctu Divinitatis

You must share some secret with that divine mind,
Constantine, which has delegated care of us to lesser
gods and deigns to reveal itself to you alone.

PANEGYRIC XII, CA. 313

On May 1, 305, Diocletian gathered his troops in his capital Nicomedia and led a procession out to a hill three miles from the city. A column had been erected on the site, topped by an image of Jupiter. Twenty years before, Diocletian had stood on this same hilltop, slaughtered the "boar" Aper, and taken command of the Roman Empire as the "son of Jupiter." On this spring day, still under the aegis of the king of the gods, he was preparing to do something no Roman emperor had ever done.

Surrounded by common soldiers wearing red or undyed tunics, centurions with breastplates adorned with ornaments of valor, senior commanders whose white helmet plumes fluttered in the breeze blowing off the Sea of Maramara, Diocletian mounted a platform and began to speak. Galerius Armentarius ("cow-keeper")[1] glared down from the dais, and Diocletian was also joined by the young commander Constantine—tall, his large head, hooked nose, and intense eyes giving him a look of confident mastery—along with Galerius's friend Maximinus Daia.

In a gesture as dramatic as it was unprecedented, Diocletian announced

---

[1]Alexander Demandt, Andreas Goltz and Heinrich Schlange-Schoningen, eds., *Diokletian und die Tetrarchie: Aspekte einer Zeintenwende* (Berlin: Walter de Gruyter, 2004), p. 41.

that he was retiring as Augustus and was prepared to name his successor. A few years before, he had suffered a sickness serious enough to raise rumors of his death, and he was weary from years of care, travel, and battle. It was time to remove himself and leave power to others. The senior Augustus of the Tetrarchy bid a tearful farewell to the troops on whose loyalty and skill the stability of his empire had depended.

According to Lactantius, who had taught rhetoric in Nicomedia until the persecution decree of 303, all eyes were on Constantine. His father was Caesar of the West, and Constantine had distinguished himself in service to the aging Diocletian. He had marched with Diocletian to Thebes and was in the emperor's army when Diocletian visited the ruins of ancient Mesopotamia.[2] He appeared to be an *imperator oriens,* a "rising emperor," groomed to take his position as Caesar. It was no surprise when Diocletian appointed Caesar Galerius as his successor as Augustus of the Eastern empire, but by Lactantius's account, everyone was astonished when Maximinus Daia[3] stepped forward to stand between Diocletian and Galerius and receive the purple cloak that Diocletian had removed from his shoulders. Constantine held his composure, but he and many in the crowd were deeply disappointed.

A civilian again, no longer Diocletian but Diocles, the former emperor descended, climbed into a cart, and returned to Nicomedia. Soon after, he retired to his splendid villa on the waterfront in the city of Salonae (now the Croatian city of Split) on the Dalmatian coast, to enjoy the subtropical warmth, tend his cabbages, and wait for death.[4]

On the same spring day on the other side of the empire, a similar event was taking place. In Milan, the Western Herculian Augustus Maximian also returned to civilian life, elevated Constantius to the position of Au-

---

[2]Little is known about Constantine's earlier career. Bits and pieces can be gleaned from later statements of Constantine, Lactantius and Eusebius and from panegyrics and later legends. For summaries of this period of his life, see Ramsay MacMullen, *Constantine* (London: Croom Helm, 1987), pp. 57-59; Charles Matson Odahl, *Constantine and the Christian Empire* (London: Routledge, 2004), chaps. 3-4; T. G. Elliott, *The Christianity of Constantine the Great* (Scranton, Penn.: University of Scranton Press, 1996), chaps. 1-2. D. G. Kousoulas, *The Life and Times of Constantine the Great: The First Christian Emperor,* 2nd ed. (author, 2007), pp. 157-59, 197-201, is vivid but not always reliable.

[3]The abundance of important figures with names beginning with "Max-" makes this history even more complicated than it would otherwise be. For clarity, I refer to Maximinus Daia as Daia throughout. His name is also sometimes rendered as Daza.

[4]The description of the scene is derived from Lactantius *Death* 19.2-6.

gustus, and appointed Severus to replace Constantius in the junior position as Caesar.

With its four armies and four emperors, the Tetrarchy was fairly successful at meeting the threats to the empire's periphery. But Diocletian's
solution to the religion problem, which was destined to be the determining
factor in the empire's future, had backfired, and so had his abortive efforts
to solve the empire's fiscal crisis. His solution to the succession program
fared no better. Diocletian had no sons, and he had constructed the Tetrarchy to ensure a peaceful transition of power to the next generation. By
this mechanism the empire would, Diocletian hoped, be spared the bloodletting that had stained the succession for generations.

If the basic rationale behind the simultaneous abdications of the emperors was obvious enough, the import of their decision was not. A panegyrist
claimed in 307 that the decision had been made some time before when
Diocletian and Maximian met behind the gold-plated doors of the temple
of Capitoline Jupiter in Rome.[5] Perhaps, as Jacob Burckhardt has argued,
Diocletian intended to initiate a system in which tetrarchs would retire
after a twenty-year term, and perhaps too he intended to initiate a system
that undermined dynastic pretentions.[6] All of this is speculation, since
neither Diocletian nor Maximian left any record of their reasons or the
plan for successions in the future.

Lactantius claimed it was a sudden and rash decision and, as usual,
blamed Galerius. Whether or not Galerius pressured Diocletian into ab-
dication, he was certainly the beneficiary of the new arrangements. Neither of the Caesars was well known prior to their elevation—except to
Galerius. The new Eastern Caesar, Daia, was Galerius's nephew, and
Severus had fought alongside Galerius for years. Behind the decision Lactantius saw a Galerian plot, an effort to isolate the one independent member of the imperial college, Constantinius, force him to retire, and replace
him with another ally, Licinius. Eventually Galerius planned to leave the

---

[5]David S. Potter, *The Roman Empire at Bay, AD 180-395*, Routledge History of the Ancient
World (London: Routledge, 2004), pp. 340-41, summarizes the evidence concerning the timing of the decision.
[6]Ibid., p. 662, n. 36. Mark Humphries, "From Usurper to Emperor: The Politics of Legitimation in the Age of Constantine," *Journal of Late Antiquity* 1, no. 1 (2008), makes it clear that the
Tetrarchy's attitude toward a blood-based dynastic succession is much more ambiguous. The
imperial college, after all, did not simply rely on the good faith of the members but rested on
the ancient method of intermarriage.

empire to Candidianus, his own son.[7]

Galerius's actions gave some support to Lactantius's suspicions. Later he "did promote Licinius to the rank of Augustus over the head of Maximinus, and he constructed a great palace for himself at Gamzigrad in Serbia on the model of Diocletian's at Split."[8] For the first time in Roman history, he imposed the census on the cities of Italy and Rome, overturning tax exemptions that had been granted centuries before.[9] Not only was this a novel act of tyranny—at least it was viewed as such by the citizens of Italy—but it indicated that Galerius was claiming the role of the senior Augustus. Under Diocletian's system, all four emperors were allowed to issue edicts, but only Diocletian himself, as senior Augustus, had the right to issue laws governing the whole of the empire. Galerius was Eastern Augustus, yet ignoring his *senior* colleague Constantius, he imposed a policy, and a controversial one, on Western territory.[10] Without the original chief Augustus, Diocletian, the Tetrarchy began to fracture.

CONSTANTINE'S EARLY YEARS

For Lactantius, the clearest sign of Galerius's ambition was his treatment of Constantine. Though his father was Western Caesar and then Augustus, Constantine had spent his life in the eastern part of the empire. He was born in Naissus, a military outpost near the Danube, on February 27, probably in the year 272,[11] when his father Constantius was an officer in the army.[12] He later claimed descent from the emperor Claudius, and medieval legend made his mother, Helena, a descendant of British royalty. Other legends made her a barmaid and claimed that Constantine's birth was illegitimate. Constantius, so the story went, stayed at an inn belonging to Helena's father while on a military excursion. Having been fed, he asked for a woman to enjoy for the night, and the innkeeper offered his beautiful daughter. During the night, portents in the sky, which the religious Constantius took as messages from Apollo, puzzled and amazed him. When

---

[7]Lactantius *Death* 18.12-13, 20.2-4; Potter, *Roman Empire,* pp. 343-44.

[8]Potter, *Roman Empire,* p. 344.

[9]Timothy D. Barnes, *Constantine and Eusebius* (Cambridge, Mass.: Harvard University Press, 1981), p. 29.

[10]Potter, *Roman Empire,* p. 343.

[11]Some scholars place his birth a decade later, but Barnes has convincingly argued, from the age of his son Crispus, that Constantine must have been born in the 270s.

[12]Barnes, *Constantine and Eusebius,* p. 3.

he departed the next morning, he left behind an embroidered purple mantle as thanks. Helena became pregnant and had a son, Constantine. Some years later, when Constantius had been promoted to the governorship of Dalmatia, some soldiers were visiting the same inn and teased Helena's child. She warned them that they were teasing the son of an emperor, and when the soldiers mocked her, she produced the mantle of Constantius. When the soldiers returned to court, they told Constantius what they had found, and he summoned both Helena and his son to be at court with him.[13] Though the story is a fanciful romance, it is likely that Helena was of humble origins, as her marriage to Constantius was not a fully endowed marriage. Helena was a concubine, and Constantine's somewhat questionable parentage cast a shadow over his claim to power.[14]

During his early years, Constantine served in Diocletian's army. He later reminisced about seeing the ancient ruins of Mesopotamian civilizations and traveling in Diocletian's entourage to Memphis in Egypt.[15] According to the anonymous *Origo Constantini*, Galerius distrusted and hated him from early on, thrusting him into military danger in the hope that he would be killed. Fighting the Sarmatians, however, Constantine seized one barbarian by the hair and dragged him back to Galerius. When Galerius sent him into a swamp, he went boldly in on horseback, making a way for the rest of the army to follow him to victory.[16]

Even when his father was transferred to the West to secure Gaul and Britain, Constantine stayed behind. After Diocletian's retirement, he re-

---

[13]The story is told in an anonymous Byzantine *Life of Constantine*, translated in Samuel N. C. Lieu and Dominic Montserrat, eds., *From Constantine to Julian: Pagan and Byzantine Views— A Source History* (London: Routledge, 1996), pp. 106-8. Kousoulas (*Life and Times*, p. 9) is virtually the only contemporary scholar who gives any credence to the story. See also Bill Leadbetter, "The Illegitimacy of Constantine and the Birth of the Tetrarchy," in *Constantine: History, Historiography and Legend*, ed. Samuel Lieu and Dominic Montserrat (London: Routledge, 1998), pp. 74-85, for a discussion of Constantine's illegitimacy.

[14]Leadbetter, "Illegitimacy," p. 79.

[15]Raymond Van Dam, *The Roman Revolution of Constantine* (Cambridge: Cambridge University Press, 2008), pp. 293-94. Van Dam emphasizes that Constantine associated these memories with the biblical accounts of Moses in Egypt and Daniel in Babylon.

[16]Translation in Lieu and Montserrat, *From Constantine to Julian*, p. 43. Eusebius clearly presents Constantine as a Moses figure in his *Life*, but the exploits recounted in the *Origo* suggest a closer analogy with David or Jonathan. To say that the *Origo* employs typology is not to cast doubt on its accuracy. Types work because similar things happen at different times. Galerius could be depicted as Saul to Constantine's David because Galerius was as paranoid as the first king of Israel.

mained in the court of Galerius. It was not a happy arrangement. Galerius was evidently suspicious of both Constantine's ambition and his father's prospects in the West, and keeping Constantine close at hand allowed the emperor to keep an eye on the rising young officer, to maintain leverage against Constantius, and to prevent a dangerous concentration of power in the West. "We beseech you, bend you to remain / Here," Claudius of Denmark said to his nephew Hamlet, "in the cheer and comfort of our eye, / Our chiefest courtier, cousin, and our son" (*Hamlet* 1.2). Galerius might have used the same rhetoric concerning Constantine, to the same effect: Stay close, so I can keep my eye on you.

Constantius repeatedly requested that Galerius send Constantine to join him in the West, and finally Galerius agreed. Fearing that Galerius might change his mind, Constantine left that same night, reputedly moving at great speed and maiming the post horses along the way to block pursuit.[17] Eusebius and other writers claim that Constantine arrived at his father's deathbed, but in fact his father was in Boulogne, in the last stages of preparation for his invasion of Britain, when his son arrived, and Constantine accompanied his father on this successful British campaign. Shortly after Constantius had brought Britain back under Roman dominion, he fell ill. On July 25, 306, scarcely fourteen months after assuming the position of Augustus, Constantius died at York and with his dying breath designated Constantine as his successor, a decision gladly confirmed by the troops.[18]

Constantine was emperor in his midthirties.

END OF THE TETRARCHY

If Galerius's plots were one reason for the breakdown of the Tetrarchy, the elevation of Constantine highlights a more basic weakness in the system. The flaw in Diocletian's plan was obvious. So long as the members of the imperial college respected one another and restrained their own ambi-

---

[17]Potter, *Roman Empire,* pp. 344-45, analyzes the alternative accounts of his escape. The *Origo* states that Constantine killed the post horses along the route (Lieu and Montserrat, *From Constantine to Julian,* p. 43).

[18]Many scholars have suggested that Constantine was first proclaimed Augustus and later demoted by Galerius to the position of Caesar. The evidence is too sketchy to allow us to know for sure, but it is clear from milestones throughout the Western Empire that Constantine for a time labeled himself *nobilissimus Caesar* (Humphries, "From Usurper to Emperor," pp. 87-88).

tions, it would work. But what would happen when one member attempted to bypass his colleagues? And what would happen to imperial sons who were not chosen for succession? As Burckhardt perceptively notes, sons must either join the imperial college or be controlled—and controlling rivals in fourth-century Rome meant killing them.[19] It is not at all surprising that in the generation following Diocletian's retirement there were periods when as many as six men claimed the position of Augustus.

The Tetrarchy's treatment of the role of family ties was ambiguous from the beginning.[20] Constantius married Theodora, daughter of Maximian, while Galerius married Diocletian's daughter Valeria. But Constantius and Galerius did not marry to join the original Tetrarchy; they joined the Tetrarchy because they were already sons-in-law of the two Augusti. Diocletian arranged the marriages ahead of time so that the Tetrarchy would be anchored in more traditional family bonds.[21] From the beginning, then, marriage tied the Tetrarchy together, and the intermarriages of the Tetrarchs continued into, and confused, the following generation as well. Maxentius, the son of Maximian, married Galerius's daughter, while Constantine married Maximian's other daughter Fausta, thus making him brother-in-law to his father and both brother-in-law and nephew of Maxentius.[22] These marriages created kin relations that resemble the fictive kin relations of the Principate, when emperors "adopted" a successor. It is not altogether clear that Diocletian intended to change the rules of succession; then again, it is not clear that he wanted to retain old rules.[23] The ambiguity proved fatal.

No doubt it seemed perfectly natural to the troops in York to acclaim a new emperor and to confer that honor on the son of the dead emperor. Armies had been making emperors for several generations, and the transfer of power from father to son was one of the most ancient of succession systems. But Burckhardt describes Constantine as "the usurper," and many

---

[19]Simon Corcoran, "Before Constantine," in *The Cambridge Companion to the Age of Constantine*, ed. Noel Lenski (Cambridge: Cambridge University Press, 2006), p. 54, points to the deaths of Licinius and of the relatives of Constantine after Constantine's death in 337.

[20]Potter, *Roman Empire*, p. 340, speaks of a "tacit" agreement that the sons of Constantius and Maximian would succeed them.

[21]Leadbetter, "Illegitimacy," p. 82.

[22]H. A. Drake, *Constantine and the Bishops: The Politics of Intolerance* (Baltimore: Johns Hopkins University Press, 2000), p. 503, n. 8; Humphries, "From Usurper to Emperor," p. 89.

[23]Drake, *Constantine and the Bishops*, p. 160.

scholars since have followed his lead.[24] That is an ahistorical designation. In Latin, "usurper" translates *tyrannus,* and a tyrant is not a ruler who attempts to gain power without authorization but a ruler who attempts but *fails* to gain power. In the fourth century, it is a retrospective designation; a ruler legitimizes his rule by hanging on to power against his rivals.[25] By the rules of the Tetrarchy, too, Constantine had a legitimate claim to the emperorship. His father was senior Augustus, and if the precedent of Diocletian was to be followed, it was the senior Augustus who selected his successor.[26] In any case, Galerius was less rigid than Burckhardt and his followers. When Constantine sent the Eastern Augustus an image of himself crowned with laurel, Galerius accepted him as a constitutionally legitimate member of the imperial college.[27] The acceptance was grudging, no doubt, but Galerius had no constitutional basis for refusing.

Yet the Tetrarchy was becoming unbalanced: Instead of two Augusti and two Caesars, there was Galerius and three Caesars (Daia, Severus, Constantine). Things became more complicated and more precarious in October 306 when Maximian's son Maxentius, envious of Constantine's elevation at York, seized power in Rome with the support of the praetorian guard and the plebs.[28] Galerius had subjected the city to census and taxation, a violation of the traditional sacred privileges of the capital. Maxentius rose to power claiming that he would restore Rome's central position in the empire and that he would defend the traditional status of the Italian cities against unconstitutional assaults from Galerius. It was no longer a Tetrarchy but a Pentarchy, and a highly unstable one: In Britain and Gaul there was Constantine; the two Caesars Daia and Severus remained in place, and Galerius continued to be the official Augustus. But Maxentius now claimed the same senior position. Maxentius sought to legitimize his

---

[24]For references, see Humphries, "From Usurper to Emperor," p. 84, n. 9.

[25]Ibid., pp. 85-87. See also Alan Wardman, "Usurpers and Internal Conflicts in the 4th Century A.D," *Historia* 33, no. 2 (1984): 220-37.

[26]Potter, *Roman Empire,* p. 346.

[27]Ibid., p. 346. Humphries, "From Usurper to Emperor," pp. 89-90, makes a strong case for the conclusion that "Constantine and Maxentius were being prepared as potential heirs," pointing out that this helps to explain "why the troops at York so readily transferred their allegiance from the father Constantius to the son Constantine; and why the former western Augustus Maximian was called out of retirement to lend an air of legitimacy to the regime of his son Maxentius. Above all, they explain why dynasty-building became one of the key tactics used by Constantine in his efforts to establish legitimacy over the next six years and beyond."

[28]Lactantius *Death* 26.

usurpation by appealing to Galerius for recognition, but Galerius, despite being Maxentius's father-in-law, refused.[29]

Victors write biography as much as history, and a later panegyrist, orating before Constantine around 313, described the defeated Maxentius as a man of "contemptibly small stature, twisted and slack of limb."[30] Whatever his physical appearance, he had some political skill. Maxentius eschewed the symbolisms and paraphernalia of the Tetrachy, adopting instead an imperial style that harked back to the rugged simplicities of Augustus and Trajan. Like Constantine, he recognized that Christians, still persecuted in the East, were a disaffected and potentially powerful constituency, and he annulled the persecution edict within his territories.[31] He was the last of the emperors to court traditional Roman elites to support his power, and when Constantine later invaded Italy, he led, by Maxentius's lights, a northern "army of Gauls" and "barbarians."[32]

Before the year was out, the Pentarchy turned into a Sextarchy, as Maxentius called his father, Maximian, out of retirement to assume the position of Augustus, joining his son in Rome. If any proof were needed of Maximian's reluctance to abdicate, this was it. If he agreed with Diocletian in principle, he did not share the senior tetrarch's self-restraint. He was all too ready to become what Maxentius called him, "Augustus for the second time." Diocletian, hearing the news in his seaside palace at Split, must have thought that all his work had been in vain. The political chaos of the third century had returned, only a few years after his retirement. The wheel turned, and Diocletian's golden age was rapidly losing its luster.

---

[29]Barnes, *Constantine and Eusebius*, p. 30.

[30]Panegyric 12.4.3, in *In Praise of Later Roman Emperors: The Panegyrici Latini*, ed. and trans. C. E. V. Nixon and Barbara Saylor Rodgers (Berkeley: University of California Press, 1994), p. 301.

[31]Drake, *Constantine and the Bishops*, pp. 170-72; MacMullen, *Constantine*, p. 62; Kousoulas, *Life and Times*, pp. 108-82.

[32]Van Dam, *Roman Revolution*, p. 37. Van Dam points out that Constantine remained north and east through most of his reign: "he never visited the provinces in Spain, Africa, southern Italy and Sicily, Greece, Western Asia Minor, Palestine, or Egypt, and he made only one round trip through central Asia Minor to Antioch in Syria" (p. 38). He also notes that under Maxentius, and then again under Constantine, the importance of Rome revived to some degree; Constantine appointed members of the senatorial class to office, and he spoke to the Senate when he entered Rome after the battle with Maxentius. He returned to Rome for anniversaries as well (pp. 45-46). Still, his conception of the Empire "plainly emphasized the northern frontiers" (p. 52), and while Helena was buried in Rome, Constantine himself was buried in the new Rome of Constantinople (pp. 58-59).

Galerius may have been reluctant to accept Constantine's elevation, but he could not oppose the decision of Constantius. Accepting Maxentius's seizure of power was impossible. Maxentius had gained support by directly opposing Galerius's policies in Italy, and he had sought legitimation not from the existing senior Augustus but from his retired father. Galerius dispatched Severus, the Western Caesar, to dislodge Maxentius. Many of the soldiers in Severus's army, however, had served under Maximian and were loath to attack their former commander. Faced with mounting desertions, Severus retreated to Ravenna, where Maximian laid siege. Unable to take the city, Maximian worked out terms and took Severus captive to the camp Tres Tabernae outside Rome, where he was later executed or committed suicide during the summer of 307.[33]

Galerius decided he would have to extricate Maxentius himself, and in the autumn of 307 he marched into Italy toward Rome. His tax policies had made him unpopular in Italy, and his campaign foundered. Despite his huge army, he lacked the manpower to mount a thorough siege of Rome itself, and Maxentius rebuffed the ambassadors he sent into the city to negotiate. Like Severus, Galerius began to lose troops to old Maximian. Fearing that remaining near Rome would be disastrous, Galerius retreated, leaving behind a wake of vindictive destruction.

Constantine waited and watched from Gaul. Observing first Severus and then Galerius retreat from Italy, Constantine realized that Galerius's recognition of his position was a precarious basis for future power. He needed a firmer tie to the Western power network, and bolstered his power with one of the oldest of political tools—marriage. Constantine had been married before, to Minervina, and had a son, Crispus, by that first marriage. Minervina was dead, and now Constantine took a second wife. To shore up his own position, and perhaps betting that the Western emperors were the winning horse, he entered an alliance with Maximian and Maxentius, sealed by his marriage to Maximian's daughter Fausta late in the summer of 307.[34] Inscriptions and panegyrics highlighted the family connection, addressing him as "grandson of Marcus Aurelius Valerius Max-

---

[33]Barnes, *Constantine and Eusebius,* p. 30. Potter, *Roman Empire,* p. 349, claims that Maxentius had Severus murdered.
[34]Drake, *Constantine and the Bishops,* p. 170.

imian Augustus" (*Marci Aureli Valeri Maximiani Augusti nepos*).[35] Maximian and Maxentius had their own reasons for the alliance. Getting rid of Severus was not going to endear them to Galerius, and they needed Constantine and his army to stare down the Eastern Augustus or to repel another invasion.[36] Constantine needed them too. He had appointed his own consuls in Gaul, defying Galerius's seniority in the imperial college. In retaliation, Galerius dropped Constantine from his coinage during the autumn of 307, a signal that he no longer considered him a member of the imperial college. For Galerius, there were only two legitimate members left—Maximian Daia and himself.[37]

The Tetrarchy was in disarray, and something had to be done about Maxentius too. On November 11, 308, Diocletian returned one last time to public life to meet with Galerius and Maximian at the Augustan military base at Carnuntum, near the Danube in what is now Austria. There the Tetrarchy was patched together. Maximian again agreed to step down, and Licinius, an old friend and ally of Galerius, leaped to the position of Western Augustus, while Constantine and Daia were confirmed as legitimate Caesars and adopted as *filii Augustorum*.[38] The Tetrarchan principle that emperors choose emperors, with the confirmation of the army, was restored.[39]

For a few years, the empire enjoyed internal calm and stability. Constantine kept himself busy with campaigns against the Franks and with building a bridge across the Rhine at Cologne. Galerius and Licinius fought the Carpi in the Balkans.[40] Maxentius remained in Rome, but Licinius had been assigned to finish him off.

For a time Maxentius had been the wild card, but his father proved difficult to handle as well. In spring 308 Maximian had attempted to depose his son. Standing before the army that he had once led, he asked the men to choose between father and son. They chose Maxentius, and Maximian, fearing his life, fled to the protection of his son-in-law, Constantine. But he was no more submissive to his son-in-law than he had been to his son.

---

[35]Humphries, "From Usurper to Emperor," p. 91.
[36]Ibid., p. 90.
[37]Ibid., pp. 90-91.
[38]Potter, *Roman Empire,* p. 349; Humphries, "From Usurper to Emperor," pp. 91-92; Barnes, *Constantine and Eusebius,* pp. 32-33.
[39]Potter, *Roman Empire,* p. 350.
[40]Ibid., p. 351.

When Constantine deployed him south on a military expedition two years later, he went to Arles, announced that Constantine was dead, and proclaimed himself emperor—again. Fearing Constantine's retribution, he fled to Marseilles, but when Constantine arrived after a forced march, the citizens opened the gates to him. Maximian was caught and allowed, or ordered, to commit suicide.[41] Later propaganda mentions a more direct plot, in which Maximian planned to kill Constantine in his sleep. Constantine's wife Fausta caught wind of the conspiracy and warned her husband, who placed a eunuch in the bed in his place. Maximian sneaked in, killed the man he thought was the sleeping Caesar, and ran out the door only to find Constantine waiting, sword drawn, to intercept him.[42] Whatever happened, Constantine had had enough of his relations and broke off the alliance he had with Maxentius to join hands with the Eastern Augustus, Licinius. The alliance was sealed, like most alliances of the time, with a promise of marriage: Licinius was to marry Constantine's sister Constantia. In this way Constantine acquired another brother-in-law with whom he would eventually be at odds.

All was not well in Rome. Maxentius ruled Rome for six years and must have had some ability to win and retain loyalty. Like most emperors, he bolstered his popularity by extensive euergetism, bestowing gifts of bread, circuses, and baths.[43] He was a busy builder. His "most extensive construction projects at Rome were just beyond the east end of the old Forum, on the north side of the Sacred Way." In that area of the city he "completely rebuilt the burned-out Temple of Venus and Roma, the largest temple in the city, which commemorated the eternity of Rome and its venerated status in the divine order," and next door went "an enormous basilica, the Basilica Nova. At one corner of the basilica he constructed a rotunda on the Sacred Way that probably was a temple dedicated in part to a cult in honor of his young son Romulus." Finally, "he may have had the colossal bronze statue (originally of Nero) that still stood next to the Colosseum rededicated in honor of his son."[44]

---

[41]Drake, *Constantine and the Bishops*, pp. 174-75. Potter, *Roman Empire*, p. 352, notes that the actual circumstances of Maximian's death are impossible to know for certain.

[42]The story is told in Lactantius *Death* 30; cf. Kousoulas, *Life and Times*, pp. 193-94.

[43]For euergetism as imperial policy in general, see Paul Veyne, "Clientele et corruption au service de l'État: La venalité des offices dans le Bas-Empire romain," *Annales* 36, no. 3 (1981).

[44]Van Dam, *Roman Revolution*, p. 82.

Over time, however, the Romans found him dangerous, and lecherous to boot. When the North African rebel Alexander stopped grain shipments to the capital in 309, riots broke out, which Maxentius brutally suppressed. Six thousand citizens "were slaughtered in the streets."[45] He made himself odious to the senatorial class, whose support he needed to maintain power. He imprisoned senators and took other men's wives for himself and for his favorites.[46] In February 312, the prefect Junius Flavianus resigned in disgrace following his wife's suicide, which reportedly was her typically Roman way of staving off Maxentius's seductions. At public events Maxentius was shouted down by Roman crowds, perhaps incited by Constantine's agents.[47] Even pagan writers who deploy every weapon they can against Constantine find nothing good to say about Maxentius. Stories of Maxentius's "tyranny" had come to Constantine, and, recognizing an opportunity to realize his own ambitions, Constantine set out toward the capital on the convenient pretext of liberating the city. Constantine and Maxentius were moving inexorably toward a showdown.

Alliances and strategies shifted again in spring 311, when Galerius died of a wasting disease. Daia moved quickly to seize Galerius's territories in Asia Minor and secured a peace with Licinius, the other remaining emperor of the east. Far from renouncing Diocletian's persecution edict, Daia set about to reform paganism.[48] Maxentius and Daia also grew close, or at least so the rumors went. The alliance was fateful for Maxentius. He had hoped to gain Christian support in Rome and Italy by canceling the persecution edict, but when he allied with the arch-persecutor Daia, he lost that constituency: "In a stroke," H. A. Drake writes, "Constantine became the true champion [of the church], Maxentius an unworthy pretender."[49] As part of his agreement with Daia, Maxentius declared war on Constan-

---

[45]Barnes, *Constantine and Eusebius*, p. 37.

[46]Linda Jones Hall, "Cicero's *instinctu divino* and Constantine's *instinctu divinitatis*: The Evidence of the Arch of Constantine for the Senatorial View of the 'Vision' of Constantine," *Journal of Early Christian Studies* 6, no. 4 (1998): 2. I am working from a printout of the article whose pagination does not match the published version.

[47]Kousoulas, *Life and Times*, p. 237.

[48]Drake, *Constantine and the Bishops*, p. 171; Potter, *Roman Empire*, p. 355; Oliver Nicholson, "The 'Pagan Churches' of Maximinus Daia and Julian the Apostate," *Journal of Ecclesiastical History* 45, no. 1 (1994); and see below, chapter 4.

[49]Drake, *Constantine and the Bishops*, p. 174.

tine. His pretext was to avenge his father's death, which he blamed on Constantine, but his treatment of his father was hardly a model of filial *pietas*. Given Maxentius's treachery toward the church, Christians viewed war between Constantine and Maxentius as a crusade for the liberation not only of the city but also of the church at Rome.

By late 311, the imperial alliances stood as follows. Constantine was allied with Licinius, who had temporarily made peace with Daia. Maxentius and Daia were allied as well. Diocletian, even in retirement, had curbed the ambitions of the other men to some degree, but the jockeying and alignments and realignments meant that the fuse was burning short. With Diocletian's death on December 3, restraint evaporated. Over the following year and a half, open war broke out between the claimants to the empire, and when all was done Constantine was emperor of the West.

It happened this way: in summer 312, with a small army of forty thousand soldiers, Constantine crossed into Italy and began moving toward Rome. He met Maxentius's forces at Susa, Turin, and Verona and was victorious in each encounter.[50] By October he was camped within sight of Rome, on the Tiber, near Milvian Bridge.

October 28 marked the sixth anniversary of Maxentius's elevation as Augustus. It seemed a propitious moment for him to confront his enemy, and his confidence was buoyed by an oracle that reported, with the ambiguity characteristic of all oracles, that "the enemy of Rome" would soon be defeated. He believed he was engaged in a battle of gods, a religious war, one in which he upheld the traditional worship of the empire.[51] Encouraged by the oracle, Maxentius decided not to wait until his anniversary festivities were finished but marched out of the impregnable city to meet Constantine by the river. It was an imprudent military decision.

By that time the Milvian bridge had been destroyed, and Maxentius had constructed in its place a pontoon bridge as a trap for Constantine's troops. He hoped that they would try to cross the bridge, which could then be cut, leaving Constantine's soldiers flailing in the deadly waters of the Tiber.[52] As it happened, Maxentius's forces were pushed back, and, caught

---

[50]On the Italian campaign, see Odahl, *Constantine and the Christian Empire*, pp. 101-4; Kousoulas, *Life and Times*, pp. 231-33; Potter, *Roman Empire*, p. 357.

[51]Odahl, *Constantine and the Christian Empire*, p. 100.

[52]Kousoulas, *Life and Times*, pp. 245-46.

between Constantine's forces and the river, they fled across the bridge. In their eagerness to escape, they broke the bridge, and many drowned. Maxentius's own body was found downstream. A panegyrist found it significant that he had not reached his seventh year of rule: "The divine spirit and the eternal majesty of the city itself robbed the cursed man of good sense, and made him rush out, after his inveterate sloth and shameful hiding, and after the passing of six indolent years to mark the very day of his accession by his final destruction, that he did not violate the sacred and holy number seven even by commencing upon it."[53]

The following day Constantine entered the city of Rome in triumph, accompanied by a soldier who displayed Maxentius's head on a pike. Tyranny had been decapitated, and the Senate proclaimed Constantine the "liberator of the city" (*liberator urbis*).[54] It was possibly his first visit to the capital, and the people received him enthusiastically. "Without a thought of resistance, crowds jammed the streets to catch a glimpse of the victor," Ramsay MacMullen writes, "cheered themselves hoarse, and were rewarded with scattered largesses and a good show." It was a show not unlike "our modern theater-in-the-round, a parade fairly bursting with drama that all could be a part of." On this day "the welcome of his *adventus* carried him through the Porta Triumphalis [Gate of Triumph] in a coach-and-four, by winding progress to the start of the Via Sacra, into the Forum Romanum, and so to his palace."[55]

Constantine's victory marked the end of the entire system of the Tetrarchy and the beginning of a new political theology. The change showed itself almost immediately. The rules of the triumph required Constantine to enter the Capitolium and offer sacrifice to Jupiter; Constantine refused.[56] Diocletian's empire was built on sacrifice, his persecutions in-

---

[53]Panegyric 12.16.2, in *In Praise of Later Roman Emperors*, ed. Nixon and Rodgers, p. 318.

[54]See Van Dam, *Roman Revolution*, pp. 135-36, for the symbolism of decapitation. The title is found on the Arch of Constantine.

[55]MacMullen, *Constantine*, p. 81.

[56]Johannes Straub, "Konstantins Verzicht auf den Gang zum Kapitol," *Historia* 4, nos. 2/3 (1955), provides the most complete examination of the evidence. R. P. C. Hanson, "The Christian Attitude to Pagan Religions up to the Time of Constantine the Great," *ANRW* 23 (1980): 962-64; MacMullen, *Constantine*, p. 81; Kousoulas, *Life and Times*, p. 249. On Roman triumphs in general, see Mary Beard, *The Roman Triumph* (Cambridge, Mass.: Belknap/Harvard University Press, 2007). Ammianus Marcellinus records this about Constantius's entry into Rome in 357: "Being saluted as Augustus with favoring shouts, while hills and shores thundered out the roar, he never stirred, but showed himself as calm and imperturb-

spired by a failed sacrifice. As soon as he defeated Maxentius, Constantine made it clear that a new political theology was coming to be, a political theology without sacrifice. It was a signal of the "opposition to sacrifice" that he would hold to "consistently for the rest of his life."[57]

Diocletian's divine patrons were also being dethroned. Years before, the second Tetrarchy had been announced in Nicomedia in the shadow of a statue of Jupiter, and in Rome statues of the four original Tetrarchs were arranged around a statue of Jupiter. When Constantine's Arch was unveiled three years after he took Rome, the emperor was depicted not facing Jupiter but with his back to the god.[58]

In the contest of the gods, Jupiter had not won. It was not yet clear to everyone who had.

---

able, as he was commonly seen in the provinces. For he both stooped when passing through lofty gates (although he was very short), and as if his neck were in a vise, he kept the gaze of his eyes straight ahead, and turned his face neither to right nor to left, but (as if he were a clay figure) neither did he nod when the wheel jolted nor was he ever seen to spit, or to wipe and rub his nose or face, or move his hands about, And although this was affectation on his part yet these and various other features of his more intimate life were tokens of no slight endurance, granted to him alone, as was given to be understood" (quoted in Drake, *Constantine and the Bishops,* pp. 123-24).

[57]Hanson, "Christian Attitude," p. 971.
[58]Van Dam, *Roman Revolution,* p. 97.

4

By This Sign

*About noon, when the day was already
beginning to decline, he saw with his own eyes the trophy
of a cross of light in the heavens, above the sun, and
bearing the inscription, Conquer by this.*

EUSEBIUS OF CAESAREA, *LIFE OF CONSTANTINE*

To Eusebius, the battle of Milvian Bridge was nothing less than a new exodus.[1] Just as "once in the days of Moses and the Hebrew nation, who were worshipers of God, Pharaoh's chariots and his host [God] cast into the sea and his chosen chariot-captains [were] drowned in the Red Sea," so now in the fourth century "Maxentius, and the soldiers and guards with him, went down into the depths like stone." Like Pharaoh and his hosts, Maxentius "sank as lead in the mighty waters." Constantine and the Christians delivered by him "obtained victory from God" and thus joined in singing the song of Moses: "Let us sing unto the Lord, for he has been glorified exceedingly: the horse and his rider has he thrown into the sea. He is become my helper and my shield unto salvation. And again, Who is like you, O Lord, among the gods? who is like you, glorious in holiness, marvelous in praises, doing wonders?" When Maxentius attempted to flee

---

[1] Eusebius used a Mosaic template to organize his entire biography of Constantine; see Anna Wilson, "Biographical Models: The Constantinian Period and Beyond," in *Constantine: History, Historiography and Legend*, ed. Samuel Lieu and Dominic Montserrat (London: Routledge, 1998), pp. 107-35.

"the divinely-aided forces of Constantine" by crossing the river, his bridge became an "engine of destruction, really against himself." Like Moses' battle with Pharaoh, it was a battle of deities: Constantine's "God stood by the one to protect him, while the other, godless, proved to be the miserable contriver of these secret devices to his own ruin." Eusebius saw in Maxentius's fall confirmation of the proverbial wisdom of the Old Testament: "He has made a pit, and dug it, and is fallen into the ditch which he made. His mischief shall return upon his own head, and his violence shall come down upon his own pate."[2]

The comparison was multifaceted. Not only was Maxentius an oppressive pharaoh who had abused the people of Rome, but Constantine entered Rome as a *Christian* conqueror. His soldier carried a new standard known as the *labarum*, a long spear made into a cross with a perpendicular bar, and "on top of the whole was fixed a wreath of gold and precious stones," within which the first letters of *Christos* were inscribed.[3] Constantine wore the same insignia on his own helmet.[4] Israel's crossing of the sea was, the apostle Paul said (1 Cor 10:1-4), a baptism, a transition from Egypt into the wilderness and toward the land of promise. For Eusebius, Rome had been baptized in the Tiber.

CONFLICTING STORIES

Exactly what happened in the days before the battle of Milvian Bridge was disputed almost from the beginning. Eusebius recorded what became the most popular version of the story. Constantine knew that within the city Maxentius, like the Babylonian Belshazzar, was deploy-

---

[2]Eusebius *Life* 1.38.

[3]Ibid., 1.31. Eusebius is describing a developed and beautified form of the labarum, not the form that it had on the day of Constantine's victory, but there is no reason to doubt that the talisman was essentially the same. For analysis, see H. A. Drake, *Constantine and the Bishops: The Politics of Intolerance* (Baltimore: Johns Hopkins University Press, 2000), pp. 201-4; Drake presses his argument about Constantine's use of deliberate ambiguity too far here, arguing that it was for Constantine more a dynastic than a religious symbol. Given the tenor of fourth-century political life, however, the distinction is another example of the "conceptual anachronism" that Drake charges against Burckhardt. Peter Weiss, "The Vision of Constantine," trans. A. R. Birley, *Journal of Roman Archaeology* 16 (2003): 254-55, claims that the word *labarum* is Celtic in origin and that it combined symbolism of Sol and the *corona* with the Christian symbol of Christ's monogram.

[4]See Andreas Alfoldi, "The Helmet of Constantine with the Christian Monogram," *Journal of Roman Studies* 22, no. 1 (1932).

ing every form of magic and incantation against his rival. Being a religious man, Constantine realized that his army alone could not stand alone against such a supernatural attack, and he considered which god he might ask for help. He had already become convinced that the Diocletian-Galerian policy of persecution was ineffectual, and worse. Even at the height of the persecution, his father had enforced the policy leniently, and Constantine could not but be struck by the contrast between Constantius's prosperous life and calm death and the frenzied panic of the dying Galerius.[5] The god of the Christians must be a very powerful god, and turning to him was worth the risk.

Almost immediately, his hopes were answered. When Constantine "called on him with earnest prayer and supplications that he would reveal to him who he was, and stretch forth his right hand to help him in his present difficulties . . . a most marvelous sign appeared to him from heaven, the account of which it might have been hard to believe had it been related by any other person." According to the emperor's story, "about noon, when the day was already beginning to decline, he saw with his own eyes the trophy of a cross of light in the heavens, above the sun, and bearing the inscription, Conquer by this."[6] His entire army saw it, and all were "struck with amazement" at "the miracle." Eusebius vouched for the truth of this account by claiming that he received it straight from Constantine: "But since the victorious emperor himself long afterwards declared it to the writer of this history, when he was honored with his acquaintance and society, and confirmed his statement by an oath, who could hesitate to accredit the relation, especially

---

[5]Eusebius calls the Christian God the "God of his father," and this, along with other evidence such as the name of Constantine's sister (Anastasia, "Resurrection") and the clearly Christian testimony of Constantine's mother Helena later in life, have led some to conclude that Constantius was already a Christian. The most sustained effort to argue this point is T. G. Elliott, *The Christianity of Constantine the Great* (Scranton, Penn.: University of Scranton Press, 1996). To make his case, however, Elliott has to dismiss a fair bit of Eusebius as unreliable. Besides, though Constantius was a much less vigorous persecutor than Diocletian or Galerius, he did destroy some churches in the Western empire after the decree of persecution was issued in 303. R. P. C. Hanson, "The Christian Attitude to Pagan Religions up to the Time of Constantine the Great," *ANRW* 23 (1980), succinctly assesses the evidence, concluding that Constantius was not a Christian but was sympathetic.

[6]In Eusebius's Greek the phrase is *en touto nika* (conquer by this), but this is rendered on the earliest Latin coinage as *hoc signo victor eris* (by this sign you will be victor) rather than, as later, *in hoc vince* or *in hoc signo vinces*. Charles Matson Odahl, *Constantine and the Christian Empire* (London: Routledge, 2004), pp. 318-19, n. 11 and the literature cited.

since the testimony of after-time has established its truth?"[7]

In the public reception area of the Vatican palace are four Stanze di Raffaello, each of which is decorated with paintings from the school of the Renaissance master Raphael. The largest is the Sala di Constantino or Hall of Constantine, and its frescoes depict episodes from the life (and legends) of Constantine—the battle of Milvian Bridge, the donation of the Vatican Hill to Pope Sylvester (who looks suspiciously like Raphael's patron, Pope Julius II), and of course the Vision of the Cross. Flanked by paintings of two popes, the *Vision* (painted in 1520-1524) shows a startled Constantine in Roman armor standing on a pedestal in front of his commander's tent. He is beginning to address the mustered troops, but something has interrupted him. His hands rise in surprise as he stares with wide eyes toward the sky. In the light that breaks through the turbulent dark clouds, three angels hold a cross, and the beams of light shining toward distant Rome double as a banner bearing the inscription EN TOYTO NIKA. A dragon twists through the sky, writhing in anger but also in abject defeat. In the seventeenth century, Peter Paul Rubens's painting of Constantine's conversion used the same imagery—light from heaven beaming onto an armored Constantine and his troops.

This seems to be what Eusebius had in mind, and this is the picture that most people have of the emperor's conversion. Earlier than Eusebius, though, Lactantius, who as the tutor to Constantine's sons was closer to the emperor than was Eusebius, recorded a simpler story. According to his account, "Constantine was directed in a dream to cause the heavenly sign to be delineated on the shields of his soldiers, and so to proceed to battle." Following the directive, he had their shields marked with the Greek letter *chi* (an "X" shape), through which a perpendicular line was drawn and then curved around at the top. The result was a *chi-rho* combination (which looks like the English letters XP), the first letters of the name of Christ. Lactantius says that "having this sign, . . . his troops stood to arms."[8]

The differences of the two accounts are obvious. Eusebius records no dream, and though Lactantius says that Constantine marked his soldiers' shields with the "heavenly sign," he does not inform us where Constantine got the idea for the sign. By Lactantius's account, Constantine's vision

---

[7]Eusebius *Life* 1.28.
[8]Lactantius *Death* 44.

could well have taken place in private, while Eusebius claims that Constantine's entire army witnessed the sign.

Pagan writers offered their own account of Constantine's conversion experience. Writing in the late fifth century, Zosimus gives a detailed account of Constantine's Italian campaign—citing troops' strength, strategy, positioning, geography, and other details—but never mentions Constantine's vision or his conversion. He admits that Constantine became a Christian but dates the event a decade and a half later and claims it was Constantine's guilty response to a horrific family and political episode, the execution of his son Crispus and his wife Fausta.[9] Zosimus's account is chronologically impossible, since it dates Constantine's conversion more than a decade after the emperor had begun to identify himself publicly with Christianity. Zosimus's history was published in a Latin translation in the late sixteenth century and was reprinted in its original Greek in the following century. It has had some influence on the image of Constantine. Without following Zosimus, many modern scholars have dismissed the Eusebian story. Jakob Burckhardt insisted that we have to give it up along with all the other legends of Constantine,[10] and James Carroll describes it as a "boy's adventure story."[11] MacMullen found in the different versions evidence that the story was blossoming over time into legend.[12]

CHRISTIAN EMPEROR?

Over the centuries, this has been *the* "Constantinian question," and it is still one aspect of the riddle of the fourth century: What, if anything, happened to Constantine on the night before the battle of Milvian Bridge? Did he become a half-committed polytheist? Was he a syncretistic monotheist, trying to split his loyalties between the Christian God and Sol the god of the sun? Was he a cynical politician ready to jump on whatever horse would carry him forward? Did he have any "subjective religious experience"?[13]

---

[9]See below, chapter 5. For a discussion of Zosimus and his influence on later writers, see Francois Paschoud, "Zosime 2,29 et la version paienne de la conversion de Constantin," *Historia* 20, nos. 2/3 (1971): 334-53.

[10]Jacob Burckhardt, *The Age of Constantine the Great*, trans. Moses Hadas (Berkeley: University of California Press, 1983), p. 296.

[11]James Carroll, *Constantine's Sword: The Church and the Jews* (Boston: Houghton Mifflin, 2001), p. 181.

[12]Ramsay MacMullen, *Constantine* (London: Croom Helm, 1987), pp. 74-77.

[13]John Howard Yoder, *Christian Attitudes to War, Peace and Revolution*, ed. Theodore J. Koontz

Eusebius claimed to have heard the story directly from Constantine, who confirmed the story with an oath. One might dismiss the oath, but this assumes a high level of cynicism on Constantine's part that is hard to believe. Credulous Eusebius may have been, but he was not the only one to hear the story. Coins issued in the middle of the fourth century by Constantine's sons depict the scene, and besides, Constantine told Eusebius of a *public* event, witnessed by soldiers—a story, in short, that could be confirmed or denied by men in Constantine's retinue. Constantine may have lied and taken a false oath; Eusebius may have lied or distorted what he heard. Neither option is plausible. The far more likely conclusion is that Constantine saw something that he took as a divine sign.

Constantine had a history of mystical experience.[14] An anonymous panegyric delivered probably in 310 refers to an earlier vision of Apollo. The orator reminded Caesar Constantine that he did "see your patron Apollo, and Victory accompanying him, offering you a crown of laurel, each of which represents a foretelling of thirty years." Referring either to the god or perhaps to the "deified" emperor Augustus, he added, "You did see him, and you recognized yourself in the image of the one to whom the sacred poems of bards prophesied that the kingdoms of the whole world were due by right. That has now come to pass, seeing that you are, Emperor, like him, young, blessed, our saviour and a very handsome one!"[15] By other accounts, after 310 Constantine changed his loyalty from the war god Mars to the sun god Sol, who also doubled as Apollo. Though practical as any successful ruler and military man, Constantine was also so deeply religious in the fourth-century way that his religion often looks to us like superstition.

A superstitious/religious Constantine would be disinclined to insult the gods by changing the standards of his army on the eve of a major battle. Roman army standards were religious objects, venerated by the troops and often credited with talismanic powers, as indeed the labarum eventually

---

and Andy Alexis-Baker (Grand Rapids: Brazos, 2009), p. 58, says no.

[14]Drake, *Constantine and the Bishops*, p. 188, calls him a "very vision-prone emperor." Weiss, "Vision," n. 68, argues that the vision of Apollo was the same as the cross vision.

[15]Panegyric 6.21.4-6, in *In Praise of Later Roman Emperors: The Panegyrici Latini,* ed. and trans. C. E. V. Nixon and Barbara Saylor Rodgers (Berkeley: University of California Press, 1994), pp. 248-50.

was.[16] Changing standards announced a change of loyalty from one divine patron to another. Constantine would not have changed the standards without powerful justification, such as a direct communication that he believed came from a different god, perhaps even from God. For the ancients generally, war was no exercise of sheer power, no secular Realpolitik. War involved bloodshed, and bloodshed was always hedged about with ritualized taboos. Diocletian's forces constituted a "sacred retinue,"[17] and Constantine would have thought of his army in the same way. Armies won by divine intervention, and the victory of an army was the victory of the army's god. If military victory depended on the patronage of a powerful god, it would be extreme folly to abandon the gods at the very moment of engagement.[18]

It was not only the standard that changed. After 312 Constantine himself turned, increasingly firmly, from paganism toward Christianity. We will trace this shift in his policies toward the church, in law, and in his conduct of the empire in the following chapters, but for now we can note the significance of the changes in his visual propaganda.[19] *Propaganda* may be the wrong term at the outset. As I have already emphasized repeatedly, fourth-century Romans were religious to the point of superstition. It is anachronistic to attribute to the political leaders of the time the kind of ironic stance toward religious legitimation that is often implied by the word *propaganda*. Diocletian, Galerius, Maxentius and Constantine—all of them believed their propaganda.

---

[16]John Helgeland has emphasized that the Roman army was a religious institution as well as an instrument of power politics. See his "Roman Army Religion," *ANRW* 2.16.1 (1978); and "Christians in the Roman Army from Marcus Aurelius to Constantine," *ANRW* 2.23.1 (1979).

[17]A. H. M. Jones, *Constantine and the Conversion of Europe* (Toronto: University of Toronto Press, 1978), p. 25.

[18]Again, the alternative is to suppose cynicism on a colossal scale and is historically incredible because it supposes that Constantine thought about war in a way that no other fourth-century Roman would think about war. The Philistines were acting in perfect accord with ancient custom when they seized Yahweh's ark and placed it in the temple of Dagon following the battle of Aphek (1 Samuel 4–6).

[19]On this, see Charles Matson Odahl, "God and Constantine: Divine Sanction for Imperial Rule in the First Christian Emperor's Early Letters and Art," *Catholic Historical Review* 81 (1995): 3. Elliott, *Christianity of Constantine*, argues that we have no need for the story of Constantine's conversion because he was raised as a Christian. Jones, *Constantine and the Conversion of Europe*, pp. 73, 75, points out that Constantine already had Hosius (Ossius) in his court before 312.

To be sure, Constantine's iconography sent multiple messages. Portraits associated him with the "good emperors" of the past. In contrast to the grizzled soldier-emperors of the Tetrarchy, Constantine had himself depicted clean-shaven and youthful, a conquering Alexander or a new Augustus restoring the glories of the early empire.[20] He was Constantine *Trachala*, Constantine of the Thick Neck, a physiognomic sign of his strength and firmness.[21] Constantine's father had taken on the name Marcus Flavius Valerius Constantius. By taking this name, Constantius associated himself with the short-lived Flavian dynasty, and Constantine maintained the connection. His full name was Caesar Flavius Valerius Aurelius Constantinus Augustus. The Flavian title was calculated to endear him to the capital, which was dotted with monuments left by the earlier Flavians—the Temple of Peace, the Arch and Baths of Titus, and, most famously, the Colosseum itself. Constantine's own arch was later placed in the same area of the city, aligned with the Arch of Titus.[22]

The religious message of Constantine's propaganda was ambiguous. In 315 the Senate acknowledged Constantine's victory over Maxentius with an honorific arch, which declared Constantine the *liberator urbis* and attributed his victory to "divine instinct" (the Latin phrase is *instinctu divinitatis*). The senators' language was general enough to appeal to a Christian or a pagan, but it is significant that they did not name Jupiter, Apollo or Mars as the inspiring deity.[23] Besides, the phrase had a well-known significance in Roman religious thought. Florus's standard account of the crimes and expulsion of Tarquin the Proud claimed that the Roman people were stirred to resist tyranny by "divine instinct" (*instinctu deorum*), and

---

[20]Odahl, *Constantine and the Christian Empire*, p. 109; David H. Wright, "The True Face of Constantine the Great," *Dumbarton Oaks Papers* 41 (1987): 493-507; and Christer Bruun, "The Thick Neck of the Emperor Constantine: Slimy Snails and 'Quellenforschung,' " *Historia* 44 (1995). Patrick Bruun, "Portrait of a Conspirator: Constantine's Break with the Tetrarchy," *Arctos*, n.s., 10 (1976), argues that Constantine's coins show a break with the ideology of the Tetrarchy as early as 310, with his adoption of *Sol invictus* as patron deity and with his emphasis on his Claudian descent.

[21]Bruun, "Thick Neck," pp. 459-80.

[22]Raymond Van Dam, *The Roman Revolution of Constantine* (Cambridge: Cambridge University Press, 2008), p. 96.

[23]Jones, *Constantine and the Conversion of Europe*, pp. 82-83, notes that the arch was constructed by the Senate and dedicated some years after 312, by which time Constantine's Christian inclinations would have been clear. He argues that the ambiguity of the inscription is evidence that the Senate acknowledged the emperor was a Christian.

now Constantine had been inspired to overthrow another tyrant by the same instinct. Cicero used the similar phrase *instinctu divino* in a discussion of divination, describing an impulse that enables the soul to see the future because of kinship with the gods (*deorum cognatione*). After Constantine's victory in 312, a panegyrist gave a twist to the Ciceronian phrase by complimenting the emperor on his ability to share secrets with "that divine mind" (*illa mente divina*), while his enemy was haunted by the Furies (*pulsus Ultricibus*). In other words, the Senate's inscription acknowledged that Constantine was in intimate contact with some divine power that gave him knowledge of future events. Even the predominantly pagan Senate of 315 recognized that its new emperor was divinely inspired.[24]

Pagan signs continued to appear on Constantine's coins and other depictions, but he added explicitly Christian symbols like the Chi-Rho and the cross, and these symbols gradually replaced the pagan signs.[25] When he did employ pagan religious symbolism, it was typically monotheistic symbolism associated with Sol/Apollo, but even these were removed from Constantine's coins between 318 and 321, before he conquered the Eastern empire.[26] Pagan symbolism never completely disappeared from Constantine's propaganda, and the monotheistic symbol of Sol continued to play double duty, but pagan significations receded. Far from being central to the imagery of his empire, they were reduced to symbols, still potent, but metaphors rather than realities.[27] Like the inscription on the arch, the inscriptions, panegyrics, and iconography adopted after 312 were ambiguous enough to be acceptable to both pagans and Christians. God was described as "the highest divinity" (*summa divinitas*) and "whatever divinity in the seat of heaven" (*quicquid divinitatis in sede caelesti*).[28]

---

[24]This paragraph summarizes Linda Jones Hall, "Cicero's *insinctu divino* and Constantine's *instinctu divinitatis*: The Evidence of the Arch of Constantine for the Senatorial View of the 'Vision' of Constantine," *Journal of Early Christian Studies* 6, no. 4 (1998).

[25]Odahl, "God and Constantine," p. 3. By contrast, Jones, *Constantine and the Conversion of Europe*, pp. 83-84, 87, concludes that Constantine remained a syncretist of sorts for some time, devoted to both Sol and the Christian God. He had attributed his conquests in the Rhine in 310 to Sol (MacMullen, *Constantine*, p. 70). Patrick Bruun, "The Christians Signs on the Coins of Constantine," *Arctos*, n.s. 3 (1962), examines the Christian symbolism of the coins.

[26]Odahl, *Constantine and the Christian Empire*, p. 168.

[27]Later in his reign, Constantine employed pagan deities in much the same way as medieval Renaissance artists. See Jean Seznec, *The Survival of the Pagan Gods* (Princeton, N.J.: Princeton University Press, 1995).

[28]Drake, *Constantine and the Bishops*, pp. 195-97, highlights the importance of the ambiguity.

Ambiguity was more than fence-sitting. In a world where Diocletian had recently identified himself *un*ambiguously with Jupiter, and where the Western Emperors were known as Heracleans, Constantine's refusal to use those titles and that imagery marks a new course. The Senate and panegyrists were not sure what divinity Constantine had contact with, but they avoided calling him Jupiter.

To those who consider such evidence trivial, Andreas Alfoldi wisely remarks:

> The tiniest detail of the imperial dress was the subject of a symbolism that defined rank that was hallowed by tradition and regulated by precise rules. Anybody who irresponsibly tampered with it would have incurred the severest penalties. Especially would this have been the case if anyone, without imperial authority, had provided the head-gear of the Emperor with a sign of such serious political importance as that attached to the monogram of Christ. Or can one imagine, for example, that the cap of the King of England could be adorned by a chamberlain or a court-painter with a swastika or a sickle and hammer—without the consent of the King?[29]

CROSS IN THE SKY

The objective, visual and tangible evidence is this: Prior to 312, Constantine's coinage and military standard honored pagan gods, particularly Sol or Apollo. After 312, he adopted a Christian standard and military insignia and put Christian symbols on his coins, which gradually replaced pagan signs. Something happened in between. Constantine said he changed because he received a sign from the Christian God. Was that true?

I believe the answer is yes. Peter Weiss has offered a convincing account of Constantine's conversion and its aftermath that merges the two contemporary versions of the story and illuminates a great deal about Constantine's entire career.[30] The two versions refer, Weiss says, to two differ-

---

Drake argues that this indicates Constantine's effort to form "the most broadly based coalition possible" (p. 196), but in making this point he mistakenly minimizes the preferential treatment Constantine gave to Christianity and the force of the legal impediments he placed on paganism. See chapter 9, below.

[29]Andreas Alfoldi, *The Conversion of Constantine and Pagan Rome*, trans. Harold Mattingly. (Oxford: Clarendon, 1948), p. 40.

[30]Weiss, "Vision of Constantine," pp. 247-50. Weiss's reconstruction is endorsed in Timothy D. Barnes, "Constantine After Seventeen Hundred Years: The *Cambridge Companion*, the New York Exhibition and a Recent Biography," *International Journal of the Classical Tradition*

ent incidents. Eusebius's was a public vision, witnessed by both Constantine and his men while the army was marching "somewhere." This probably occurred in Gaul in 310, two years prior to the battle of Milvian Bridge, at the time when other evidence indicates that Constantine began to devote himself to the invincible sun god, *Sol invictus*.[31] Constantine kept the vision in the back of his mind for some time, pondering what it could mean. On the eve of the crucial battle with Maxentius, he had a dream. When he discussed the dream with some Christians in his entourage, they told him that Christ had appeared, and they gave him a Christian interpretation of the sign he had witnessed two years before.

Weiss makes a convincing case that the sign was not the flying scroll[32] envisaged by Raphael, Rubens and the popular imagination, but a sun halo, a circular rainbow formed when ice crystals in the atmosphere refract sunlight. In a sun halo, the sun is at the center of the circle and often radiates beams in a cross or asterisk shape.[33] In 310, Weiss concludes, "Constantine, with his army, unexpectedly witnessed a complex halo-phenomenon. He saw a double-ring halo, each ring with three mock suns arranged in cross-formation around the sun, tangent arcs or points of intersection with the circle, presumably with a more or less distinct light-cross in the middle. He saw it in the spring and in the afternoon, which is when the phenomenon mainly occurs."[34] A cross of light in the sky, encircled by a "crown"—for fourth-century Christians, how can that be anything other than a sign of conquest by the cross?

Weiss's scenario explains a great deal about Constantine's subsequent career and faith: his recurrent use of light and sun imagery, his tendency to use solar imagery when referring to Christ and to merge Christ with Sol the sun god, his sense of divine commission and his confidence of success, his devotion to the cross as a sign of victory and kingship, and the iconog-

---

14 (2008; but I am relying on an unpublished 2007 version of this review essay generously provided by the author). Jones, *Constantine and the Conversion of Europe*, p. 85, also suggests a sun halo.

[31]Patrick Bruun, "The Disappearance of Sol from the Coins of Constantine," *Arctos*, n.s. 2 (1958). Weiss makes this connection by claiming that the appearance of Apollo mentioned by the panegyric of 310, when Constantine was marching between Massilia to the Rhine frontier, is the same as the cross-vision.

[32]Eusebius reports that the phrase "in this conquer" was "written," but the verb can mean "signify" or "mean."

[33]Google "sun halo" for some striking images.

[34]Weiss, "Vision of Constantine," p. 250.

raphy of the sun that appears on Constantine's constructions and those of his heirs.[35]

If David Petraeus had recommended a surge in Iraq based on an eclipse or a sign in the heavens, he would have been forced into psychiatric treatment, followed by early retirement. Constantine, though, was a fourth-century Roman who, like everyone else in his time, believed that the gods guided humanity with signs and portents. He saw *something*, something he interpreted as a sign that committing himself to the God of the Christians would give him victory.

CONSTANTINE THE CHRISTIAN?

Constantine's conversion is one aspect of the "question of Constantine." A bigger and more important question is whether this experience, whatever it was, had an effect on his personal and political conduct. After he defeated Maxentius, did he conduct himself like a Christian? Was his conversion a *real* conversion?

Modern historians, as H. A. Drake points out, often project the very modern notions of conversion found in William James and Arthur Darby Nock back into the fourth century and expect Constantine to experience what Nock, in one of his most striking phrases, called the "clean and beautiful newness" of a spiritual epiphany.[36] Perhaps Constantine did, but the more important question is whether this is the right model of conversion to apply to a fourth-century Roman commander. Though later writers, and perhaps Constantine himself, saw parallels between the emperor's vision and Paul's Damascus Road experience, it is clear that the two experiences were quite different and had different effects.

Modern conceptions of conversion often assume a dichotomy of political and religious spheres that is foreign to the fourth century. There is no reason to deny that Constantine's vision was a political as well as a spiritual epiphany. As Drake puts it, "Three and a half centuries earlier, under similar pressure to find a more stable counterweight for the heavy reliance he had heretofore placed on the army to support his claim to rule, the first Augustus had turned instinctively to the Senate. In the new climate of the

---

[35]Ibid., pp. 250-56.
[36]See the very sharp discussion of models of conversion in Drake, *Constantine and the Bishops*, pp. 187-89.

late empire, Constantine turned equally instinctively to the heavens."[37] Constantine knew that his position in the empire depended on his highly competent, highly successful armies. He also knew, from Diocletian not least of all, that sheer brute force was an insufficient basis for political order. He also knew that the empire faced a "Christian problem," and he had witnessed the failure of Diocletian's attempt to solve it. The Christian interpretation of the sun halo cut the political knot. From 312 on, Constantine had both a personal calling and mission and, inseparably, a political program. It is no contradiction to say both that God called Constantine and that he "emerges as one of several talented and ambitious players seeking a formula to reconcile the imperial need for religious justification with the refusal of Christians to pay divine honors to any other deity."[38] Constantine had discovered a way to solve the Christian problem. Not only would he cease to persecute, but he would actively promote the church. It was not only good politics; the God of the Christians, Constantine believed, had given him a sign that this was the *right* thing to do.

We can never uncover exactly what Constantine experienced in 310 and 312. But we do not have to. More important for assessing Constantine's sincerity is the question of Constantine's words and actions following 312. Did he talk like a Christian after his conversion? Did he act like one?

Zosimus certainly did not think so. He characterized the emperor as untrustworthy in alliances, addicted to luxury, wasteful in finance, and destructive of the empire's security.[39] Zosimus's analysis influenced Voltaire, who wrote his *Philosophical Dictionary* that Constantine was a "scoundrel," not to mention "a parricide who smothered his wife in a bath, butchered his son, assassinated his father-in-law, his brother-in-law, and his nephew," "a man bloated with pride and immersed in pleasures," as well as a "detestable tyrant, like his children." But Voltaire recognized that Constantine could not have achieved the heights he did without some good sense, which he manifested in a "belligerent letter" to Arius and Alexander of Alexandria, urging them to give up the "trifling matter" of their quarrel concerning the divinity of the Son.[40] Burckhardt thought Constantine a

---

[37]Ibid., p. 187.
[38]Ibid., p. 191.
[39]Zosimus *New History* 2.
[40]See Odahl, *Constantine and the Christian Empire*, p. 282, for a publishing history of Zosimus; Voltaire, "Arianism," in *Philosophical Dictionary, Volume 1*, available online at Google Books.

"genius" and did not begrudge the traditional title "the Great," but argued that Constantine was "driven without surcease by ambition and lust for power." He was a "murderous egoist who possessed the great merit of having conceived of Christianity as a world power." His only concern was success, though he may have had a "superstition" in favor of Christ.[41] James Carroll likewise claims that Constantine was "infinitely shrewd" for making use of the Christian church as he did.[42] Edward Gibbon aimed at providing a "balanced portrait" that combined the virtues celebrated by Constantine's promoters with the vices decried by his detractors, but Gibbon ended up with a schizophrenic Constantine whose early greatness trailed off into elderly sensuality. Gibbon gives us a young Eusebian Constantine and an old Zosimian one.

Dan Brown's smashingly popular *The Da Vinci Code* continues in the same vein, and then some. For Brown's oh-so-highly educated characters, if not for Brown himself, Constantine was a lifelong pagan whose decision to support Christianity was nothing more than "backing the winning horse." Pagan symbols dominated Constantinian iconography, Brown's character claims, and his shift of the sabbath to Sunday signifies his continuing adherence to the god Sol. Constantine was responsible for elevating the all too human Jesus to deity, and he did it to buttress his imperial power: "By officially endorsing Jesus as the Son of God, Constantine turned Jesus into a deity who existed beyond the scope of the human world." To ensure that the church conformed to the divine Jesus of Constantine, he called the Council of Nicaea, suppressed all the earlier gospels, and compiled the New Testament canon.[43]

Bits and pieces of the pagan and post-Enlightenment assessment of Constantine's Christianity are commonly invoked among contemporary theologians, evidence that prejudice against Constantine crosses the cultural spectrum from popular novelists to sophisticated theologians. Theo-

---

[41]Burckhardt, *Age of Constantine,* pp. 245, 261, 292-93. Burckhardt's analysis of Constantine needs to be historicized. It was a response to the state-building thugs of his own time as much as historical analysis of Constantine and his era, and imposes what Drake calls the "conceptual anachronism" of secular politics onto a fourth-century emperor for whom religion and politics are inseparable (see Drake, *Constantine and the Bishops,* pp. 13-18; Timothy D. Barnes, "Constantine, Athanasius and the Christian Church," in *Constantine: History, Historiography and Legend,* ed. Samuel Lieu and Dominic Montserrat (London: Routledge, 1998), pp. 8-9.
[42]Carroll, *Constantine's Sword,* p. 182.
[43]Dan Brown, *The Da Vinci Code* (New York: Doubleday, 2003), pp. 231-34.

logian Craig Carter is certainly no Dan Brown, but he is nearly as hostile to the first Christian emperor and gives nearly as distorted an account of Constantine's career. Carter argues that Constantine's support of the church had nothing to do with his real convictions, since it was a rational policy decision. More damningly, Carter claims that Constantine never really promoted Christian faith per se but adhered to and supported a synthetic monotheism that could hold Christians and pagans together in a single empire. He "never had much to say about Jesus," Carter claims.[44]

CONSTANTINE IN HIS OWN WORDS

I beg to differ. Constantine's own writings reveal, in my judgment, a seriously Christian ruler.[45] Constantine does not display the polemic acuity of an Athanasius or the subtlety of a Gregory of Nyssa, but that is not surprising given his background and vocation. Still, he was not so ignorant as many have claimed. According to Eusebius, he was educated in the liberal arts,[46] a claim that is consistent with his presence in the court of Diocletian as a young man, a court where philosophers were welcome. After 312, Eusebius informs us, Constantine became a student of the Scriptures, listening to the doctors and spending long hours in study and reading.[47]

One simple conviction was central to Constantine's beliefs: the Christian God was the heavenly Judge who, in history, opposes those who oppose him. He believed that God destroys those who destroy his temple. Convinced of Lactantius's arguments concerning God's vengeance on emperors who persecuted the church, he feared arousing that wrath.[48] Lactantius, who wrote a history of the persecutions based on this conviction,

---

[44]Craig A. Carter, *Rethinking Christ and Culture: A Post-Christendom Perspective* (Grand Rapids: Brazos, 2006), pp. 81-82, 86. In a later chapter I will explore the irony that Constantine is condemned both for imposing religion on an unwilling populace and for failing to be explicitly Christian.

[45]Norman H. Baynes (*Constantine the Great and the Christian Church*, Raleigh Lecture on History [London: Humphrey Milford, 1929]) bases his similar conclusion on a survey of Constantine's own writings.

[46]Eusebius *Life* 1.19.

[47]Ibid., 1.32; 4.17.

[48]Depending on your angle of vision, you can call this "betting on the winning horse," or you can call it a healthy fear of God. Given the religious instincts that Constantine showed even before becoming a Christian, it is as likely the latter as the former. And the simple faith is a biblical one: my summary above—God destroys those who destroy his temple—comes from Paul (1 Cor. 3:17), no simpleton.

was no simpleton. Known as "the Christian Cicero," he was the first Christian to write polished Latin, the first to write a "systematic theology" in the *Divine Institutes,* and the holder of an imperial post in rhetoric in Nicomedia. Yet he shared Constantine's conviction that God frustrates enemies of the church and blesses those who defend, befriend and support it. Eusebius adhered to the same conviction. It was an essential part of the theology of the martyr church, one of the bases for their utter confidence that someday their blood would be avenged.

Constantine also worried that the church would destroy itself, that the attacks on God's temple would come from God's own priests. As soon as he secured control of the Western empire and decreed that the Christian church would be tolerated alongside paganism, Constantine was greeted with appeals from the Donatists, who wanted him to intervene to solve the crisis in North Africa. No sooner had he secured the Eastern empire by defeating Licinius (324) than the Arian controversy broke out. Fierce controversies in the church grieved Constantine for several reasons. One of the reasons was certainly political. Constantine was a formidable politician,[49] and his letters reveal an emperor who, unsurprisingly, was interested in gaining and maintaining power, preserving the unity and health of the empire, and determining how the church fit into his political aims. Constantine believed that a unified church was essential to the health of the empire. Like Diocletian, he continued to think of religion in political terms: as the old priesthoods kept the gods propitious, so the ministry of the priests and bishops would keep the Christian God from becoming displeased with Constantine.[50]

Constantine's reasoning here was less sociological than many of the modern accounts suggest. When he rebuked Christians for their quarrels, he was not arguing that the church should remain unified so it could serve

---

[49]Repoliticizing Constantine is one of the central themes of Drake, *Constantine and the Bishops.* Unfortunately, Drake regularly falls back into a religious-political dichotomy that he recognizes was not available in the fourth century. He claims, for instance, that Constantine's efforts to reform the judicial system were part of a social program rather than an effort to secure the triumph of the church, but in this he fails to recognize that the social program was itself religiously motivated. As Drake himself knows, there was little support within Roman social or religious life for the kind attention that Constantine showed toward *humiliores.*

[50]Johannes Roldanus, *The Church in the Age of Constantine: The Theological Challenges* (London: Ashgate, 2006), p. 37. He notes (p. 41) that after Constantine the traditional religions no longer guaranteed the Empire's *salus,* since "this vital function was from now on assigned to the Christian religion."

as the glue of imperial power. Such a claim would be nonsensical, since at the time of Constantine's conversion the Christian population—cohesive and well organized to be sure—amounted to about 10-15 percent of the population.[51] The church did not provide enough glue to stick the empire together. Constantine's argument was directly theological. Divisions in the church displease the one God whose church it is, and God in his anger might well, Constantine thought, take his vengeance not only on the church but on the emperor himself. Constantine learned from Diocletian that politics and theology are inextricably mixed, and he operated in a similar framework. He had a different political theology from Diocletian's, but it was equally political, equally theological.

For Constantine, it was specifically "catholic" worship that would secure the empire. After his efforts to heal the Donatist schism ended in frustration, he wrote to an official threatening to come to Africa to settle things personally. "By diligent examination," he wrote in a tone that verged on petulance, "I shall acquaint myself to the full with the things which at the present time some persons fancy they can keep dark through the allurements of their ignorant minds, and shall drag them into the light. Those same persons who now stir up the people in such a war as to bring it about that the supreme God is not worshipped with the veneration that is His due, I shall destroy and dash in pieces."[52] In a letter of 314 to Ablavius, he stated his intention to summon bishops and priests to the Council of Arles to deal with the Donatist controversy, and again castigated those who bring war into the church. "I confess to your Lordship," the emperor wrote, "since I am well aware that you also are a worshipper of the most High God, that I consider it by no means right that contentions and altercations of this kind should be hidden from me." He feared that "God may be moved not only against the human race, but also against me myself, to whose care, by His heavenly Decree, He has entrusted the direction of all human affairs, and may in His wrath provide otherwise than heretofore." Divisions in the church left him fearful, and he claimed that he could be "truly and most fully without anxiety, and may always hope for all most prosperous and excellent things from the ever-ready

---

[51]Jones, *Constantine and the Conversion of Europe*, p. 73, notes that Christians were such a minority that favoring them brought little immediate political advantage.

[52]Optatus *Against the Donatists*.

kindness of the most powerful God," only if he could ensure "that all, bound together in brotherly concord, adore the most holy God with the worship of the Catholic religion, that is His due."[53] Pagans charged that the church endangered the empire because Christians failed to honor the ancestral gods, and Constantine's perspective here reversed the pagan criticism. He believed that his own safety, and therefore the safety of the empire whose management had been given into his hands, depended on the church maintaining right worship of the Christian God. And right worship involved, at least, unity.

In a conciliatory 324 letter to Alexander of Alexandria and Arius at the beginning of the Arian controversy, Constantine returned to this theme, explicitly using language from Paul concerning the unity of the body: "A dissension arose between you, fellowship was withdrawn, and the holy people, rent into diverse parties, no longer preserved the unity of the one body. Now, therefore, do ye both exhibit an equal degree of forbearance, and receive the advice which your fellow-servant righteously gives."[54] When the Arian controversy dragged on for a decade after Nicaea, Constantine wrote to summon the bishops to the Council of Tyre, reminding them of their duty of unity: "Surely it would best consist with and best become the prosperity of these our times, that the Catholic Church should be undivided, and the servants of Christ be at this present moment clear from all reproach."[55] Constantine recognized that maintaining unity in the church required forbearance and patience. In his final intervention in the Donatist controversy, he gave up his earlier threatening tone and urged the bishops to return no evil for evil but to bear with their enemies patiently.

Constantine could have found ample New Testament warrant for both this emphasis and his fiery response to disharmony. Nothing provoked Paul's wrath more immediately or more fiercely than division within the body of Christ. Paul's astonished "Is Christ divided?" is a fair summary of Constantine's perspective in these letters. There is even some similarity here to Augustine's later view of the nature of justice in the *res publica*. A commonwealth is truly a commonwealth only when it embodies justice.

---

[53]Ibid. MacMullen (*Constantine,* p. 111) doubts that the letter is wholly from Constantine.
[54]Eusebius *Life* 2.64-72.
[55]Ibid., 4.42.

Without justice, a commonwealth is just a glorified robber band. Justice means giving to everyone his or her due, and "everyone" here must include the most important party to the commonwealth, God himself. Without right worship, there is no justice and no commonwealth.[56] Where Augustine and Constantine differed, profoundly, was in the results they expected to see. Constantine and his theological supporters, flush with the victory of the church, believed that a Christian empire could only go from victory to victory. "Success," as John Howard Yoder charges, became a central criterion of Christian political ethics.[57] A century later, Augustine knew better. Constantine hoped his commonwealth would be secured by right worship of the true God; Augustine saw before his eyes that a putatively orthodox empire was crumbling. Constantine was right; God is the Judge. Augustine agreed but emphasized equally that his judgments are inscrutable, his ways past finding out.

MISSIONAL EMPEROR

The emperor was concerned with the internal conflicts of the church also because they gave ammunition to pagans to attack the church and reason to remain pagan. Division interfered with the church's universal mission. A letter to bishops Eusebius and Theognis (324) celebrated the union of various peoples in the empire and expressed the emperor's dismay that Christians should be divided. Calling himself a "fellow-servant" of the Christian God, he reminded the bishops of "the pledge of your salvation which I have in all sincerity made my care and through which we have not only conquered the armed force of our foes, but have also enclosed their souls alive to demonstrate the true faith of the love of man." His greatest success, though, was "the renewal of the *oikoumene*." He marveled that "so many peoples should be brought to the same mind—peoples which but yesterday were said to be in ignorance of God." But this marvel was diminished by the petty infighting that plagued the church: "Think of what they

---

[56]Augustine *City of God* 19.21. See Robert Dodaro, *Christ and the Just Society in the Thought of Augustine* (Cambridge: Cambridge University Press, 2004).

[57]This is one of Yoder's central charges against the "Constantinian church," and it was true of some Christians in Constantine's time. But it was most true for a brief moment in the early fourth century. As I argue throughout this book, what happened in the early fourth century, insofar as it fits Yoder's paradigm at all, was more a "Constantinian moment" than a "Constantinian shift."

might have learnt if no shadow of strife had come upon them! Why, then, my beloved brothers, tell me, why do I bring a charge against you? We are Christians, and yet we are torn by pitiable disagreements."[58]

At the outset of the Council of Nicaea, he reminded the bishops of the urgency of Christian unity and noted that their divisions had brought calumny on Christ's body. His "chief desire," he claimed, was "to enjoy the spectacle of your united presence." Seeing the assembled bishops, he added, "I feel myself bound to render thanks to God the universal King" for letting him "see you not only all assembled together, but all united in a common harmony of sentiment." Constantine warned the bishops to make the best use of the elimination of persecuting tyrants and begged them to resist the devil, who in Constantine's mind is almost always associated with conflict: "Now the impious hostility of the tyrants has been forever removed by the power of God our Savior, that spirit who delights in evil may devise no other means for exposing the divine law to blasphemous calumny." The blasphemy he had in mind was "intestine strife within the Church of God," which he considered "far more evil and dangerous than any kind of war or conflict; and these our differences appear to me more grievous than any outward trouble." He knew that he had been victorious by "the will and with the co-operation of God," but he thought that once the battle was done "nothing more remained but to render thanks to him, and sympathize in the joy of those whom he had restored to freedom through my instrumentality." Instead, he received unwelcome and unexpected "intelligence," namely, "the news of your dissension."

Eager to heal the divisions, "I immediately sent to require your presence." Constantine's joy would be fulfilled only when he saw the bishops "all united in one judgment, and that common spirit of peace and concord prevailing among you all, which it becomes you, as consecrated to the service of God, to commend to others." He ended his speech with an exhortation to overcome their differences as quickly as possible: "Delay not, then, dear friends: delay not, you ministers of God, and faithful servants of him who is our common Lord and Savior: begin from this moment to discard the causes of that disunion which has come among you, and remove the perplexities of controversy by embracing the principles of peace.

---

[58]Quoted in Baynes, *Constantine the Great*, pp. 27-28.

For by such conduct you will at the same time be acting in a manner most pleasing to the supreme God, and you will confer an exceeding favor on me who am your fellow-servant."[59] He reminded the assembly that "it would be a terrible thing—a very terrible thing—that now that wars are ended and none dares to offer further resistance we should begin to attack each other and thus give cause for pleasure and for laughter to the pagan world."[60]

Constantine was not just a Christian; he was a *missional* Christian.

CONSTANTINE ON CHRIST

Constantine frequently used ambiguous expressions like "most high God," "Divine Power," "Providence" and "Supreme God" in his correspondence, but these expressions too should be seen in their historical context. Fourth-century Rome was a world of many gods, and the notion that there was a single supreme God beyond and above all those pointed not to modern deism but to monotheism or "henotheism."[61] Constantine did not shy away from sharp polemics against paganism. Still, he was aware that a large proportion of his empire was still pagan, and especially when addressing a pagan audience, he expressed himself in ways that minimized offense.

In one sense, it is hardly surprising that we find comparatively few explicit references to Jesus in Constantine's writings. So far as we know, he did not keep a spiritual journal, nor did he write hymns or mystical poetry. Most of the writing we have from Constantine's own hand consists of official correspondence with subordinate civil rulers or bishops, a genre not known for pious flourishes. Given the nature of most of the extant writing of Constantine, the striking thing is how often he turns to theological, and frequently specifically Christian, themes. I dare say that one will find more frequent references to Christ in Constantine's official pronouncements than one could find in the *Federalist Papers*.

In the 314 letter summoning bishops to Arles, he repeatedly referred to "Christ our Savior" and warned that the "mercy of Christ" has departed from hardened Donatists. He expressed surprise that the Donatists had

---

[59]Eusebius *Life* 3.12.
[60]Quoted in Baynes, *Constantine the Great,* p. 27.
[61]Drake, in *Constantine and the Bishops,* goes too far in claiming that Constantine aimed to articulate an "inclusive" Christianity with a low bar to the entry of pagan monotheists.

appealed to him to judge in this case, since he himself was under judgment, awaiting the "judgment of Christ." An assembly of bishops would heal the division, he hoped, since bishops could speak or teach nothing but what they learn from the "teaching of Christ." He accused the Donatists of being traitors to the church and wondered what their behavior said about their regard for "Christ the Savior."[62] Elsewhere, he praised Eusebius for his treatise on Easter, since it so clearly explained the "mysteries of Christ."[63] In another letter to Eusebius, he reminded him of the tyrants who once persecuted the "servants of our Savior."[64] He urged Alexander and Arius to resist the "temptations of the devil" that would lead to dissension and to recognize that "our great God and common Savior of all has granted the same light to us all."[65] Summarizing the findings of the Council of Nicaea on the date of Easter, he distinguished the church from Judaism, contending that "we have received from our Savior a different way."[66] After Nicaea, he wrote to the church of Alexandria to express his horror at Arius's errors and his gratitude to God for the council's wisdom, and along the way he expressed a hope that "the Divine Majesty pardon the fearful enormity of the blasphemies which some were shamelessly uttering concerning the mighty Savior, our life and hope."[67]

Not only is Constantine's God the Savior, but he is a God who saved through the cross and passion of the incarnate Son. In 325, during Constantine's mother Helena's pilgrimage to Palestine, excavators uncovered a tomb believed to be the empty tomb of Jesus. Later accounts add that they also found three crosses, one of which, reportedly after controlled testing, was found to be the cross of Jesus.[68] Constantine breathlessly wrote to Macarius about the "Savior's grace" in giving this "monument of his most holy Passion."[69] Constantine personally accepted the christological deci-

---

[62]Optatus *Against the Donatists.*
[63]Eusebius *Life* 4.35.
[64]Ibid., 2.46.
[65]Ibid., 2.64-72.
[66]Ibid., 3.17-20.
[67]Eusebius *Church History* 1.9.
[68]The testing comes from later tradition: a piece of each cross was touched to a corpse, which sprang to life when touched by the true cross's wood. Two versions of the story are available in Mark Edwards, trans., *Constantine and Christendom* (Liverpool: Liverpool University Press, 2003).
[69]The cross is so central to Constantine's piety that Carroll, *Constantine's Sword,* suggests that he virtually invented a cross-centered, and therefore anti-Semitic, Christianity.

sions of Nicaea. He claimed that the voice of assembled bishops was equivalent to the voice of God, and though he probably did not, as some have alleged, suggest the use of *homoousios* as the appropriate creedal word, he grasped and defended the Nicene findings.

Constantine believed that one of God's central acts in Christ was to restore human beings to "soundness of mind,"[70] and as a result he emphasized the teaching of Jesus and the need for Scripture. In a letter of 332 urging the people of Antioch to desist from their efforts to call Eusebius as their bishop, he referred to "our Savior's words and precepts as a model, as it were, of what our life should be."[71] He rebuked the Arians for "declaring and confessing that they believe things contrary to the divinely inspired Scriptures."[72] He was acting on this faith when he provided fifty copies of the Bible to the churches under Eusebius's care.[73]

By Eusebius's account, Constantine was regular in prayer and even erected a Mosaic tabernacle outside his army camp, to which he retreated for prayers before battle.[74] He was generous to the poor and to widows and treated prisoners with humane kindness.[75] He recognized his complete dependence on God[76] and had a strong personal sense of destiny. He had been chosen, he believed, not only to deliver the church from persecution but to spread the truth of God throughout the world.[77] Constantine believed that his calling was to proclaim the Son of God to the Romans.[78]

ORATION TO THE SAINTS

Eusebius recorded that Constantine preached so often in his palace that he virtually turned it into a temple, though he added that the members of the court found the emperor's preaching wearisome. Eusebius promised to provide examples of Constantine's sermons but unfortunately appended only one to his *Vita Constantini*. One wishes there were more, but it is enough. The authenticity of his "Oration to an Assembly of Saints," also

---

[70]Eusebius *Oration* 11.
[71]Eusebius *Life* 3.60.
[72]Eusebius *Church History* 1.9.
[73]Eusebius *Life* 4.36.
[74]Ibid., 2.4, 12, 14; 4.22.
[75]Ibid., 1.42-43; 2.13.
[76]Ibid., 2.29.
[77]Ibid., 2.28; 4.9.
[78]Ibid., 1.41.

known as Constantine's "Good Friday Sermon," has been doubted;[79] the date is still controversial, and the existing manuscript of the sermon is complicated by the fact that it is a Greek translation of a Latin original. Yet most scholars today accept that the sermon is genuine and that it was written by Constantine, no doubt with assistance from Christian scholars in his court.[80]

Scholars have combed through the "Oration" for signs of Arian sympathies and for clues to Constantine's theology of empire. There is material in the sermon for such pursuits, but my interest is more traditional and more basic. My question is, is the "Oration" the work of a Christian? More modestly: is it, at least, the work of someone who wants to be *thought* a Christian?

Though the sermon was delivered to a Christian audience, much of it is an extended antipagan polemic and apologetic that employs Plato and Plotinus, includes an intricate analysis of Virgil's *Fourth Eclogue* and a discussion of an acrostic prophecy from the Erythraean Sibyl, offers a précis of Lactantius's arguments concerning the death of persecutors (sec. 24) and shows an interest in the natural world as well as in history and ethics.

The opening sections of the sermon provide a generic defense of monotheism. Creation is diverse because God created it from different elements (sec. 13), but it is harmonized by the one Creator. Only monotheism can guarantee the "harmonious concord of the whole" (sec. 3). Polytheistic paganism is not just philosophically indefensible; it produces "unrighteousness and incontinence, raging against righteous works and ways." So evil did paganism become that pagans sacrificed not only "irrational creatures" but also human beings: "according to Egyptian and Assyrian laws, people sacrificed righteous souls to idols of bronze and clay." Memphis and Babylon paid

---

[79]Cf. Baynes, *Constantine the Great,* pp. 50-56. Baynes's doubts about the authenticity of the sermon were sufficient to keep him from using the text as evidence of Constantine's religious beliefs.

[80]H. A. Drake, "Suggestions of Date in Constantine's 'Oration to the Saints,' " *American Journal of Philology* 106, no. 3 (1985): 335; Timothy Barnes "The Emperor Constantine's Good Friday Sermon," *Journal of Theological Studies* 27 (1976): 414-23; M. J. Edwards, "The Arian Heresy and the Oration to the Saints," *Vigiliae Christianae* 49, no. 4 (1995); Edwards, *Constantine and Christendom,* pp. xvii-xxix; Bruno Bleckmann, "Ein Kaiser als Prediger: Zur Datierung der Konstantinischen 'Rede an die Versammlung der Heiligen,' " *Hermes* 125 (1997). Barnes, "Constantine After Seventeen Hundred Years," claims that the "Oration" is today "universally accepted." Edwards, *Constantine and Christendom,* provides a lucid, heavily footnoted translation.

the price: "I myself have been present to behold it, and have been an eyewitness of the miserable fortune of the cities." As Constantine remembers it, "Memphis is waste," destroyed from the time of Moses not by "shooting arrows or launching javelins, but just by holy prayer and meek adoration" (sec. 16). Because of its "ontological violence,"[81] polytheism is incompatible with peace; it inevitably brings violence, envy, greed, as gods seek to "dominat[e] according to their power," just as we find in ancient myths. Only a single divine ruler can ensure harmony and moral uprightness (sec. 3).

As the sermon progresses, it is clear that Constantine was also interested in specifically Christian questions. He showed his awareness of the issue of divine generation that was central to the Arian disputes and Nicene orthodoxy.[82] Why is Jesus called the Son? he asked. "Whence this generation of which we speak, if God be indeed only One, and incapable of union with another?" He answered by distinguishing two types of generation: "one in the way of natural birth, which is known to all; the other, that which is the effect of an eternal cause, the mode of which is seen by the prescience of God, and by those among men whom he loves. For he who is wise will recognize the cause which regulates the harmony of creation" (section 11).

God's begotten Son has come to deliver human beings from the evils of the past and restore the race to soundness of mind. Along the way, Constantine summarized the incarnation, life, ministry, and death of Jesus at some length and explained some Old Testament prophecies of his coming. He mentioned Jesus' selection of apostles, his miracles, and his teaching. At the climax of his life Jesus went to the cross not, as pagans said, for his own crimes but to gain victory over sin, a victory that inspires confidence amid the hardships of life. No doubt thinking back to the martyrs, Constantine said that the support of faith does not falter even in "the trial of evils." When God has taken hold of a soul and "takes his seat in the intellect," a "person is invincible, and thus the soul that possesses this invincibility in its own intellect will not be overcome by the evils that surround it." God himself is the great example: "this we have learned from the vic-

---

[81]The phrase is John Milbank's, but it expresses, I think, Constantine's point.

[82]Lewis Ayres, *Nicaea and Its Legacy: An Approach to Fourth-Century Trinitarian Theology* (Oxford: Oxford University Press, 2006), argues that the fourth-century debates were debates about different notions of divine generation.

tory of God, who, exercising his providence over all things, suffered the besotted iniquity of the impious, yet reaped no harm from his affliction, but donned the greatest victory tokens and an eternal crown in defiance of wickedness" (sec. 15).

In place of violence, greed, brutality, God in Christ brings peace and justice. It is a sign of the sea-change in sensibility that a Roman emperor could say, toward the close of his "Oration," "This indeed is heavenly wisdom, to choose to be injured rather than to injure, and when it is necessary, to suffer evil rather than to do it" (sec. 15); or when the same emperor, writing to Sapor king of Persia, insists that the only sacrifice the true God desires is "purity of mind and an undefiled spirit," "moderation and gentleness," humility and gentleness.[83] He refused the sacrifice at the Capitoline in 312, and in the "Oration" he gives part of his rationale. He had entered a world without sacrifice and embraced a faith that proclaimed the end of sacrifice.

ISOAPOSTOLOS

When Constantine died in 337, shortly after his baptism, he was buried in the Church of the Apostles in his eponymous city of Constantinople, "the New Rome." Surrounding his tomb were twelve other tombs, indicative of Constantine's conviction that he was the "thirteenth apostle," charged, like Peter and Paul, with extending the gospel to a new region of the globe, with converting the Roman Empire.

There is another way to read the arrangement of Constantine's tomb: not that he was the thirteenth apostle but that he viewed himself as an *alter Christus*. Other evidence points in the same direction. Some Christians wondered whether the heavenly sign of the cross that Constantine witnessed fulfilled Jesus' prophecy of the "sign of the Son of Man in heaven" that preceded his second coming. Constantine may have thought the same. If he did not identify his empire with Christ's reign itself, he may have viewed it as the prelude to the second advent.[84] Constantine's interest in locations in Palestine associated with Jesus increased over the years, and both he and his

---

[83]Eusebius *Life* 4.10.
[84]The evidence is explored in Oliver Nicholson, "Constantine's Vision of the Cross," *Vigiliae Christianae* 54, no. 3 (2000).

mother Helena sponsored the building of churches there.[85] By donating "ornaments and embroideries" to churches in Bethlehem and Jerusalem, Constantine "essentially incorporated Jesus' entire life on earth into his own family's traditions."[86] When the Church of the Holy Sepulcher was dedicated, one bishop's fervor overwhelmed his sense, and he declared that Constantine would rule beside Jesus in the future kingdom.[87]

Throughout his New Rome, Constantine left hints of the same identification. "Although named after the emperor," Raymond Van Dam writes, "Constantinople was also known as 'Christoupolis,' 'Christ's city.' In a new forum the emperor erected a giant statue of himself on top of a tall porphyry column." The story was that Constantine had put "a relic of the True Cross in his statue, and some even offered prayers to it 'as if to a god.'" Further, "over the entrance to the palace Constantine hung a portrait depicting himself and his sons with a cross over their heads and a serpent beneath their feet. This portrait commemorated the emperor's military success over Licinius, an imperial rival whom he had himself once characterized as a 'serpent.'" The picture "presented the emperor as another savior who had defeated evil with the assistance of the cross."[88]

All this seems damning, more an expression of Roman *superbia* than of Christian *humilitas*. These icons expressed Constantine's sense of mission, which sometimes exceeded its bounds. The emperor had a high opinion of himself, a sense of destiny, a deep conviction about his own importance in the history of Christ's kingdom. Yet in one sense, all of this is perfectly orthodox. As Christ, Jesus is the head of a body, a body that shares in his resurrection and victory as much as in his cross. Though it is certainly Jesus the Seed of the Woman who crushes the serpent's head, Paul also assured the Romans that the Lord would crush Satan under *their* feet (Rom 16). Constantine thought too highly of himself, but in thinking he could join Christ in crushing Satan, he was simply thinking like a Christian.

CONCLUSION

There are various ways to escape the force of this evidence. The most plau-

---

[85]Van Dam, *Roman Revolution*, p. 285, links the interest in Palestine with Constantine's self-image and his inclination toward Arianism.
[86]Ibid., p. 307.
[87]Ibid., pp. 307-8.
[88]Ibid., p. 308.

sible is to raise doubts about the reliability of the sources. Burckhardt considered Eusebius the most dishonest historian of antiquity. That was not the case, but Eusebius did idealize his subject, and some of his claims about Constantine's personal piety strike jaded modern readers as overdrawn. Constantine was rough and blunt and could be violent. Even if we dismiss Eusebius entirely, however, we still have the evidence of Constantine's letters and the "Oration," in which he expresses a soldierly faith in the powerful God of Christians, in the cross of Jesus as a victory over evil, and in the church as the unifier of the human race.[89]

Still, there are other ways to escape the evidence. Burckhardt does not deny that Constantine delivered sermons to his court, but he concludes that they served a political purpose, proffering warnings to members of the court with whom Constantine was displeased. He assumes that Constantine was a purely political animal who merely used the Christian religion for his own ends. Such a theory supposes an extraordinary degree of cynicism on the part of the emperor. It would mean he referred regularly to "our Savior," the truth of the "Catholic religion," the divine inspiration of Scripture, the demand for unity among Christian brothers, the veneration of the "Supreme God" all without believing a word of it. If the "Oration" is genuine, then the cynicism increases exponentially, for then Constantine defended monotheism against polytheism, summarized the life of Jesus "our Savior," argued that Jesus was prophesied by seers Jewish and pagan, and worked out ingenious christological puzzles from non-Christian texts—again without believing a word of it. If Constantine was motivated only by policy, he was one of the most monstrous political cynics of all time. Monstrously cynical, and politically inept cynicism to boot: his expressions of revulsion at paganism might be calculated political maneuvers to win over the bishops, but in winning the support of Christians he would risk offending some 90 percent of the population of the empire. The "evil genius" explanation does not work. He might have been evil, but if so he was dumb, a "useful idiot" whose strings were pulled by the bishops.

Far more likely, Constantine was what the letters and *Oration* indicate he was, and once we discount the sepia hues of the *Vita Constantini*, Euse-

---

[89]Baynes, *Constantine the Great*, attends to Constantine's own writings and draws a similar conclusion, though he sets aside the "Oration to the Saints" because he doubts its authenticity.

bius's portrait is genuine. Timothy Barnes, in my judgment, gets the "Constantine question" right:

> From the days of his youth Constantine probably had been sympathetic to Christianity, and in 312 he experienced a religious conversion which profoundly affected his conception of himself. After 312 Constantine considered that his main duty as emperor was to inculcate virtue in his subjects and to persuade them to worship God. Constantine's character is not wholly enigmatic; with all his faults and despite an intense ambition for personal power, he nevertheless sincerely believed that God had given him a special mission to convert the Roman Empire to Christianity.[90]

That gets us a bit ahead of our story, since we still have to examine Constantine's conquest of the Eastern empire and his policies and practices, religious and otherwise, during his years as emperor. But it gives us a starting point: I assume throughout the remainder of this book that the Constantine we are examining was a Christian. Flawed, no doubt; sometimes inconsistent with his stated ethic, certainly; an infant in faith.

Yet a Christian.

---

[90]Barnes, *Constantine and Eusebius*, p. 275.

5

Liberator Ecclesiae

Open and free exercise of their respective religions
is granted to all others, as well as to the Christians.

EDICT OF MILAN

Jupiter did not come through. Again.

A year before the battle of Milvian Bridge, the Eastern Augustus Galerius, wracked by his final illness and desperate for supernatural aid, ended the Eastern persecution, permitted Christians to worship, and asked the church to pray for him. Persecution had not worked, and Galerius concluded that it was "fit to extend our indulgence to those men, and to permit them again to be Christians, and to establish the places of their religious assemblies," so long as they "offend not against good order."[1] It is one of the ironies of history that it was neither the Christian Constantine nor his erstwhile ally Licinius who ended Diocletian's persecution in the east but Constantine's nemesis, Galerius.

Galerius died shortly after, and within weeks the Caesar Daia, inspired and encouraged by Theotecnus, a city *curator* in Antioch, began rolling back Galerius's deathbed edict. He prevented Christians from assembling to honor martyrs at cemeteries[2] and executed Bishop Peter of Alexandria. In Ancyra seven virgins were drowned, and when another Christian pro-

---

[1]Lactantius *Death* 34.
[2]Stephen Mitchell, "Maximinus and the Christians in A.D. 312: A New Latin Inscription," *The Journal of Roman Studies* 78 (1988): 113-14.

tested, he was burned.[3] Sword, fire and water were back. Knowing that he could not fight Christianity with nothing, Daia attempted to reform pagan devotion. He appointed high priests throughout the cities in his realm with cult responsibilities and the power to arrest Christians, compel sacrifice and hand those who refused to the magistrates.[4] The *Acts of Pilate* became required reading in schools.

Daia issued no edict of persecution. For the first time in Roman history, an emperor governed by rescript, answering requests from civic and provincial officials begging him to deal with the dangerous infection.[5] An appeal from Antioch stopped just short of asking for permission to expel all Christians from the city. A similar letter arose from Nicomedia. Eusebius did not think the requests were accidental. Daia, he said, arranged for the requests to come to him, so he could shrug and pretend he was only responding to popular outrage.[6]

At the same time, Daia saw that he was being isolated in the imperial system. Constantine and Licinius wedded east and west by virtue of Licinius's 313 marriage to Constantine's sister Constantia. But the crisis for Daia went deeper. Constantine and Licinius had adopted a common solution to the Christian problem, and it did not involve devotion to Jupiter and Heracles. After 313 Daia was alone, the only member of the imperial college still clinging to Jupiter and hoping for his aid.

"EDICT OF MILAN"

Every schoolchild knows that shortly after his victory over Maxentius, Constantine issued the Edict of Milan, giving freedom to Christians to worship as they pleased. By the standard account, the edict was issued jointly from Milan by Constantine and Licinius in 313, when they were together to celebrate Lincinus's marriage. But the standard account is a

---

[3]David S. Potter, *The Roman Empire at Bay, AD 180-395,* Routledge History of the Ancient World (London: Routledge, 2004), p. 365.

[4]Oliver Nicholson, "The 'Pagan Churches' of Maximinus Daia and Julian the Apostate," *Journal of Ecclesiastical History* 45, no. 1 (1945): 4. Daia's reforms of the priesthood and his efforts to revive paganism are often compared to the later pagan revival of Julian, who drew his plans for reform from the church. Nicholson makes a compelling case against this interpretation, arguing that Daia's priests, though sincere in their paganism and their desire to eliminate Christianity, were political appointees who had little in common with Christian or Julianic priesthood.

[5]Potter, *Roman Empire at Bay,* pp. 364-65.

[6]Mitchell, "Maximinus," p. 117; he cites Eusebius *Church History* 9.9.4.

fiction.[7] Constantine and Licinius issued no edict from Milan. What *was* issued was not an edict, it was neither issued from Milan nor applied to that city, and it did not legalize Christianity. There was no need, after all, in either east or west, to decree toleration for Christians. As soon as Constantine was acclaimed as Augustus of the West at York in 306, he ended the persecution of Christians. Maxentius granted freedom to Christians in Rome and Italy during his six years of rule there.

Constantine and Licinius did meet at Milan in 313, they did discuss the imperial policy toward Christianity and religion in general, and they did arrive at a common policy, which is expressed in two letters jointly signed by the two Augusti, one a Latin letter posted in Nicomedia in June 313 and the other a slightly different Greek version posted in Caesarea some time later.[8] Lactantius preserved the first, a letter to the governor of Bithynia. Licinius and Constantine referred to their "interview at Milan," at which they "conferred together with respect to the good and security of the commonweal" and concluded that "reverence paid to the Divinity merited our first and chief attention" and that "it was proper that the Christians and all others should have liberty to follow that mode of religion which to each of them appeared best." Their intention was to ensure that "God, who is seated in heaven, might be benign and propitious to us, and to every one under our government," and that "the supreme Divinity, to whose worship we freely devote ourselves, might continue to vouchsafe His favour and beneficence to us." Considering it "highly consonant to right reason," they adopted the policy that "no man should be denied leave of attaching himself to the rites of the Christians, or to whatever other religion his might directed him." Thus all Christians "are to be permitted, freely and absolutely, to remain in it, and not to be disturbed in any ways, or molested." The letter made clear that this "indulgence which we have granted in matters of religion to the Christians is ample and unconditional" and intended to help the provincial officials to "perceive at the

---

[7]In what follows I am particularly indebted to Timothy D. Barnes, "Constantine After Seventeen Hundred Years: The *Cambridge Companion,* the New York Exhibition and a Recent Biography," *International Journal of the Classical Tradition* 14 (2008). Simon Corcoran, *The Empire of the Tetrarchs: Imperial Pronouncements and Government, AD 284-324,* rev. ed., Oxford Classical Monographs (Oxford: Oxford University Press, 2000), p. 189, also notes that the "edict" is not in fact an edict.

[8]Barnes, "Constantine After Seventeen Hundred Years."

same time that the open and free exercise of their respective religions is granted to all others, as well as to the Christians." Given the "well-ordered state and the tranquility of our times," "each individual" should be permitted "according to his own choice, to worship the Divinity; and we mean not to derogate anything from the honor due to any religion or its votaries."

Thus far, the decision merely confirmed the status quo determined by the decree of Galerius and Constantine's own earlier cessation of persecution. The legal substance of the letter was to order the return of church property that had been seized during the persecution: "Now we will that all persons who have purchased such places, either from our exchequer or from any one else, do restore them to the Christians, without money demanded or price claimed, and that this be performed peremptorily and unambiguously." Even those who had received church properties as gifts from another party must return them to the Christians. In short, "all those places are, by your intervention, to be immediately restored to the Christians," not only "places appropriated to religious worship" but also other property that belonged to "their society in general, that is, to their churches." The emperors promised that "the persons making restitution without a price paid shall be at liberty to seek indemnification from our bounty." By diligently carrying out these orders, Licinius and Constantine declared, the local and provincial officials of the East will secure "public tranquility" and guarantee "that divine favor which, in affairs of the mightiest importance, we have already experienced, continue to give success to us, and in our successes make the commonweal happy."[9]

Liberis mentibus—"with free minds"—all are to worship their gods. It is a remarkable policy, an unexpected one, since "it would have been natural for a ruler after his conversion to Christianity to shift all the previous relations."[10] Was this a concession to the pagan majority? A sign of Con-

---

[9]Lactantius *Death* 48. Eusebius's version is in *Church History* 10.5.

[10]Hermann Dorries, *Constantine and Religious Liberty*, trans. Roland Bainton (New Haven, Conn.: Yale University Press, 1960), p. 23. On the "edict" of Milan, Craig A. Carter, *Rethinking Christ and Culture: A Post-Christendom Perspective* (Grand Rapids: Brazos, 2006), is a bundle of contradictions. He faults Constantine for establishing religious freedom without any explicit acknowledgment of the truth of Christianity (p. 80) but then complains that Constantine set the trajectory for the persecution of non-Christians and heretics (p. 96). He suggests that Constantine might have used his power "to promote religious liberty and increase respect for human life and dignity" (p. 96), but he has already told us that the edict accomplished the

stantine's syncretic monotheism? A principled decision?

Beyond the policy, Daia could see that Constantine and Licinius had differing degrees of personal commitment to the faith. Constantine was already publicly identified with Christianity, while Licinius' attachment to the church was looser and more indirect. Licinius's wife was a devout Christian, and Licinius was close enough to the new faith to replace the traditional prebattle sacrifice with a monotheistic, though not explicitly Christian, prayer.[11] These differences might, Daia thought, be exploited for his benefit, if he could find some way to use them as a wedge to drive the two Augusti apart. Militarily, Daia knew he had to act. Eventually, Daia thought, the Augusti would strike, and Daia decided to preempt that attack by striking first. He began to prepare for war, and in the meantime, to gain support of the Christians in his realm, he issued two decrees of toleration at the end of 312 and again in 313. His heart was not in it. Prior to the battle with Licinius, he "vowed to Jupiter that if he gained the victory, he would utterly extinguish Christianity."[12]

Jupiter did not come through. When on April 30, 313, Daia's army faced Licinius's across a "bare and desolate plain" near Campus Ergenus, Licinius's soldiers put aside their shields and helmets, knelt to pray Licinius's prayer three times, and then stood up and proceeded to win a thoroughgoing victory. Daia fled to Nicomedia, gathered his family, and sped on to Tarsus, where he may have hoped to wait out a siege. He did not have the patience. When Licinius marched on the city, Daia committed suicide and his family was slaughtered.[13]

Licinius continued to Antioch, where he secured his power by wiping out all he could find of the family of Galerius. Galerius's wife, Diocletian's daughter Valeria, and her mother, Diocletian's widow Prisca, fled, and lived in hiding and wore disguises until Licinius's agents tracked them down and beheaded them. Two years before, six men had claimed the purple. By the end of 313, Diocletian and Galerius had died of natural causes, Maxentius and Daia had fallen in battle. Constantine and Licinius

---

first. It is not at all clear what Carter wants: if Constantine's laws are explicitly Christian, he's a theocratic tyrant; if not, then he's promoting vanilla monotheism.

[11]For the prayer, see Potter, *Roman Empire at Bay,* p. 366.

[12]Timothy D. Barnes, *Constantine and Eusebius* (Cambridge, Mass.: Harvard University Press, 1981), p. 63.

[13]Potter, *Roman Empire at Bay,* p. 366.

were the only Augusti left standing, and they had jointly agreed to a policy
of toleration of Christianity.

EMPEROR OF THE EAST

Marriage alliances rarely work, and the marriage alliance of Constantine
and Licinius did not work for long.[14] Political and dynastic issues initially
raised tensions and led to war in 316-317. Tensions were exacerbated because Licinius did not keep the commitment made at Milan and expressed
in the letters that confirmed the policy of religious toleration. But the decisive factor was Constantine himself, perhaps beginning to wonder if a
tetrarchy could function in a world ruled by one God, gripped with a sense
of divine mission, annoyed with the limits of shared power, and hugely
ambitious.

The first issue to crack the alliance had to do with children and the future
shape of the imperial college. Licinius and Constantia had their first child
in the middle of 315, and Constantine and Fausta followed with a child of
their own, named for Constantine's father, in August 316. Sensing rising
tensions between Licinius and himself, Constantine sent his half-brother
Constantius to Sirmium in the late summer of 316 with a proposal. Constantine suggested that the two Augusti appoint Bassianus, Constantine's
brother-in-law by marriage to Anastasia his half-sister, as Caesar of Italy,
thereby eliminating Italy as a possible bone of contention between them.
Bassianus was a shrewd choice, related to both Augusti. According to the
official story, Licinius refused the offer and also persuaded Bassianus's
brother Senecio to turn Bassianus against the Western emperor. When the
plot was discovered, Constantine condemned and executed Bassianus and
then demanded that Licinius turn over his coconspirator Senecio.[15] Licinius

---

[14]The history of this period is complicated and controversial, and what follows is a sketch of
events. For a more thorough treatment, see Barnes, *Constantine and Eusebius*, pp. 62-77; Potter,
Roman Empire at Bay, pp. 364-66, 377-80. For Daia's role, see Nicholson, "Pagan Churches,"
pp. 1-10; Mitchell, "Maximinus," pp. 105-24.

[15]Charles Matson Odahl, *Constantine and the Christian Empire* (London: Routledge, 2004), pp.
162-64; A. H. M. Jones, *Constantine and the Conversion of Europe* (Toronto: University of
Toronto Press, 1978), p. 109. The *Origo* (5.14) claims that Constantine's aim was to set up a
buffer (*medius*) between the two Augusti (Samuel N. C. Lieu and Dominic Montserrat, eds.,
From Constantine to Julian: Pagan and Byzantine Views—A Source History [London: Routledge,
1996], p. 45). Barnes (*Constantine and Eusebius*, pp. 66-67) claims that "chronology suggests
a cynical view of Constantine's conduct." Constantine's initial aim in offering Bassianus as a
Caesar was to head off Licinius's attempts to put his own infant son in that position. Once

refused and toppled statues of Constantine at the border between their territories. By Roman reckoning, it was an act of war.

Constantine attacked and won a battle near Cibalae on October 8, 316, more than two hundred miles into Licinius's territory and well on the way to Licinius's central city of Sirmium. Constantine won again at Adrianople and pressed on toward Byzantium. Licinius was able to cut his lines of communication and force Constantine into negotiations. They signed a peace treaty at Serdica in spring 317, entirely to Constantine's advantage. Licinius acknowledged Constantine as senior Augustus, gave up all his claims to the Western empire except Thrace, and deposed and executed Valens, whom he had appointed as Caesar in the lead-up to the war. They agreed to a revived Tetrarchy of sorts, Constantine and Licinius serving as Augusti, assisted by three Caesars: Crispus, the infant Constantius, and Licinius's son, also an infant. Crispus, Constantine's son from his first marriage, was the only one who could exercise any real power. He was able, well-liked, a rising commander in Constantine's army destined, as we will see, to play a decisive role in his father's conquest of the Eastern empire.[16]

The arrangement lasted six years, and then, by Eusebius's account, Licinius went mad. He abandoned the policy of mutual toleration agreed to at Milan[17] and revived persecution, mild by fourth-century standards. After application of the sacrifice test, Christians were expelled from the imperial court and army. Licinius prohibited church councils, forced Christian assemblies to take place outside the city walls, prevented men and women from worshiping together, and revoked some of the tax privileges granted to churches and clergy.[18] In the provinces, officials realized that they could use the mechanisms of Roman law to attack Christians. Magistrates treated Christians as criminals, punished them when they confessed Christ, and released apostates immediately.[19] During the celebra-

Constantine had his own child, Bassianus was a rival rather than an ally, both "expendable, and vulnerable." Whatever Bassianus's follies, Barnes suggests, the charges against him bear too much resemblance to the charges against Maximian to be taken seriously. Potter, *Roman Empire at Bay*, p. 377, tells a similar story.

[16]I am dependent primarily on Barnes, *Constantine and Eusebius*, p. 67. See also Odahl, *Constantine and the Christian Empire*, pp. 164-65; Potter, *Roman Empire at Bay*, pp. 377-78.

[17]Ramsay MacMullen, *Constantine* (London: Croom Helm, 1987), p. 132.

[18]Jacob Burckhardt, *The Age of Constantine the Great*, trans. Moses Hadas (Berkeley: University of California Press, 1983), pp. 279-80.

[19]This information is taken from Eusebius's *Proof of the Gospel* and summarized by Barnes, *Constantine and Eusebius*, pp. 71-72. Accounts of martyrs under Licinius are almost universally

tion of the fifteenth year of his rule (*quindecennalia*) in 323, Licinius's officials threatened Christians with death or exile if they refused to sacrifice, which elicited a stinging rebuke from Constantine.[20] Despite agreeing to liberate the Christians and despite the early respect granted to him by Eusebius, Licinius had remained a pagan. Political and religious concerns overlapped. The older Licinius, envious of Constantine's evident successes, plausibly suspected that the Christians of the East would prefer to have Constantine as their emperor, though Christians assured him that they prayed for both emperors equally.[21]

The alliance between Constantine and Licinius frayed further when Constantine fought back against the Sarmatians along the Danube in 323, intruding deep into Licinius's eastern territories.[22] Both Augusti felt they had reason for war—Licinius because Constantine had trampled the boundary between them, Constantine because his colleague was apparently incapable of protecting the frontier.[23]

Over time, other reasons were presented. Praxagoras of Athens, a pagan historian writing in the late 320s, said that Constantine went to war to deliver Licinius's subjects, who were being treated "in a cruel and inhuman manner." Constantine hoped to "change him from a tyrant into a kingly ruler." The later *Origo* charged Licinius with "a frenzy of wickedness, cruelty, avarice, lust" in putting "many men to death for the sake of their riches" and violating their wives.[24]

According to the Christian historians, the aim of Constantine's war against Licinius was liberation of persecuted Christians. The Western Augustus, "perceiving the evils of which he had heard to be no longer

---

regarded as fictions. Potter (*Roman Empire at Bay*, p. 378) goes so far as to say that there is no evidence that Licinius was hostile to Christians at all. Barnes (*Constantine and Eusebius*, p. 70) argues instead that Licinius "drifted from toleration of Christianity to implicit disapproval, and finally toward active intolerance."

[20]Odahl, *Constantine and the Christian Empire*, p. 174. Odahl also credits the claims that there were some martyrs in eastern Anatolia during 323-324 and says that it was on this basis that Christians came to regard Licinius as a tyrant and "savage beast" who plunged his territories into "the darkness of a gloomy night."

[21]Odahl, *Constantine and the Christian Empire*, p. 163.

[22]Many historians see Constantine as the instigator of this conflict, but Odahl (*Constantine and the Christian Empire*, pp. 174-75) argues that Licinius, not Constantine, provoked the final showdown by initiating the persecution of Christians in the Eastern Empire.

[23]Potter, *Roman Empire at Bay*, p. 379.

[24]Both sources quoted in T. G. Elliott, *The Christianity of Constantine the Great* (Scranton, Penn.: University of Scranton Press, 1996), pp. 127-28, 131.

tolerable, took wise counsel, and tempering the natural clemency of his character with a certain measure of severity, hastened to succor those who were thus grievously oppressed." Constantine considered it a "pious and holy task to secure, by the removal of an individual, the safety of the greater part of the human race" and worried that "if he listened to the dictates of clemency only, and bestowed his pity on one utterly unworthy of it, this would, on the one hand, confer no real benefit on a man whom nothing would induce to abandon his evil practices, and whose fury against his subjects would only be likely to increase." Meanwhile, "those who suffered from his oppression would thus be forever deprived of all hope of deliverance."[25]

Open war broke out in 324, and larger armies than had been seen for centuries and would not be seen again for a millennium converged in Eastern Europe.[26] During the summer, Crispus's eighty ships defeated Licinius's three hundred at the Sea of Maramara, and the next day winds broke up all but four of Licinius's ships against the shore. Constantine followed with victories at Byzantium and Adrianople, but Licinius escaped to Chalcedon, where he still had enough support to raise an army. On September 18, Constantine defeated him conclusively at Chrysopolis. Constantia, half-sister of Constantine and wife of Licinius, negotiated a peace, and Licinius and his son were promised their lives and sent off to Thessalonica. By the spring of the following year, however, Constantine had found reason to suspect that Licinius was plotting against him, and he was strangled.

Both parties saw their struggle as a religious war. Licinius sought the guidance of soothsayers and magicians, and he condemned Constantine for being "false to the religion of his forefathers." As the sacrificial smoke arose before the battle, he told his troops that this battle would "decide between our gods and those whom our adversaries profess to honor." For his part, Constantine prepared for battle with prayers in his tabernacle and went to the field following the labrum and probably wearing a helmet marked with the initials of Christ; before the battle his men knelt to pray the generic monotheistic prayer he had prepared for them. Eusebius claimed that Constantine's victory was over his enemies "and their gods," and in the celebrations that followed the soldiers sang "hymns of praise" in

---

[25]Eusebius *Life* 2.3.
[26]MacMullen, *Constantine*, pp. 134-35.

which they "ascribed the supreme sovereignty to God."[27] As at Rome, Constantine was hailed as *liberator* and *salvator*—Liberator and Savior.

Chrysopolis 324 stands close to Milvian Bridge 312 as a decisive moment in the history of European civilization, and especially of Christianity in Europe. Not only did Constantine become the sole Christian emperor of the Eastern and Western empire, but he also laid the foundations for a new Christian capital city near ancient Byzantium, named for himself.

LIBERATOR OF THE CITY, LIBERATOR OF THE CHURCH?

Constantine's conquest of the East was, more than one historian has suggested, the first crusade.[28] Hardly surprising, say critics of Constantine. A Christianized *imperium* is inherently a crusading *imperium*, intolerant, oppressive to minorities and other religions, likely to burn heretics at a moment's notice. As we have seen, the "edict of Milan" set out a quite different policy. That means that the story of Constantine's religious policies is more complicated, and therefore more interesting, than is often supposed. But would he be consistent with the principle of religious liberty articulated there? Now that he had sole control, would he press his advantage and force the empire to embrace Christ? Would Christ simply fill the vacuum left by the removal of the Roman gods? Would Christ become the patron of Rome, Christianity a new form of civic religion?

In a number of works H. A. Drake has argued that the question "Did Constantine become a Christian?" is the wrong question.[29] The more per-

---

[27]Ibid., 2.4-19.

[28]MacMullen, *Constantine*, p. 135; Jones, *Constantine and the Conversion of Europe*, p. 112. Odahl (*Constantine and the Christian Empire*, pp. 176-77) describes it as a religious war.

[29]Drake, *Constantine and the Bishops*. Drake is correct that Constantine did not impose Christianity or completely suppress paganism and that he established a form of religious toleration. As I argue below, however, Drake overstates his case, and besides that, elements of Drake's analysis are self-contradictory. On the one hand, he argues that Constantine's religious beliefs should not be confused with his policy decisions (p. 200), yet a few pages later he argues, on the basis of Constantine's religious policy, that the emperor tried to secure "a definition of Christianity which would include a broader array of Roman beliefs" (p. 205), and later argues that Constantine saw "Christianity in broadly inclusive terms" (p. 242) and that he "favored an umbrella faith of compromise and inclusion" (p. 306). But these are policy decisions, and Drake has warned us against attempting to read the emperor's religious beliefs from policy. Constantine did not offer a definition of Christianity at all; that was something he rightly left to the bishops. Rather, he sought a policy that both expressed his support for the church and the God of Christianity and also honored the humanity of pagans. Drake's formulation on p. 315 is more accurate: Constantine adopted as "conscious policy to achieve Christian objectives by concentrating on the broad areas on

tinent political question is "What *kind* of Christian did Constantine become?" Christians disagreed on all manner of practical and theological issues in the early fourth century, and they disagreed about politics too. Some hoped for escape from persecution so that they could take the reins of power and apply a retributive "good-for-the-goose" policy. (You made us sacrifice; here, eat this Host!) Others developed a principled understanding of religious freedom, rooted in a particular understanding of the nature of religion and the nature of humanity.

Most of the apologists who defended the church in the early centuries advocated freedom of religion. For some it may have been only tactical, the rhetoric of an oppressed minority. The Latin rhetor Lactantius, however, developed a *theological* argument for religious freedom. Lactantius was close enough to Constantine later to serve as tutor to the emperor's sons, and his influence is evident in many ways in Constantine's own writings. I noted above that Constantine was convinced, either by Lactantius or by his own observation, of Lactantius's claim that God would avenge those who persecute his people. Lactantius also wrote a short treatise on the anger of God (*De ira Dei*), again a theme central to Constantine's own religious outlook. Lactantius's Christianity was a hardy, tough-minded, very Latin Christianity that appealed to the sensibilities of a soldier and a politician.

Though he detested the persecuting emperors and merrily detailed their gruesome deaths, Lactantius's basic plea was for freedom of conscience. "Religion is the one field in which freedom has pitched her tent," Lactantius wrote, "for religion is, first and foremost, a matter of free will, and no man can be forced under compulsion to adore what he has no will to adore." At best, coercion will force people to make a "hypocritical show" of devotion, but force cannot make a man or woman will to worship. "If, then, anyone, out of fear of the tools of torture or vanquished by the torture itself, finally assents to the accursed pagan sacrifice, he never acts of his own free will, as compulsion was involved." This is obvious from the fact that "as soon as opportunity offers and he recovers his freedom, he comes back to his God and begs with tears for forgiveness, doing penance for that which he did, not of his own free will, which he did not possess, but under the

---

which Christians and at least educated, monotheistic pagans could agree."

compulsion to which he submitted, and the Church will not withhold its forgiveness." To the persecutors, he asked, "What good can you do, then, if you defile the body but cannot break the will?"[30] It is a surprisingly modern statement, arguing, as modern theorists like John Courtney Murray and George Weigel do, that religious liberty is the "first freedom," rooted in the very nature of religious life as an exercise of free will.

In the *Divine Institutes,* Lactantius was responding to Porphyry's arguments in his treatise against Christians and also his treatise *Philosophy from Oracles.* Porphyry believed that many roads led to the truth and bliss, and this included the road of Jesus. This did not lead Porphyry to endorse a policy of toleration. Christians worshiped a man—a good man, to be sure, but only a man. Porphyry did not think the Roman Empire should be willing to put up with the man-worshiping Christians indefinitely for some greater good. Christianity's humanism offended the gods and needed to be stopped. Porphyry advocated "threatening the use of force against those who worshiped a human being" but at the same time "suggested that Christianity, by forsaking its worship of Jesus, might be made compatible with traditional worship and philosophy."[31] Christians, he argued, should conform to Roman practice, offer the prescribed sacrifice. They could believe whatever they liked, so long as they did what the empire and its gods demanded. But Rome could not condone Christian worship in its current form.

Lactantius' response draws in part on earlier strands of Roman political theology. Cicero had claimed that God should be approached chastely and with piety, and Lactantius takes this to mean that a true God will not want to have force used in religion, since one cannot be chaste and pious in religion if one is coerced to worship. Force pollutes rather than purifies religion. "For religion is to be defended," he wrote, "not by putting to death, but by dying; not by cruelty, but by patient endurance; not by guilt, but by good faith: for the former belong to evils, but the latter to goods; and it is necessary for that which is good to have place in religion, and not that which is evil. For if you wish to defend religion by

---

[30]Lactantius *Divine Institutes* 49, quoted in Andreas Alfoldi, *The Conversion of Constantine and Pagan Rome,* trans. Harold Mattingly (Oxford: Clarendon, 1948), p. 53; cf. Drake, *Constantine and the Bishops,* p. 211.

[31]Elizabeth DePalma Digeser, *The Making of a Christian Empire: Lactantius and Rome* (Ithaca, N.Y.: Cornell University Press, 2000), p. 108.

bloodshed, and by tortures, and by guilt, it will no longer be defended, but will be polluted and profaned."[32]

Lactantius also deployed traditional Roman ideals of freedom. As in the "edict of Milan," the keynote of Lactantius's argument is liberty (*libertas*). *Libertas* pitches her tent in the area of religion, and religion belongs in the realm of will rather than in the realm of necessity (*necessitas*). *Libertas* has a long history in Roman political theology.[33] Caesar and Octavian both posed as liberators of Rome from tyranny and as conservative restorers of the Roman past. Constantine's imperial propaganda rings the same note. The triumphal arch completed in 315 titles him "Liberator of the City" (*liberator urbis*), other inscriptions in the capital acclaim him as "Restorer of Public Liberty" (*restitutor libertatis publicae*), and coins claim him to be "Restorer of Rome" (*Restitutor Romae*) and "Recoverer of His City" (*Recuperator urbis suae*). Much the same is implied by the designation of Constantine as emperor (*princeps*), for the emperor was expected to be a "suppressor of tyranny and the surety for freedom."[34] Coins declare him to be "greatest emperor" (*optimus princeps*), and on one coin the goddess Roma herself hands over imperial power to the new prince.[35]

While continuing to employ the terminology of the traditional imperial ideology, Lactantius revised the concept significantly, and Constantine followed suit in his imperial propaganda. Though still making play with the imperial ideology of the past, they redefined tyranny in terms of religious compulsion, thus branding Diocletian, Maxentius, Licinius, and the rest as enemies of Christian *libertas*, as sub-Roman tyrants. Perhaps inspired by the arguments of Lactantius, Constantine forged a religious policy that seamlessly knitted Christian and Roman themes together and set the ideological foundations for a Christian, but tolerant, Roman Empire. The theory was expressed in the inscription on the statue of Constantine in Rome. He holds the sign of Christ, and the inscription reads: "In this sign of salvation I have restored to Rome, her senate, and her people, their ancient liberty and glory, delivering them from the lawless

---

[32]Lactantius *Divine Institutes* 5.20; see Digeser, *Making of a Christian Empire*, pp. 57-60.

[33]Chaim Wirszubski, *"Libertas" as a Political Idea at Rome During the Late Republic and Early Principate* (Cambridge: Cambridge University Press, 1950).

[34]Alfoldi, *Conversion of Constantine*, p. 64.

[35]All the details are in ibid.

yoke of the tyrant."[36] The inscription could have adorned a statue of Octavian, who also claimed to fight for the *libertas* of the "Senate and the People of Rome" (long abbreviated as *SPQR*) and who claimed to bring "salvation" of the people. But the Christian symbol changes everything: Rome's
libertas is now secure only *in hoc signo*—in *this* sign.

What kind of Christian did Constantine become? He became a Lactantian Christian.

Practically, that meant toleration of paganism. That was the policy established in 313, and it was the policy Constantine reiterated, more elabo-
rately, after he defeated Licinius and assumed the sole *imperium* in 324.
His edict to the Eastern Provinces attacked the irrationality of polytheism
and defended monotheism. He recalled his father's kindness to the church
with fondness and recounted the arrogance and stupidity of the persecuting emperors, "unsound in mind" and "more zealous of cruel than gentle
measures." They turned a period of peace and prosperity into a virtual civil
war and proved themselves more savage than the barbarians, among whom
Christians found refuge. Like Lactantius, he rejoiced that the persecutors
"have experienced a miserable end, and are consigned to unceasing punishment in the depths of the lower world." He insulted the Pythian oracle
as "impious" and "delusive" and described Christianity as a "holy"
religion.

Having exposed the error, the savagery, and the political evils of paganism, and just as the reader is ready for the hammer to fall, Constantine
revealed the thrust of the edict. Insisting that his desire was "for the common good of the world and the advantage of all mankind, that your people
should enjoy a life of peace and undisturbed concord," he declared that
"anyone who delight[s] in error, [should] be made welcome to the same
degree of peace and tranquility which they have who believe." He did not
want such persons to remain in their ignorance and error but hoped that
"this restoration of equal privileges to all will prevail to lead them into the
straight path." Perhaps addressing himself to militant Christians, Constantine declared that no one is to molest anyone else: "Let every one do as

---

[36]Alfoldi (ibid.) makes the case for this policy very effectively and concisely. The inscription is
in ibid., p. 83. He reconstructs the Latin as "Hoc salutari signo . . . senatui populoque Romano
et urbi Romae iugo tyrannicae dominationis ereptae pristinam libertatem splendoremque red-
didi."

his soul desires." It is true that it is possible to live a life of "holiness and purity" only if one relies on the "holy laws" of "men of sound judgment." But Constantine was willing to permit "those who will hold themselves aloof from us" to keep their "temples of lies." He gave a Lactantian rationale for the policy: "The battle for deathlessness requires willing recruits. Coercion is of no avail." There is a vast difference between pursuing immortality "voluntarily" and compelling "others to do so from the fear of punishment." As it comes to a close, the edict modulates from imperial pronouncement to prayer: "We"—he meant "we Christians"—"have the glorious edifice of your truth, which you have given us as our native home. We pray, however, that they too may receive the same blessing, and thus experience that heartfelt joy which unity of sentiment inspires."[37] Though framed as an official imperial document, from "Victor Constantinus, Maximus Augustus, to the people of the Eastern provinces," it is more a sermon than a law. Constantine is less a theocrat imposing Christianity than Billy Graham issuing an altar call.

His concluding remarks suggest that Constantine issued the decree in part to cool down hot-headed Christians who might want to shut down all pagan shrines immediately, or even believed that paganism had suddenly died. He went on at length "because we were unwilling to dissemble or be false to the true faith; and the more so, since we understand there are some who say that the rites of the heathen temples, and the power of darkness, have been entirely removed." While he wished it were true, the emperor recognized that "the rebellious spirit of those wicked errors still continues obstinately fixed in the minds of some, so as to discourage the hope of any general restoration of mankind to the ways of truth." Instead of attacking pagans, Christians should be mixing with and evangelizing them. "Once more," he added, "let none use that to the detriment of another which he may himself have received on conviction of its truth; but let every one, if it be possible, apply what he has understood and known to the benefit of his neighbor; if otherwise, let him relinquish the attempt."[38]

That Constantine was serious about giving freedom to pagans is evident from pagan reaction. For most, Constantine's conversion was a "bear-

---

[37]Eusebius *Life* 2.56.
[38]The whole edict comes from Eusebius *Life* 2.48-60. See also Corcoran, *Empire of the Tetrarchs*, p. 189, for Constantine's treatment of public and private divination.

able evil," and Constantine continued to have pagan philosophers in his court for years after his conversion.[39] Pagans continued to serve in his administration and army; he gave pagans high positions; a pagan helped him gather materials from around the East to adorn his great "Christian" city of Constantinople. His policies toward the army were particularly significant. Diocletian, Galerius, and Licinius had expelled Christians from their army because their presence offended the gods and might lead to defeat. Theodosius II operated this principle when he reversed, or revived, Diocletian's policy and restricted the army to Christians. Wearing his chi-rho helmet and bearing his shield painted with a cross, Constantine kept pagan troops and led them in a monotheistic prayer that he knew would not violate their conscience.[40]

John Howard Yoder to the contrary, Constantine did not decide that everyone in the empire had to be a Christian.[41] Under the arrangements of Milan and the letter to the Eastern provinces, the Roman Empire appeared to offer all religions a level playing field.

But is there any such thing?

PUBLIC SPACE

Drake argues that Constantine's goal "was to create a neutral public space" in which Christians and pagans could participate, a "peaceful coexistence."[42] Above I have noted some of the grounds for that claim. Still, Drake's is a one-sided conclusion. Though Constantine followed the principles and rhetoric of the Lactantian policy of religious freedom, he did not pretend to establish a neutral religious freedom. In the very same decree where he granted pagans freedom to maintain their temples, he condemned them for their persistent errors and prayed for their conversion. Everyone knew on which side of the pagan-Christian divide Constantine stood, and Constantine's preference for Christianity was more than verbal. It showed up in iconography, in privileges granted to the church and clergy, and in efforts to suppress some aspects of

---

[39]Drake, *Constantine and the Bishops*, pp. 247-49. Drake quotes the phrase "bearable evil" from Friedhelm Winkelmann. See also Raymond Van Dam, *The Roman Revolution of Constantine* (Cambridge: Cambridge University Press, 2008), p. 31: "Both Christians and pagans seemed to recognize that Constantine was quite tolerant in religious matters."

[40]Dorries, *Constantine and Religious Liberty*, pp. 37-39.

[41]John Howard Yoder, *The Royal Priesthood: Essays Ecclesiological and Ecumenical*, ed. Michael G. Cartwright (Grand Rapids: Eerdmans, 1994), p. 254.

[42]H. A. Drake, "Constantine and Consensus," *Church History* 64 (1995): 7.

paganism. Pagans were tolerated, but they were tolerated within an empire that everyone could see was increasingly Christian.

As we saw in the previous chapter, Constantine's iconography was initially ambiguous but became more explicitly Christian over time. He often had himself depicted with his eyes turned toward heaven, and the hand that remains from the monumental statue erected at Rome appears to be folded in a gesture of benediction. At Constantinople, the mint busied itself with producing a coin inscribed with the motto *spes publica*—the hope of the public—with an emblem of Christ piercing a dragon on the reverse side. To Eusebius, Constantine wrote after his victory over Licinius that the occasion was ripe for restoring churches "now that freedom is restored, and that dragon, through the providence of God, and by our instrumentality, thrust out from the government of the Empire" and thereby "the divine power has become known to all, and that those who hitherto, from fear or from incredulity or from depravity, have lived in error, will now, upon becoming acquainted with Him who truly is, be led into the true and correct manner of life."[43] By 320, images of the old gods completely disappeared from Constantine's coinage. Constantine is surrounded and adorned by traditional Roman battle gear—horse, shield, helmet. But on the helmet is the chi-rho insignia.

More than any other instrument of propaganda, architecture expressed the complexity of Constantine's religious policy. Architecture had a double significance for Roman emperors. Most obviously, it was a direct formation of public space. By laying out cities and building baths, public meeting halls, arches, temples, and governmental buildings, emperors literally shaped the pathways of civic life. An emperor's largess could turn a provincial backwater—like Byzantium—into the booming capital of a dream-empire that would last a thousand years. During the Tetrarchy, Augusti and Caesars had left their imprint on Trier, Serdica, Surmium and Nicomedia, and the one Rome-based figure, Maxentius, was involved in massive building in the venerable capital.

Building was an act of euergetism, one of the main forms of gift-giving by which emperors established and nurtured alliances, enhanced their reputation for generosity and clemency, and offered conspicuous displays

---

[43]Theodoret *Ecclesiastical History* 1.14.

of wealth that increased their regal *auctoritas*. Augustus was patron of the city of Rome, and during the Principate only the emperor or Senate was permitted to build within the sacred walls of the *urbs*. His patronage extended throughout the empire; Augustus built the ramparts of Trieste, Fanum and Nimes and an aqueduct at Venafrum, as well as public buildings throughout Italy and the Roman provinces. Elsewhere, local and provincial officials imitated the emperors by building fortifications or buildings in their own territories.[44] Constantine had the disposition, the resources and, just as important, the time to engage in massive and widespread building projects,[45] and he used his time and resources to expand his popularity and promote his policies, particularly his religious policies.

STUDIED AMBIGUITY

No one questions the scale of Constantine's artistic and architectural achievement. Many have contested its quality, and more broadly the quality of the culture in the age of Constantine. Charles Freeman traces the "closing of the Western mind" to the triumph of Christianity in the time of Constantine.[46] The squat, expressionless figures on the frieze of the Arch of Constantine have come in for particular scorn, symbolic markers of the end of ancient artistry and the beginning of medieval incompetence. In a famous report on the art of Rome prepared for Pope Leo X, Raphael found the arch architecturally "beautiful and well conceived" but the sculptures "very tasteless."[47] Bernard Berenson complained that "individual figures suggest nothing so much as an assemblage of rudely carved chessmen. . . . We find huge heads out of all proportion to their bodies." The "stunted bodies," he observed, "are swathed in heavy blankets or covered with scanty shifts, both with the folds of the draperies as unfunctional, as helplessly chiseled as ever European art sank to in the darkest ages."[48]

---

[44]Paul Veyne, *Bread and Circuses: Historical Sociology and Political Pluralism,* trans. Brian Pearce (New York: Penguin, 1990), p. 362. Veyne is the chief source on imperial euergetism.

[45]Mark J. Johnson, "Architecture of Empire," in *The Cambridge Companion to the Age of Constantine,* ed. Noel Lenski (Cambridge: Cambridge University Press, 2006), pp. 278-97.

[46]Charles Freeman, *The Closing of the Western Mind: The Rise of Faith and the Fall of Reason* (New York: Vintage, 2002).

[47]Elizabeth Gilmore Holt, ed., *A Documentary History of Art,* vol. 1, *The Middle Ages and the Renaissance* (Princeton, N.J.: Princeton University Press, 1981), p. 294.

[48]Quoted in R. Ross Holloway, *Constantine and Rome* (New Haven, Conn.: Yale University Press, 2004), pp. 37, 48.

Burckhardt's criticism of Constantinian art was more wide ranging. Everywhere he looked he saw signs of degeneration and aesthetic corruption. Because of the penetration of Goths and Franks and their incorporation into the empire, arts and customs took on a disturbingly un-Roman character, evidence of a widespread "barbarization." Mosaics splashed upward from floors to walls, and finally to ceilings, and "with the introduction of Christianity, mosaic became the principal decoration, wherever means sufficed, for all walls and ceilings in churches." The speeches of rhetors were filled with bombast and poets undertook strained efforts to represent Christian truth symbolically.

Part of the reason, Burckhardt explained in his Teutonic nineteenth-century way, was that people themselves were getting uglier. Most of the blame, though, went to the church. Once victorious, the church felt compelled to announce its victory, resulting in a "tendency toward heightened magnificence" in architecture; the aim was to "make the entire structure and every stone in it a symbol of its power and its victory." Christians were so insistent on their message that form mattered little, and in arches, sarcophagi and other places "representation grew altogether impoverished and childish." Burckhardt's charge is that Christianity introduced a corruption—"domination of subject over form."[49]

Judgments about the value of Roman art in Constantine's age turn on questions of preference—"whether one prefers the classical naturalism of the bulk of Graeco-Roman art to the more abstract schematism of medieval art, of which the arts under Constantine were a harbinger"—and questions about Constantine's religion: "whether the Christianization inaugurated by Constantine was more or less of a good thing."[50] Burckhardt's commitment to classicism blinds him here. Deviation from classical forms, genres and styles is necessarily a decline from a great height.

Burckhardt, further, was less informed about the interests and aims of classical Roman art than he realized. Subject matter had long shaped style. In depicting battle scenes, artists strove to capture the passion, chaotic motion and tragedy of war. When Augustus wanted to be represented as the embodiment of Roman *dignitas, maiestas, pondus* and *auctoritas*, how-

---

[49]Burckhardt, *Age of Constantine*, chap. 7.
[50]Jas' Elsner, "Perspectives in Art," in *The Cambridge Companion to the Age of Constantine*, ed. Noel Lenski (Cambridge: Cambridge University Press, 2006), pp. 255-77, esp. 272.

ever, he distanced himself from the "Asiatic" Anthony by having himself portrayed according to "an ideal of calm serenity and cheerfulness." Battle scenes, in short, demanded "Hellenistic" treatment, but portraiture demanded "Hellenic, classical" treatment. Linkages of subject matter and form were not mechanical. Bacchus could be depicted in the nude as a soft, feminine youth, his posture sensuous and his hand resting languidly on his head. But he could also be depicted as an old man, fully clothed, with archaic stylized beard and hair. Though the connections were not rigid, subject matter shaped style; different depictions of Bacchus intended to bring out different aspects of his complex character. As Tonio Holscher puts it, "State ceremonies were shown as being conducted with religious or official dignity, battles portrayed in terms of pathos, emotion and straining effort. The choice of the form was thus based on the content."[51]

Even those stumpy figures on the frieze of the arch have precedents in Greek art. Constantine's battle scenes "are reminiscent of the work of another group of sculptors, from the finest period of Greek art in Greece and Asia Minor, who undertook to carve battle scenes, including a siege, on the basement of the tomb known as the Nereid Monument at Xanthos." Though completed in the heyday of classicism, around 400 B.C., the figures "show the same tendencies toward distortion of the human figure (venturing toward dwarfism) and the same rendering of fortifications in a Lilliputian fashion that we see on the Arch of Constantine." The issue is not artistic skill but "the result of the problems of achieving wide perspective on a narrow frieze without making it look gigantic and without allowing the figures to all but disappear if they are to be kept in proportion to the buildings." Similarly, on Constantine's arch "the dwarfish figure with head too large for his body and the stunted building [were] part of an effort to keep the action from being lost and to keep the setting subordinate to the figures involved."[52]

Artistic values were indeed changing during the Tetrarchy and into Constantine's time. Depictions of the Tetrarchs suggest that the change

---

[51]This entire paragraph is dependent on Tonio Holscher, *The Language of Images in Roman Art,* trans. Anthony Snodgrass and Annemarie Kunzl-Snodgrass (Cambridge: Cambridge University Press, 2004). The quotation comes from p. 58, and photos of different depictions of Bacchus are found on pp. 66-68.

[52]Holloway, *Constantine and Rome,* p. 49.

was partly forced by political considerations.[53] Not all artistic shifts were politically motivated, however. Fourth-century artists had a taste for pattern, geometry and flat surfaces without perspective or clear spatial distribution. Mosaic was ideal for such a sensibility, and mosaic reached a pinnacle in the fourth century, in the peacocks and fruit that adorn the Santa Costanza in Rome, the hunting scenes in a villa at Hippo Regius, the hunting scene and "bikini girls" on the walls in a villa at Piazza Armerina, Sicily.[54] It is impossible to tell in the last of these how the animals in the hunt scene are spatially related. In another mosaic, a charioteer, hand raised in triumph, faces the viewer. His two horses turn impossibly in opposite directions so that the artist could depict them at three-quarter view, while his chariot wheels twist at a right angle to the chariot itself. It is difficult to prove that these shifts are the product of a decline in talent; it is just as plausible to account for them as a change rather than as a collapse of taste. Burckhardt's animus toward Constantinian art simply states a preference and a prejudice: he prefers classical to medieval and pagan to Christian, and so pre- to post-Constantinian art.

The Arch of Constantine has, moreover, a more unified design than often credited to it.[55] One of the complaints against the art of late antiquity and after was its extensive use of spolia. Sculptors recut the faces of statues to resemble the latest patron, architects reused columns, builders moved figures and designs from their original location to a new location. Though spolia in fact had long been used in Roman art,[56] it reached a "veritable flood" in the fourth century and into the medieval period.[57] But this "recycling" was not necessarily driven (merely) by lack of materials or

---

[53]See chapter 1.

[54]Nancy H. Ramage and Andrew Ramage, *Roman Art*, 5th ed. (Upper Saddle River, N.J.: Pearson/Prentice Hall, 2009), pp. 334-40, 355-57.

[55]See Holloway, *Constantine and Rome*, pp. 19-53; Mark Wilson Jones, "Genesis and Mimesis: The Design of the Arch of Constantine in Rome," *Journal of the Society of Architectural Historians* 59 (2000): 50-77; Jas Elsner, "From the Culture of Spolia to the Cult of Relics: The Arch of Constantine and the Genesis of Late Antique Forms," *Papers of the British School at Rome* 68 (2000). Dale Kinney (" 'SPOLIA. DAMNATIO' and 'RENOVATIO MEMORIAE,' " *Memoirs of the American Academy in Rome* 42 [1997]: 117) attributes this conclusion to Hans Peter L'Orange.

[56]See Kinney, "SPOLIA," pp. 117-48; see also Kinney, "Roman Architectural Spolia," *Proceedings of the American Philosophical Society* 145, no. 2 (2001): 138-61. Kinney ("SPOLIA," pp. 118-20) argues that the term itself is an anachronistic projection of modern standards of artistry, and provides evidence of pre-Constantinian spolia at pp. 124-26, 134.

[57]Elsner, "From the Culture of Spolia," p. 154.

talent. It could also be motivated by a "positive choice aimed at identifying Rome's new ruler with the 'good' emperors of the past, particularly Trajan, Hadrian, and Marcus Aurelius."[58] On Constantine's arch, the spolia was not an act of *damnatio,* literally effacing images of earlier emperors. Spolia rather was an architectural typology, associating the *vetera* or old things (Trajan) with the fulfillment in the *nova* or new things (Constantine).[59]

Its religious message was also one of continuity and change. Eight tondo relief carvings were taken over from Hadrian's arch, with the imperial faces recut to resemble Constantine. These too show a unity of design. They move from a hunt—traditional artistic symbol of the taming of chaos—through various acts of government and end with sacrifices to Apollo, Diana and Hercules.[60] Yet the figures who perform the sacrifice are not cut to resemble the new emperor. Earlier emperors engaged in animal sacrifice, and Constantine's arch pays due homage to that traditional mode of worship. But Constantine himself has left that form of worship behind, and with it the gods of the Roman past.[61]

Earlier triumphal arches declared the victory of the *princeps* and the favor of his gods, and Constantine's did the same. The way it makes the point is, however, significant. Its famously inscrutable inscription attributes his victory over Maxentius to the inspiration of an unidentified deity. The fact that it was not attributed to Jupiter or Mars is itself a sign that the Senate that awarded the arch to Constantine in 315 recognized that its new emperor served a different deity.[62] The arch's inscription places Constantine in continuity with his predecessors, while it hints silently that a new God has taken residence in Rome. The same subtle neutrality is evident in its placement and in the reliefs that adorn its various levels. Constantine's arch imitates that of Septimus Severus in many particulars, establishing continuity with the previous imperial dynasty and with the most impressive arch in the Forum. Constantine's arch is set at the entry to the Forum, thus claiming it for Constantine and his followers, and the

---

[58]Jones, "Genesis and Mimesis," p. 70.
[59]Elsner, "From the Culture of Spolia," makes this connection and links it to literary habits of the time, as well as to the cult of the saints. My student Lisa Beyeler offered the same analogy of spolia and typology.
[60]Holloway, *Constantine and Rome,* pp. 21-25; Jones, "Genesis and Mimesis," pp. 69-70.
[61]Jones, "Genesis and Mimesis," pp. 70-71.
[62]Ibid., p. 70, quotes Jose Ruysschaert's "masterful remark" that "the arch is pagan for that which it says, Christian for that which it doesn't."

arch was designed to line up with a statue of Sol, Constantine's pagan patron and, at least for the later Constantine, a symbol of the Christian Sun of Righteousness.[63]

Constantine's arch thus sends multiple messages in the way it mimics "the grandest arch in the Forum Romanum," in its "orchestration of spolia and the sculptural program," and especially in "its sweeping synthesis of past masterpieces of composition, proportion, sculpture, and iconography" to produce a design that both honored the "old ways of design and heralded the new."

NEW ROME

Constantinople displayed a similar subtlety. Inspired by a dream,[64] Constantine founded the city shortly after his victory over Licinius and dedicated it on May 11, 330. Eusebius found no hint of ambiguity. In celebration of his victory over the "tyrant" Licinius, Constantine established the city as an explicitly and thoroughly Christian civic space, having first cleansed it of idols. Thereafter "he embellished it with numerous sacred edifices, both memorials of martyrs on the largest scale, and other buildings of the most splendid kind, not only within the city itself, but in its vicinity." By honoring the martyrs, the emperor was simultaneously consecrating the city "to the martyrs' God." The emperor insisted that the city be free of idolatry, "that henceforth no statues might be worshipped there in the temples of those falsely reputed to be gods, nor any altars defiled by the pollution of blood." Above all, he prohibited "sacrifices consumed by fire," as well as "demon festivals" and all "other ceremonies usually observed by the superstitious."[65]

On the positive side, Constantine filled the city with Christian symbols: "one might see the fountains in the midst of the market place graced with figures representing the good Shepherd, well known to those who study the sacred oracles, and that of Daniel also with the lions, forged in brass, and resplendent with plates of gold. Indeed, so large a measure of Divine love possessed the emperor's soul." Eusebius was most impressed with a "vast tablet displayed in the center of its gold-covered paneled ceil-

---

[63]Ibid., pp. 50, 69.
[64]Potter, *Roman Empire at Bay,* p. 383.
[65]Eusebius *Life* 3.48.

ing" in the palace, where Constantine ordered "the symbol of our Saviour's Passion to be fixed, composed of a variety of precious stones richly in-wrought with gold." For Eusebius, "this symbol he seemed to have in-tended to be as it were the safeguard of the empire itself."[66]

From what we can tell at this distance,[67] Constantinople's break with the pagan past was not so self-evident.[68] Constantine included no coli-seum but built a hippodrome for racing that mimicked the Circus Maxi-mus at Rome. Notable churches dotted the city, including the first form of the Church of Holy Wisdom and the Church of the Apostles, where for a time the emperor was buried.[69] Christian imagery was evident through-out. Yet he also treated the city as a project continuous with the Roman past. As a celebration of his victory over the tyrant, Constantinople was the city of *Rome's* victory, not merely of Constantine's personal triumph.[70] Further, he erected a statue to Tyche, the goddess of good fortune,[71] and at the top of a porphyry column that still stands in the center of the old square of Constantinople, he placed a golden statue of Apollo looking to-ward the rising sun, whose face was remade into the face of Constantine, with an inscription that "intended to signify that instead of being a sun-god Constantine gave his allegiance to the God who made the sun."[72] He moved so much existing art into his new city that Jerome complained that all the cities of the East had been stripped bare.[73] Constantinople was newly founded, but it deliberately evoked the Roman past as well, reli-giously as well as politically.

HOUSES OF THE LORD

In the main, Constantine's buildings in Rome and elsewhere left no room

---

[66]Ibid., 3.49.

[67]Richard Krautheimer, *Early Christian and Byzantine Architecture,* Pelican History of Art, 3rd ed. (New York: Penguin, 1979), p. 72, notes that the city today has few remains of the original Constantinian constructions.

[68]A general discussion of the founding and adornment of Constantinople is found in Gilbert Dagron, *Naissance d'une capitale: Constantinople et ses institutions de 330 a 451,* 2nd ed. (Paris: Presses universitaires de France, 1984), pp. 13-47.

[69]Krautheimer, *Early Christian and Byzantine Architecture,* pp. 72-73.

[70]Dagron, *Naissance d'une capitale,* p. 26.

[71]Ibid., pp. 43-47.

[72]R. P. C. Hanson, "The Christian Attitude to Pagan Religions up to the Time of Constantine the Great," *ANRW* 23 (1980): 968.

[73]Potter, *Roman Empire at Bay,* p. 384.

for ambiguity. He was a great builder of churches, *Christian* churches. He studded Rome with churches and baptisteries[74] and erected church buildings throughout the empire, including several in Palestine, where his mother Helena traveled. He built other buildings and monuments, but church building was his main architectural preoccupation. Not only did this preoccupation demonstrate Constantine's official approval of the church, but erecting churches took the place of the temple building sponsored by earlier emperors. The location of his buildings in the capital was significant. Now the site of a bustling urban center, St. Peter's was originally built on the margins of the city, a sign of Constantine's departure from the earlier imperial focus on the Forum.[75]

Constantine's church building often embodied his self-image as a victor over paganism.[76] In his construction projects Constantine was once again Moses, plundering Egypt for materials with which to erect the house of God. None so thoroughly expressed this victory over paganism as the church erected at Mamre. Sacred to Jews, Arabs and even Greeks, Mamre, a place Abram visited during his sojourns in Canaan, had become a hotspot of pagan revelry and idolatry. When Constantine heard, he was incensed. According to Sozomen, he "rebuked the bishops of Palestine in no measured terms, because they had neglected their duty, and had permitted a holy place to be defiled by impure libations and sacrifices." In a letter to Macarius, bishop of Jerusalem, and other Palestinian bishops, he commanded that "these bishops . . . hold a conference on this subject with the Phœnician bishops, and issue directions for the demolition, from the foundations, of the altar formerly erected there, the destruction of the carved images by fire, and the erection of a church worthy of so ancient and so holy a place." Prohibiting sacrifice, he demanded that Mamre "should be exclusively devoted to the worship of God according to the law of the Church." In the event that "any attempt should be made to restore the former rites, the bishops were to inform against the delinquent, in order

---

[74]Holloway, *Constantine and Rome*, chap. 3.

[75]Gregory T. Armstrong, "Imperial Church Building and Church-State Relations, A.D. 313-363," *Church History* 36, no. 1 (1967): 7. Thanks too to my student Lisa Beyeler for a helpful conversation on this point.

[76]Ibid., p. 8, points out that Constantine's buildings were selective, often erected in order to embody a Christian conquest of a pagan site.

that he might be subjected to the greatest punishment."[77] At Mamre, at least, Constantine intended to bring an end to sacrifice.

The very form of Christian church buildings communicated the triumph of Christianity in the Roman world and Christ's victory over the Roman gods. The choice of the basilica form for church buildings was virtually forced on Constantine and other church builders. Domestic spaces could no longer house the crowds that now crammed into meeting places for worship, and ancient temples were designed to house an image of the god, not to accommodate mobs of worshipers. In the Roman world, only one style met all the needs of the church—the basilica.[78]

Today a "basilica" is a church basilica, but in the Roman world basilicas were used for many purposes. Whenever there was a need for a large assembly—for political gatherings, markets, court sessions, military drills, adjacent to temples—basilicas were serviceable. Basilica plans were no more uniform than their uses. There were "single-naved halls with or without apses; halls with two naves; halls composed of a nave and aisles, the latter parallel to or enveloping the nave on four sides; broad and short, or very long structures." Entryways were variable as well. They could be "placed on one of the long sides, thus intimating a transversal or central reading of the plan; or they are placed on one short side, on the longitudinal axis, or indeed, on both one long and one short side." In public basilicas, "the tribunal for the presiding magistrate may project into the nave or an aisle; or apses sheltering tribunals may extend outward from one, two or three flanks of the building. Nave and aisles may be of one height; or the nave may be higher and provided with clerestory windows, small or large. Also, the aisles may or may not be surmounted by galleries."[79] In the early fourth century, the only common elements of the basilica form were a timber roof and the presence of at least one raised platform or tribunal in the apse or standing free in the nave. By the early part of Constantine's reign, the single-nave basilica, whether or not flanked by aisles, had become the predominant form.[80]

---

[77]Sozomen *Ecclesiastical History* 2.4. On Constantine's building at Mamre, see Van Dam, *Roman Revolution,* pp. 301-2.

[78]Krautheimer, *Early Christian and Byzantine Architecture,* pp. 41-42. There is evidence that the few pre-Constantinian church buildings were also basilicas.

[79]Richard Krautheimer, "The Constantinian Basilica," *Dumbarton Oaks Papers* 21 (1967): 122.

[80]Ibid., p. 125.

Basilicas already carried a religious charge. They "shared the architectural vocabulary of the temples," such as "colonnaded orders, entablatures, stone masonry . . . vaulting or coffered ceilings." By the beginning of the fourth century, these associations were overlaid with allusions to the imperial cult: "the presence of the emperor, in effigy or in the flesh, had become increasingly the predominant element in any basilica." Any boundary between secular and civic disappeared, and "any basilica was, or carried the connotations of, a sanctuary of the god on earth."[81]

Constantine continued to build monumental civic buildings in basilica form, the most prominent of which is at Trier. It is a long-nave basilica, without aisles, one hundred by two hundred Roman feet (95 by 190 English feet), and a hundred Roman feet high. The nave has two rows of windows on each side, nine windows per row, and the curved apse has two rows of smaller windows, five in each row.[82] Today the exterior is simple brick, and the building sticks out awkwardly like a prematurely tall teen, but it was once covered by pink stucco and nestled among other buildings that have since collapsed. When Constantine first built it, the interior was lavishly decorated: "the walls carried a marble revetment of many colors rising in successive tiers to the upper row of windows and articulated, it seems, by inlaid pilasters, panels, and friezes; above, there followed a zone of painted stucco or possibly mosaic; five niches in the apse wall bore ornamental glass mosaic; on the floor, pavement slabs of white and dark marble formed a geometric pattern."[83]

A few of Constantine's basilica churches were on the same scale.[84] Begun shortly after his victory over Maxentius, the Lateran basilica in Rome was a long-nave structure flanked by side aisles. It was over three hundred feet long, and its ceiling rose to one hundred feet.[85] If the *Liber Pontificalis* is to be believed (it probably is not), the ornamentation of the Lateran basilica was as luxurious as any pagan temple, with "a hammered silver *fastigium*," on the front of which was "the Saviour seated in a chair, 5 ft in size,

---

[81]Ibid., pp. 123-24.

[82]Ramage and Ramage, *Roman Art,* p. 354.

[83]Krautheimer, "Constantinian Basilica," p. 118.

[84]For detailed discussion of particular churches, see Krautheimer, *Early Christian and Byzantine Architecture,* pp. 39-70; for churches in Rome, Holloway, *Constantine and Rome.*

[85]Gregory T. Armstrong, "Constantine's Churches: Symbol and Structure," *Journal of the Society of Architectural Historians* 33, no. 1 (1974): 6.

weighing 120 lb, and 12 apostles each 5 ft and weighing 90 lb with crowns of the finest silver." Another image of Christ was visible to someone looking down the nave from the apse: "the Saviour sitting on a throne, 5 ft in size, of finest silver weighing 140 lb, and 4 spear-carrying silver angels, each 5 ft and weighing 105 lb, with jewels of Alabanda in their eyes."[86]

Constantine's original church of St. Pietro at the Vatican was the largest of all Christian churches of the time. The nave alone was 295 feet long, and the entire interior 390 feet long and 210 feet wide. Distinctively, however, it had a transept as tall as the nave itself that separated the nave from the large apse. Before the apse was the tomb of Peter, marking the transept as the *martyrium* proper.[87] After St. Pietro, the cruciform shape made from the long-nave basilica with transept became a standard cathedral form. Constantine's conversion was a response to the sign of the victorious cross, and the cross had been painted on military gear and impressed on coins. Fittingly, the cross also became the shape of sacred space.

The sheer fact of church buildings gave the church a fixed physical presence that it had never had before. Church buildings had existed, but their existence was precarious, dependent on the unreliable favor of the emperor. Constantine secured the church's legal status and in building churches gave that establishment physical form. After Constantine, church building became the most characteristic of the emperor's building projects, a signal of the changed status of the Christian religion.[88] The size of Constantine's churches, especially the Lateran cathedral, spoke of the new prominence of Christianity in Constantine's world. The Christian God had proved himself the most powerful of all deities, and this had to be expressed in the design and scale of his houses of worship.

The basilica form was fitting, since Constantine had drawn the church into the imperial orbit and delegated to bishops some of the functions of the state. As we shall see in a later chapter, Constantine broke the logjam of legal appeals by allowing complainants to take their case to episcopal courts, and bishops were increasingly responsible for social welfare in the cities. Given the bishops' expanded public role, the basilica was the most natural architectural form to use. Since the basilica had been a form as-

---

[86]Quoted in Elsner, "Perspectives on Art," pp. 255-77, 266.
[87]Armstrong, "Constantine's Churches," pp. 13-14.
[88]Krautheimer, "Constantinian Basilica," p. 128.

sociated with the imperial cult, the churches also suggested a union of civic and religious life on a different level. The Lateran was "the throne hall of Christ Basileus and of the bishop, His representative, just as the basilica at Trier was the seat of the Emperor's Divine Majesty, or, in his absence, the seat of his local representative."[89]

Some of the vocabulary of pagan temples carried over into the Christian basilicas, but the distinction between church and temple was equally important. On the one hand, churches "were meeting halls for the congregations (*basilicae ecclesiae*) or meeting halls for burial and funeral rites (*basilica quae sunt cemeteria*)," but "they were also audience halls of the Lord." According to the Pilgrim of Bordeaux, the church built on Golgotha (wrongly described as the Church of the Holy Sepulcher) is "*basilica, id est dominicum*," and Eusebius uses terms such as *basileios neos* or *basileios oikos* instead of *basilike*. Such language "establishes the church as the throne room of the Emperor of Heaven, comparable to the sanctuary where the living god-emperor received the obeisance of his subjects."[90]

This might be evidence that Constantine was trying to rope Christ into service to the imperial cult, but it seems more likely that it was a confession of his subordination to the greater Lord. He had baptized public space. Paganism still had its place, but temples were increasingly overshadowed by large, and numerous, churches.

---

[89]Ibid., p. 121.
[90]Ibid., p. 129.

6

End of Sacrifice

[Constantine] intended to restrain the idolatrous abominations
which in time past had been practiced in every city and country;
and it provided that no one should erect images,
or practice divination and other false and foolish arts,
or offer sacrifice in any way.

EUSEBIUS, *LIFE OF CONSTANTINE*

Constantine's architectural expressions of favor toward the church were backed up by legislative and administrative initiatives. Soon after he defeated Maxentius, Constantine exempted the Christian clergy from tax burdens, explaining that this would protect them from being harassed by heretics (cf. CTh 16.2.1-2). He mounted various attacks on paganism. Early church historians celebrate the fact that he closed notorious temples,[1] removed cult items and melted down metal objects for his own Christian buildings. He tore doors off some temples and removed the idolatrous images from others. Eusebius exaggerated the degree of destruction of pagan centers, but it happened.

In recent decades, the question of whether Constantine intended to

---

[1] R. P. C. Hanson, "The Christian Attitude to Pagan Religions up to the Time of Constantine the Great," *ANRW* 23 (1980): 969, notes that temples were closed that "encourage immoral practices" or "occupied ground specially holy to Christians." Yet "there was no general policy of closing temples." Pagan shrines, in fact, continued to be built during Constantine's reign (p. 970).

suppress paganism by force has focused on whether he issued a law prohibiting sacrifice.[2] There is general agreement that he suppressed sacrifices on certain occasions and in certain settings. He prohibited his provincial governors from offering sacrifice at official functions, thus opening up civil offices to Christians, and he regularly expressed his personal unwillingness and revulsion at sacrifice in sometimes caustic terms. But did he issue a blanket prohibition against sacrifice?[3]

Eusebius claimed he did. In his *Vita Constantiani*, he referred to a law passed around 324 that "was intended to restrain the idolatrous abominations which in time past had been practiced in every city and country; and it provided that no one should erect images, or practice divination and other false and foolish arts, or offer sacrifice in any way."[4] Shortly after Constantine's death, his son Constans issued an imperial constitution reinforcing this prohibition by requiring punishment for anyone who violated the law of Constantine by celebrating sacrifice.[5] Taking Eusebius at face value, "it may be argued that in 324 Constantine established Christianity as the official religion of the Roman Empire, and that he carried through a systematic and coherent reformation, at least in the eastern provinces."[6]

Can Eusebius be believed? Some think not, and Drake's Lactantian interpretation of Constantine's religious policies requires a negative answer.[7] If Constantine allowed everyone to follow his own conscience in

---

[2]We could follow a similar line of argument by examining Constantine's legislation regarding haruspication.

[3]Andreas Alfoldi, *The Conversion of Constantine and Pagan Rome*, trans. Harold Mattingly (Oxford: Clarendon, 1948), arranges the evidence chronologically and concludes that Constantine's policies toward paganism became increasing repressive over time, especially in the final period of his reign (A.D. 330-37).

[4]Eusebius *Life* 2.45.

[5]The constitution of 341 appears in the Codex Theodosianus 16.10.2: "Contra legem divi principis parentis nostri et hanc nostrae mansuetudinis iussionem ausus fuerit sacrificia celebrare." Quoted in Timothy D. Barnes, "Constantine's Prohibition of Pagan Sacrifice," *American Journal of Philology* 105 (1984): 71.

[6]Ibid., p. 70. This is a crucial point in Timothy D. Barnes, *Constantine and Eusebius* (Cambridge, Mass.: Harvard University Press, 1981); part of the evidence of his claim is that Constantine considered himself a chosen instrument of God for the Christianization of the Roman Empire.

[7]Following Drake's lead, Elizabeth DePalma Digeser (*The Making of a Christian Empire: Lactantius and Rome* [Ithaca, N.Y.: Cornell University Press, 2000]) likewise minimizes Constantine's antipagan legislation. She finds (p. 128) only two "minor instances" of Constantine's taking "direct action against polytheists," and though she admits (pp. 131-32) that Constantine

worship, how could he suppress the central liturgical act of the majority cult? One reason for doubting the existence of this decree is that there is no record of enforcement in the early fourth century.[8] So was there any law against sacrifice? Was the law issued and never enforced? And if the latter, why issue the decree at all?

We can resolve this issue by attending carefully to the nature of imperial decrees in the fourth century.[9] Imperial edicts always depended on enforcement by provincial or local officials, who might be too lazy or busy to carry out the emperor's business. A provincial governor surrounded by convinced pagans would be hesitant to bear down. More important, emperors "never *expected or intended* that their anti-pagan legislation be vigorously enforced."[10] Leafing through the codices, one gets the impression that the decrees of the early Christian emperors were concise and legally framed legislation, but when we examine the full text of certain decrees in Eusebius, we find that the legislative portion is fairly minor and often concludes a prolix moral lecture. The Codex Theodosianus consists of excerpts from Constantine and his immediate successors, but excerpting changes the genre and tone. In its original setting, much imperial legislation functioned more as moral appeal than as law in our modern sense of the term.[11] Given the nature of "law" in Constantine's empire, there was no necessary contradiction between his "We wholly forbid the existence of gladiators" and his permission to an Umbrian town to honor the emperor with combats.[12] Nor was there any necessary contradiction between a decree suppressing sacrifice and continued toleration of sacrifice.

Constantine cannot keep himself from preaching. He did it in court, and when he issued decrees in his official capacity he was still the mission-minded preacher. Eschewing sacrifice entirely was the best way to go, and

---

"razed" temples, she insists that there were not many. She also admits that there might have been some fairly minor prohibition of sacrifice. These details are much more damaging to her overall thesis, however, than she admits.

[8]Scott Bradbury, "Constantine and the Problem of Anti-pagan Legislation in the Fourth Century," *Classical Philology* 89, no. 2 (1994): 134.

[9]My conclusions here follow those of Bradbury (ibid.), and see also Scott Bradbury, "Julian's Pagan Revival and the Decline of Blood Sacrifice," *Phoenix* 49, no. 4 (1995).

[10]Ibid., p. 134.

[11]Bradbury (ibid.) quotes Paul Veyne: "Il existe beaucoup de legislations qui legiferent, non pour indiquer et imposer des conduits ou des procedures, mais pour proclamer a la face du ciel quelle est la bonne conduite, ou un ideal moral."

[12]Ibid., p. 135.

so he prohibited sacrifice; yet everyone should be free to follow conscience, so he did not enforce the prohibition. He was a politician-preacher, and his sharp language also pacified militant Christians in his empire who muttered that their pseudo-Christian emperor was soft on idolatry. His law against sacrifice was part of an effort to "clear public spaces of that aspect of the pagan cult considered most unacceptable in the eyes of Christians," and by the 350s sacrifice was rare enough that it took some daring to perform one. Constantine did not have to take up the sword against pagans. His "legislation" created an "atmosphere" in which sacrifice gradually faded away.[13]

AGAINST ALL HERESIES

The results of Constantine's wide-ranging antiheresy legislation (ca. 324) were similar. Around the time of his final war with Licinius, he issued a decree condemning a variety of heretics—Valentinians, Montanists, the Novatianists of Alexandria, and some others. Heretics, he said, were "haters and enemies of truth and life" and their heresies a "tissue of falsehood and vanity," promoting "destructive and venomous errors" that can only lead to "everlasting death." Their crimes were too many to catalog, and in a fit of rhetorical self-rebuke, he claimed that his policy of "protracted clemency" had only encouraged them to spread.

Given the menace of heresy, he said, he had no choice but to act. Since "it is no longer possible to bear with your pernicious errors," he wrote, "we give warning by this present statute that none of you henceforth presume to assemble yourselves together." Heretical church buildings were to be seized, and Constantine's "care in this respect extend[ed] so far as to forbid the holding of your superstitious and senseless meetings, not in public merely, but in any private house or place whatsoever." He reiterated the point:

> We have commanded, as before said, that you be positively deprived of every gathering point for your superstitious meetings, I mean all the houses

---

[13]Ibid., p. 138. The idea of an "atmosphere" comes from Peter Brown. Bradbury, "Julian's Pagan Revival," shows that Constantine's legislation did have a chilling effect. Combined with declining funding for pagan cults, his edict led to a weakening of paganism. Hanson, "Christian Attitude to Pagan Religions," pp. 913-15, 968, makes the important observation that many pagans already disapproved of animal sacrifice, and so Constantine was on relatively safe ground in prohibiting it.

of prayer, if such be worthy of the name, which belong to heretics, and that these be made over without delay to the catholic Church; that any other places be confiscated to the public service, and no facility whatever be left for any future gathering; in order that from this day forward none of your unlawful assemblies may presume to appear in any public or private place. Let this edict be made public.

Heretics were, of course, always welcome to return to the "holy fellowship" of the catholic church, "whereby you will be enabled to arrive at the knowledge of the truth." But "the delusions of your perverted understandings must entirely cease to mingle with and mar the felicity of our present times: I mean the impious and wretched double-mindedness of heretics and schismatics." Constantine believed he enjoyed prosperity because of God's favor, and the poison of false teaching spewing from the church endangered him. He saw it as his duty "to endeavor to bring back those who in time past were living in the hope of future blessing, from all irregularity and error to the right path, from darkness to light, from vanity to truth, from death to salvation."[14]

Like many of his edicts, this was something less than it seemed. For one thing, he concluded two years later that the Novatianists had been wrongly condemned. They were separatist schismatics but not heretics, and in a rescript of 326 he restored their rights.[15] Further, there is no evidence that the law was ever enforced, since "Valentinian, Marcionite, and Montanist conventicles long continued to exist."[16] Like Constantine's edicts against pagans examined above, Contantine's decree against heresies functioned more as moral exhortation than as a legally binding decree, and it was a rhetorical display that kept the orthodoxy-hounds satisfied. Still, the result was that by 324 heresy had officially been declared illegal. Orthodox Christianity, as defined by church councils, was the only unrestricted faith still permitted in the Roman Empire. And the edict, and other of Constantine's decisions, did have an effect. Heretics were exiled, and Arius's books were burned, just as the anti-Christian treatise of Porphyry was destroyed by imperial order. Constantine's religious policy created an "atmosphere" of hostility to heresy as much as to paganism.

---

[14]Eusebius *Life* 3.64-65.
[15]Barnes, *Constantine and Eusebius*, p. 224.
[16]Ibid.

One suspects fourth-century Christians had the same question we do: was this man the liberator of the church, or its new lord?

JEWS IN THE CHRISTIAN EMPIRE

Though for different reasons, both historians and theologians have objected to Constantine's policies regarding Jews. James Carroll sees in Constantine's policies a coherent, if not entirely conscious, plot to suppress Judaism. Above all, Carroll argues, Constantine was a politician looking for some principle of unification in the empire, and the Jews, like the pagans, were a standing challenge to his ambitions. By Carroll's reading of history, Constantine was responsible for making "unity" a mark of the church, as he suppressed the delightfully diverse Christian expressions of earlier centuries. More subtly but more dangerously, Constantine elevated the cross to its central importance in Christian faith. Prior to Constantine, Christianity had been centered on resurrection, but Constantine's vision and then the discovery of the true cross coalesced in a cruciform faith that had dangerous political ramifications for Jews. For if the cross is central, so is the guilt of the Jews for the death of God's Son. Specific laws, Carroll argues, also worked against Jews. Constantine did not impose the death penalty for proselytizing, but his successors did, and Constantine's criminalization of proselytizing laid the foundations for legal persecution of Jews throughout the Middle Ages.[17]

Like many critics of Constantine, Carroll is ill-informed about facts. He overstates the degree of diversity in early Christianity and also understates Christians' devotion to unity prior to Constantine. The New Testament itself is sufficient refutation of the idea that it took an emperor to introduce the notion of unity into the faith. Carroll also claims that Constantine is being innovative when he is being quite traditional. Jews had considerable liberty under the Roman Empire, but proselytizing was the point where they were most restricted. Long before Constantine, Jews had been prohibited from circumcising converts, with the exception of slaves.[18]

---

[17]This summarizes James Carroll, *Constantine's Sword: The Church and the Jews* (Boston: Houghton Mifflin, 2001), chaps. 17-20. Marcel Simon, *Verus Israel: A Study of the Relations between Christians and Jews in the Roman Empire AD 135-425*, trans. H. McKeating (London: Littman Library of Jewish of Jewish Civilization, 1996), p. 291, baselessly attributes to Constantine a law threatening the death penalty to converts.

[18]David S. Potter, *The Roman Empire at Bay*, Routledge History of the Ancient World (London:

Constantine had a contempt for Jews that almost rivaled his contempt for pagans. In a letter sent to bishops following the Council of Nicaea, the emperor neglected to mention Arius or the christological controversy but celebrated the conciliar consensus on the date of Easter. One of his main reasons for rejoicing was that the church chose not to follow the Jews in dating their celebration of the resurrection of the Messiah whom the Jews had killed. But apart from his "violently prejudicial language,"[19] and it *is* both violent and prejudicial, his legislation changed the lives of Jews very little. Jews were permitted to serve on municipal senates, and Constantine extended the same tax exemption to synagogue heads and other Jewish leaders that he offered to Christian priests (CTh 16.8.2, 4), thus enabling "a system of Jewish self-government that strengthened Jewish life and identity."[20] For the first time since Hadrian's devastation of Palestine, Jews were permitted to travel to Jerusalem, albeit only once a year and only to mourn its destruction. Jews did return to Palestine during his reign.[21] The Jewish patriarch of Constantinople could judge not only religious issues but even civil cases among Jews.

Some of Constantine's severe laws regarding Jews prohibited the Jews from attacking converts to Christianity (CTh 16.8.1). He threatened Jews who harassed converts to Christianity with burning; he forbade Jews to own Christian slaves and strengthened the rules against circumcision, extending the prohibition to slaves, whether pagan or Christian.[22] Carroll's leading evidence is a decree that he dates to 315, in which Constantine threatened unspecified punishments to anyone who converted to Judaism (CTh 16.8.1.1).[23] This was new but not revolutionary, since Roman law

---

Routledge, 2004), pp. 424-25.

[19]Potter (ibid., p. 425) denies that it is possible to discern a coherent plan of persecution in Constantine's legislation regarding Jews. Jacob Neusner (*Judaism and Christianity in the Age of Constantine: History, Messiah, Israel and the Initial Confrontation* [Chicago: University of Chicago Press, 1987], p. 18) agrees that the destruction of Jews during the medieval period and later is *not* attributable to Constantine's policies. Robert L. Wilken (*John Chrysostom and the Jews: Rhetoric and Reality in the Late 4th Century* [Eugene, Ore.: Wipf & Stock, 1983], p. 50) claims that Constantine's laws, though making harsh references to Jews like "feral" and "nefarious," still "remain, in the main, within Roman legal tradition."

[20]Wilken, *John Chrysostom and the Jews*, p. 51.

[21]Ibid.

[22]The evidence is taken from the Codex Theodosianus and is summarized concisely in T. G. Elliott, *The Christianity of Constantine the Great* (Scranton, Penn.: University of Scranton Press, 1996), pp. 112-13.

[23]Cf. Barnes, *Constantine and Eusebius*, pp. 252, 392 n. 74. Barnes suggests a date of 329. If this

already prevented Jewish proselytizing.

Even when a law seems to be directed against Jews, other concerns were more decisive than hostility to Judaism per se. In 321, for instance, Constantine legislated that Jews who were members of the curial class would be required to fulfill their civic duties, even if those duties conflicted with Jewish custom. Though this treated Jewish custom lightly, the point of the legislation was not to beat down Jews but to address the long-standing shortage of men willing to serve, and fund, city governments. Constantine backed off in any case, issuing a later law that gave Jews with synagogue offices exemptions from curial responsibilities.[24]

Theological critics also attack the stance of the church toward Judaism during Constantine's day and after. "Constantinianism," if not the emperor himself, rests on and reinforces an untenable, perhaps even "heretical," supersessionism, the notion that the new covenant with the Christian church "fulfills" or "replaces" the Abrahamic promises and the Mosaic covenant with Israel. Constantine advanced this heresy because by forming a Christian empire he offered a this-worldly fulfillment of Old Testament prophecies. Instead of being fulfilled in the spiritual realities of redemption, or the church, Abraham's promise of blessing to the nations was fulfilled in the Christian Roman Empire. The Old Testament was increasingly used as justification for imperial policies, and the Jews were essentially robbed of their Scriptures and their continuing place in redemptive history.

In a wide-ranging revisionist account of early Jewish-Christian relations, John Howard Yoder placed "Constantinianism" at the center. Jesus and Paul were thoroughly Jewish, and the earliest church operated within a Jewish conceptual and practical world. Jesus' commands were treated as commands, the Torah was not played off against the gospel, and the Christians patterned their communal life after the example of diaspora Judaism. Constantine's rise to power, and the shift in Christian con-

---

is true, then Simon (*Verus Israel*, p. 126) is quite wrong to say that Constantine's legislation against Jews was "one of his first official acts" after the defeat of Maxentius. The decree is found in the Codex Theodosianus 16.8.1.1: "Si quis vero ex populo ad eorum nefariam sectum accesserit et conciliabulis eorum se applicaverit, cum ipsis poenas meritas sustinebit." Simon and Carroll claim that the decree requires the death penalty for converts, but that makes the decree more precise than it is.

[24]Potter, *Roman Empire at Bay*, p. 425.

sciousness associated with that, changed everything. By merging Christian faith with the power of the empire, Constantinianism de-Judaized Christianity. In place of the transcendent demands of the Torah, Constantinianism put the judgment of a general, producing a morality "serviceable to present power structure." Christians abandoned the specificity of Jewish law, which was now played off against the gospel; they abandoned Jewish universalism for the pseudo-universalism of Greek culture and Roman power; and when they picked up the sword they left behind the "Jewish pacifism" of Jesus. The Judaism that the West has known since is a product of Christianity, and specifically of the Constantinian apostasy.[25] In an ironic twist of providence, the isolation of Judaism forced the Jews to adopt a communal lifestyle closer to that of the original community envisioned by Jesus than the imperial church, so that Judaism serves as a continuing witness against the Constantinian attempt to seize godlikeness and control history.[26]

As usual, Yoder is aware of antecedents. Conflicts between Christians and Jews in the New Testament were, he argues, intramural conflicts within Judaism, and he acknowledges that the pre-Constantinian Christians were virulently hostile to Jews. Christian writers prior to Constantine already claimed that the Jews' status as people of God had been revoked, often pointing gleefully to the destruction of the temple in Jerusalem as proof of God's abandonment. Christians prior to Constantine were, moreover, often flirting with a de-Judaized form of Christianity. Though he wrote in reply to Marcion, Tertullian repudiated the carnality of the Old Testament, its sacrifices and circumcisions, almost as vigorously as did his opponent.[27] Origen believed that Old Testament sacrificial law was a test; God never wanted the Jews actually to *offer* animals. Faustus the Manichaean hit his target when he noted how "daintily" the Catholics sipped from the Old Testament.[28]

[25]John Howard Yoder, *The Jewish-Christian Schism Revisited*, ed. Michael G. Cartwright and Peter Och (Grand Rapids: Eerdmans, 2003).

[26]This point, which comes from Yoder, is neatly summarized by Stanley Hauerwas and Chris K. Huebner, "History, Theory and Anabaptism: A Conversation on Theology after John Howard Yoder," in *The Wisdom of the Cross: Essays in Honor of John Howard Yoder*, ed. Stanley Hauerwas et al. (Grand Rapids: Eerdmans, 1999), p. 396.

[27]Paula Fredricksen, *Augustine and the Jews: A Christian Defense of Jews and Judaism* (New York: Doubleday, 2008), pp. 224-28.

[28]Ibid., p. 218.

Yet it was one of Yoder's main "Constantinian" theologians, Augustine, who stemmed the tide. Augustine's sermons are nearly as full of the themes of *adversus Iudaeos* as those of any church father,[29] but after working through his "literal" commentary on Genesis and formulating a response to Faustus, he came to a quite different position.[30] Crucially, he affirmed that the sacrifices and rites of the Old Testament were commanded by God and, moreover, that precisely by putting the law into bodily practice, the Jews became fitting types of the coming Lord. Their dignity in salvation history depended on obedience to what earlier Christians had dismissed as "carnal" law. God told them to sacrifice, and when they did, they foreshadowed the passion of the incarnate Son. It was a brilliant maneuver, striking down the anti-incarnational and anti-Jewish elements of Faustus's theology at a single blow while simultaneously correcting the soft Marcionism of Catholics by binding Old and New unbreakably together.[31]

Augustine's pro-Torah and pro-Jewish theology had direct policy implications. The Jews' complicity in the death of Jesus was foreshadowed by Cain's slaughter of righteous Abel, but Augustine insisted on following the story through to the end. Just as Cain received a mark that protected him from vengeance for his fratricide, so the Jews had been marked for protection and given a promise of perpetuity to the eschaton. "Slay them not," Augustine warned, and even when he crowed about the destruction of pagan altars and defended the forcible suppression of Donatists, he never wavered in his opposition to persecution of Jews.[32]

Through Augustine, Western theology inherited a large theological problem that never went away, even to the present, the problem of relating Old to New. Medieval theologians differed about how to relate the sacraments of the "Old Law" to the Christian rites, and the Lutheran and Reformed gave different answers still. No one in the mainstream of the tradition, however, believed, as some early fathers had suggested, that the Old could simply be ignored or condemned as unworthy of God. Marcion

---

[29]Ibid., p. 311.

[30]R. A. Markus, *The End of Ancient Christianity* (Cambridge: Cambridge University Press, 1990), p. 51, emphasizes the role of the Genesis commentary in the "re-direction" of Augustine's thought on sexuality, the body and many other topics.

[31]Fredricksen, *Augustine and the Jews*, pp. 242-44.

[32]Ibid., chaps. 11-12. For an account of Christianity and Judaism that stresses the continuity, see Oskar Skarsaune, *In the Shadow of the Temple: Jewish Influences on Early Christianity* (Downers Grove, Ill.: InterVarsity Press, 2002).

made a comeback, but that was much later, in the modern period.

I do not suggest any causal relation. I only note the fact: contrary to Yoder, Christian theology was *re*-Judaized in the century following Constantine.

NEW JERUSALEM

Though Jews like pagans were granted "limited toleration" in Constantine's empire,[33] they were, also like pagans, living in a public environment that was increasingly Christian. Again, architecture provides a helpful gauge of the situation, particularly Constantine's architectural efforts in Palestine and Jerusalem. Memories and remnants of the ancient Jewish Jerusalem had been so thoroughly buried by the Hadrianic-era Roman city that replaced it, known as Aelia Capitolina, that Roman officials thought Christians who identified their home as Jerusalem were referring to a secret Christian military base in the east.[34] There is no overt evidence that Constantine's project to erect a "new Jerusalem" on the ruins of the old was motivated by an anti-Jewish agenda. Like his building projects that used pagan spolia or basilica forms for churches, however, Constantine's buildings in Jerusalem advanced his Christianization of public space, a triumph over the old world by their erection on space once claimed by Jews. By building grand churches in Jerusalem he rivaled Solomon[35] and went some way toward satisfying Christian "temple envy."[36] It was perhaps, Eusebius thought, the fulfillment of the prophecies of Ezekiel concerning the restored temple.[37] *Vetus* Israel was giving way to *nova* Israel.

When the Augusta Helena, Constantine's mother, made her pilgrimage to Palestine, she found the site of the death and resurrection of Jesus

---

[33]The phrase is from Neusner, *Judaism and Christianity*, p. 18.

[34]Robert L. Wilken, *The Land Called Holy: Palestine in Christian History and Thought* (New Haven, Conn.: Yale University Press, 1992), p. 83.

[35]E. D. Hunt ("Constantine and Jerusalem," *Journal of Ecclesiastical History* 48, no. 3 [1997]: 422) denies any connection with Solomon. There is no overt association, but given the typological imagination of the fourth-century Christians, it beggars belief to think that the thought never crossed Constantine's mind.

[36]See Hugh Nibley, "Christian Envy of the Temple," pts. 1-2, *Jewish Quarterly Review*, n.s. 50, nos. 2-3 (1959), quoted by Wilken, *Land Called Holy*, p. 97. The church was equally a declaration of triumph over paganism. It is probably no accident that the church was dedicated on September 13, the Roman festival of Jupiter Optimus Maximus, to whom Hadrian had dedicated Aelia (Hunt, "Constantine and Jerusalem," pp. 421-22).

[37]Wilken, *Land Called Holy*, p. 96.

encrusted with paganism. To Eusebius, it looked like a deliberate plot to obscure the truth about Jesus:

> For it had been in time past the endeavor of impious men (or rather let me say of the whole race of evil spirits through their means), to consign to the darkness of oblivion of that divine monument of immortality to which the radiant angel had descended from heaven, and rolled away the stone for those who still had stony hearts, and who supposed that the living One still lay among the dead; and had declared glad tidings to the women also, and removed their stony-hearted unbelief by the conviction that he whom they sought was alive. This sacred cave,[38] then, certain impious and godless persons had thought to remove entirely from the eyes of men, supposing in their folly that thus they should be able effectually to obscure the truth.[39]

Constantine ordered the site cleared of idolatry, initiated an excavation, and soon discovered the cave in which Jesus had been entombed. Later legend added to this the discovery of the true cross, whose genuineness was confirmed by the fact that its wood brought a boy back from the dead. In those later accounts, Helena was said to have tortured a Jew to discover the whereabouts of the cross—a Jew who later became a bishop.[40] Of that there is no word in Eusebius.[41]

Instead, Eusebius told the story of the sepulcher and of Constantine's decision to erect a magnificent church on the site. Eusebius's description of the church is breathless and not altogether clear, but the overall impression is unmistakable. It had the same massive size and luxurious ornamentation as the other structures Constantine built. Though the original church focused more on Golgotha than on the site of the resurrection, Eusebius was obsessed with the cave:

> For at the side opposite to the cave, which was the eastern side, the church itself was erected; a noble work rising to a vast height, and of great extent both in length and breadth. The interior of this structure was floored with

---

[38]Ibid., p. 89, argues that Eusebius is deliberately evoking the sacred caves of classical paganism.

[39]Eusebius *Life* 3.26.

[40]Alison Futrell, *Blood in the Arena: The Spectacle of Roman Power* (Austin: University of Texas Press, 1997).

[41]Even if this is not quite sufficient reason to conclude that it had not been found, the absence of mention of the cross from the account of the Bordeaux Pilgrim confirms it. See Hunt, "Constantine and Jerusalem," p. 415.

marble slabs of various colors; while the external surface of the walls, which shone with polished stones exactly fitted together, exhibited a degree of splendor in no respect inferior to that of marble. With regard to the roof, it was covered on the outside with lead, as a protection against the rains of winter. But the inner part of the roof, which was finished with sculptured panel work, extended in a series of connected compartments, like a vast sea, over the whole church; and, being overlaid throughout with the purest gold, caused the entire building to glitter as it were with rays of light.[42]

The Holy Sepulcher was the place of the theophany of all theophanies, and its church paralleled the design of ancient temples. "It was a place to be set apart, to be enclosed—or, more precisely, one that set itself apart." This was done partly through the erection of "a monumental entrance, a gate of heaven in the sense that in this holy place earth meets heaven and one may pass between." Beyond the gate was an atrium, "a place of preparation for the worshiper, of separation from the world." Another liminal area followed, "the house of prayer which afforded an opportunity for further preparation and a place for congregational worship." Finally, the worshiper "came to the place of the theophany proper. At the Holy Sepulchre there was an inner atrium enclosing another inseparable holy place, the rock of Calvary." Above the site of the resurrection was a dome, "the dome of heaven or of the cosmos which had an oculus at the apex like the Pantheon in Rome. This oculus gave direct access to heaven from the holy place, and the rotunda was the focal point of the whole, structurally and symbolically."[43]

Set in Jerusalem, however, the church was more than the center of the city. It was conceived of as the new temple, the *umbilicus mundi*. "The twelve columns in the hemisphere of the apse symbolized the twelve disciples and the twelve tribes of Israel, and perhaps the columns and pillars of the Holy Sepulchre were echoes of the sacred forest of religious mythology, just as the inner atrium was in fact understood as a sacred garden or paradise."[44] Jerusalem was, in imagination if not in administration, the hub of Constantine's Eastern empire, so much so that he celebrated his

---

[42]Eusebius *Life* 3.36.
[43]Gregory T. Armstrong, "Constantine's Churches: Symbol and Structure," *Journal of the Society of Architectural Historians* 33, no. 1 (1974): 16.
[44]Ibid.

tricennalia in Jerusalem rather than in Constantinople.[45] Medieval maps that show Jerusalem as the center of the world perpetuated the Constantinian vision.

With the Christianization of the architecture of Jerusalem, the baptism of public space was complete. At the place where ancient sacrifices had been offered, in a building that rivaled the splendor of Solomon, Christians now gathered to offer their bloodless sacrifice of praise.

TOLERATION OR CONCORD?

Given his evident preference for Christianity and his restrictions on paganism, it seems that Constantine was less Lactantian than the "Edict of Milan" suggests. And that creates a fundamental incoherence at the heart of Constantine's religious policy: If religion was a matter of free will, why did Constantine so vigorously oppose paganism in his decrees, letters and speeches, and how could he justify any restrictions on religion at all? If Constantine thought that religion should be free, what was he doing forbidding sacrifice?

Elizabeth Digeser offers terminology and categories that help make sense of Constantine's policies. She distinguishes forbearance from toleration, and tolerance from "concord."[46] Forbearance is a pragmatic policy, not guided by moral or political principle. Forbearance might change to persecution if political conditions change. The periods of Roman acceptance of Christianity were periods of forbearance. Toleration is "disapproval or disagreement coupled with an unwillingness to take action against those viewed with disfavor in the interest of some moral or political principle." This principle could arise, as for Lactantius, from a theory concerning the nature of religion, or, alternatively, from a theory about human nature or about the limits of state power. By this definition, toleration does not involve an idea of the equality of all viewpoints but the opposite. Toleration assumes *disapproval* of certain religious expressions but refrains for principled reasons from using state power to suppress the dis-

---

[45]Hunt, "Constantine and Jerusalem," p. 420; Wilken, *Land Called Holy,* p. 94. Jas Elsner's brilliant analysis of the "sacred journey" of the Bordeaux Pilgrim reinforces this point ("The Itinerarium Burdigalense: Politics and Salvation in the Geography of Constantine's Empire," *Journal of Roman Studies* 90 [2000]: 181-95).

[46]This is in part based on Mario Turchettti, "Religious Concord and Political Toleration in Sixteenth- and Seventeenth-Century France," *Sixteenth Century Journal* 22, no. 1 (1991).

approved religion. Beyond toleration, Digeser introduces the category of "concord": "(1) its attitude of forbearance is dictated by some moral, political, or even religious principle and (2) it expects that by treating its dissenters with forbearance it is creating conditions under which they will ultimately change their behavior to conform to what the state accepts."[47] These three categories of religious policy build on one another: toleration assumes forbearance but is principled; concord assumes toleration, but in addition to basing forbearance on principle, it expects that the forbearance will have the ultimate outcome of unity if not complete uniformity.

Digeser concludes that Constantine remained Lactantian but gradually moved from a policy of toleration to one of concord, especially after his defeat of Licinius in 324. "Constantine's newly disparaging attitude toward some elements of traditional cult," she argues, "marked a move away from a policy of religious liberty—in which traditional cult was not criticized—toward a policy of concord, in which forbearance toward the temple cults was intended as a means of achieving ultimate religious unity."[48] Digeser's argument is persuasive. Constantine's religious policy, expressed in law and architecture, formed a Christianized public that provided limited freedom for paganism while simultaneously pressuring pagans, more or less gently, to embrace the God of Christians, the God of the emperor.

CONSTANTINIAN FREEDOM, LOCKEAN TYRANNY

Historian H. A. Drake exaggerates Constantine's toleration of paganism when he concludes that Constantine embodied Jesus' exhortation to "turn the other cheek" in religious law, but his exaggeration gets at an important truth of Constantine's policy.[49] Still, Constantine's religious policies had flaws, some significant. His rhetoric regarding Judaism, if not the specifics of his legislation, created an atmosphere in which Jew-baiting gained imperial approval. Augustine's re-Judaizing of the faith was not known to everyone and did not convince everyone who knew of it. Enforcing civil penalties for heretics and schismatics risked compromising the indepen-

---

[47]Digeser, *Making of a Christian Empire*, p. 110.
[48]Ibid., p. 125.
[49]H. A. Drake, "The Impact of Constantine on Christianity," in *The Cambridge Companion to the Age of Constantine,* ed. Noel Lenski (Cambridge: Cambridge University Press, 2006), p. 122.

dence of the church as a holy polity.[50] Constantine's policies toward paganism were, as noted above, relatively mild; the main pagan practice he forbade was animal sacrifice, which is illegal even in hypertolerant twenty-first-century America.

Theoretically, Constantine's policy has much to recommend it. On the one hand, he retained the virtues of toleration. In principle, he treated religion as a matter of choice and conscience, an area free of state meddling. At the same time, he saw this freedom as a time for conversion. He made no pretense of being neutral among religions but both verbally and practically supported the work of the one religion he regarded as true.[51] Here, perhaps surprisingly, at one of the main points of criticism of Constantine, we find a policy that Christian political theory might in certain respects honor and emulate.

Constantine's position is certainly more politically and theologically coherent than that offered by many early modern defenders of religious toleration. According to John Locke's "A Letter Concerning Toleration,"[52] freedom in religion requires a sharp distinction between religious and civil realms:

> The end of a religious society . . . is the public worship of God, and, by means thereof, the acquisition of eternal life. All discipline ought, therefore, to tend to that end, and all ecclesiastical laws to be thereunto confined. Nothing ought nor can be transacted in this society relating to the possession of civil and worldly goods. No force is here to be made use of upon any occasion whatsoever. For force belongs wholly to the civil magistrate, and the possession of all outward goods to his jurisdiction.

Behind this is Locke's assumption that the essence of religion is internal: "All the life and power of true religion consist in the inward and full persuasion of the mind; and faith is not faith without believing." Outward professions are nothing "if we are not fully satisfied in our own mind that the one is true." The church's realm is the care of souls, and everything

---

[50]I return, briefly, to this question at the end of the next chapter.

[51]For the failure of this Constantinian policy and the growing intolerance of the Christian empire through the fourth century, see H. A. Drake, *Constantine and the Bishops: The Politics of Intolerance* (Baltimore: Johns Hopkins University Press, 2000), pt. 4. Drake, mistakenly in my judgment, does not find the distinction between concord and toleration very meaningful.

[52]John Locke, "A Letter Concerning Toleration," is available online at <www.constitution.org/jl/tolerati.htm>.

external is committed to the civil magistrate.[53] Such a definition of religion as nothing more than inward "belief" or piety is at odds with most major world religions, and is certainly at odds with Christian orthodoxy. Besides, how does Locke go about locating the boundary between "inward" and "outward"? He does not try; it is self-evident.

In addition, Locke's claims about the character of religion depend on an equally radical disjunction of Old and New. If you want a de-Judaized faith, Lock provides it. He describes the Jewish commonwealth as "an absolute theocracy" and contrasts it with the faith of the New Testament. "If anyone can show me where there is a commonwealth at this time, constituted upon that foundation [i.e., established by God]," he wrote, "I will acknowledge that the ecclesiastical laws do there unavoidably become a part of the civil, and that the subjects of that government both may and ought to be kept in strict conformity with that Church by the civil power." It is nowhere to be found: "there is absolutely no such thing under the Gospel as a Christian commonwealth." Though "many cities and kingdoms . . . have embraced the faith of Christ," yet "they have retained their ancient form of government, with which the law of Christ has not at all meddled."[54]

Locke's position is, besides, politically fragile and quickly collapses into tyranny. Though he claims to be arguing for toleration and freedom for religion, he ends up ceding final determinative authority over religion to the civil authorities. Locke asserts in his "Letter Concerning Toleration" that since "speculative opinions and religious worship" have "no direct influence upon men's lives in society," these matters have "a clear title to universal toleration, which the magistrate ought not to entrench on."[55] But there's absolute and then there's absolute. Believers cannot always tell what counts as a matter of speculative opinion and religious worship, and they are in-

---

[53]To this I would only say: "Take, eat; take, drink." Lockean politics are possible only when sacramental theology has been deleted.

[54]Cities and kingdoms that "embraced the faith of Christ" retained "their ancient form of government"? Tell that to all the medieval kings who had to swear fealty to Jesus or the Trinity; tell that to the emperors who sought papal anointing; tell that to Alfred the Great, whose laws were expressly based on the Ten Commandments; tell that to Henry standing in the snow outside Gregory's castle at Canossa. Locke's is precisely the conception of Christianity that Yoder identified as "Constantinian." I share Yoder's abhorrence of this non- and antiecclesial brand of Christianity, but I submit that it is better described as "Lockean" than "Constantinian."

[55]*Locke: Political Essays,* ed. Mark Goldie, Cambridge Texts in the History of Political Thought (Cambridge: University of Cambridge Press, 1997), pp. 134-59.

clined to "mix with their religious worship and speculative opinions other doctrines absolutely destructive to the society wherein they live." Catholics are especially apt to do this, in Locke's view, since they blend "opinions with their religion, reverencing them as fundamental truths, and submitting to them as articles of their faith," and therefore "ought not to be tolerated by the magistrate in the exercise of their religion, unless [it] can be secured that he can allow one part without spreading the other, and that those opinions will not be imbibed and espoused by all those who communicate with them in their religious worship."

Even if the opinions themselves are tolerable, there might be a danger that too many people will begin to hold opinions that isolate them from the general public. People tend to attach themselves to fellow believers more strongly than to fellow citizens. Magistrates have to put a stop to such things too: "When . . . men herd themselves into companies with distinctions from the public, and a stricter confederacy with those of their own denomination and party than other [of] their fellow subjects, whether the distinction be religious or ridiculous matters not, otherwise than as the ties of religion are stronger, and the pretenses fairer and apter to draw partisans, and therefore the more to be suspected and the more heedfully watched." When a sect like this becomes numerous, it is "convenient" for the magistrate to do what he can "to lessen, break, and suppress the party, and so prevent the mischief." Quakers are tolerable because they are few, but "were they numerous enough to become dangerous to the state," they "would deserve the magistrate's care and watchfulness to suppress them." Magistrates should act even if Quakers are "no other way distinguished from the rest of his subject but by the bare keeping on their hats." Hats are a "very indifferent and trivial circumstance," yet too many people wearing the same hat might "endanger the government," and thus it is the magistrate's duty to "endeavour to suppress and weaken or dissolve any party of men which religion or any other thing hath united, to the manifest danger of his government." Locke's argument is little more than a theoretical endorsement of Tocqueville's "tyranny of the majority." Not that this is an attack on religion, or a limit of toleration of worship and speculative opinion. Not at all: "they are not restrained because of this or that opinion or worship, but because such a number, of any opinion whatsoever, who dissented would be dangerous."

These limits are on the surface of Locke's essay, but the suppressed issue is the question of classification. Worship and speculative opinions are left more or less free, but practical opinions and actions, even if indifferent, might have to be suppressed for the peace and prosperity of the state. But who decides? One man's speculative opinion is another man's practical opinion. Locke never addresses this directly; it's as if the distinctions are self-evident. But the only possible answer is, of course, the magistrate. What guides the magistrate in deciding what religions are tolerable? For Locke, that guidance cannot come from any particular religious tradition, because that would favor one religion and violate the fundamentals of toleration. The only guidance he provides is that of state interest. Religions are tolerable if they do not threaten public peace and order, as defined by the state. Thus Locke's doctrine of religious toleration deconstructs in practice into tyranny over religion.

Locke is the great theorist of religious freedom? Constantine, more like.

Constantine's policy is more coherent than Locke's because it is more honest. Locke pretends to offer a level playing field but tilts it in the direction of a latitudinarian and sectarian Protestantism. Constantine openly favored one religion, Christianity, and dedicated the empire's pulpit, its incentives, its persuasive powers to encourage ultimate unity in religion. He allowed other religions to continue, in the hope that their adherents would convert. As we have seen and will see more in the following chapter, Constantine at times resorted to force, and he sometimes made things worse by resorting to force clumsily. When he did attempt to shut down Donatist churches or exile Arians (and Athanasius!), he was at least open about what he was defending and what he was attacking, open that he was using the power of the empire to defend the church and arrest its enemies.

Constantine's system was by Augustinian standards more just. Like Augustine, Lactantius insisted that no society could be just while it ignored the living God, while it failed to "give what is due" to the Creator. For all the dangers and drawbacks of its practice, Constantine's policy embodied that insight. He was intent on ensuring not only that the Christian God be worshiped but that he be rightly worshiped.

Space must be organized somehow. *Something* must be at the center of a city, and that something is, in practice, going to be higher, bolder, bigger, more dazzling than the surrounding cityscape. Modern cities, where even great cathedrals cower in the shadows of insurance companies, banks, law firms, investment companies, high-tech corporations, are certainly not religiously neutral. To a Christian sensibility, modern cities are organized to lift up the idol Mammon above all others and to leave just enough space for the church to be a cheerleader or a marginal, cranky critic. Constantine had many faults and committed many wrongs, but he apparently knew this much: neither society nor social space, neither public life nor the space in which it takes place, can be religiously neutral.

CONCLUSION

Pagans came under attack soon enough.[56] Jews too.[57] Before the fourth century ended, the "atmosphere" of disapproval for paganism had turned into direct action, as monks and mobs tore down pagan temples and altars and Christian bystanders suffered the reprisals. Early in the fifth century, Christian mobs incited by bishops set synagogues aflame. Eventually, Christian emperors abandoned Constantinian religious policy, perhaps believing they were advancing it. Theodosius issued an edict in 380 that expressed the imperial "desire" for all Romans to "live in accord with the religion which the Apostle Peter committed to the Romans" (CTh 16.2.2) and in doing so effectively "returned to the presuppositions and policy of Diocletian."[58] Emperors attempted to treat the church as a department of state. Bishops fought back, as we will see, often vigorously and successfully.

None of this happened in the early fourth century, in the time of Constantine. Under Constantine's policy of concord, the church was flooded with new converts, not through coercion but by force of imperial example and patronage.[59] Under Constantine, Jews retained their traditional privileges, and pagans were tolerated and found conditions tolerable. Constan-

---

[56]For the East, and for a somewhat later period, see K. A. Harl, "Sacrifice and Pagan Belief in Fifth- and Sixth-Century Byzantium," *Past and Present* 128 (1990); for North Africa, Fredricksen, *Augustine and the Jews*, p. 354. Constantius pursued a short-lived and unsuccessful program to shut down pagan temples and prevent sacrifice.

[57]Fredricksen, *Augustine and the Jews*, pp. 357-60.

[58]Hermann Dorries, *Constantine and Religious Liberty*, trans. Roland Bainton (New Haven, Conn.: Yale University Press, 1960), pp. 49-51.

[59]J. H. W. G. Liebeschuetz, *Continuity and Change in Roman Religion* (Oxford: Oxford University Press, 1979), p. 296.

tine favored the church, but he also gave serious attention to protecting the rights of non-Christians. Pogroms and antipagan mob action were products of the *abandonment,* not the application, of Constantinianism. One cannot help but muse how European history would have been different if Christians had had the patience to let Constantine's original settlement alone.

What of the church? Constantine's favor was too good to be true, and at least for a moment some bishops and other church leaders were careless about the dangers. If the emperor pays for the church building, what happens if he withdraws the funding? Will a softened, fattened bishop have the fortitude to return to the catacombs? Can Christian worship continue to be centered on a common meal when some of the members are 295 feet away from the minister? Won't space shape liturgy, nudging it away from participation toward performance? The city of Jerusalem mattered now as it never had; should it? Were the awesome basilicas too sacred for mere plebs? Would the leaders learn habits of dependence and lean on the next Constantine to suppress the next heresy? They had met the test of Egypt; could they meet the test of conquest? They had borne the cross; could they meet the challenges of vindication? Initially, euphoria may have swept them away.

It was not long before they and the emperor would come down to earth. Supporting the church was, as it turned out, not nearly so easy as the emperor might have expected. As soon as Constantine assumed the throne, he discovered, if he did not know before, that the church was at war with itself. Support the church—but *which* church? Constantine's policy of tolerant concord was to be severely tested by Christian discord.

7

Common Bishop

Like some general bishop constituted by God,
[Constantine] convened synods of his ministers.

Eusebius, *Life of Constantine*

On a spring day in 325, more than two hundred bishops sat in silent expectation. They had come to Nicaea, a city on Lake Iznik in northwest Asia Minor, by imperial transit, responding to a call from the emperor Constantine. Never before had representatives from all over the empire assembled in council. Most were from the East, most from Asia Minor, more were simple pastors than subtle theologians. But in the crowd were two Roman deacons and one Italian bishop. Ossius of Cordoba was there, more as chair and adviser to the emperor than as a member of the council. Exotic bishops from outside the empire—from the Crimea, from Armenia, even one from Persia—vindicated the bishops' boast that their council and church were not only Roman and ecumenical (*oikoumenē*) but truly catholic (*katholikos*).[1] Eventually, legend inflated the number of bishops to 318, but that is a tad too typological to be believed, corresponding as it does to the number of fighting men in Abraham's entourage (Genesis 14).

They had come to settle a dispute that had begun in Egyptian Alexandria, in a conflict between the bishop, Alexander, and a popular presbyter named Arius. Other issues were on the agenda. The Melitian

---

[1]A. H. M. Jones, *Constantine and the Conversion of Europe* (Toronto: University of Toronto Press, 1978), pp. 130-31.

schism, also arising in Alexandria, needed to be put to rest, and the council needed to resolve the disputed question of the date for the celebration of Easter.

Not only was the assembly at Nicaea the first general council ever called, but it had been called by the emperor Constantine. The year before he had defeated the Eastern Augustus Licinius in a series of battles that ended at Chrysopolis, and he had already traced the boundary for and begun to build a grand new city in Constantinople, just across the Bosphorus from Nicaea. For the past decade, the bishops knew, he had identified himself as a worshiper of the Christian God, and most were aware that he had repealed the edicts of persecution, stopped Licinius's mild opposition to the church, and devoted substantial imperial funds to building churches in Rome and elsewhere. Constantine had initially called the bishops to assemble at Ancyra, in central Asia Minor, but then thought better of it. Western bishops would have an easier time getting to Nicaea, he said, and so would the emperor, from his palace in Nicomedia. Besides, the lakeside air would be pleasant.[2] What he did not mention was that the bishop of Ancyra was a defiant enemy of Arius and his crowd, which might have made it more difficult for the council to evaluate his theology fairly. Holding the council at Nicaea also meant that the bishops would have an easy trip to Nicomedia, where Constantine, emperor since 306, was planning a splendid celebration of his twentieth anniversary as emperor (*vicennalia*) at the conclusion of the council.

There was much to anticipate, including an appearance of the emperor himself. First three members of his family entered, then a few others, Constantine's friends in the faith. There was no show of force, no soldiers or bodyguard. A signal was given, and the bishops stood as the emperor entered, tall, dignified, vigorous, serenely confident, clothed in a purple robe so glittering with jewels and gold that he looked to the giddy Eusebius, bishop of Caesarea, like an angel of God. His downcast eyes, the faint blush on his cheek, and his carriage, however, all expressed to Eusebius his humility and faith. Constantine moved to the end of the row of seats and stood waiting. A low chair of gold was brought, but he sat only

---

[2]R. P. C. Hanson, *The Search for the Christian Doctrine of God: The Arian Controversy, 318-381* (Grand Rapids: Baker Academic, 2005), p. 152.

after being invited by the bishops.[3] Later accounts embellish this as well, claiming that Constantine waited to sit until all the bishops had sat down first.

Augustus had shown a similar deference to the Senate, and every other successful emperor knew the arts of humility.[4] Constantine was a master of imperial protocol, and his unwillingness to sit before being invited was the first of many consummate political acts performed at the council, several of them calculated to demonstrate that he, the emperor, had changed sides, no longer a persecutor but a friend of martyrs. He kissed the empty eye-sockets of an aged victim of the Great Persecution. When the bishops entered the banquet hall for the *vicennalia,* they walked through a gauntlet of bodyguards and troops with drawn swords, but knew they could pass without fear to the emperor's own table, where they could recline to feast as if they were in Christ's kingdom itself.[5] Had the word been current, they would have described the experience as "surreal."

The opening ceremonies of the council of Nicaea focus a central aspect of the Constantinian question: "What chair should the Emperor occupy at the Council?"[6] He was, after all, no bishop. He was not even baptized. Councils had previously been reserved for clergy: by what right did Constantine appear here at all, much less in a golden chair? And that question immediately raises others. From what we can tell from the sources, there were no protests. Why not? Did no one see the anomaly of an unbaptized emperor sitting in on a church council? And what exactly did Constantine do from that golden chair? Did he force decisions on the bishops? Did he threaten to renew persecutions? Did the bishops spend their time reading his reactions? Did he frown, and if so, how did the bishops respond when they saw a passing glower of imperial displeasure?

Though not officially a member of the church, Constantine played a

---

[3]Eusebius *Life* 3.10. Eusebius is more fashion reporter than historian or theologian throughout this passage.

[4]H. A. Drake, *Constantine and the Bishops: The Politics of Intolerance* (Baltimore: Johns Hopkins University Press, 2000); Andrew Wallace-Hadrill, "*Civilis princeps*: Between Citizen and King," *Journal of Roman Studies* 72 (1982).

[5]Eusebius *Life* 3.15.

[6]Alexander Murray, "Peter Brown and the Shadow of Constantine," *Journal of Roman Studies* 73 (1983): 192, poses this as one of three "consubstantial and coeternal" questions of the Constantinian shift. The others are "the problem that arises when a small church of underdogs becomes a church of the dominant majority" and what happens "when capitals are removed nearly nine hundred miles."

large role in theological disputes and church politics from the time he converted around 312 through the Arian crisis of the 320s and the aftermath of Nicaea (325) to the end of his life (337). For some writers, though, "large role" is a massive understatement; a more appropriate phrase would be "absolute authority over the entire church."[7] He "supported, *administered,* and finally joined the church."[8] In submitting to the control of the emperor, who regarded himself as something akin to a "common bishop,"[9] the church and especially the bishops surrendered their independent status as shepherds and overseers of God's city and flock and became instead the religious arm of the empire, a Constantinian party at prayer.

For Craig Carter, this was Constantine's conscious intention. Constantine's main interest was in unifying the empire to achieve his political ambitions. To that end, he decreed religious freedom in the "Edict of Milan," but without any acknowledgment of the truth of Christianity or the reality of Jesus. He wanted to formulate a monotheistic civil religion to which both Christians and pagans could subscribe, a "vague monotheism" that downplayed Jesus and emphasized politically useful doctrines like "providence." It was to be a "respectable, rational religion"—a fourth-century version of gentry Deism.[10] Along the way, he had to mute and muzzle the inherent exclusivism of Christianity so that it could be "coopted as the religious arm of the empire" and "absorbed" by the state. Church councils were part of Constantine's strategy. He "presided over" the Council of Nicaea and permitted discussion of the theological issues for a time, before "lowering the boom on the minority." Throughout, his "long-term plan" was to imitate Diocletian in his persecution of heretics. The only thing that had changed was the identity of the heretics. Carter faults the bishops for letting themselves be taken in by the plan as much as Constantine himself for forming it. They could have prohibited Constantine from attending the council, since he was unbaptized, but they feared that might lead to confrontation and persecution. They could have allowed him to

---

[7]James Carroll, *Constantine's Sword: The Church and the Jews* (Boston: Houghton Mifflin, 2001), p. 188.

[8]John Howard Yoder, *The Royal Priesthood: Essays Ecclesiological and Ecumenical,* ed. Michael G. Cartwright (Grand Rapids: Eerdmans, 1994), p. 245, emphasis added.

[9]Jacob Burckhardt, *The Age of Constantine the Great,* trans. Moses Hadas (Berkeley: University of California Press, 1983), p. 311.

[10]Craig A. Carter, *Rethinking Christ and Culture: A Post-Christendom Perspective* (Grand Rapids: Brazos, 2006), pp. 80, 105.

attend but not "dominate" the proceedings. They could have urged Constantine not to impose civil penalties on heretics. No one got the point, which is "that the emperor does not have the right to define Christian orthodoxy."[11]

Burckhardt likewise viewed Constantine as a meddler in ecclesiastical disputes. He indirectly influenced episcopal elections, and his prominence in councils affected the outcome because "many sought to discover his desires so that they might vote accordingly." He went so far as to reserve "for himself the right of approval, without which no conciliar decree was valid," and once the decree was approved, it "was raised to imperial law." At Nicaea, Constantine ended the debate by insisting "upon the questionable expression *homoousios* against the will of the majority," but when they saw where Constantine's wind was blowing, "the majority patiently submitted." Constantine went away from Nicaea with contempt for the bishops, who had "cringed before him." His utter indifference to theology turned out to be a political advantage. He could play now one side, now the other; his very "energetic interventions" were a frightful reminder of his power.[12]

I agree completely with critics to this extent: emperors have no right to define orthodoxy. The question is, *did* Constantine do that? Emperors have no business "dominating" church councils; but did he? Carter is right that it would be exceedingly odd for an unbaptized man, albeit an emperor, to "preside over" a church council; but did he?

Is Carroll right to say that he exercised "*absolute* authority" over the church? On the face of it, Carroll's is a remarkable claim. Does "absolute authority" mean that Constantine selected the bishop for every see, that he decreed the sermon texts for every preacher in the empire, that he was responsible for every act of discipline, that he signed every paycheck? If Constantine was exercising "absolute authority," why did he call those councils in the first place? Charitably, we can chalk Carroll's language up to sloppiness and possession by the demon of polemic (the very spirit I am currently indulging). The softer claim would be that Constantine exer-

---

[11]Ibid., pp. 82, 84, 96-97, 103-4.
[12]Burckhardt, *Age of Constantine*, pp. 311-15. Yoder (*Royal Priesthood*, p. 259) claims that Constantine formulated the conclusions of the council and that the emperor had the "decisive voice" in shaping these conclusions (Yoder, *Christian Attitudes to War, Peace and Revolution*, ed. Theodore J. Koontz and Andy Alexis-Baker [Grand Rapids: Brazos, 2009], p. 58).

cised *final* authority in the church. But we still must ask, *did* he?

Burckhardt's assessment of Constantine's role at Nicaea—"insisting" on *homoousios* and cowing the majority into submission—is as unfounded as Carroll's claims. Both rest on the same evidence, which is to say, on nothing. Eusebius left us an account of the council, which he attended, but he provided very little information about the course of debates and motivations of the participants, and certainly no transcript. Burckhardt's suggestion that Constantine grew to despise the obsequiousness of the bishops sits uneasily with the emperor's stated belief that "whatever is determined in the holy assemblies of the bishops is to be regarded as indicative of the Divine will."[13] We may call Constantine cynical, but as I argued in chapter four, such towering cynicism is highly implausible.

Equally implausible is Carter's hint that Constantine or the bishops would have been better off to pursue a separation of church and state. As we saw in the last chapter, Constantine did in fact follow a policy of tolerant concord. Beyond that, no one in the fourth century would have thought that a political regime could function without religious sanction, and it is naive to think that Constantine's conversion would have instantly turned him into James Madison. The conclusions of chapter one are especially relevant here: The question is, what were Constantine's historical options *in the fourth century?* What were the constraints on his action? What, perhaps more important, were the limits of his imagination? Only when we have considered those questions are we capable of doing justice to Constantine's interventions in church politics.

Constantine was a very skilled politician,[14] and he had definite preferences, strategies, goals. As we saw in chapter four, his understanding of Christianity was inherently political, structurally similar to Diocletian's Tetrarchic political theology: right worship of the Christian God would ensure the prosperity and peace of Rome, and right worship demanded the unity of the church. Much of what he attempted and did was experimental, pursued in fits and starts and not in a single grand strategy. If he had a grand aim, it was to unify the church, and he employed myriad tactics to achieve that end. He had to experiment, because neither he nor any other emperor had ever encountered anything like the church:

[13]Eusebius *Life* 3.17-20, from a letter written to the bishops after Nicaea.
[14]Drake, *Constantine and the Bishops,* is particularly good on this.

The Church could never be simply the religious department of the *respublica*, as the old religion had been. The Church had its own officers, the clergy, who were absolutely distinct from the officers of the state. It accepted the authority of sacred writings and of traditions which were not part of Graeco-Roman civilization. . . . The weekly services, sermons, the discipline of penance, and religious instruction offered the clergy means of indoctrination which had no precedent. . . . The incorporation of the Church involved a fundamental transformation of Roman institutions, with consequences that were bound to be very great indeed.[15]

Constantine was not, besides, the only one with an agenda.[16] He was not capable of simply imposing his will on the bishops, even if he had wanted to, and there are clear signs that he did not want to. Bishops had wills too.

It was a gesture, but Constantine knew it would be a meaningful one: Constantine refused to take a place in the council until *invited*. So we must ask not only what Constantine intended and did but what the bishops thought he, and they, were doing. Polemics about "Constantinianism" focus, rightly, less on Constantine himself than on the question of the church's accommodation to power. Just as we must ask whether Constantine did the things he is charged with doing, we must also ask whether the bishops did in fact bend to Constantine. How craven were they? Though the issues in these disputes were not directly to do with the relation of the church and empire, that was among the underlying concerns in both cases. Through disputes about *traditores*, Christology and Easter, and through less known but historically important disputes about murders, offended widows and broken chalices, the church was hashing through the Constantinian question: Should he sit at the council? If so, where?

CONSTANTINE AND THE DONATISTS

The Arian controversy is the most famous theological contest in which Constantine intervened, but it was not the first.[17] He had no sooner con-

---

[15]J. H. W. G. Liebeschuetz, *Continuity and Change in Roman Religion* (Oxford: Oxford University Press, 1979), pp. 292-93.

[16]Drake, again, is crucial here. His fundamental methodological and substantive point is given in the plural of his title—not "Constantine and the Church" but "Constantine and the Bishops." To grasp what Constantine attempted and accomplished, accurately, we need to put faces on "the church" (see especially Drake, *Constantine and the Bishops*, p. 24).

[17]Nor, indeed, was this the first time the church had appealed to the emperor for resolution of

quered Maxentius (312) and become the sole Western Augustus than the Donatist schism was placed before him for adjudication. He might have known something of the controversy before this, but it came sharply to his attention as word spread that the Western emperor had started painting the Chi-Rho on his helmet and shields.[18]

The origins of the controversy were disputed. At one extreme is the account of the anti-Donatist Optatus of Milevus. According to his reconstruction, written in Numidia during the 360s and 370s, it all started with ambition, avarice and, of course, a humiliated woman. During the Diocletian persecution, Bishop Mensurius of Carthage was arrested and taken to Rome for harboring a fugitive deacon, Felix, who was wanted by the Roman authorities. Before leaving, Mensurius left some church property in the hands of certain "seniors," Botrus and Celestius, for safekeeping, but he died before returning to his see. Borus and Celestius wanted to keep the treasure—hence the avarice. Meanwhile, Botrus and Celestius wanted to be leaders in the church and hoped that one or the other would succeed Mensurius—hence the ambition. Avarice and ambition make a heady mixture: when the archdeacon Caecilian was chosen instead, their hopes were dashed, and when Caecilian asked for the return of the valuables, Botrus and Celestius refused and broke communion with the church at Carthage, allying in the meantime with a widow, Lucilla. She had her own reasons for hating Caecilian, since as archdeacon he had severely rebuked her for kissing a bone during the Eucharist, charging that she preferred bones to the life-giving bread and wine—hence the humiliated and vindictive woman. Botrus and Celestius, of course, had to invent some pretext for opposing Caecilian, and their rationale was that he had been ordained by Felix of Abthungi, a *traditor*, one who was guilty of handing

---

an internal dispute. The church had appealed to Aurelian to resolve the Donatist controversy earlier (Drake, *Constantine and the Bishops*, pp. 117, 217-18). Like Constantine later, Aurelian had referred the question to the "bishops of Rome and Italy."

[18]For summaries of Constantine's involvement in the Donatist controversy, see David S. Potter, *The Roman Empire at Bay, AD 180-395*, Routledge History of the Ancient World (London: Routledge, 2004), pp. 402-10; Henry Chadwick, *The Early Church*, Pelican History of the Church 1 (New York: Penguin, 1967), pp. 121-24; W. H. C. Frend, *The Rise of Christianity* (Philadelphia: Fortress, 1984), pp. 488-501; Geoffrey Grimshaw Willis, *Saint Augustine and the Donatist Controversy* (1950; reprint, Eugene, Ore.: Wipf & Stock, 2005), pp. 1-8; Timothy D. Barnes, *Constantine and Eusebius* (Cambridge, Mass.: Harvard University Press, 1981), pp. 54-56; Jones, *Constantine and the Conversion of Europe*, pp. 91-107; Ramsay MacMullen, *Constantine* (London: Croom Helm, 1987), pp. 101-8.

over (*traditio*) sacred books during the Diocletian persecution.[19] Felix had been defiled by his unfaithfulness, and all his episcopal acts were nullified.

The Donatists themselves told a different story. Caecilian, they claimed, not only had been illegitimately ordained but had been disqualified by his treatment of confessors during the persecution. Instead of supporting imprisoned Christians, the Abitinian martyrs, he had interfered with family members who attempted to bring them food and drink. He was virtually a persecutor himself.[20]

Whatever the precise origins of the conflict, it reflected sharp differences in Christian responses to the persecution. Some were so eager to join the martyred saints that they provoked persecution, while others, such as Mensurius, urged caution and warned the faithful not to break the laws or be unnecessarily disruptive. He not only considered some martyrs unwise but charged, in a letter to Secundus, that some sought martyrdom to escape debts, to absolve themselves of sin or to gain a reputation for Christian heroism. Mensurius admitted that he handed some books over to the authorities, but he said they were heretical writings and not copies of the Bible. That, he thought, was shrewd. Others disagreed—Secundus of Tigisis, the leading bishop of Numidia, for one. He had refused to give the Romans anything and had suffered in prison as a result.[21] How could Mensurius look him in the eye? When the persecution ended, these differences showed up in disputes about *traditores*. All sides agreed that *traditores* should be dismissed from office. The question had to do with the status of their actions between the time they were unfaithful and the time they were dismissed.[22] Did their ordinations and baptisms "work"? Did baptisms and ordinations they had performed need to be redone? Did *they* need rebaptism?

The conflict soon divided the church in Carthage and swept through North Africa. Some Numidian bishops came to investigate the situation in

---

[19]Optatus *Against the Donatists* 1.15-21, summarized in Potter, *Roman Empire at Bay*, p. 403. G. E. M. De Ste. Croix ("Aspects of the 'Great' Persecution," *Harvard Theological Review* 47 [1954]) points out that *traditio* was not considered a serious sin, if a sin at all, in the East and that *sacrificio* rarely appears in debates about martyrdom and persecution in the West. He draws the conclusion that the edict requiring sacrifice was never issued for the West.

[20]Potter, *Roman Empire at Bay*, pp. 404-6; Frend, *Rise of Christianity*, p. 489.

[21]Barnes, *Constantine and Eusebius*, pp. 54-55.

[22]Drake, *Constantine and the Bishops*, p. 117.

Carthage and appointed a replacement for Caecilian. Tempers were getting out of hand: the replacement was murdered in his church. A council of seventy bishops, presided over by Secundus of Tigisis, determined that Felix had been a *traditor* and that as a result his consecration of Caecilian was invalid. The council looked at Carthage and saw an empty see, and named Majorian bishop of Carthage.[23]

None of the parties quite grasped what was actually happening in the dispute. Personalities clashed, ambitions were frustrated, and African Christians debated about martyrs and *traditores*, but the battle was not most fundamentally about the surface issues. Some of the Numidian bishops, after all, had also been *traditores*.[24] Underneath, it was a dispute about how the church should relate to the Roman world. It was a question of purity.[25] Did *traditores* become unclean? Did they communicate this pollution in their official acts? In the interests of purity, must the church keep itself at arm's length from the Roman world? North African Christians had long nurtured a strongly legalistic, rigorist and pharisaical version of the faith. To be Christian meant to avoid worldly contaminants. The opposing view developed alongside and took various forms. For Eusebius, the church had conquered the world. A century later, Augustine, a North African himself, was less sanguine on that point, but his Christianity was still expansive enough to absorb much of the outside world.

When Constantine defeated Maxentius in 312, he decreed that property seized during the persecution should be returned to the church and that Christian clergy should be exempted from public services or "liturgies." In Carthage, the questions "What counts as a church?" and "Who is a Christian clergyman?" needed answers. Majorian wanted the exemption and the property. So he appealed to the proconsul of North Africa, Anullinus, de-

---

[23]Barnes, *Constantine and Eusebius*, p. 56.

[24]Peter Brown, *Augustine of Hippo: A Biography*, new ed. (Berkeley: University of California Press, 2000), p. 210.

[25]Brown (ibid.) has a few brilliant pages that illuminate the whole controversy (pp. 209-14). When Donatists took over Catholic buildings later in the fourth century, they "scraped off, smashed up, or simply removed the altars, whitewashed the walls, and either actually washed out the interior of the building or symbolically sprinkled it with salt water. Chalices and other serving vessels used by Catholic priests in their perverted sacraments had to be melted down. The Donatists regarded the Catholics' consecrated host as useless and tainted, and accordingly they threw it to the dogs, which the Catholics of course considered to be terrible sacrilege" (Michael Gaddis, *There Is No Crime for Those Who Have Christ: Religious Violence in the Christian Roman Empire* [Berkeley: University of California Press, 2005], pp. 120-21).

nouncing Caecilianus as a false bishop and asking for a judgment from Constantine. On April 15, 313, Constantine wrote to Miltiades, bishop of Rome, worrying over the fact that Christians were "following the baser course, and dividing, as it were, into two parties," submitting to bishops "at variance" precisely in "those provinces which Divine Providence has freely entrusted to my devotedness, and in which there is a great population." Constantine's solution was to summon Caecilian "with ten of the bishops that appear to accuse him, and with ten others whom he may consider necessary for his defense," to Rome to have a hearing before Miltiades and other bishops. Constantine passed on his record of the case to Miltiades, advising him to note "that I have such reverence for the legitimate Catholic Church that I do not wish you to leave schism or division in any place."[26]

Constantine did not take upon himself the responsibility of intervening in the church's dispute. The Donatists appealed to him. If anyone is to blame for starting a process that subordinated the church to the emperor, it is not Constantine but the Donatists. He was *invited* to sit. Constantine did not let the Donatists get away with bypassing church authorities to whom they should be subject. Rather than accepting the appeal directly, Constantine deflected responsibility to the bishops who were to be assembled at Rome. Initially, he treated the church as a separate polity, governed by its own bishops. Eventually Constantine intervened directly in the dispute, but only after several councils had proved ineffectual. The letter makes clear Constantine's desire for unity and concord within the church. He wanted no "schism or division" in the "catholic" church. His stated reason is that he has "reverence for the legitimate Catholic Church." One might, again, read that as a cynical bit of political propaganda, but it is equally plausible to consider it a sincere, and very early, statement of his personal attachment to the church.

This rancorous context is crucial for assessing Constantine's actions. The question that faced him was not, how can I control the church, which lives peaceful and at ease in my kingdom? The question was, how can I get two North African churches that hate each other enough to kill to recognize each other as brothers? As noted above, he was not the only one with an agenda.

---

[26]Eusebius *Church History* 10.5.

Donatist Twists and Turns

Unfortunately, the bishops were not as interested in concord as Constantine was.[27] By the time the bishops assembled in Rome in early October 313, Donatus—"charismatic, eloquent, tireless, and utterly convinced of the justice of his cause"[28]—had taken over as the "shadow bishop" of Carthage. In the meantime, Miltiades had done what he could to ensure the outcome by stacking the court with anti-Donatist bishops.[29] Unsurprisingly, they decided against Donatus, particularly condemning his practice of rebaptizing those who had been baptized by *traditores* or those consecrated by them. Perhaps aware of Miltiades' manipulation of the decision, Constantine felt compelled the following summer to call bishops to a second council at Arles. In summoning them, he offered imperial transport and issued an exhortation. He reviewed his efforts to settle the controversy at Rome and his hopes that the Donatist dispute could be put to rest. Information from sources in North Africa made it clear that the controversy was continuing because of the bad will and disgraceful conduct of some of the participants. "After I had read your letters," he wrote, "I recognized clearly that they would not place before their eyes either considerations of their own salvation, or (what is of more importance) the reverence which is due to Almighty God." This is clear from the fact that "they are persisting in a line of action which not merely leads to their shame and disgrace, but also gives an opportunity of detraction to those who are known to turn their minds away from the keeping of the most holy Catholic Law."[30]

His final exhortation reminded the bishops of the dangers that their divisions posed to Constantine and the empire:

> Since I am well aware that you also are a worshipper of the most High God,
> . . . I consider it by no means right that contentions and altercations of this
> kind should be hidden from me, by which, perchance, God may be moved
> not only against the human race, but also against me myself, to whose care,
> by His heavenly Decree, He has entrusted the direction of all human af-
> fairs, and may in His wrath provide otherwise than heretofore. For then

---

[27]Gaddis, *There Is No Crime*, pp. 60-61.
[28]Drake, *Constantine and the Bishops*, p. 213.
[29]Ibid., pp. 118, 219.
[30]Optatus *Against the Donatists*.

shall I be able to remain truly and most fully without anxiety, and may always hope for all most prosperous and excellent things from the ever-ready kindness of the most powerful God, when I shall know that all, bound together in brotherly concord, adore the most holy God with the worship of the Catholic religion, that is His due.[31]

Constantine's interest in a unified church is evident. He wanted a unified church, among other things, for the good of the empire. His stated concern, however, is to preserve God's kindness, not to manipulate the church. He planned to use the tools available to an emperor to restore "brotherly concord" so that the whole church can "adore the most holy God with the worship of the Catholic religion."

The council that met at Arles in August 314 was the first council called by a Roman emperor.[32] It had a negligible impact on the Donatist controversy. The bishops reiterated the decision of Rome, condemning Donatus and reaffirming Caecilianus as bishop of Carthage, and passed a canon requiring bishops to provide evidence when leveling charges of *traditio*. Far more important for the future of the church and its relation to Constantine than the decision was the fact of the council itself. Despite the imperial summons, Constantine stood back to let the bishops do their work.[33] He may have attended sessions, but he was informed of the bishops' decision after it had been made. Still, the very decision to convene a second assembly to deal with the question already answered at Rome was the first time an emperor had "effectively nullified" the decision of a council.[34] Necessary as it may have been, it set a dangerous precedent, for after Arles any emperor might claim the right to summon councils to revisit earlier decisions with which he disagreed.

The Donatists did not rest satisfied with the decision of Arles for even a month. On August 19, Maximus of Carthage asked that the case be argued directly to Constantine, presenting evidence to the North African officials that Felix of Abthungi had indeed been a *traditor*. This was new information for Constantine, and he ordered his *vicarii*, first Aelius Paulinus and then Aelianus, to investigate. They found Felix innocent again,

---

[31]Ibid.

[32]Drake, *Constantine and the Bishops*, p. 118.

[33]Potter (*Roman Empire at Bay*, p. 408) says that during the early stages of the conflict, Constantine honored the independence of the church.

[34]Drake, *Constantine and the Bishops*, p. 220.

and Constantine summoned Caecilian and representatives of the Donatists to appear before him. They did so in Milan on October 315, where Constantine rendered what he thought was a final verdict: Caecilian was innocent, and he returned to Africa as bishop of Carthage, with support both from bishops and from the emperor.[35]

Constantine had shifted and appeared to be indecisive. New evidence, or allegedly new evidence, or tricks, kept arising and forcing him to take up another appeal. Now that he had rendered a final decision—simply reiterating the decision of Rome two years before—he became frustrated. Riots were breaking out in the streets of Carthage, and when Roman soldiers joined some citizens in attacking a Donatist church in 317 and killed two bishops, a rumor spread that Caecilian had egged them on. A Donatist sermon described "bands of soldiers serving the furies of the *traditores*." For the Donatists, "bloodshed marked the end of this hatred. Now the soldiers endorsed the contract and the covenant of crime in no other way than by the seal of blood." Children and women were slaughtered in the basilica, while others shielded their eyes. Though anticipating a slaughter, the brave Donatists stood firm, and many "flew undaunted to the house of prayer with a desire to suffer."[36] To make matters worse, Constantine had of course not overhauled the army overnight; the same soldiers who had seized books from *traditores* on Diocletian's orders were still on duty in North Africa.[37]

Constantine threatened to visit Africa to destroy and annihilate the Donatists, and in another letter he launched some choice invective in their direction. He claimed that the "mercy of Christ" had departed from them, "in whom it is as clear as the sun of noon-day, that they are of such a character, as to be seen to be shut off even from the care of Heaven, since so great a madness still holds them captive, and with unbelievable arrogance they persuade themselves of things which cannot lawfully be either spoken or heard." They were "departing from the right judgment that was given, from which, as through the provision of Heaven I have learnt they are appealing to my judgment—Oh, what force has the wickedness which even

---

[35]Barnes, *Constantine and Eusebius,* pp. 58-60.
[36]Quoted in Gaddis, *There Is No Crime,* p. 54.
[37]Gaddis (ibid.) notes that soldiers, magistrates, judges and other officials remained in place when Constantine assumed power. The head had changed, the body very little.

yet is persevering in their breasts!" In Constantine's opinion, "the judgment of Bishops ought to be looked upon as if the Lord Himself were sitting in Judgment." Perhaps thinking of 1 Corinthians 6's prohibition of Christians' taking fellow believers to court, he added, "For it is not lawful for them to think or to judge in any other way, excepting as they have been taught by the teaching of Christ. Why then, as I have said with truth, do wicked men seek the devil's services? They search after worldly things, deserting those which are heavenly. Oh, mad daring of their rage!"[38]

At some point in the following two years, Constantine ordered Donatists' property to be confiscated and their churches closed. He imprisoned Donatist bishops, and some were tortured and put to death.[39] The precedent was not lost on Augustine. Though he dismissed Constantine's policy as a "most disgraceful indulgence" (*indulgentia ignominiossima*), he gave an evangelical defense of the coercive suppression of heresy. For their own sake, they should be forced back into communion with the true church: "Compel them to come in." Constantine, who had ascended to the throne as *liberator ecclesiae,* had begun to persecute Christians—schismatic Christians, but Christians.[40]

In the end, Constantine admitted defeat. He recalled Donatist exiles[41] and in a letter to the bishops and people of North Africa counseled patience. "You know right well," he reminded them, "that, as Faith required, so far as Prudence permitted, as much as a single-minded intention could prevail, I have endeavored by every effort of kindly government to secure that, in accordance with the prescriptions of our law, the Peace of the most holy Brotherhood, whose grace the supreme God has poured into the hearts of His servants, should, through complete concord, be preserved secure." His decrees and threats, however, "have not prevailed to subdue the obstinate violence of crime, which has been implanted in the breasts of certain men," and there is no hope except in "that source to which all good

---

[38]Optatus *Against the Donatists.*

[39]Jones, *Constantine and the Conversion of Europe,* pp. 101, 105-6.

[40]Still, it is not accurate to say, as Yoder does, that Christian emperors from Constantine on ruled "on what constitutes orthodox belief" (John Howard Yoder, *The Priestly Kingdom: Social Ethics as Gospel* [Notre Dame, Ind.: University of Notre Dame Press, 1984], p. 136). Constantine came the closest to doing this, and even he was enforcing decisions of episcopal councils, not making the decisions himself. After Constantine, emperors had no direct role in deciding theological issues.

[41]Barnes, *Constantine and Eusebius,* p. 60.

desires and deeds are referred." Peace cannot be forced, and "until the Heavenly medicine shows itself, our designs must be moderated so far as to act with patience, and whatever in their insolence they attempt or carry out, in accordance with their habitual wantonness—all this we must endure with the strength which comes from tranquility." Alluding to Jesus' Sermon on the Mount, he urged them not to return wrong for wrong and reminded the bishops that "it is the mark of a fool to snatch at that vengeance which we ought to leave to God." This was especially true for Christians, whose "faith ought to lead us to trust that whatever we may endure from the madness of men of this kind, will avail before God for the grace of martyrdom." Overcoming means enduring "with an unshaken heart the untamed savagery of men who harass the people of the Law of Peace." Through patient endurance, he hopes, "these men, who are making themselves the standard-bearers of this most miserable strife, may all come to recognize, as their laws or customs fall into decay, that they ought not, through the persuasion of a few, to give themselves over to perish in everlasting death, when they might, through the grace of repentance, be made whole again, having corrected their errors, for everlasting life."[42] Having done all he could to glue the fractured pieces of the African church back together, he found he had to leave it to God. He did not want to make martyrs, nor to be another Diocletian, sacrificing Christians for the good order of the empire.

CONCLUSION

It is an overstatement to say that Constantine treated the bishops as "imperial commissions" or "state functionaries," addressed them as if they were no more than "minor bureaucrats," and asserted his rights as an "arbiter of worship."[43] Constantine tried to limit himself to facilitating the bishops' work by calling councils and providing venues and transport. Even his legal recognition of the conciliar decisions was unavoidable. After all, if he granted exemptions to Christian churches and clergy, he needed to know whom he was exempting.

---

[42]Optatus *Against the Donatists.*
[43]Jones, *Constantine and the Conversion of Europe,* p. 98; D. G. Kousoulas, *The Life and Times of Constantine the Great: The First Christian Emperor,* 2nd ed. (Author, 2007), pp. 301, 307-8; MacMullen, *Constantine,* pp. 105, 114.

With the Donatists, further, he faced an intractable challenge. Memories of the persecution were still sharp, and readily invoked. Donatists cried persecution when Constantine turned on them, as later Athanasius would consider himself a latter-day martyr. A Christian emperor could not pacify unruly Christian groups without being branded a persecutor or making martyrs, yet some of the Christian groups were deadly. Throughout the fourth century, Circumcellions in North Africa terrorized with their clubs, called "Israels," and "around 406 they began blinding Catholic clergy by forcing a mixture of powdered lime and vinegar . . . into their eyes."[44] Somebody had to stop them, and the emperor happened to be that somebody. But then he risked being labeled another Diocletian. Given these dynamics, it is not so surprising that Augustine, after many peaceful overtures to the Donatists, finally determined that they should be compelled to reenter the church, nor that Constantine went beyond his initial minimalism by calling new councils and using coercion in his effort to heal a schism.

Constantine could have, and ultimately did, stand back and stand down, but the murderous factionalism of the church had tempted him to dangerous precedents. Filled with both passion for Catholic unity and ambition for the empire, he did not always have the resources to resist those temptations when they appeared. They would appear again.

---

[44]Gaddis, *There Is No Crime*, pp. 126-27.

8

Nicaea and After

*I know that the plentitude of the Father's and the Son's
pre-eminent and all-pervading power is one substance.*

CONSTANTINE, *LETTER TO ARIUS*

The controversy between Arius and Alexander erupted in Alexandria around 318 and eventually engulfed the Eastern Church.[1] It was, however, preceded by the much less known but important Meletian controversy, a replay of the Donatist controversy now in the eastern part of Africa. During the Diocletian persecution, Bishop Peter of Alexandria fled from the city. In fact, he fled more than once. During one of his absences, Meletius found the city bereft of pastoral care and promptly ordained some men to

---

[1]Recent scholarship presents a fairly radical revision of many details concerning Nicaea—from the chronology of events and the reliability of sources such as Athanasius to the context, background and importance of Arius himself, to the force of the Nicene formula, the effect of its creed, and the question of the relation of orthodoxy and heresy. The best recent treatments are found in Timothy D. Barnes, *Constantine and Eusebius* (Cambridge, Mass.: Harvard University Press, 1981), pp. 191-244; Lewis Ayres, *Nicaea and Its Legacy: An Approach to Fourth-Century Trinitarian Theology* (Oxford: Oxford University Press, 2006), chaps. 2-3; Rowan Williams, *Arius: Heresy and Tradition*, rev. ed. (Grand Rapids: Eerdmans, 2001), pp. 29-91; R. P. C. Hanson, *The Search for the Christian Doctrine of God: The Arian Controversy, 318-381* (Grand Rapids: Baker Academic, 2005), pp. 13-273; Timothy D. Barnes, *Athanasius and Constantius: Theology and Politics in the Constantinian Empire* (Cambridge, Mass.: Harvard University Press, 1993), pp. 1-33. Deft and still useful older treatments are found in Henry Chadwick, *The Early Church*, Pelican History of the Church 1 (New York: Penguin, 1967), pp. 129-36; W. H. C. Frend, *The Rise of Christianity* (Philadelphia: Fortress, 1984), pp. 492-517. David S. Potter, *The Roman Empire at Bay, AD 180-395*, Routledge History of the Ancient World (London: Routledge, 2004), pp. 401-22, is out of his depth in the theology.

fill the vacuum. Peter returned and wondered what had happened to his bishopric.

In part, the Meletian schism was another war concerning the proper response to persecution and whether to encourage or discourage the zeal of voluntary martyrs. Peter, like Mensurius in Carthage, urged moderation and was mild toward those who lapsed; Meletius was of a Donatist disposition. The division was so acute that, according to legend, Peter and Meletius were not even able to cooperate when they were, ironically, forced to share a prison cell. Peter hung a curtain down the middle of the cell and urged his supporters to remain on his side of the curtain.[2] The Meletian schism reminds us that there were multiple layers of conflict in the Alexandrian church and that it is misleading to describe it all on an "Arian versus orthodox" model. Athanasius had at least as much trouble from Meletians as from Arians, though he had the rhetorical shrewdness and bravura to brand all his opponents as "Arians."

Peter, despite his prudent escapes, died a martyr in 311. Achillas briefly followed him, but he too died, and Alexander was installed in 313. Sometime around 318, he and a local priest, Arius, came into conflict over Christology. A charismatic preacher, Arius was tall, stooped and curved—as one ancient historian put it—like a snake, wore the garb of an ascetic and a philosopher, and oversaw a large number of devoted virgins within the Alexandrian church. Possibly a student of Lucian of Antioch (as Arius's ally Eusebius of Nicomedia was), he followed one strain of the Origenist tradition of theology that had been bubbling in the church of Alexandria for decades. In various writings, Origen had expressed a subordinationist Christology that considered Christ to be ontologically secondary and inferior to the Father. Arius pushed the point further, complaining in a letter to Eusebius of Nicomedia that he was being persecuted for teaching that the Logos exists "by will and counsel," that "before he was begotten, or created, or determined or established, he did not exist,"

---

[2]The Melitian controversy is briefly summed up in Chadwick, *Early Church*, p. 124; Frend, *Rise of Christianity*, pp. 493-94; Williams, *Arius*, pp. 32-41. Potter, *Roman Empire at Bay*, p. 412, tells the story of the prison-house schism. Records list an "Arius" as a supporter of Melitius, and Frend (*Rise of Christianity*, p. 493) believes it is the same Arius who later emerged in conflict with Alexander. That implies that Arius was a very slick operator, changing from loyalty to Melitus to Peter's successor, and recent scholars have doubted that the two are the same man (Williams, *Arius*, p. 40; Hanson, *Search for the Christian Doctrine*, p. 5).

and that he "derives from non-existence" (*ex ouk onton estin*).[3] To be sure, the Logos is not a creature as other creatures are, but neither is he unbegotten, since there can be only one Unbegotten, the Father.[4]

A document preserved by Athanasius in his treatise *On the Synods* provides a fuller explanation of the Arian viewpoint:

> For when giving to him [the Son] the inheritance of all things [Heb 1:2], the Father did not deprive himself of what he has without beginning in himself; for he is the source of all things. Thus there are three subsisting realities [*hypostaseis*]. And God, being the cause of all that happens, is absolutely alone without beginning; but the Son, begotten apart from time by the Father, and created [*ktistheis*] and founded before the ages, was not in existence before his generation, but was begotten apart from time before all things, and he alone came into existence [*hypestē*] from the Father. For he is neither eternal nor co-eternal nor co-unbegotten with the Father, nor does he have his being together with the Father, as some speak of relations, introducing two unbegotten beginnings. But God is before all things as monad and beginning of all. Therefore he is also before the Son, as we have learned also from your public preaching in the church.[5]

Alarmed not only at Arius's teaching but also at his popularity, Alexander summoned a synod of one hundred Egyptian bishops, who roundly condemned Arius. Banished from the city, he journeyed to Nicomedia, where he knew he would gain a sympathetic hearing from the powerful bishop Eusebius, intimate of Constantia, the wife of Licinius and sister of Constantine. Arius had chosen a good ally. Eusebius summoned a council in Bithynia, which reversed the decision of the Egyptian council by finding Arius orthodox.[6] Another council was held at Caesarea, the other Eusebius presumably at the head, and this too found Arius innocent of heresy, though it recommended that he return to Alexandria to attempt a reconciliation with his bishop. Reconciliation did not happen, and instead Arius's presence in Alexandria only provoked further quarreling. Meanwhile, a council in 324 held in Antioch condemned and excommunicated Eusebius of Caesarea.[7]

---

[3]All quoted in Hanson, *Search for the Christian Doctrine*, pp. 6-7.
[4]Ayres, *Nicaea*, emphasizes the central importance of theories of "begetting" in the debate over Arius's views.
[5]Athanasius *On the Synods* 16.
[6]Barnes, *Constantine and Eusebius*, pp. 203-4.
[7]Frend, *Rise of Christianity*, p. 497.

Resolution of the controversy was made difficult by Licinius's prohibition of Christian assemblies in 322 (which may have been a response to the controversy), and so it was not until Constantine took over the East that the bishops felt they could resolve the question. When Constantine first learned of the dispute, his first instinct, as usual, was to urge concord. "Do ye both exhibit an equal degree of forbearance," he wrote to Arius and Alexander, "and receive the advice which your fellow-servant righteously gives." For himself, the emperor considered it "wrong in the first instance to propose such questions as these, or to reply to them when propounded," since "those points of discussion which are enjoined by the authority of no law, but rather suggested by the contentious spirit which is fostered by misused leisure, even though they may be intended merely as an intellectual exercise, ought certainly to be confined to the region of our own thoughts, and not hastily produced in the popular assemblies, nor unadvisedly entrusted to the general ear." It is a rare thinker who is able accurately to "comprehend, or adequately to explain subjects so sublime and abstruse in their nature," and even those competent few will find it difficult to convince others. "Who," he demanded, "in dealing with questions of such subtle nicety as these, can secure himself against a dangerous declension from the truth?" When faced with such mysteries, "it is incumbent therefore on us in these cases to be sparing of our words, lest, in case we ourselves are unable, through the feebleness of our natural faculties, to give a clear explanation of the subject before us, or, on the other hand, in case the slowness of our hearers' understandings disables them from arriving at an accurate apprehension of what we say, from one or other of these causes the people be reduced to the alternative either of blasphemy or schism." Both the one who asked "unguarded questions" and the one who offered an "inconsiderate answer" should seek "mutual forgiveness." After all, "the cause of your difference has not been any of the leading doctrines or precepts of the Divine law, nor has any new heresy respecting the worship of God arisen among you. You are in truth of one and the same judgment: you may therefore well join in communion and fellowship."[8] Voltaire did not care for Constantine, but he approved this letter, particularly Constantine's characterization of the Arian con-

---

[8]Eusebius *Life* 2.64-72.

troversy as a quarrel over "small and very insignificant questions."

It is not clear whether we should take this at face value.[9] After the council, and after several feints and shifts in his jousting with Arius, Constantine's views hardened considerably. After Nicaea, he commended the "three hundred bishops" who unanimously affirmed "one and the same faith, which according to the truth and legitimate construction of the law of God can only be the faith," and argued that only Arius himself remained "beguiled by the subtlety of the devil."[10] In another letter to the churches in 325, he threatened death to anyone who possessed a copy of Arius's writings and failed to burn it.[11]

At the beginning, though, his inclination was to settle the dispute by negotiation. Constantine dispatched his advisor Ossius to Alexandria, armed with the imperial letter, to resolve things, but Ossius found the situation far worse than he had expected. Soon after his mission failed, Constantine summoned the bishops of East and West, and even, as we saw, from outside the empire, first to Ancyra and then to Nicaea to put the issue to rest once and for all.

EMPEROR IN COUNCIL

Despite the mythology that has grown up around Constantine's "dominance" and "control" of the council of Nicaea, his approach to the Arian controversy was consistent with his initial approach to the Donatist dispute. He had, however, learned some lessons from that earlier encounter. In dealing with the Donatists, he had finally resorted to persecution; apart from the instrument of exile, he would not do the same with the Arian controversy. Doubtless, too, he entered the Arian dispute disabused of any naive expectation that the bishops were going to be easy to work with. They would not be. Arius was a strong personality, and persistent; Eusebius of Caesarea was a widely respected scholar and writer, a force to be reckoned with; Athanasius, who attended the council as a diaconal assistant to Alexander, would prove to be the strongest of all, willing to rebuke an emperor to his face.

---

[9]Charles Matson Odahl (*Constantine and the Christian Empire* [London: Routledge, 2004], p. 192) argues that Constantine did recognize the importance of the theological issues but aimed first and foremost at *concordia* among the bishops.
[10]Socrates *Ecclesiastical History* 1.9.
[11]Ibid.

Ossius of Cordoba ran the council.[12] Though he knew Greek, Constantine gave the opening address in the imperial language, Latin, and his speech was translated to the largely Greek-speaking council. He stressed, as he had in his initial letter to Arius and Alexander, his desire to see the church united in brotherhood. According to Eusebius, he dramatically burned copies of complaints that the bishops had brought to him against one another. Throughout the council he was present, though probably sitting apart from the bishops. He participated in the discussion, often urging the bishops to practice moderation and puruse peace.[13] Eusebius thought this all to his credit, but Eustathius later complained that the pleas for peace had the effect of shutting down debate and silencing the most effective speakers.

The actual course of debate is impossible to reconstruct with assurance. Socrates later described the council as a battle carried on in the dark, everyone striking out at indistinct but threatening shadows.[14] Apparently contradictory accounts come from Eustathius and Eusebius. The latter claimed that he offered a creed himself, which was accepted with enthusiasm by the emperor and approved, with some amendments, by the council. Eustathius recorded that the initial creed was shouted down and torn up. Perhaps these are simply two accounts of the same event: Eusebius exaggerated the enthusiasm for his own creed, and Eustathius exaggerated the opposition. Or perhaps the two offerings came from different Eusebii. It may be that Eusebius of Caesarea offered a local creed that met with approval, while Eusebius of Nicomedia offered an Arian creed that was rejected outright.[15] Our ignorance of the basic structure of the debate should

---

[12]Odahl, *Constantine and the Christian Empire*, p. 197; Timothy D. Barnes, "Constantine, Athanasius and the Christian Church," in *Constantine: History, Historiography and Legend*, ed. Samuel Lieu and Dominic Montserrat (London: Routledge, 1998); Ayres, *Nicaea*, p. 89; most thoroughly, Hanson, *Search for the Christian Doctrine*, pp. 154-155. A. H. M. Jones (*Constantine and the Conversion of Europe* [Toronto: University of Toronto Press, 1978], p. 132) claims that Constantine chaired the meeting and that it was organized like a meeting of the Senate or town council, in which the chair of the meeting fully participated in the deliberations. H. A. Drake (*Constantine and the Bishops: The Politics of Intolerance* [Baltimore: Johns Hopkins University Press, 2000]) also notes the parallels with the Senate, as does Francis Dvornik, "Emperors, Popes and General Councils," *Dumbarton Oaks Papers* 6 (1951), but the latter makes the crucial point that the emperor had no vote in the Senate but was an admittedly powerful moderator of senatorial deliberations.

[13]Barnes, "Constantine, Athanasius," pp. 10-11.

[14]Quoted by Frend, *Rise of Christianity*, p. 498.

[15]Hanson, *Search for the Christian Doctrine*, pp. 157-63.

make us very cautious about deciding what role Constantine played in the process.[16]

In any case, the crucial innovation was the introduction of the term *homoousios,* "one substance," to describe the relationship of the Father and Son. Eusebius credits Constantine with offering the term,[17] but Ossius and Alexander may have had a prior agreement to introduce it as a way of weeding out Arius's allies.[18] If Constantine indeed suggested this solution, he did it in collusion with the two bishops. When some of the bishops objected, Constantine offered an interpretation that satisfied all but two Libyan bishops, who may have acted in defense of Arius, a fellow Libyan. Arius was excommunicated and sent into exile. Not long after, Eusebius of Nicomedia and Theognis extended hospitality to some Arians, and as a result they too were deposed and excommunicated, and Constantine even charged Euesbius with treachery in allying with Licinius.[19]

We should not underestimate Constantine's achievement. Of at least two hundred often irascible bishops, only two refused to sign off on the creed. Many had come to the council with sympathy for Arius, and it is implausible that they quietly accepted "an openly Sabellian creed." It is also unlikely that Origenists would have abandoned their belief in three *hypostases.* Somehow the formula worked for almost everyone, with *homoousios* "not a flag to be nailed to the masthead, a word around which self-conscious schools of theology could rally," but instead "an apotropaic formula for resisting Arianism."[20] Constantine did not dominate the council. He did not formulate the final creed, nor did he sign off on it—being, again, an unbaptized nonbishop. It is difficult, however, to believe that the bishops could have come to such a thoroughgoing conclusion without his political skill and strength of personality.

At the same time, Nicaea was not what it is often said to be. Later legend treats the council at Nicaea—a city named "Victory"—as the decisive

---

[16]On Constantine's role at the council, see Ayres, *Nicaea,* pp. 89-90; Hanson, *Search for the Christian Doctrine,* p. 171, both of whom conclude that we have no way of knowing what exactly he did. Jones, *Constantine and the Conversion of Europe,* pp. 133-34.

[17]Athanasius does not say that Constantine introduced this term.

[18]Odahl (*Constantine and the Christian Empire,* p. 197) attributes the introduction of the term to Lactantius and Ossius.

[19]Barnes, *Constantine and Eusebius,* pp. 215-17; Williams, *Arius,* p. 71; Hanson, *Search for the Christian Doctrine,* p. 173; Jones, *Constantine and the Conversion of Europe,* pp. 138, 146.

[20]Hanson, *Search for the Christian Doctrine,* p. 172.

triumph of christological orthodoxy. In fact, it was only the first round of a theological, political and intensely personal controversy that consumed the Eastern Church through the middle decades of the fourth century. At first no one treated the Nicene Creed as exclusively definitive, and most churches continued to use their pre-Nicene confessions and creeds. Only with the formulation of the theory, late in the fourth century, that ecumenical creeds outranked local creeds did the Nicene formula take on its aura of final authority. Over the last decade of his life, Constantine was in the thick of the controversy, attempting reconciliations between Arius and the church at Alexandria, exiling a bishop here and restoring one there. Councils throughout that decade met without Constantine's initiative, and they often came to contradictory conclusions.

Constantine had given the Donatists several chances, and he did the same for Arius. In 327 he reconvened the Council of Nicaea, where Arius insisted that he could accept the Nicene Creed. Constantine invited him to court with hopes of ending his exile, and the following year he wrote to Alexander urging him to receive Arius back into communion. Arius proved intransigent, as did both Alexander and his successor Athanasius. Eusebius and Theognis claimed to accept *homoousios,* arguing that they objected only to the anathemas, which they did not think applied to Arius, and asked the bishops at the second convening of Nicaea to petition the emperor for an end to their exile. Constantine agreed, recalled the two excommunicated and exiled bishops, and reinstalled them into their sees, forcing out the bishops who had replaced them.[21]

When Arius, perhaps inadvertently, seemed to threaten schism by referring to the support he enjoyed in his native Libya, Constantine lost patience and sent him a railing letter. Condemning him for his similarity to the war god Aries, he asked, "Are you, then, really blameless, gallows rogue? Have you not, then, really perished, sorry fellow, surrounded by such great horror? We know, we know your undertaking; what kind of anxiety, what kind of fear troubles you, wretched and miserable person, has not escaped our notice. Oh, the dullness of your wits, you profane person, who do not restrain your soul's sickness and helplessness, who un-

---

[21]Barnes, *Constantine and Eusebius,* p. 229; Jones, Constantine and the *Conversion of Europe,* pp. 148-49.

dermine the truth by varied discourses."[22]

Constantine was no longer of the opinion that the Arian conflict was over trivial matters:

> Do you say that the "the Word of his essence is the Word without beginning and without end?" I acquiesce in this; believe so. If you add anything further, this I abrogate. If you join anything to an impious separation, I confess that I neither see nor perceive this. . . . If you say that "the spirit of eternity was born in the pre-eminent Word," I receive it. Who has known the Father, unless he who comes from the Father? Whom has the Father known, unless him whom he has begotten from himself eternally and without beginning? You think that you ought to substitute a "foreign hypostasis," believing doubtless badly; I know that the plentitude of the Father's and the Son's pre-eminent and all-pervading power is one substance.[23]

Constantine knew how to insult, but what is most striking in his correspondence from the period is the pleading tone. Theoretically allpowerful within the empire, the emperor begs bishops to get along. Meanwhile, vocal pro-Nicene bishops were deposed and exiled. Marcellus of Ancyra was condemned at Constantinople for going overboard in his criticisms of Eusebius, and Eustathius of Antioch was condemned as a Sabellian and for insulting the queen mother, Helena.[24] Not everyone accepted his deposition, and in Antioch a separate church was rapidly assembled with Eustathius as bishop. When riots broke out, Constantine had to send in troops to quell them and to oversee a new election, which ended with the selection of Eusebius of Caesarea, who, in conformity with the canons of Nicaea, refused.[25]

The church in Alexandria was also in turmoil. Alexander of Alexandria died on April 17, 328, and Athanasius was elected on May 9, in an election that was later challenged as shady and underhanded. If Constantine's relations with Alexander were strained, his spars with Athanasius threw off sparks. Both were domineering personalities. Athanasius, for all his repu-

---

[22]Athanasius *Defense* 40. Translation from P. R. Coleman-Norton, *Roman State and Christian Church* (London: SPCK, 1966).

[23]Ibid.

[24]Hanson, *Search for the Christian Doctrine*, pp. 208-38; Williams, *Arius*, p. 80; Ayres, *Nicaea*, pp. 101-2. Behind the falls of these Nicene supporters, Chadwick (*Early Church*, pp. 134-35) sees the hand of Eusebius of Nicomedia.

[25]Jones, *Constantine and the Conversion of Europe*, pp. 150-51.

tation for piety and theological acumen, was a tough, skillful infighter, a community organizer and rabble rouser, willing to use intimidation or other tools in pursuit of his aims. Above all, the clash was one between an emperor whose main hope for the church was concord and a bishop who wanted no part of a consensus not based on truth.[26]

Once Athanasius was made bishop, Constantine renewed his efforts to get Arius readmitted to the church. When Athanasius refused, Constantine threatened to depose him. The situation was exacerbated by the side conflict between Athansius and the Meletians of Alexandria, who accused Athanasius of trying to impose a levy on Egyptian linen and of bribery and sacrilege. The latter charge rested on allegations about the actions of one of the bishop's agents, Macarius. The Meletians claimed that Macarius burst in on Ischyras, whose right to priestly office Athanasius contested, while Ischyras was celebrating Mass, overturned the altar, burned a book, and broke a Eucharistic chalice.[27] Constantine summoned the bishops to Nicomedia in 332, where Athanasius produced a letter in which Ischyras admitted that the charge was false. Athanasius was exonerated, but the Meletian bishops were not satisfied with the outcome and appealed again to Constantine, repeating the charge that Athanasius was responsible for the chalice and adding a charge that Athanasius had murdered Arsenius. They brought a burned hand as evidence, the only surviving limb of Arsenius. At Antioch, the story goes, Athanasius produced Arsenius, who had been hiding in a monastery, and the charges were again dropped.[28]

Arius was still eager to be vindicated, and he found allies in the Meletians who also wanted to remove Athanasius. In 334 Constantine called yet another council, this one at Caesarea, to resolve the dispute once and for all. Athanasius refused to attend, and Constantine backed down. The following year the bishops were assembled in Tyre, Athanasius among them, and he again had to answer the charge of breaking the sacred chalice. Ischyras had retracted his retraction in the meantime and added to the

---

[26]Barnes, *Athanasius and Constantius,* pp. 10-14, on the background of Athanasius as a lower-class biblicist. See also Hanson, *Search for the Christian Doctrine,* pp. 239-73; Jones, *Constantine and the Conversion of Europe,* p. 153.

[27]Barnes, *Athanasius and Constantius,* p. 21; Potter, *Roman Empire at Bay,* p. 422; Jones, *Constantine and the Conversion of Europe,* pp. 155-56.

[28]Jones, *Constantine and the Conversion of Europe,* pp. 156-57.

charges the claim that Athanasius had imprisoned him on the false charge that he, Ischyras, had stoned a statue of the emperor. Five other Meletian bishops claimed they had been flogged on orders from the bishop of Alexandria. Recognizing that the council was set against him, Athanasius slipped away one night in disguise and was condemned by the council in absentia.[29]

Athanasius sailed to Constantinople, where he confronted the emperor in disguise in one of the most dramatic scenes in the series of dramatic events:

> As I was making my entry into the city which bears our name, in this our most flourishing home, Constantinople,—and it happened that I was riding on horseback at the time,—suddenly the Bishop Athanasius, with certain ecclesiastics whom he had around him, presented himself so unexpectedly in our path, as to produce an occasion of consternation. For the Omniscient God is my witness that at first sight I did not recognize him until some of my attendants, in answer to my enquiry, informed me, as was very natural, both who he was, and what injustice he had suffered. At that time indeed I neither conversed, nor held any communication with him. But as he repeatedly entreated an audience, and I had not only refused it, but almost ordered that he should be removed from my presence, he said with greater boldness, that he petitioned for nothing more than that you might be summoned hither, in order that in our presence, he, driven by necessity to such a course, might have a fair opportunity afforded him of complaining of his wrongs.[30]

Constantine was persuaded and issued a blistering condemnation of the proceedings at Tyre. Within a few days a delegation of Athanasius's enemies arrived in Constantinople to see the emperor, including Eusebius of Caesarea and Eusebius of Nicomedia, and they persuaded the emperor to reverse himself. The bishop of Alexandria was not deposed, but he was exiled—not for the last time—to Trier.[31]

---

[29]Ibid., pp. 160-63. Athanasius never completely denied the charges of breaking a chalice or of intimidation. His response to the chalice episode was usually that it did not matter since Ischyras was not a priest and therefore the chalice was not holy. Anyone with small children will recognize the maneuver, a denial that is as good as an admission.

[30]Socrates *Ecclesiastical History* 1.34, p. 96; Hanson, *Search for the Christian Doctrine*, p. 263.

[31]Hanson (*Search for the Christian Doctrine*, p. 263) notes that we do not know why Athanasius was exiled. Ayres (*Nicaea*, p. 103) says that the last straw was the charge that Athanasius threatened to interrupt the transport of grain from Alexandria to Constantinople. See also

Arius meanwhile continued his appeals to the emperor. He professed to accept the orthodox faith in a letter to Constantine, and Constantine, ever eager to reunite the church, accepted his profession. It was not to be. Reputedly on his way to church to be readmitted, he suffered a bizarre death, perhaps by poisoning, in what James Joyce called a "Greek watercloset" where "with beaded mitre and with crozier, stalled upon his throne, widower of a widowed see, with uplifted omophorion," he died "with clotted hinderparts."[32] Legend has it that no one used the seat again for some time, and other legends say that Theodosius set up statues of Arius in Alexandria so that people could amuse themselves by spattering it with shit and piss.[33]

This confusing and convoluted history is not the history of a Constantine with absolute control of the church. If anything, he was too easily persuaded by whatever powerful episcopal personality happened to be speaking to him, too ready to change course when he saw a chance for reconciliation. Now Athanasius, now Arius, now Eusebius had his ear, and imperial policy changed accordingly. One may interpret this as cynical and calculating. It is more likely uncynical politics: Constantine was willing to work with team players but marginalized divisive zealots.[34] Whatever policy and calculation were involved, we ought not discount the role of sincere but blundering clemency.

WHAT HAS BISHOP TO DO WITH PALACE?

As used by John Howard Yoder, "Constantinianism" is a "heresy" and represents the "fourth-century shift" that created a gap between biblical Christianity and us, a "disavowal and apostasy."[35] For Yoder, "Constantinianism" is not identical with the work and achievements of Constantine. Nor is it confined to a particular period of Western history, or necessarily linked with any particular form of church-state settlement. In his most complete discussion, an essay in *Priestly Kingdom,* he multiplies

---

Jones, *Constantine and the Conversion of Europe,* pp. 163-64.

[32]*Ulysses.*

[33]Raymond Van Dam, *The Roman Revolution of Constantine* (Cambridge: Cambridge University Press, 2008), p. 257.

[34]This is Drake's plausible thesis.

[35]John Howard Yoder, *The Priestly Kingdom: Social Ethics as Gospel* (Notre Dame, Ind.: University of Notre Dame Press, 1984), p. 144.

neo- prefixes to show that even after the Reformation, even after dises-
tablishment, even in liberation theologies, some form of the protean heresy of Constantinianism still dominates.

Instead of a particular man, a particular set of policies, or a particular era,
Constantine has a "code function": "the first emperor to tolerate, then to
favor, and then to participate in the administration of the Christian churches
is the symbol of a shift in relationships which had begun before he came on
the scene and was not completed until nearly a century after his death." Yoder believes "his thoughts and his deeds are eminently representative of the
nature of the shift."[36] "Constantinianism" refers to a theology and ecclesial
practice that took form when the church assumed a dominant position in
Roman society. Constantinianism is the wedding of piety to power,[37] the
notion that the empire or state, the ruler of civil government rather than the
church, is the primary bearer of meaning in history. When the church succumbs to Constantinianism, Christians think they need to link themselves
to the "real powers" in the palace or White House in order to get things
done, in order to take some control of history.

Stanley Hauerwas has taken up and popularized Yoder's critique,
though he has not treated it as systematically as Yoder. In a penetrating
summary of Hauerwas's work, R. R. Reno suggests that Hauerwas uses
the word to describe "the ways in which Christian truth becomes in-
nocuous and weightless." *Constantinianism* is a "rhetorical device for
sharpening contrasts."[38] Christianity can become weightless in different
ways. Cultural accommodation is the most obvious form of Constantinianism; when the culture gets sufficiently "Christianized" that everyone behaves in a roughly Christian fashion, it is hard to see how to be a
disciple, what difference it makes. On the other hand, appeals to transcendence can also be Constantinian if they contribute to the invisibility
of the faith. Thus "Hauerwas rages against a mistaken view that the
church gains weight through alliances to 'real' forces (regnant regimes of
political, cultural, and intellectual power), and at the same time he attacks modern theological attempts to make Christian invisibility into a

---

[36]Ibid., pp. 201-2, n. 3.
[37]Ibid., 140.
[38]R. R. Reno, "Stanley Hauerwas," in *Blackwell Companion to Political Theology*, ed. Peter Scott
   and William T. Cavanaugh (Oxford: Blackwell, 2006), p. 310.

spiritual virtue."[39] In sum, Reno sees the coherence of Hauerwas's position as a rhetorical coherence:

> To enter this heavenly city, one leaves behind, often in painful turns of repentance, the earthly city we thought our only possible home. Hauerwas' polemics against Constantinianism should be understood as *ad hoc* criticisms of the many ways in which the church has tried to demolish the walls of separation and moderate the wrenching turn of repentance, whether by so distancing faith from practical affairs that "spiritual" becomes a synonym for "impotent," or by so intertwining faith with the habits and practices of the wider culture that the Christian life becomes invisible.[40]

INVISIBLE CHURCH?

I will return to the more subtle theological aspects of Yoder's anti-Constantinianism in the final chapter. Here my question is a more or less strictly historical one: Did the church of the fourth century allow itself to be absorbed into the machinery of power? Did the bishops of the fourth century who accommodated themselves to Constantine lose their critical, prophetic edge? Did they become yes-men to a brute and a tyrant? Did the church become weightless and invisible? Yoder, I submit, misrepresents the fourth century, and his answers to these questions are misleading or outright false.

Some regard criticism of Yoder's historical imprecision as a "significant misreading" of his intentions.[41] Yoder is, after all, skeptical that we can know much of anything about Constantine himself, and more important, he wonders whether asking detailed questions about Constantine's sincerity, his control of councils, his self-image as "savior of the church" is a fruitful enterprise.[42] He is concerned not with Constantine the man but rather with the shift that Constantine symbolizes: "The shift is what matters," he regularly reminds us. Yet it is not so easy for Yoder to escape the charge of inaccuracy, distortion or misrepresentation. He portrays himself as, and is, a notably particularist theologian, and if he gets his facts wrong,

---

[39]Ibid., p. 311.
[40]Ibid., p. 312.
[41]Michael Cartwright, introduction to Yoder, *The Royal Priesthood: Essays Ecclesiological and Ecumenical*, ed. Michael G. Cartwright (Grand Rapids: Eerdmans, 1994), p. 10.
[42]Yoder, *Priestly Kingdom*, p. 245, n. 3.

he is being inconsistent with his fundamental historiographical outlook.[43] Yoder makes specific historical claims, and specific historical mistakes, and those historical mistakes contribute to distortions within his complex concept of "Constantinianism."

Yoder to the contrary, Constantine did not call himself "bishop of bishops."[44] That was a concept his son, Constantius II, promoted, and it was roundly condemned by the real bishops. Yoder claims that throughout the Middle Ages "church government was in the hands of the civil government,"[45] which, true in many cases, would be news indeed to Hildebrand and Henry. He contrasts the hardy heroic church of the martyrs to the accommodated post-Constantinian church by pointing out that earlier the catechumenate demanded that converts learn the faith and take time for baptism,[46] but much of the information we have about the catechumenate and the awe-inspiring rites of initiation comes from the mystagogical catecheses of Chrysostom and Ambrose, both doubly disqualified by Yoder as being Constantinians and sacramentalists.[47]

These are not quibbles, but they are comparatively small matters. Yoder also gets more central and substantive issues wrong—or, more modestly, Yoder's interpretations of key figures are misinterpretations. He sums up Eusebius's political eschatology with a brief paraphrase, "God gave Constantine the victory, so this must be the millennium,"[48] and claims that for Eusebius the state is brought entirely within the realm of redemption.[49]

---

[43]I return to the contradictions between Yoder's historiographic theory and practice in chapter 13.

[44]John Howard Yoder, *Christian Attitudes to War, Peace and Revolution*, ed. Theodore J. Koontz and Andy Alexis-Baker (Grand Rapids: Brazos, 2009), p. 58. Gilbert Dagron (*Emperor and Priest: The Imperial Office in Byzantium*, trans. Jean Birrell [Cambridge: Cambridge University Press, 2003], p. 135) attributes the phrase to Lucifer of Cagliari, a fourth-century bishop.

[45]Ibid., p. 60.

[46]Ibid., p. 71.

[47]On the development of baptismal liturgy, see Paul Bradshaw, *The Search for the Origins of Christian Worship*, 2nd ed. (Oxford: Oxford University Press, 2002). The elaborate catechetical rites of the fourth century look for all the world like efforts to do something quite different from what Yoder claims. Far from making "it easy for people to get in" (Yoder, *Christian Attitudes*, p. 71), the church is responding to the post-Constantinian growth and mainstreaming of the church by making sure that baptismal candidates know what they are getting into. Yoder's claim is also refuted by the well-known fourth-century practice of delaying baptism, sometimes, as in Constantine's case, until near death. Not only did the church *not* accommodate unquestioningly to Constantine; at some points, it overreacted in the opposite direction!

[48]Yoder, *Priestly Kingdom*, p. 158.

[49]Ibid., p. 59.

Yoder is right that Eusebius believed that God's work was discernible in history, in the rise and fall of rulers and princes.[50] Yet Yoder's overall summary of Eusebius is misleading. To be sure, Yoder is not entirely to blame for this, since mainstream scholarship has long considered Eusebius nothing more than a "political propagandist, a good courtier, the shrewd and worldly advisor of the Emperor Constantine, the great publicist of the first Christian emperor, the first in a long succession of ecclesiastical politicians, the herald of Byzantinism, a political theologian, a political metaphysician, and a caesaropapist," not to mention a toady whose obsequiousness can only make us cringe until it makes us vomit.[51]

Yet Eusebius has been misread, largely because his biography and panegyric in praise of Constantine have been studied without reference to his apologetic and biblical works, which make up the bulk of his corpus. Eusebius was not in fact a court insider but probably met the emperor only four or five times.[52] While he did muse that Constantine's buildings in Jerusalem might be the new Jerusalem of prophecy[53] and did find hints of a Christian empire in Old Testament prophecies like Micah 5 and Isaiah 2, he did not reinterpret prophecy wholesale so that Christ was displaced by Constantine and the church by the empire. In his commentary on Isaiah, published soon after the Council of Nicaea, he writes—using terminology that Yoder would endorse—that the *church* is the "godly polity" (*theosebes politeuma*) and "city of God" (*polis tou theou*), ruled by bishops, not by the emperor. On Isaiah 11:6, Eusebius interprets the wild animals "as imperial officials, and the little child who leads them symbolizes the Christian clergy."[54] Yoder's claim that Eusebius identifies the millennium with Constantine's empire is doubly wrong, first because Eusebius was antimillenarian and second because Eusebius regularly refers to the future advent of Christ.[55] Craig Carter claims that "Constantinianism for Yoder is an eschatological heresy which tries to reach forward and pull the future kingdom of God back into the present sphere of history with no regard for

---

[50]Ibid., p. 324.

[51]Michael J. Hollerich, "Religion and Politics in the Writings of Eusebius: Reassessing the First 'Court Theologian,'" *Church History* 59 (1990): 309.

[52]Ibid., p. 313; Barnes, *Constantine and Eusebius*, p. 266.

[53]Eusebius *Life* 3.33.

[54]Hollerich, "Religion and Politics," p. 313-15.

[55]Ibid., p. 318; cf. Frank S. Thielman, "Another Look at the Eschatology of Eusebius of Caesarea," *Vigiliae Christianae* 41 (1987): 226-37.

the necessity of a still-future Second Coming of the Messiah, thus turning the kingdom into a human political project."[56] If Carter is correct that Yoder's "Constantinianism" is nothing more than a complete immanentization of the eschaton ("*no* regard for . . ."), then it becomes difficult to find any Christian theologian who qualifies as a Constantinian. Eusebius certainly does not, and he is one of the prime candidates.

Even when Eusebius celebrated Constantine's role in the church, he hedged. When he described Constantine as a "sort of bishop," the "quasi" was as important as the "bishop." By "opening the door to a conception of the emperor as a *quasi-bishop,* Eusebios [*sic*] was closing it to a more radical conception" adopted by Constantine's son Constantius, the notion that the emperor was *episcopus episcoporum.*[57] In any case, Eusebius's enthusiasm was slowly cooled and curbed by later historians. Rufinus's translation or paraphrase of Eusebius's history reworked Constantine's career to highlight the emperor's respect for bishops: the emperor "did not think it was appropriate for the clerics of God if he presented himself as an equal or if he did not greatly privilege them."[58] Socrates and Sozomen are more distant still from Eusebius, both theologically and politically.[59] Augustine is the high point of this revisionism. On Yoder's reading, Augustine merges New Testament teaching on reconciliation with classical notions of peace, especially the *pax Romana,* "as if they were all the same thing." Augustine wrote a large book on that subject, and the basic thrust of it was the opposite—to *distinguish* the Roman peace from the peace of the kingdom. Yoder regularly places Eusebius and Augustine together as chief representatives of Constantinian theology, but Augustine wrote *City of God* as an *antidote* to Eusebianism.[60]

Yoder also makes questionable claims about the relationship between Christology and politics in the fourth century. He disputes the "Catholic axiom" that the early creeds and councils are above criticism. While we

---

[56]From "Politics of the Cross Revisited," Carter's blog.

[57]Dagron, *Emperor and Priest,* p. 135. He adds, "We may suspect that the rhetoric of Eusebios [*sic*] was specifically intended to detach the new sovereign from 'caesaropapism' by systematically locating imperial priesthood within the Christian empire, certainly, but outside the Church and by treating it as a metaphor."

[58]Rufinus *Church History* 10.8.1-2. Quoted in Van Dam, *Roman Revolution,* pp. 331-32.

[59]Van Dam, *Roman Revolution,* pp. 335-42.

[60]R. A. Markus, *Saeculum: History and Society in the Theology of Augustine* (Cambridge: Cambridge University Press, 1970).

must learn from the council and sympathize "deeply with what it tried to say," we cannot help but be struck by the fact that "heretics" were often more politically faithful than the "orthodox": "it must mean something to us that the Arians and the Nestorians—each in their own age—were less nationalistic, less politically bound to the Roman Empire, more capable of criticizing the emperor, more vital in missionary growth, more ethical, and more Biblicist than the so-called orthodox churches of the Empire."[61] While there is some truth here (heretics were expelled from the Christian empire and therefore naturally were less attached to it as a result), it is so oversimplified as to be misleading. In the fourth century at least, it was the orthodox Athanasius who resisted Constantine when he believed the emperor wrong, while it was the soft Arian Eusebius of Caesarea who delivered orations in praise of Constantine and the harder Arian Eusebius of Nicomedia who was more likely to be hobnobbing at the Nicomedian court. The relation of Christology and politics is complex, and I do not mean simply to reverse Yoder's equation. Since Erik Peterson's *Monotheism as a Political Problem* (*Monotheismus als politisches Problem*), many scholars have believed that Arianism lent itself to accommodation to empire while trinitarian orthodoxy resisted it.[62] The truth is probably that there simply was no one-to-one correspondence between political and theological convictions.

More fundamentally, Yoder utterly fails to grasp the motivations and passions of fourth-century actors. This is part of his deliberate avoidance of a "great man" historiography of the period, but given his claims about how history should be done, it is a significant historical lacuna. For all his interest in martyrs and the suffering church, Yoder makes virtually no effort to enter into the mentality of beleaguered Christians or to understand the relief they felt at the gradual realization that Constantine was on their side and he was going to be there for a long time.[63] I have

---

[61]John Howard Yoder, *Preface to Theology: Christology and Theological Method* (Grand Rapids: Brazos, 2002), p. 223.

[62]The classic discussion in English is George Huntston Williams, "Christology and Church-State Relations in the Fourth Century," pts. 1-2, *Church History* 20, nos. 3-4 (1951); see also Rousas John Rushdoony, *The Foundations of Social Order: Studies in the Creeds and Councils of the Early Church* (Fairfax, Va.: Thoburn, 1978), chap. 2. Rushdoony states with characteristic bluntness: "Everywhere, pagan statism found Arianism to be an ideal doctrine" since "Arianism was humanism and statism" (p. 14).

[63]Interestingly, he accurately credits Galerius for ending persecution in the Eastern Empire but

not found in Yoder a single word of gratitude to Constantine for keeping
Roman officials from killing Christians for being Christians. I have not
found a single word that shows any effort to get under the "psychic skin"
of bishops (like Eusebius) who witnessed Christians being roasted alive
and then witnessed Constantine kissing the empty eye-sockets of a persecuted brother. Yoder shows little sign of trying to understand why the
bishops answered the question "Where should the emperor sit in Council?" the way they did.

Yoder also pays little attention to the intellectual, legal and constitutional context in which Constantine arose. Constantine, and everyone in
the empire, inherited a set of assumptions about the responsibilities of the
Roman emperor. Caesar was responsible for the defense of the empire, for
the administration of justice, and, equally important, for the *sacra* and
sacerdotes of Rome. Cult was within his jurisdiction as one who had care of
the *status rei Romanae*.[64] That the emperor had oversight ("episcopacy") of
religious life was as natural to fourth-century Romans as the First Amend-
ment separation of church and state is to modern Americans. It is hardly
fair to expect Constantine and all the bishops of the fourth century instantly to abandon centuries of imperial practice as soon as Constantine
converted.

I return to a point made earlier: no emperor had ever had to deal with
something like the church. The Romans knew of Jews, but they were a
recognizable ethnic group, and their independence from the Roman way

---

gives no credit to Constantine for having ended Western persecution several years earlier or for
securing the toleration of Christians permanently after 312. J. Alexander Sider (" 'To See History Doxologically': History and Holiness in John Howard Yoder's Ecclesiology," Ph.D. diss.,
Duke University, 2004, p. 154) notes that from Yoder's account one would gain the impression
"that the persecution under Diocletian and Galerius was in fact not terribly consequential for
the formation of Christian consciousness in the fourth century."

[64]Dvornik, "Emperors, Popes and General Councils,"; and Walter Ullmann, "The Constitutional Significance of Constantine the Great's Settlement," *Journal of Ecclesiastical History* 27
(1976)—both crucial articles. See the similar claims of Drake, *Constantine and the Bishops*, p.
289: "Christians in the late empire recognized the emperor as a sacrosanct individual, with
the right and duty to regulate religious affairs." Johannes Roldanus, *The Church in the Age of
Constantine: The Theological Challenges* (London: Ashgate, 2006), p. 39, misses the point when
he claims that "according to traditional Roman thought, the cultic domain was sacred and
the Emperor's responsibility was rather to guarantee unimpeded worship than to intervene
in questions concerning the legitimacy of priests." Diocletian's policy matched this only if we
define "unimpeded worship" narrowly to include the worship of the traditional Roman gods.
The emperors always had the right, though few exercised it, of suppressing dangerous cults.

of life, unique as it was, made some sense to Romans. A new Israel, an independent "nation" *within* the empire without ethnic or social or geographic boundaries—this was unprecedented. Gibbon recognized the problem: the church was already a state within a state before Constantine, and with the conversion of Constantine the church and the empire both were faced with the challenge of figuring out how the Christian polity and the Roman polity were to relate. For many Christians, such as Eusebius, the task of the hour was not to integrate the church into the empire. The empire had lost the battle with the church, and it was the empire that should make concessions. The church was not incorporated but victorious; the martyrs' faith had been vindicated, and the task was now to integrate the emperor into the church.[65]

NOT CHAPLAINS

It is hardly astonishing that the first Christian emperor had his hands full trying to make legal and constitutional sense of the church, and hardly astonishing that churchmen themselves took some time to recover their balance and learn how to maintain a proper "vis-à-vis" toward a Christian emperor.[66]

Yet even with a Christian on the imperial throne, the church had not lost the capacity to be critical.[67] Even before the days of Ambrose and Augustine, churchmen began to act in critical judgment toward ruthless powers. Opposition was already taking shape in the fourth century, even before Constantine died. It is certainly a testimony to Constantine's political skills, the overwhelming power of his personality, and the relief that many bishops felt at the end of the persecution that Constantine maintained as much sway in the church as he did. We should also recall that the persecution had weeded out many of the hardiest church leaders, and the ones who survived were often the ones who knew how to go along to get along. Still, battles there were, and the bishops very quickly asserted their independent authority. There were bishops who refused to be reduced to "chaplaincy."[68]

---

[65]Dagron, *Emperor and Priest*, p. 129.

[66]This phrasing is from O'Donovan.

[67]As Yoder, *Priestly Kingdom*, p. 144, charges.

[68]Yoder (ibid., pp. 82-83), says, with some accuracy, that we have no record of "strong advocacy" of the need for Constantine to change. It is likely this is because the bishops believed

Eusebius was not as obsequious or unthinking, or as knavish, as he is often made out to have been, and besides, not every bishop was a Eusebius. When Athanasius showed up unexpectedly in Constantinople to plead his case directly to the emperor, he was initially successful. Something went wrong, and before long there was a "blistering exchange." As Epiphanius later told the story, "Angry as the emperor was, Pope Athanasius spoke painful words to him: 'The Lord will judge between me and you, since you yourself agree with those who calumniate your humble servant.'" [69] Constantine did not take this well and summarily dispatched Athanasius to Trier, his first exile. Athanasius was not one to be reduced to a functionary, and he was not. He desired and sought Constantine's support for Nicene orthodoxy and wanted the emperor to judge in his favor against his Meletian and Arian enemies. But if Constantine failed to render a just verdict, Athanasius had a clean conscience about defying the emperor, just as he defied councils that were stacked against him. His relations with Constantine's successor, Constantius, were even sharper. [70] In a remarkable rebuke to the emperor, he demanded to know "what concern the emperor had" with a judgment "passed by bishops." "When," he protested, "did a judgment of the church receive its validity from the emperor, or rather when was his decree ever recognized by the church?" [71] One is tempted to say, "In 325, don't you remember?" Perhaps the bishop had forgotten Nicaea, or perhaps he worked himself into a rhetorical froth. Or, perhaps, these questions expressed his own understanding of what was actually happening in 325. Even in 325, he did not think of the emperor as the leader of Christ's church.

After Constantine's death, Athanasius had to confront a Roman gover-

---

he had already done so. Yoder argues that in a Constantinian system the church is reduced to a chaplaincy, "part of the power structure itself." He admits that chaplains can be more or less faithful; critics and even radicals have found their way into king's palaces. But so long as the chaplain is dependent on the ruler financially and administratively and so long as he owes his position to the ruler, he does not have a "properly ecclesiastical base within the people 'served,'" and under such circumstances the chaplain's radicalism can only go as far as "the elasticity of the ruler's tolerance" permits (ibid., pp. 138, 210, n. 8).

[69]Drake, *Constantine and the Bishops*, p. 7; this incident is a touchstone scene in Drake's account of Constantine's relation with the bishops.

[70]Barnes, *Athanasius and Constantine*.

[71]From Athanasius *History of the Arians*, quoted in Michael Gaddis, *There Is No Crime for Those Who Have Christ: Religious Violence in the Christian Roman Empire* (Berkeley: University of California Press, 2005), p. 77.

nor in Libya whose life, by Basil of Caesarea's account, was "marked by cruelty and crime." He had been persecuting Christians, and Basil wrote in a letter to Athanasius that the heavenly Judge would repay the persecuting governor with similar scourges. Basil promised Athanasius that he would publicize the man's crimes so that "he shall be held by all as abominable, cut off from fire, water and shelter."[72] Given Athanasius's previous dealings with Meletians and Arians, this leaves one with disquieted suspicions, but it also makes it evident that the church had lost none of its capacity for criticism.

Athanasius did not write any treatises of political theology, but his *Life of Anthony* was arguably an early counter to Constantinianism. Not only did he record Anthony's insistence that Constantine was no more than a man and that "Christ is the only true and eternal Emperor," but he also laid out an alternative way of life for Christians in a Constantinian system. Rather than conform to the standards of the political world, Athanasius implicitly urged, Christians were called to follow the ascetic example of humility found in Anthony. Athanasius's argument was not missed by later emperors, who, without leaving the palace, conformed their personal lives to Anthony's example.[73] Eugene Rosenstock-Huessy claimed that St. Francis won political vindication when Lincoln walked unarmed into defeated Richmond. Anthony too had his political victory.

At his death, Constantine was buried in the Church of the Apostles in Constantinople, the thirteenth apostle, or even Jesus himself among the Twelve. Within a few generations, the church was redesigned and Constantine's remains were reinterred in an imperial mausoleum, some distance from the apostles. John Chrysostom got the point: emperors should be buried in a place that shows their real position in the church, not apostles but "doorkeepers."[74] Constantine's elevation to sainthood may seem the most blatant of capitulations, but it meant that Constantine was in a unique position among the emperors. His special personal charisma, deriving from his visions and dreams, was not expected to be repeated in later emperors. To say he was a saint was to say that he was

---

[72]Basil *Epistles* 61.
[73]Van Dam, *Roman Revolution*, pp. 327-29.
[74]Dagron, *Emperor and Priest*, p. 143.

not a typical emperor.[75] Later emperors took that hint too. Theodosius did not sit in on the deliberations of the Council of Ephesus, and he and Valentinian sent their representative, Candidianus, with the concession that he would "take no part whatsoever in the enquiries and proposals which would be made there on the subject of dogmas," since it would be "contrary to religion for someone not belonging to the list of holy bishops to meddle in the discussion of ecclesiastical matters." Constantine IV in the seventh century asked the pope to bring an end to the Monothelite controversy, declaring by the way that he had no desire to influence the bishops.[76]

During the reign of his son, Constantius, one of Constantine's primary advisers, Ossius, formulated a version of the two-swords theory that dominated church-state relations throughout the medieval period. Writing to Constantius, the nonagenarian bishop ordered him to

> stop [compulsion], and remember that you are a mortal man: fear the day of judgment and keep yourself pure for it. Do not intrude into the affairs of the Church, and do not give us advice about these matters, but rather receive instruction on them from us. God has given you kinship, but has entrusted us with what belongs to the Church. Just as the man who tries to steal your position contradicts God who has placed you there, so you should be aware of becoming guilty of a great offense by putting the affairs of the Church under your control. It is written: "Render to Caesar the things that are Caesar's and unto God those that are God's." . . . Hence neither do we [bishops] have the right to rule over the world nor do you, emperor, have the right to officiate in the church.[77]

Ossius was mild by comparison with Hilary of Poitiers, who wrote a series of letters to correct the wayward son of Constantine. When around 360 the Arian Constantius changed from harsh persecution of the orthodox to seductive flattery and favor, Hilary was incensed. Bring on the fires and axes, he said, but do not seduce the faithful:

> Now we are contending against a deceitful persecutor, against a flattering enemy, against an Antichrist Constantius, who does not scourge the back, but pampers the appetite; who does not issue proscriptions that lead us to

---

[75]Ibid.
[76]Ibid., pp. 296-97.
[77]Ossius, letter to Constantius, quoted in Roldanus, *Church in the Age of Constantine*, p. 98.

immortal life, but rich gifts that betray to endless death; does not send us from prison to liberty, but loads us inside the palace with honours that bribe to slavery; does not torture the body, but makes himself master of the heart; does not strike off heads with the sword, but slays the soul with gold; does not in public threaten with fire, but in secret is kindling for us a hell.

Christian though he may be, Constantius was worse than the pagan emperors:

To Thee, O Constantius, do I proclaim what I would have uttered before Nero, what Decius and Maximin would have heard from me. Thou art warring against God, raging against the Church, persecuting the Saints. Thou hatest those that preach Christ, thou art overthrowing religion, tyrant as thou art, no longer merely in things human but in things divine.[78]

These are not the words of a "Constantinian," nor of a pliant court chaplain. They are prophetic words. The harder you look for chaplains in the fourth-century church, the fewer there seem to be. That is because chaplains rarely make much difference in history. But it is also because bishops were not seduced or co-opted.

Far from demonstrating or securing the emperor's dominance of the church, Nicaea had the opposite effect:

What the Church discovered in the painful years after Nicaea was that its own inner tensions could not after all be resolved by a *deus ex machina* on the imperial throne; and that its relationship with the empire intensified rather than solved the question of its own distinctive identity and mission. It was unable to avoid reflection on its defining conditions, unable to avoid a conscious and critical reworking of its heritage, unable, in short, to avoid theology.[79]

Yoder's statements are generalizations, and intended as such. If they had no truth, they would not have any persuasive power. The problem is not that they are generalizations but that they are often misleading generalizations, particularly when they are applied to Constantine, generalizations that ignore counterevidence and counternarratives that would balance the

---

[78]Hilary of Poitier, quoted in John Gibson Casenove, *St. Hilary of Poitier and St. Martin of Tours*, The Fathers for English Readers (London: SPCK, 1883), pp. 75-76. See also Timothy D. Barnes, "Hilary of Poitiers on His Exile," *Vigiliae Christianae* 46, no. 2 (1992).
[79]Williams, *Arius*, pp. 236-37.

picture. It is simply not the case, as Yoder in his more unguarded moments implies, that the church was turned into a chaplaincy and lost its capacity to criticize. The church since Constantine has not seen an almost uninterrupted run of obsequious bishops, one neo-Constantinian followed by another. In regard to the church's stance over against power, the "Constantinian" moment of the fourth century was comparatively brief. Before the end of the fourth century, indeed by the middle of the century, once-awestruck bishops had recovered their voices if they ever lost them. They spoke truth to power, in words that Yoder and Hauerwas would be proud of. There was no Ambrose in Constantine's court, but the movement was already beginning that would produce one. Bishops had not so fully identified with the imperial palace that they lost the ability to call emperors to "modesty."[80]

THE EMPEROR AND THE QUEEN

"Kiss the Son," Psalm 2 exhorts, addressing itself to kings of the earth. Constantine kissed the Son, publicly acknowledging the Christian God as the true God and confessing Jesus as "our Savior."

For Constantine and the emperors who followed him, after kissing the Son and Lord, it made sense to do homage to Jesus by supporting his Queen, the church—building and adorning cathedrals, distributing funds for poor relief and hospitals, assisting the bishops to resolve their differences by calling and providing for councils. Constantine did not always show restraint. Sometimes he took over business that belonged to the King and Queen alone. But if we want to judge Constantine fairly, we have to recognize that the Queen often had issues. A queen's bodyguard ought to keep his hands off the queen, but what does he do when she turns harpy and starts scratching the face of her lady-in-waiting?

Once they noticed there was a Queen in their midst, some emperors and kings were often not satisfied with kissing the Son. Some could not keep their hands off her. Some wanted to steal a kiss or two from the Bride and seduce her. Plenty did, but it is important to notice the difference: adorning and protecting someone else's queen, even protecting her from

---

[80]Contra Yoder, *Royal Priesthood*. In saying all this, I do not pretend that I have "refuted" Yoder. Yoder's thesis is partly a historical thesis, but it is more fundamentally a thesis about eschatology and ecclesiology, and on those points I must defer discussion to later chapters.

herself, is not the same as raping her.

And the Queen had some responsibility to be true to her King. She was not supposed to be flattered by the blandishments of a Constantine or a Justinian or a Charlemagne. She was not to look wistfully at the emperor's court, as she too often did, and remodel her own courtiers into the image of the emperor's.[81] If the emperor tried to steal a kiss, he should be greeted with a good hard slap. That happened, as we have seen, but it did not always happen, and at times the Queen was only too happy to take a tumble with the emperor, provided he paid her handsomely for the pleasure— there's a good biblical word for that (see Revelation 17–18), and neither Wycliffe nor Dante nor Luther was afraid to use it.

All these were real, and often horrific, acts of unfaithfulness. But they do not imply a structural flaw. Once the emperor has kissed the Son, should he not honor the Son's Bride?

---

[81]J. H. W. G. Liebeschuetz (*Continuity and Change in Roman Religion* [Oxford: Oxford University Press, 1979], pp. 298-99) notes that the church was being "Romanized" as "more members of the ruling classes were converted" and "the social status of bishops and that of secular dignitaries began to converge." The church's organization mirrored "the imperial administration based on cities, provinces, and dioceses."

9

Seeds of Evangelical Law

Bloody Spectacles are not suitable for civil ease and domestic quiet.

CONSTANTINE, THEODOSIAN CODE 15.12.1

In the middle of the ancient Roman Forum was a small pond that the Romans knew as the Curtian Lake. Ancient historians disagreed about the origin of its name. In one version of the story, Curtius was a Sabine who abandoned his horse in what was then a swamp. Another version is more dramatic, and more revealing. Around 362 B.C., a growing chasm had opened in the middle of the Forum, threatening buildings and citizens. For moderns, this would be an engineering project; for ancient Romans, it was an omen. Priests consulted the Sibylline books and concluded that the earth would close if the Romans filled it with their most precious treasure, and added the promise that the earth would return the favor by giving the Romans an abundance of whatever they deposited. Citizens dutifully filled the gap with sacred cakes, silver and other treasures. Nothing worked.

Finally Marcus Curtius, already renowned as a warrior despite his youth, addressed the Senate. What is more precious, he asked, than the virtue of its armed soldiers (*an ullum magis Romanum bonum quam arma uirtusque esset*)? He promised that Rome would have a continuous supply of courage if one man would throw himself into the pit. Donning his armor, he raised his hands to the sky and lowered them to the gods of the earth, then mounted his horse and charged into the gap, devoting himself to the infernal gods (*se deuouisse*), horse and all. People threw animals, silver, cloth into the hole over him, and the earth immediately closed.[1] Everyone knows the rest of the story: the soil of Rome produced a consistent crop of military heroes.

Curtius was not the only Roman famed for devoting himself to the gods and Rome. Several decades after Curtius, the consul Decius was leading the Romans in battle against the Latins at Campania. The Romans were beginning to lose, and auspices were ambiguous. Decius consulted the pontiff Valerius, who told him to dress in a toga, cover his head and stand with one hand touching his chin. Standing on a sword, Decius invoked Janus, Jupiter and Mars, as well as new gods, gods of nation, the infernal gods and even the gods who ruled the enemy (*Diui, quorum est potestas nostrorum hostiumque*), and then declared that he was devoting himself with the legions to the chthonic deities (*legiones auxiliaeque hostium mecum Deis Manibus Tellurique deuoueo*). Throwing back his toga, he charged alone against the opposing army. Surprised at the attack, the Latins fell back and fled. Decius died, but earned the *laus,* the eternal praise of the Romans, because in a sort of substitutionary propitiation he had "averted onto himself alone all the menace and danger from the gods above and below" (*ab deis superis inferisque in se unum uertit*).[2] In offering himself to the gods, he was taking the Latin legions to death with him, so that Rome might live.

Suicide was an honorable escape from illness, tyranny, slavery or shame in the Roman world,[3] but Curtius and Decius were doing something more overtly religious than Cato the Younger when he messily killed himself to escape the prospect of life under King Caesar. Their deaths were not apolitical. On the contrary, both devoted themselves in service to Rome as much as to the gods. Whatever the general truth of Émile Durkheim's dictum "Society is god," it holds true for Rome: Rome is god. Shakespeare knew his Romans. Volumnia, the mother of Coriolanus, representing

---

[1]This version of the story is told by Livy, *From the Foundation of the City* 7.6. It is summarized in Alison Futrell, *Blood in the Arena: The Spectacle of Roman Power* (Austin: University of Texas Press, 1997), pp. 191-92, and Florence Dupont, *Daily Life in Ancient Rome,* trans. Christopher Woodall (Oxford: Blackwell, 1993), p. 74.

[2]Livy *From the Foundation of the City* 8.9-10; summarized in Futrell, *Blood in the Arena,* pp. 192-93.

[3]See now Catherine Edwards, *Death in Ancient Rome* (New Haven, Conn.: Yale University Press, 2007).

mother Rome, is a devouring mother with a taste for her children's blood.

ROMAN MICROCOSM

This complex of interlocking ideas—*devotio*, patriotism, self-sacrifice to chthonic deities—supported a military and political practice closely resembling human sacrifice.[4] And this is the set of ideas that Tertullian found at the basis of the Roman *munera*, the gladiatorial shows. Explaining that *munera* (duties, obligations) were so called because in combats "they rendered offices to the dead," he argued that they were simply a commuted form of human sacrifice. Earlier, it was believed that "the souls of the departed were appeased by human blood," and like Achilles at the funeral of Patroclus, Romans bought "captives or slaves of wicked disposition, and immolat[ed] them in their funeral obsequies." Over time, this seemed too barbaric, and someone decided to "throw the veil of pleasure over their iniquity." Thus they trained and armed men so that "they might learn to die," and at a funeral they killed them before the dead: "they alleviated death by murders." This is the way of all idolatry, Tertullian declared, since idolatry is "a sort of homage to the departed," humans deified by death, and thus spectacles are as idolatrous as the worship of the pagan temples.[5] Tertullian would not have been surprised to learn that the arena in Lugdunum was immediately adjoined by a temple complex.[6]

This connection between the *munera* and patriotic self-sacrifice reveals only one of the cultural and political values reinforced by the shows. Combats in the arena reenacted the founding sacrifice of Remus by Romulus. According to Rome's founding myth, Romulus "killed his brother for jumping over the walls which would define Rome and separate it from the non-Roman." For republican Romans like Cicero and Seneca, "the gladiator plays Remus to the normative aristocrat's Romulus: he is the brother

---

[4]Futrell, *Blood in the Arena*, pp. 184-203, carefully reviews all the evidence, concluding that "human sacrifice can be found in the oldest strata of Roman religious practices, used, as elsewhere, as a means of propitiating angered deities" (p. 205). George Heyman, *The Power of Sacrifice: Roman and Christian Discourses in Conflict* (Washington, D.C.: Catholic University of America Press, 2007), also connects *devotio* to sacrifice (pp. 180-84).

[5]Tertullian *De spectaculis* 12. Though not all modern historians make so direct a connection between human sacrifice and gladiatorial combats, most recognize that the shows originated as funeral games. See Carlin A. Barton, "The Scandal of the Arena," *Representations* 27 (1989); Futrell, *Blood in the Arena*, pp. 2-4, 10; Edwards, *Death in Ancient Rome*, p. 59.

[6]Futrell, *Blood in the Arena*, pp. 84-85.

who must be slain that an empire may be founded." Just as "the murder of Remus permanently establishes the validity of this boundary and secures the name of Rome for the city," so the death of the gladiator helps "to found the nobility of the *nobilis*."[7]

Further, the games provided an opportunity for Romans, at Rome and at the many amphitheaters throughout the empire, to see Rome on parade. The *maeniana* or levels of seating offered a public view of the hierarchy of Roman society and of the centers of power. Social classes were distinguished by their proximity to the games, with the senators occupying the "box seats" and members of other orders further back. Some priesthoods and other associations had their own sections of seating, but commoners had to settle in the back rows, with only the women behind them. At the games, the variegated social order of men was represented and distinguished visually and spatially from the homogenous collection of women.[8] Ovid noted the double spectacle: *Spectatum veniunt, veniunt spectentur ut ipsae*—"they come to a spectacle, they come to make a spectacle of themselves."[9]

Games were also political events. Prominently seated so his reactions to the show could be viewed, the emperor served as *editor*, or master of games, and decided the fate of the fighters. His presence at the games was an exercise of power just as surely as was his place at the head of a triumphal procession.[10] Crowds carefully monitored the emperor's behavior. If he answered correspondence (as Julius Caesar did) or heard appeals during the combats, he was criticized, but if, like Augustus, he enjoyed the games, he won the admiration of the crowd.[11] For perceptive emperors, the games

---

[7]Erik Gunderson, "The Ideology of the Arena," *Classical Antiquity* 15, no. 1 (1996): 139. Futrell (*Blood in the Arena*, p. 208) agrees that the *munus* "cloaks another foundation sacrifice in Rome's mythical history."

[8]Gunderson, "Ideology of the Arena," pp. 123-26; Futrell, *Blood in the Arena*.

[9]Ovid *Ars amatoria* 1.99.

[10]The more subtle impact of the games was to reinforce a specular notion of power within Roman society (Shadi Bartsch, *The Mirror of the Self: Sexuality, Self-Knowledge and the Gaze in the Early Roman Empire* [Chicago: University of Chicago Press, 2006]; Florence Dupoint, *L'acteur-roi: Le théâtre dans le Rome antique* [Paris: Societé d'édition, 1985], pp. 19-40). Power flowed from spectacle; to have power was to be the object of an adoring or fearful gaze, or to be the subject of the gaze, able to fix eyes on others and subject them to your scrutiny. In the colosseum the emperor was on stage, the object for thousands of fans. He exercised power by being seen in glory, in awesome splendor.

[11]Gunderson, "Ideology of the Arena," examines the reviews of Suetonius and others concerning the emperors' conduct at games; see also Fergus Millar, *The Emperor in the Roman World*, 2nd

provided an opportunity to display the *levitas popularis*, the "common touch" so important in a principate that still claimed to be rooted in republican values.[12] At the same time, the games provided one of the few opportunities the people still had to voice their grievances in the hearing of the emperor. Chants about oppressive taxation or the high price of bread mingled with cheers for favorite fighters.[13]

The arena was also an instrument of imperial policy in the provinces. The spread of Roman power was marked architecturally by the spread of amphitheaters. Not only were the arenas—built in a distinctively Roman style—visual reminders of the sometimes distant power of the emperor, but the bloody combats that took place on the sands reminded viewers of Rome's willingness to use violence and gave restless provincials pause. Arenas embodied the empire; the gladiatorial shows and their amphitheaters were the "imperial process in microcosm."[14]

Gladiatorial shows captured the very "essence of *Romanitas*."[15] Gladiators were often slaves, and socially despised, yet at the same time aristocrats recognized a common bond between the gladiators' pursuit of glory and their own. War was one of the main arenas for aristocratic advance, so that the bloody sand of the literal arena mirrored the bloody sands where aristocratic soldiers fought for the empire. Despite legal bans, some aristocrats even went so far as to join the gladiators in the coliseum.[16] *Romanitas* was a masculine ideal, and Pliny the Younger commended Trajan's games because there was "nothing spineless or flabby, nothing that would soften or break the manly spirit of the audience," but rather "a spectacle that inspired the audience to noble wounds and to despise death, since even in the bodies of slaves and criminals the love of praise and desire for victory could be seen."[17] For Cicero, the games played on the dynamics of *dignitas* and *ignominia* to exhort Romans to *devotio:* "If the state [*res publicae*] . . . has come to its moment of truth, let us do as worthy gladiators do to die with honour, let us, the leaders of all

---

ed. (London: Duckworth, 1992), pp. 368-75.

[12]Futrell, *Blood in the Arena*, p. 46, with note (p. 245).

[13]Ibid., pp. 45-46.

[14]Ibid., pp. 209-10. Futrell dedicates much of her book to examining the arenas themselves—where they were built and by whom, how they were funded and by whom.

[15]Ibid., p. 207.

[16]Gunderson, "Ideology of the Arena," p. 141.

[17]Pliny the Younger *Panegyric* 33.1, quoted in Barton, "Scandal of the Arena," p. 7.

peoples, fall with dignity rather than submit with shame."[18]

Cicero, and Seneca even more, found not only politico-religious but philosophical meaning in the combats.[19] Though often cited as a philosophical critic of the shows, Seneca, his fantasies filled with tragedies of erotic violence, never mounted a criticism of the shows as such. In a famous letter, he warned Lucilius to "stay away" because he would "either be corrupted by the multitude, or, if you show disgust, be hated by them." He admitted to being "bitterly disappointed" when he attended the games "hoping for a little wit and humor." He found "mere butchery." The morning show was good enough. Men were thrown to lions and bears, but in the afternoon the crowd became bestial. Though "the slayer was kept fighting until he could be slain," still the crowed cried out, "Kill him! flog him! burn him alive. . . . Why is he such a coward? Why won't he rush on the steel? Why does he fall so meekly? Why won't he die willingly?"[20]

Seneca was a critic not of violent spectacles but only of useless violence. Violent spectacles could, he believed, be socially and even philosophically beneficial. Identifying more with the defeated than with the winner, he found the gladiator a model of courage in adversity, of dignified death. "The gladiator considers it a disgrace to be matched with an inferior and knows that he who has conquered without danger has conquered without glory." Philosophers face similar dangers: "Fortune does the same; she seeks out the bravest for her opponents, and passes over some with contempt. She attacks the most unyielding and upright against whom she may exert her strength. She tried Mucius by fire, Fabricius by poverty, Rutilius by exile, Regulus by tortures, Socrates by poison, Cato by death. Misfortune alone reveals great examples."[21] Like the gladiator, human beings are thrown *sine missione* into an arena of combat from which there is no escape, save death. Philosophers aim, like gladiators, to make their death a brave one.

Gladiators were "*both* a version of the Stoic *sapiens*, offering a metaphor

---

[18]Quoted in Edwards, *Death in Ancient Rome*, p. 70.

[19]For Cicero, see ibid., pp. 69-72.

[20]Seneca *Epistle* 7.

[21]Seneca *On Providence* 3.4. On Seneca and the games generally, see Pierre Cagniart, "The Philosopher and the Gladiator," *Classical World* 93, no. 6 (2000): 607-18; Gunderson, "Ideology of the Arena," pp. 135-38; Barton, "Scandal of the Arena," p. 13; Edwards, *Death in Ancient Rome*, pp. 72-77.

of apathy, independence, and contempt for the opinions of society, *and* an expression of intense interaction with, and acceptance of, others, a longing for esteem and appreciation, in other words, glory."[22] Spectacles lent the powerless a sense of power, gave the curious something to watch, provided a cathartic outlet for violence, and encouraged the fundamental virtues of Roman citizenship—courage, patriotism, self-sacrifice. They gave emperors opportunities to display their godlike munificence and magnificence, as well as their potential for violence, while at the same time sharing the enthusiasm of commoners for high-stakes competition. Gladiators had something for everyone. The shows were as basic to Rome as sacrifice.[23] Rome *was* the arena, and the arena was Rome. What would the empire be without it?

CONSTANTINE AND THE SPECTACLES

With Constantine, Rome had a chance to find out. In 325, he issued an edict concerning spectacles. "Bloody spectacles are not suitable for civil ease and domestic quiet," he declared, and therefore "since we have proscribed gladiators, those who have been accustomed to be sentenced to such work as punishment for their crimes, you should cause them to serve in the mines, so that they may be punished without shedding their blood" (CTh 15.12.1). The emperor's hedging in the first sentence is intriguing. The prohibition is not absolute but is fitting for a time of domestic ease (*in otio civili et domestica quiete non placent*), which leaves open the possibility that Constantine thought the games might be fitting in another time and condition. The final clauses prohibit condemnation to the arena as a criminal punishment, replacing it with bloodless exile to the mines, and the law has been interpreted as if Constantine's *only* intent were to outlaw confinement to the arena as a punishment, not to outlaw the games themselves.[24] Eusebius took this law as an absolute prohibition, and that is what

---

[22]Carlin Barton, *The Sorrows of the Ancient Romans: The Gladiator and the Monster* (Princeton, N.J.: Princeton University Press, 1993), p. 39.

[23]Robert Dodaro (*Christ and the Just Society in the Thought of Augustine* [Cambridge: Cambridge University Press, 2004], p. 50) notes that Augustine discerned connections between priests and actors, shows and sacrifice. So too Tatian (quoted in Maria-Zoe Petroupoulou, *Animal Sacrifice in Ancient Greek Religion, Judaism and Christianity, 100 BC to AD 200* [Oxford: Oxford University Press, 2008], p. 250).

[24]This is the view of David S. Potter, *The Roman Empire at Bay, AD 180-395*, Routledge History of the Ancient World (London: Routledge, 2004), pp. 428-29. He argues that Constantine

the law actually says. If so, Constantine's views on the shows had shifted over time. In 315 he had issued a rescript (CTh 9.18.1) condemning kidnappers to the beasts or to gladiatorial schools, but a decade later he had become disgusted by the whole business and prohibited gladiators as a part of a reorganization of public entertainments.[25] It is notable that there was no arena in Constantinople; instead, a hippodrome was to be the place of public entertainments. This was a major departure from imperial custom.

CONSTANTINE AS LEGISLATOR

Constantine's legislation on gladiatorial shows illustrates some important dimensions of the impact of his reign on Roman government, law and society. Constantine was an active legislator, responsible for about three hundred extant laws as well as others that we have lost.[26] Like the laws of other Roman emperors, these take various forms. Some are *decreta,* oral decisions made by the emperor in a court case, some of which became widely known but, so far as we know, were not published. Others were edicts initiated by the emperor to address a particular problem in the empire, or some part of the empire, and published in the affected provinces and cities. Others were "rescripts" composed in answer to questions com-

---

was "simply abolishing the penalty of *damnatio ad ludos,*" which, he points out, is not a sentence to become a gladiator but to be "condemned to fight other humans to the death." He also notes that Constantine does not take the opportunity to abolish *damnatio ad bestias,* which would be expected "if he were indeed reforming the penal code to eliminate all penalties that might be thought offensive to Christian sentiment." This law, he says, was only a "minor step." Potter also notes (p. 683 n. 134) that Constantine granted Hispellium the right to have gladiatorial shows. Finally, Constantius prohibits soldiers and men of palatine rank from participating in the shows at Rome (CTh 15.12.2), which assumes that the shows were still being held in the capital. In the same passage where he records Constantine's prohibition of pagan sacrifice, Eusebius (*Life of Constantine* 4.25) claims that he made it illegal "to pollute the cities with the sanguinary combats of gladiators." Potter, to the contrary, says that is the import of the first part of the edict (Potter is forced to say that the law "belies the force of the opening clause," p. 429), the beginning of whose second sentence he translates as "Since therefore we altogether forbid those who would be accustomed to receive this status and sentence, to become gladiators." My colleague Tim Griffith tells me that the Latin will not bear this meaning and that the edict explicitly outlaws gladiatorial shows. Even if Potter is correct, however, Constantine's legislation would damage the *munera,* since gladiators were frequently condemned criminals.

[25]Timothy D. Barnes, *Constantine and Eusebius* (Cambridge, Mass.: Harvard University Press, 1981), p. 53.

[26]Christopher Bush Coleman, *Constantine the Great and Christianity,* Columbia Studies in History, Economics and Public Law 146 (New York: Columbia University Press, 1914), p. 26, available in full at Google Books. T. G. Elliott (*The Christianity of Constantine the Great* [Scranton, Penn.: University of Scranton Press, 1996], p. 97), estimates that we have 420 laws from Constantine.

ing from provincial governors and were published in the place of origin.[27] Most of the Constantine's legislation comes from the period after 323-324 when he assumed sole imperial power in the empire.

Constantine's legislation was collected by the later Christian emperors, Theodosius, who commissioned the codification of Roman law, and Justinian, who commissioned both a codification of the law and a *Digest* and *Institutes* for lawyers, judges and law students.[28] The Codices include only the strictly legislative portions of edicts and rescripts and leave out preambles that offer the rationale and explain the intent of a particular law. As a result, the Codices give a somewhat distorted portrait of imperial legislation. Still, it is far better than nothing, and more complete versions of some laws found their way into the works of Eusebius and Lactantius.

Constantine's legislation is uneven in both substance and style.[29] It has been charged that some of his laws were composed in haste, even in anger, though the tone of some laws may be no more than evidence that Constantine had mastered the rhetorical bombast fashionable in his time. His sarcasm about the details of the law is so pervasive that the Codices attribute to Constantine virtually any law that manifests this "Constantinian" tone. In substance, the legislation is not consistent. In one law he shuts down the imperial cult, but in another he permits a city in Bithynia to erect a temple in his honor, with the limitation that no images should be erected or venerated there.[30]

Is there any consistent pattern here? Did Constantine have a legislative agenda? More specifically, did his legislation have the effect of incorporating Christian principles into law? Did his laws make any difference in forming a Christian political order?

No, says Ramsay MacMullen. Constantine's legislation, he argues, shows two main features: obsession with sexual crimes and increased bru-

---

[27]A. H. M. Jones, *The Later Roman Empire, 284-602: A Social, Economic and Administrative Survey*, 2 vols. (Baltimore: Johns Hopkins University Press, 1964), 1:471-73; see also Simon Corcoran, *The Empire of the Tetrarchs: Imperial Pronouncements and Government, AD 284-324*, rev. ed., Oxford Classical Monographs (Oxford: Oxford University Press, 2000), p. 2.

[28]The Codex Theodosianus is available in Latin online at <http://ancientrome.ru/ius/library/codex/theod>, and an English translation of the Codex Justianius at <http://uwacadweb.uwyo.edu/blume&justinian/default.asp>.

[29]Coleman, *Constantine the Great and Christianity*, p. 25, says that he was "not a systematic nor a careful legislator."

[30]Ramsay MacMullen, "What Difference Did Christianity Make?" *Historia* 35, no. 3 (1986): 329-32.

tality in punishment.[31] Constantine's sexual legislation of April 326 demonstrates the presence of both of the alleged obsessions. "Constantine totally forbade married men to have concubines. He restricted the right to bring a charge of adultery to husbands, fathers, brothers, uncles, and cousins. He laid down that when a female ward grows up and wishes to marry, her guardian must furnish proof that she is a virgin inviolate; if the guardian has seduced her, he shall be deported and all his property confiscated." Sexual crimes were punished severely. "Constantine decreed that rapists should be punished by being burned alive, and he disallowed any appeal against the sentence." If a man abducted "a girl against her parents' wishes, he could no longer marry her, even if she was willing; on the contrary, her acquiescence rendered her too liable to be burned alive." Accessories to elopement were also in danger: "nurses who encouraged girls to elope were to have boiling lead poured down their throats, while anyone of either sex who aided the lover would also be burned alive." In short, he "treated seduction like a ritual impurity which can in no way be cleansed." Parents of seduced virgins who tried to hide their daughter's disgrace were "liable to deportation," and "even a virgin who was violently raped deserved punishment, since she could have stayed safely at home."[32]

There were some ameliorations of punishment. Crucifixion was outlawed, apparently in respect to the cross of Jesus that had given Constantine his throne, and after Constantine no one appears to have been condemned to death by wild animals.[33] But many of his decrees suggest a horror show. Corrupt bureaucrats were to have their hands cut off by the sword, tax evaders were put to death "with exquisite tortures," informers "shall be strangled in the very throat, and the tongue of envy cut off from its roots and plucked out" (CTh 10.10.2). The most colorful punishment was Constantine's re-

---

[31]Ibid. See also similar judgments in Ramsay MacMullen, *Constantine* (London: Croom Helm, 1987), p. 203; A. H. M. Jones, *Constantine and the Conversion of Europe* (Toronto: University of Toronto Press, 1978), p. 188.

[32]Barnes, *Constantine and Eusebius*, p. 220. On the sexual legislation, see Charles Matson Odahl, *Constantine and the Christian Empire* (London: Routledge, 2004), p. 204. Hermann Dorries, *Constantine the Great*, trans. Roland Bainton (New York: Harper Torchbooks, 1972), p. 213, speaks of the irresponsible sexuality of the age. Barnes describes the legislation as "morbid and unwholesome" and immediately connects it to the mysterious events surrounding the execution of Constantine's son Crispus and the empress Fausta. On Crispus and Fausta, see chapter 10 below.

[33]A panegyrist in 307 states that Constantine himself condemned Frankish captives to the beasts after a victory.

vival of the antiquated practice of tying an offender in a leather sack with snakes and throwing the sack into water to drown.[34] After Constantine, death penalties increased throughout the fourth century.

As we saw in chapter six, however, it is not entirely clear whether these punishments were ever enforced or whether they were ever intended to be enforced. Imperial legislation often functioned more as moral exhortation than as a code, and Constantine might well have been expressing his disgust at sexual criminals, informants and corrupt bureaucrats rather than instructing his agents to initiate a bloodbath. Even the focus on sexual legislation is not as obviously wrongheaded as it appears to us. For moderns, sexual activity is a purely private matter, so long as the parties are consenting adults; public law, we think, ought to have nothing to say about seduction, homosexual activity and the like. But this was hardly the perspective of Constantine or his age. Not only did they recognize that sexuality was a matter of public interest, but Constantine was faced with a sexual culture that would make even jaded postmoderns blush.

More generally, Craig Carter charges that Constantine squandered the opportunity to "promote religious liberty and increase respect for human life and dignity."[35] Other critics have complained that Constantine permitted slavery to continue, did little to reform law in a Christian direction and generally continued imperial business as usual. Yoder muses yearningly on the lost opportunity. He can imagine a genuinely Christian Constantine. If Constantine's faith had been stronger, he "would be just as free as anyone else to take risks in faith."[36] Elsewhere Yoder rightly argues that no one ever has to deal with a "state as such" but only with particular states. For the early Christians, he says, there could only be a "polarity between Caesar and the God of the Bible." Caesar's empire was founded on idolatry, was prideful, demanded oaths and killed, and the early Christians totally rejected the system and operated by a "total dualism" that was practical rather than theoretical. Caesar was inescapable, and his "idolatry, violence, circuses, public abuse of minorities and enemies, feeding people to the lions for the crowd's amusement, war, and empire" were all "one

---

[34]MacMullen, "What Difference," pp. 333-34.
[35]Craig A. Carter, *Rethinking Christ and Culture: A Post-Christendom Perspective* (Grand Rapids: Brazos, 2006), p. 96.
[36]John Howard Yoder, *The Priestly Kingdom: Social Ethics as Gospel* (Notre Dame, Ind.: University of Notre Dame Press, 1984), p. 146.

package."[37] Still, from the beginning Christians acknowledged the presence of the state and that it had a role in protecting the innocent and punishing the wicked, and by the time of Tertullian, the notion of "good government" was becoming "thinkable." What would good government have looked like? It would be a Roman empire that "would not persecute Christians, in which they would have their say and rights, and in which the laws could be judged from their perspective."

It would have looked, in fact, a lot like the government that Constantine established.

CHRISTIAN LEGISLATION?

While he almost never cited explicit Christian or biblical justification for a law,[38] Constantine did reform the law in a Christian direction in several respects. Most important, of course, he solidified Christianity's status as a legal religion and granted the church the exemptions enjoyed by pagan priesthoods and religious groups. Clergy were exempted from taxes, and a number of Constantine's laws included exhortations to pagans to abandon their false religion and sacrifices in order to worship the true God. Applying biblical precedent to the "Lord's Day" but using ambiguous terminology, he established the *dies Solis* as a day of rest, especially rest from lawsuits since the courts were closed. In his own palace, he honored the day with Christian worship.[39] He not only abolished crucifixion but also prohibited torture that would damage the face, justifying this law by with the biblically based argument that a scar on the face does damage to the beauty of God's image in man. This has been mocked, and it is a somewhat trivial example; doesn't plucking out the tongue or cutting off the hands also

---

[37]John Howard Yoder, *Christian Attitudes to War, Peace and Revolution*, ed. Theodore J. Koontz and Andy Alexis-Baker (Grand Rapids: Brazos, 2009), pp. 43-48.

[38]Alan Watson (*The Spirit of Roman Law* [Athens: University of Georgia Press, 1995], p. 45) points out the more curious fact that Justinian's *Institutes* rarely mentions God or Jesus either, even though Justinian insisted that law involves "knowledge of things divine and human" (CJ 1.1.1).

[39]Eusebius saw this as a *Christian* calendrical change, and Christians in the empire drew the same conclusion; even some magistrates took to naming the day as *hiera kuriake*, the "Lord's day," a designation that found its way into a number of European languages (Potter, *Roman Empire at Bay*, p. 427; see also Dorries, *Constantine the Great*, pp. 118-29; Odahl, *Constantine and the Christian Empire*, p. 173). On the development of the week in Roman culture, see Eviatar Zerubavel, *The Seven Day Cycle: The History and Meaning of the Week* (New York: Free Press, 1985), pp. 20-25, 45-46.

damage the image of God? But it shows that at least in this one instance Constantine was thinking about Christian teaching when he legislated.[40]

Though there is no overt Christian reference in the edict concerning spectacles, in all likelihood this legislation was inspired by Christians, who had long complained about their cruelty. Pagans voiced objections as well, arguing that the games encouraged the baser members of society toward irrationalism.[41] Constantine may have known of these arguments, but it is likely that whatever inclinations he had against combat were reinforced by Christian polemics. Lactantius said that a man "who reckons it a pleasure, that a man, though justly condemned, should be slain in his sight, pollutes his conscience as much as if he should become a spectator and a sharer of a homicide which is secretly committed." But Romans "call these sports in which human blood is shed." Fellow-feeling with other humans has departed when men watch a show and think "they are amusing themselves with sport, being more guilty than all those whose bloodshedding they esteem a pleasure."[42]

Lactantius was drawing on a long tradition. Pungent as always, Tertullian asked, "Why, the authors and managers of the spectacles, in that very respect with reference to which they highly laud the charioteers, and actors, and wrestlers, and those most loving gladiators, to whom men prostitute their souls, women too their bodies, slight and trample on them, though for their sakes they are guilty of the deeds they reprobate." The contradiction was obvious: "they doom them to ignominy and the loss of their rights as citizens, excluding them from the Curia, and the rostra, from senatorial and equestrian rank, and from all other honours as well as certain distinctions," yet at the same time "have pleasure in those whom yet they punish." While "they put all slights on those," they also "award their approbation; they magnify the art and brand the artist." To Tertul-

---

[40]I concur with Barnes, *Constantine and Eusebius*, p. 51: "Constantine . . . began to mold Roman law and the attitudes of Roman society in a Christian direction." See also A. D. Lee, "Decoding Late Roman Law," *Journal of Roman Studies* 92 (2002); Michele Renee Salzman, "The Evidence for the Conversion of the Roman Empire to Christianity in Book 16 of the 'Theodosian Code,'" *Historia* 42, no. 3 (1993), notes the various ways in which post-Constantinian legislation encouraged conversion.

[41]Thomas Wiedemann, *Emperors and Gladiators* (London: Routledge, 1992), chap. 4. Weidemann calls these arguments "elitist" and concludes that no pagan opposition to the arena was strictly "humanitarian."

[42]Lactantius *Divine Institutes* 6.20.

lian it was an outrage "to blacken a man on account of the very things which make him meritorious in their eyes!"[43]

Cyprian likewise complained that the shows made killing into an art. Games are cannibalistic feasts, in which gladiators "are prepared, that blood may gladden the lust of cruel eyes. The body is fed with stronger food, and the vigorous mass of limbs is enriched with brawn and muscle, that the wretch fattened for punishment may die a harder death. Man is slaughtered that man may be gratified, and the skill that is best able to kill is an exercise and an art." Crime itself is bad enough, but gladiatorial shows not only commit but teach and train in crime. "Training is undergone to acquire the power to murder, and the achievement of murder is its glory." Gladiators "of ripe age, of sufficiently beautiful person, clad in costly garments," are only being "adorned for a voluntary death." When they fight with beasts, it is "not for their crime, but for their madness." Family members watch and cheer: "Fathers look on their own sons; a brother is in the arena, and his sister is hard by; and although a grander display of pomp increases the price of the exhibition, yet, oh shame! even the mother will pay the increase in order that she may be present at her own miseries. And in looking upon scenes so frightful and so impious and so deadly, they do not seem to be aware that they are parricides with their eyes."[44] When he decreed that blood shows should be ended, Constantine was probably drawing on teaching such as this.

Tracing effects, even unintentional effects, is often more important than identifying the sources of Constantine's legislation.[45] Wherever he picked up his hostility to gladiatorial shows and it may be simply from his own personal revulsion at needless bloodletting, a common enough trait among military menhis legislation struck at an institution that, as we have

---

[43]Tertullian *De spectaculis* 22.

[44]Cyprian *Ad Donatum* 7.

[45]Judith Evans Grubbs, *Law and Family in Late Antiquity: The Emperor Constantine's Marriage Legislation* (Oxford: Oxford University Press, 1999), is indispensable but suffers from an insistent, even pedantic focus on the "influence" of Christianity on Constantine's marriage legislation. This misses the bigger picture that she herself glimpses, as from a great distance through heavy fog. She concludes that Constantine encouraged the church's growth as an alternative social organization; he helped the church be the church, rather than attempting to Christianize Rome by legislation (319). Surely, though, empowering and funding an already well-organized Christian counterpolity counts as a Christianizing program, and one that Constantine pursued *legislatively*. Did Constantine *intend* to Christianize the empire in this fashion? No one can know, and no one needs to know: his intentions did not determine the outcome.

seen, embodied many of the political, religious and cultural values of the empire. When Constantine outlawed gladiatorial contests, he may have believed he was doing no more than opposing the decadence of bloody spectacles. But his law had much wider effects on Roman culture. Gladiators continued to perform for some time after Constantine, and Christian emperors were still legislating against them into the middle of the fifth century. Already with Constantine, however, we see the beginning of a revolution in public spectacle, and that revolution, perhaps unwittingly, subverted much of what made Rome Rome. Not only did he outlaw bloody entertainments, but by eliminating one of the main public venues for the display and inculcation of *Romanitas* he began to chip away at the pagan civilization that had preceded him. It is too much to say that Constantine's legislation "Christianized" public entertainments, but he clearly de-Romanized them. Rome had been baptized; now it needed to begin the slow work of Christian *paideia*.

Like his legislation against pagan sacrifice, Constantine's legislation against spectacles created an "atmosphere" of public disapproval and played its part in forming a world without sacrifice.

MARRIAGE AND FAMILY

Whatever his intentions, and whatever his sources of inspiration, Constantine's legislation, and the legislation of the Christian emperors who followed him, on sex, women, marriage and divorce strengthened the church and improved the lot of women in the empire. Under the laws of Augustus, the unmarried were penalized. To encourage a restoration of the traditional Roman family, Augustus decreed that the unmarried could not bequeath an inheritance to anyone who was not within six degrees of relation, childless couples could pass on only half of their property in inheritance, and spouses were allowed to pass on only one-tenth of their wealth to the other, unless they were within six degrees of relation. Married men, by contrast, were given preference for senatorial rank and civic offices, and women with more than three children were permitted to carry out their financial affairs without the oversight of a guardian.[46]

Constantine reversed the Augustan policy, removing penalties against

---

[46]Ibid., p. 103.

the celibate and the childless by treating everyone as "married" before the law and every married couple as having children. Unmarried men and women thus could pass on an inheritance to whomever they pleased, and parents could pass on a full inheritance to their children. Constantine did not change Augustus's restrictions on inheritance from spouse to spouse, however. Constantine's marriage legislation has often been cited as a clear example of Constantine's Christianizing legislation, since it extended the privileges of married Roman citizens to celibates, who would mostly have been Christian. That may not have been the intention of the law. But its effects did assist the church. Not only did it enable celibates to retain property rights, but by changing the laws of inheritance, it made it easier for Christians to grant bequests to the church.[47]

Other marriage legislation extended the rights of women. Established by Romulus and reinforced by the Twelve Tables, the traditional Roman *patria potestas* granted the *paterfamilias* "unfettered legal right" over his wife and children, including the power of life and death.[48] Male privileges in sexuality and property associated with the *patria potestas* were already weakening in the early empire, but Constantine's legislation undermined them further, granting women significantly improved status.

The legal deprivations of women were manifold. Women often married in their teens to men decades older, but under previous legislation when their husband died they were required to marry within two years of the death or forfeit all their property. Women who retained property and inheritances were forbidden to manage the marital property themselves. During the second and third centuries, jurists admitted that the law prohibiting widows from managing their own property was merely customary, but only under Constantine did the rules begin to change. He passed a law that "permitted women of good character over the age of eighteen to control their own property, although they still seem to have had to retain legal guardians." By the end of the century, women had gained the same rights as men over their property, and the *tutela mulierum* had disappeared completely. A law of 414 declared that "all

---

[47]Ibid., pp. 120-23, 137.
[48]Alan Watson, *The Law of the Ancient Romans* (Dallas: Southern Methodist University, 1970), pp. 11-12.

contracts made by women be considered as binding."[49]

Divorce laws also worked against women. Men were legally permitted to divorce wives at will, and they frequently satisfied their sexual urges with slaves and prostitutes.[50] Men frequently gave up one wife to secure a more socially advantageous marriage or a new wife of proven fertility. Constantine denounced divorce "for trivial reasons" and specified the conditions under which a man could sue for divorce. During the second century, women had gained the right to initiate divorce, and Constantine confirmed that right, with restrictions.[51] Women were allowed to sue for divorce from a murderer, tomb robber or *medicamentarius*—Mathew Kuefler thinks this means "an abortionist or poisoner." A double standard remained.[52] While men could divorce wives for adultery, a woman could not divorce a *muliercularius*, which Kuefler suggests is "a man who visited prostitutes," which did not come under the legal definition of adultery. Still, the law treated extramarital sexual dalliances as breaches of marriage.[53] Under Constantine, penalties for unjustified divorce were sharpened. Earlier, a man who divorced his wife without cause would lose her dowry. Under Constantine's legislation, a woman could face deportation, and an ex-husband was forbidden to marry again.[54] Significantly, Julian bowed to pressure from the Roman nobility, and Constantine's divorce legislation was overturned during his reign.

Despite remaining inequities, Constantine's legislation undermined

---

[49]Mathew Kuefler, *The Manly Eunuch: Masculinity, Gender Ambiguity and Christian Ideology in Late Antiquity* (Chicago: University of Chicago Press, 2001), p. 73.

[50]Ibid., pp. 70-87.

[51]Grubbs (*Law and Family*, pp. 256-57) claims that "at no time in the pre-Constantinian Empire had Roman law attempted to restrict the right of husbands or wives in general to terminate their marriages." This oversimplifies the situation. Marriage in Roman law was of two types, *cum manu* and *sine manu*. Under the first the wife came under the oversight of her husband as *paterfamilias*, while in the second she remained under the oversight of her own father's *patria potestas* (Watson, *Law of the Ancient Romans*, p. 32). Marriage *sine manu* was well established by the second century B.C., and sometime in the early first century B.C., in Cicero's time, *cum manu* marriage became very rare (ibid., p. 33). A woman married *sine manu* was never under her husband's *potestas* to begin with and could divorce only through her father, who sent his son-in-law the messenger who delivered the *repudium*. Until the mid-second century A.D., though, women married *cum manu* had difficulty divorcing (Susan Treggiari, "Divorce Roman Style: How Easy and How Frequent Was It?" in *Marriage, Divorce and Children in Ancient Rome*, ed. Beryl Rawson [Oxford: Oxford University Press, 1996], pp. 31-46).

[52]Grubbs, *Law and Family*, pp. 255-56.

[53]Kuefler, *Manly Eunuch*, p. 76.

[54]Watson, *Law of the Ancient Romans*, p. 36.

some of the double standard of Roman sexual custom. Sex with slaves was discouraged in strong terms, and Constantine also appears to have been the first to legislate against rape.[55] More deeply, Constantine's legislation embedded the new Christian masculinity within the Roman legal system. Roman men had always expressed their masculinity in sexual prowess, victory in battle, political power. By removing the legal penalties against the unmarried, Constantine signaled that sexual potency was no longer the test of manhood, nor an essential duty of citizenship. By outlawing gladiatorial games, he showed that violence was not the way of manhood. Sexual self-control—something on which Constantine seems to have prided himself personally—was encouraged by the state.

CONSERVATIVE INNOVATOR

Constantine appears, especially in his legislation, to have been an impatient man. He was certainly impatient with the technicalities, exceptions, and tiny twists and turns of the law, and this accounts for the sometimes sarcastic tone of his legislation. No piece of legislation illustrates this tendency better than that concerning wills. Wills were cumbersome for most Romans. Seven witnesses were required, and the one making the will had to seal a written text to authenticate the will. Exceptions were made for soldiers, whose wills were valid without formal confirmation by witnesses and who could therefore declare a binding will on their deathbed. Constantine's legislation on wills extended the military exception to citizens of the empire generally,[56] and did so in a way that made it clear that he disliked the way earlier laws allowed the wishes of the dying to be overridden if someone forgot to use the proper formula:

> Since it is undignified that testaments and last wishes of decedents should become invalid through useless technicalities, we deem it best to dispense with formalities, the value of which is imaginary, and in instituting an heir no particular form of words is necessary, whether that is done by imperative, direct or indirect words. 1. For it makes no difference whether it is stated "I make an heir," or "I institute," or "wish," or "I charge," or "I desire,"

[55]Kuefler, *Manly Eunuch*, pp. 83-84.

[56]This is how Barnes characterizes the legislation: Timothy D. Barnes, "Constantine After Seventeen Hundred Years: The *Cambridge Companion,* the New York Exhibition and a Recent Biography," *International Journal of the Classical Tradition* 14 (2008).

or "let him be," or "he will be"; but an appointment should be valid, by whatever expressions or by whatever form of words that is made, provided only that the intention is thereby made clear. No solemnity of words which are uttered, perchance by a half-dead and stuttering tongue is necessary. 2. The necessity of use of customary words is, accordingly, dispensed with in making a will, and persons who desire to arrange their affairs, may do so by writing their will on any material suitable for documents by using any words they wish. (CJ 6.23.15)

There is a charming irritation with lawyers and legalisms in the multiplication of possible formulas: "'heredem facio' vel 'instituo' vel 'volo' vel 'mando' vel 'cupio' vel 'esto' vel 'erit.'" Constantine was the kind of man who laughed at, and probably told, lawyer jokes. But there is a more substantive concern driving Constantine's law concerning wills, a principle enunciated in various ways in his legislation. In a law of September 17, 325 (CTh 11.39.1), Constantine mentioned a former law requiring a "plaintiff" to prove a claim to property. "Moved by a sense of justice and equity" (*nos aequitate et iustitia moti*), he added to this requirement the demand that claimants to property prove *how* the object belongs to them. In a law ascribed jointly to Constantine and Licinius (CJ 3.1.8), the emperors declare, "It has been accepted as law that the foremost aim in all things should be justice and equity, rather than to follow the strict letter of the law."

The first principle of Constantine's legislation is nicely summarized in a statement from a later emperor: Man is more than law (CTh 9.45.4.2).

PROTECTING THE WEAK

And the second principle is like unto it: Constantine's legislation is frequently driven by a concern to protect the rights of the forgotten little people of the empire from the venality of officials, the burdens of landlords, the petty manipulations of the wealthy and powerful.[57] Over the course of the century between Caracalla's expansion of Roman citizenship and Constantine, citizenship had suffered the effects of inflation: If everyone is a citizen, what privilege does it confer? None, except the privilege of paying heavy taxes to support the army. Legal distinctions between citizen and noncitizen no longer defined the boundaries of social order, giving

---

[57]See Dorries, *Constantine the Great,* pp. 83-84. Even MacMullen (*Constantine,* p. 194) admits that Constantine turned a kind legal face toward slaves and *humiliores.*

way instead to differences of wealth and social connection, usually described in terms of the distinction between *honestiores* and *humiliores*. Constantine knew that *honestiores* were wont to abuse their privileges. An undated decree from Constantine and Licinius condemned municipalities for colluding to transfer tax burdens from "the more powerful men to persons of inferior status" (*per collusionem potentiorum sarcinam ad inferiores transferunt*), and announced that anyone who can prove he has been oppressed in this manner "shall assume only his original tax declaration" (CTh 13.10.1). He required that tax assessments be developed "in accordance with plans and regulations of the governor" so as to prevent the "multitude of lower classes" from being "subjected to the wantonness and subordinated to the interests of the more powerful." Commoners were to be relieved of "grave and iniquitous outrages" (CTh 11.16.3).

Constantine increased penalties on officials who overcollected on imposts, and he provided recourse for small landowners who were abused by the system:

> The serf [*colonus*], from whom more is demanded by the proprietor than is customary or more than was paid in former times, may go before the first judge whom he can find, and make complaint, so that the proprietor, convicted of demanding more than is customary, may be restrained from doing so thereafter, first returning what he has extorted as overpayment. (CJ 11.50.1)

> If it shall appear by the complaint of our provincials and it shall be proved that the desire for gain of the farmers of revenue has been such that they have demanded imposts beyond the customary amount and beyond the limits of our permission, they will be punished for such crime by perpetual exile. The sale of the right [to collect imposts] shall be made under your inspection or under that of those who succeed Your Gravity. (CJ 4.62.4)

Constantine's interest was not confined to human abuses. He also legislated (in 316) concerning the humane treatment of animals. He worried that many Romans abused animals with "knotty and very stout clubs" and thus "use up whatever strength they have." Constantine thus forbade clubs to be used on animals and decreed that drivers should "employ either a switch or at the most a whip in the tip of which a short prick has been inserted, by which the lazy limbs of the animals may be gently tickled into action." He was serious: ranked soldiers who violated the rule would be demoted, and common soldiers might be deported (CTh 8.5.2).

There is a third principle, and it clashes rather violently with the first two: traditional Roman social distinctions are good and should be preserved when possible and restored where they have eroded. In one law, Constantine said that the force of the law against adultery would not be brought against a woman who serves drinks in a tavern. It is not clear whether he considered the woman a slave, a free woman or the tavern owner. Given her profession, though, she is more likely to be seduced and loose than other women. Perhaps Constantine intended his law to protect such women when he wrote that they were outside the law because of their "mean status" and are thus "immune from judicial severity" (CTh 9.7.1). But it is hard to escape the implication that Constantine's law codified a distinction between the good girls and the sluts and that it left the sluts to fend for themselves.[58] In Constantine's legislation we first meet with *coloni*, free peasants, who were often much poorer than slaves. Constantine legislated to protect them against voracious tax officials but also required them to stay on the land. Similarly, he restricted the freedom of sons to choose a profession different from that of their fathers.[59] Criminal punishments had differed from class to class for centuries, and Constantine did nothing to remove the inequity.[60] While Constantine may have agreed with Lactantius that social status meant nothing in the church,[61] the emperor ensured that it continued to mean a lot outside.

Such legislation intentionally maintained social divisions, hardening or reestablishing them as necessary. Other decisions inadvertently widened social and economic divisions. Establishing a gold standard for the Roman world was one of the great achievements of Constantine's reign, one of the few monetary reforms in history that worked. The gold *solidus* remained in circulation for centuries after and retained its value. Though he did not

---

[58]Grubbs, *Law and Family*, pp. 206-7. Constantine's definition of adultery is similar, defined in terms of social status (ibid., p. 255).

[59]Ibid., pp. 26-27; Georges Depeyrot, "Economy and Society," in *The Cambridge Companion to Constantine*, ed. Noel Lenski (Cambridge: Cambridge University Press, 2006), p. 249.

[60]See Peter Garnsey, "Legal Privilege in the Roman Empire," *Past and Present* 41 (1968): 3-24; John A. Crook, "Ivs Romanvm Doli Revm," review of *Social Status and Legal Privilege in the Roman Empire* by Peter Garnsey, *Classical Review* 22 (1972): 238-42; P. A. Brunt, review of *Social Status and Legal Privilege in the Roman Empire* by Peter Garnsey, *Journal of Roman Studies* 62 (1972): 166-70.

[61]Lactantius *Divine Institutes* 5.14.

mention it, Eusebius might have found some Mosaic significance in the fact that Constantine removed gold from pagan temples and put it into circulation—the plunder of Egypt distributed to Israel. At the same time, however, Constantine continued the inflation of bronze coinage, which was used by the majority of laborers, *coloni* and small-hold freemen. The result was an astonishing inflation of bronze over against the *solidus,* a situation made all the worse because taxes were increasingly demanded in gold. While the wealthy traded in stable gold coinage, bronze-money poor farmers and laborers paid higher and higher prices for goods and had to resort to patrons to pay their taxes.

CONCLUSION

Constantine's marriage legislation nicely illustrates the tendency of much of his legal activity. On the one hand, he was perfectly willing to overturn laws of centuries-long standing if they violated reason,[62] as he did with the Augustan restriction on inheritance. At the same time, much of his legislation seems, in intent, to be aimed at securing or restoring traditional Roman social patterns. We will observe this dialectic at several points in what follows.

---

[62]See CJ 8.52.2.

10

Justice for All

The ears of the judge shall be open equally to the poorest as well as to the rich.

Constantine, from the Theodosian Code

Rome was always famed for its legal system, but that system was developed almost exclusively for civil rather than criminal law, "private" rather than "public." Nothing exposed the weakness, arbitrariness and cruel tyranny of Roman criminal law more clearly than the persecution of Christians. Charges against Christians rested on no foundation "other than a prosecutor, a charge of Christianity, and a governor willing to punish on that charge." Though the church has sometimes been considered a *collegia illicita,* that classification played no role in the actual decisions regarding Christians. No "Christian was ever prosecuted as a member of a *collegium illicitum.*" Christians were punished for being Christians, punished for the name alone. Not only the law but also the personnel needed to change, for if the persecutions revealed the arbitrary underside of Roman criminal procedures, they also revealed that the justice system was populated by feeble Pilates. Despite the theoretical primacy of the emperor—the emperor is the law—enforcement of the law was not directed from the center but left in the hands of provincial and municipal officials. Governors were advised "to consider not so much what was the practice at Rome as what the circumstances required; and the principle that in the exercise of his criminal jurisdiction the governor should act according to the circumstances existing in his particular province was well recognized." Many martyrs were made because judges thought sacrificing a few Christians a small price to pay to keep the province peaceful and quiet (*pacata atque quieta*).[1]

Private law was more developed but in practice little better. The law was "obscure and uncertain, and riddled with archaic technicalities," while "the administration of justice was excessively slow, largely owing to the wide latitude given to appeal." Justice was expensive "because of the heavy court fees charged, especially in the higher courts, not to speak of barristers' fees and of the long journeys and delays often imposed on parties and their witnesses." As if that were not enough, "the judges who administered the laws were not chosen for their legal learning, had a very brief tenure of office, and were as a rule venal and subject to social pressure and intimidation."[2] Most judges sought the position in order to advance economically and socially, and posts were filled by the highest bidder: "provincial governors . . . had paid considerable sums for their appointment, and had to recoup themselves in a hurry, for their period of office was short."[3] Both in the fourth century and over the centuries, many have complained about the corruption of the late Roman system of justice, but the complaint assumed the decay of an uncorrupt "normal" system. There was none. Corruption was not a flaw in the system; it was the system.

CONSTANTINE AND APPEALS

Constantine issued twenty-five laws concerning the process of appeals, the most intricate and challenging aspect of the imperial legal system.[4] He addressed the money problem head-on. In addition to the normal court fees, bribes were common, and even the official fees (*sportulae*) originated as "illicit tips." Fees made it impossible for the poor to move up the system of appeals. A poor man could not afford to make the appeal himself, and if his richer opponent made the appeal, the poorer could not afford to de-

---

[1]G. E. M. De Ste. Croix, "Why Were the Early Christians Persecuted?" *Past and Present* 26 (1963).

[2]A. H. M. Jones, *The Later Roman Empire, 284-602: A Social, Economic and Administrative Survey*, 2 vols. (Baltimore: Johns Hopkins University Press, 1964), 1:470. Simon Corcoran (*The Empire of the Tetrarchs: Imperial Pronouncements and Government, AD 284*-324, rev. ed., Oxford Classical Monographs [Oxford: Oxford University Press, 2000], p. 240) also notes Constantine's frequent railings against the venality of his officials and his desire to give access to justice to poor and rich alike.

[3]Jones, *Later Roman Empire*, 1:502.

[4]T. G. Elliott, *The Christianity of Constantine the Great* (Scranton, Penn.: University of Scranton Press, 1996), p. 100.

fend himself. If a richer opponent kept appealing, the poor would have to concede defeat, which would likely involve additional monetary loss.[5]

Constantine fumed against the piling up of fees. He recognized that the system worked against the *humiliores*, the wretched poor who could not pay for justice. "The chamber curtain of the judge shall not be venal," he demanded. "Entrance shall not be gained by purchase, the private council chamber shall not be infamous on account of the bids," and "the appearance of the governor shall not be at a price." Rather, "the ears of the judge shall be open equally to the poorest as well as to the rich." He aimed at specific abuses—chiefs of staff charging litigants for the privilege of being escorted to the judge, or subordinates who extorted from powerless people looking for justice. Finally, "the intolerable onslaught of the centurions and other apparitors who demand small and great sums will be crushed; and the unsated greed of those who deliver the records of a case to litigants shall be restrained." If anything unjust is taken from those who are involved in a civil case, "armed punishment will be at hand, which will cut off the heads and necks of the scoundrels" (CTh 1.16.7).[6]

This law contains some of the most pointed invective in Constantine's corpus and threatens horrors against violators. But it is important to notice the object of his attack and who is being defended. He lashed out with all his considerable rhetorical energy at rich scoundrels who wanted to make some extra money by selling justice, and he did so in defense of common litigants abused by the system.[7]

Fees were only part of the problem. People of high social status had access to governors and judges that commoners lacked. Members of the elite stuck together. Aristocrats were allowed to visit the governor's residence and "were entitled if they so wished to sit beside him on the bench in court."[8] The system of patronage and clientage overlay the justice system, and men of rank who happened to be judges were often beholden to other persons of rank who appeared in their courts. In response, poorer men had to find patrons of their own, transferring property to them for the duration

---

[5]Jones, *Later Roman Empire*, 1:499.
[6]H. A. Drake, *Constantine and the Bishops: The Politics of Intolerance* (Baltimore: Johns Hopkins University Press, 2000), p. 331.
[7]Diocletian launched similar efforts to curb the corruption of the court system; Corcoran, *Empire of the Tetrarchs*, pp. 239-44.
[8]Ibid., 1:503.

of the case.[9] Like other emperors, Constantine pinned legal sanctions on court officials who showed favoritism (CTh 11.30.5).

Appeals were also frustrated by violence, intimidation or imprisonment by judges or legal opponents. Judges took appeals as affronts to their honor and sometimes tried to prevent them from going forward. Appeals, Constantine insisted, did not cast "contumely on the judge" but were instead the legal privilege of everyone who appeared in court. Judges who blocked appeals were "arrogant through vainglory" (CTh 11.30.11; cf. 11.30.13, 15). Constantine warned that appellants in civil suits were not to be put in prison or suffer "any kind of outrages or torments or even contumely" (CTh 11.30.2). When he heard a report about appellants being "treated with contempt," he decreed that if it occurred through "fault or negligence of the governors," then he would take it up personally and see to it that the governor would be "fittingly punished" (CTh 1.5.1). Judges would sit on appeals, and Constantine not only demanded that cases be advanced speedily (CTh 11.30.3) but also threatened capital punishment to anyone who failed to deliver an appeal to the emperor's court within twenty days of its arrival and to members of his "office staff" who failed to deliver his own sentence to the judge (CTh 11.30.8). Any judge who suppressed the report of a case, thus forcing a litigant to appeal to the emperor, was guilty of "sacrilege" (CTh 11.30.6). Constantine threatened to "break and shatter" any judicial decision made "to the prejudice of the laws" (CTh 1.5.2). Judges were not to be allowed to hide in anonymity. Trials should be public, before "throngs of people," so that judges could not make back-door deals with those who would bribe them. Constantine even called on citizens to help reform the judicial system by praising "by public acclamation the most just and vigilant judges" and by complaining against "unjust and evildoers" (CTh 1.16.6).

Constantine addressed this knot of problems on several levels. As we have been seeing, he castigated his own officials for their abuses of power. He showed little confidence in his provincial judges, and his laws attempted to curb pointless appeals and make appeals easier for those who had little money.[10] The most substantive change was the permission that

---

[9]Ibid.
[10]Elliott, *Christianity of Constantine*, p. 100.

Constantine granted, in 323, for litigants to appeal from the civil courts to the courts of bishops:

> Pursuant to his own authority, a judge must observe that if an action should be brought before an Episcopal court, he shall maintain silence, and if any person should desire him to transfer his case to the jurisdiction of the Christian law and to observe that kind of court, he shall be heard, even though the action has been instituted before the judge, and whatever may be adjudged by them shall be held as sacred; provided, however, that there shall be no such usurpation of authority in that one of the litigants should proceed to the aforementioned tribunal and should report back his own unrestricted choice of a tribunal. For the judge must have the unimpaired right of jurisdiction of the case that is pending before him, in order that he may pronounce his decision, after full credit is given to the facts as presented. (CTh 1.27.1)

The intention of this law is unclear at several points, but fortunately we have a second document that provides clarification. In 333 Constantine sent a rescript to Ablabius, explaining the operation of the system. Collected as the first of the Sirmondian Constitutions, the decree "On the Judgment of Bishops" is one of the important pieces of legislation in Constantine's reign, not only for the specific effect it had on the administration of justice but also for what it reveals about the "agenda" that Constantine pursued.[11] His interest, he says, was to curb "the wicked seeds of litigation, so that wretched men, entangled in long and nearly endless snares of legal procedure, may have a timely release from mischievous pleadings or absurd love of *disputatio*."

---

[11]For a revealing analysis, see Drake, *Constantine and the Bishops,* pp. 325-44; the text is included as an appendix in Drake. Unfortunately, Drake concentrates so heavily on refuting Norman Baynes's view that Constantine's policies were motivated by a desire to ensure the success of the church that he misses the important religious thrust of the legislation. He rightly notes that Constantine's concern was for "fair and speedy trials" (p. 327) and an effort to empower the poor (p. 339). He also recognizes that the emperor's solicitousness for the poor had little support in traditional Roman legal practice, where social privilege played an enormous role. Yet he doesn't put these two insights together to ask how Constantine came to be convinced of the need to use the power of the emperor to open up avenues of redress for those who could not afford the Roman courts. The answer, it seems clear, is that Constantine was following Christian imperatives and impulses. Drake, somewhat contradictorily, claims that the purpose of the legislation on appeals was to "correct the notorious tilt of Roman courts in favor of the rich and powerful," adding that the emperor did this "in the belief that by this means he will secure divine favor" (p. 336). If he is courting divine favor by attending to the poor, how is the legislation "social" rather than "religious"?

Ecclesiastical courts of one sort or another existed already in the first century. By making use of these, Constantine solved "one of the most intractable problems of late antiquity, a judicial system that works to the advantage of the rich and powerful" and against what Constantine considered "oppressed lower classes."[12] His ruling had a number of immediate effects on legal practice. It sped up the process because bishops generally rendered judgment after a single hearing with the litigants. Because the bishops charged nothing, it opened up an appellate court for those who could not afford the fees or the bribes that the civil courts demanded. The bishop rendered a final judgment, no appeal permitted, reflecting Constantine's conviction that the voice of a bishop is the voice of God. Church courts were used, as is evidenced in the next century by Augustine's by then commonplace complaint that he had no time for contemplation because he spent so much time rendering judgment on his litigious North African congregants.[13] Augustine's court, like most, was open to non-Christians, such as the Jew Licinius, who had been defrauded of his property by a bishop until Augustine intervened to put things right.[14]

Constantine's efforts to provide justice to the weak and poor had a twofold aim. On the one hand, he wanted to replace a corrupt imperial bureaucracy with what he hoped would be superior judges, who operated with a tradition of church law already in formation in the early centuries.[15] Bishops stepped in to take that position. On the other hand, he saw it as his duty as emperor, in Lactantius's words, "to protect and defend orphans and widows who are destitute and stand in need of assistance."[16] Personally, he was liberal, distributing "money largely to those who were in need" and "showing himself philanthropist and benefactor even to the heathen." Beggars, "miserable and shiftless," approached him in the Forum and he

---

[12]Ibid., pp. 333-35. The phrase "oppressed lower classes" is from CTh 1.16.4.

[13]One of Yoder's examples of living out the gospel is the judge who opens "the court system to conflict resolution procedures" and resists "the trend toward more and more litigation." Perhaps he would have had some sympathy with the intentions of Constantine's legislation on appeals (*Body Politics: Five Practices of the Christian Community Before the Watching World* [Scottdale, Penn.: Herald, 2001], p. 27).

[14]Paula Fredricksen, *Augustine and the Jews: A Christian Defense of Jews and Judaism* (New York: Doubleday, 2008), pp. 312-14. A. D. Lee ("Decoding Late Roman Law," *Journal of Roman Studies* 92 [2002]: 192) notes that bishops often played the role of arbitrator or mediator.

[15]See Jean Gaudemet, *Formation du droit canonique et gouvernement de l'Église de l'antiquité à l'âge classique* (Strasbourg: Presses universitaires, 2007).

[16]Lactantius *Divine Institutes* 6.12.

provided money, food or clothing. Those who had fallen into poverty received land and titles. To orphans he was "as a father," and he "relieved the destitution of widows, and cared for them with special solicitude." To losers in lawsuits he decided, Constantine gave money from his private funds.[17] Constantine not only changed the rules for appeals to remove some of the advantage of the rich but also provided resources to bishops and encouraged them to dispense charity, and urged his own officials to do the same.[18]

OUTCASTS AND SLAVES

Constantine's concern for the poor and vulnerable in the Roman Empire was also evident in some of his legislation regarding children and slaves. Despite occasional eccentric denials, most historians recognize that child exposure had been practiced from the republican period of Roman history into the empire. This was not an odd divergence from Roman law but was sanctified by both basic principles of law and the antiquity of the practice. Though the text is somewhat obscure and subject to emendations, the Twelve Tables that served as the foundation of the Roman law appear to require Romans to kill "monstrous" infants: *Cito necatus insignis ad deformitatem puer esto* (An obviously deformed child must be put to death quickly; Table IV).

The legal foundation for this practice lies in the *patria potestas* of the Roman *paterfamilias*. Again according to the Twelve Tables, this was a power of life and death (*vitae necisque potestas*). Cicero reiterated the principle,[19] and there are examples from the early imperial period of the rule in operation. By Hadrian's time in the early second century, a son could be killed only if condemned by a family council, but this was a procedural restriction and not a substantive change.[20] Exposure of children because of deformity, illegitimacy, poverty or superstition,[21] which usually

---

[17]Eusebius *Life* 1.43; 4.1, 4. This is perhaps overdrawn, but Zosimus too comments on Constantine's generosity but describes it as "voluptuousness" (*New History* 2.53).

[18]Drake, *Constantine and the Bishops*, p. 342; Hermann Dorries, *Constantine the Great*, trans. Roland Bainton (New York: Harper, 1972), pp. 160-62.

[19]Cicero *De Domo* 29, 77.

[20]Max Radin, "The Exposure of Infants in Roman Law and Practice," *Classical Journal* 20, no. 6 (1925): 338-39. Cf. W. V. Harris, "Child-Exposure in the Roman Empire," *Journal of Roman Studies* 84 (1994).

[21]Harris, "Child-Exposure," pp. 11-15, summarizes the reasons for exposing children.

ended in death, was simply one manifestation of this basic paternal power. Not all Romans endorsed the practice, but there was no prohibition until a law of Valentinian in 374.

Christians had long condemned exposure, and Lactantius declared explicitly that the practice was a form of parricide. "Let no one imagine that even this is allowed, to strangle newly-born children," he urged, "for God breathes into their souls for life, and not for death." Such violence will only breed more violence: "can any one, indeed, expect that they would abstain from the blood of others who do not abstain even from their own?" But exposure does not just lead to murder; it is murder: "it is therefore as wicked to expose as it is to kill." If someone exposes his children from poverty, "it is better to abstain from marriage than with wicked hands to mar the work of God."[22]

Constantine did not prohibit child exposure, but in an edict of 318 sent to the *vicarius* of Africa, he undermined the legal foundation of the practice:

> Whoever, secretly or openly, shall hasten the death of a parent, or son or other near relative, whose murder is accounted as parricide, will suffer the penalty of parricide. He will not be punished by the sword, by fire or by some other ordinary form of execution, but he will be sewn up in a sack and, in this dismal prison, have serpents as his companions. Depending on the nature of the locality, he shall be thrown into the neighboring sea or into the river, so that even while living he may be deprived of the enjoyment of the elements, the air being denied him while living and interment in the earth when dead. (CJ 9.17.1)

In 322 he backed up his opposition to child exposure with an edict, similar to the edicts of earlier emperors, that promised imperial aid to parents to prevent them from selling their children to slavery,

> We have learned that provincials suffering from lack of sustenance and the necessities of life are selling or pledging their own children. Therefore, if any such person should be found who is sustained by no substance of family fortune and who is supporting his children with suffering and difficulty, he shall be assisted through our fisc before he becomes a prey to calamity. The proconsuls and governors and the fiscal representatives . . . shall bestow

---

[22]Lactantius *Divine Institutes* 6.20.

freely the necessary support on all persons whom they observe to be placed in dire need. (CTh 11.27.2)

A later law reiterated this pledge to families in Italy, but now with explicit reference to the emperor's desire to prevent child exposure. It would, he wrote, be "at variance with Our character [*Abhorret enim nostris moribus*] that we should allow any person to be destroyed by hunger or to break forth to the commission of a shameful deed" (11.27.1-2).[23] By this law Constantine treated exposure as a form of *parricidium*.[24] Another law, however, indicates that parents could reclaim their exposed children, provided they paid for them. Earlier emperors had allowed anyone finding a newborn child "to hold it in the condition of slavery," but if later someone wants "to restore the child to freedom or should defend his right to it as his slave," the claimant has to pay an adequate price (CTh 5.10.1). For Constantine exposure was not yet considered a crime, but it was discouraged in his legislation.

Laws regarding child exposure were closely bound up with laws regarding slavery. Foundlings by and large became slaves. For some Romans, exposing their children and, by all odds, killing them would be preferable to selling them to slavery.[25] That is the dynamic that helps to explain several odd laws of Constantine. In one piece of legislation, Constantine decreed that the adopting parents of a foundling were allowed to determine the slave or free status of the foundling, in perpetuity: "Every disturbance of suits for recovery by those persons who knowingly and voluntarily cast out from home newly born children, whether slaves or free, shall be abolished" (CTh 5.9.1). Though this was harsh, and certainly was unjust in disallowing the possibility of manumission, it was not a sacrifice of "the freedom of the free-born to the interests of slave-owners."[26] Rather, it is

---

[23]For a summary of the complexities of this legislation, see Harris, "Child-Exposure," pp. 20-21.

[24]This is evidence against Raymond MacMullen's claim ("What Difference Did Christianity Make?" *Historia* 35 [1986]: 160) that Constantine did not attack the practice of exposing children. While it is true that he never outlawed the practice, his legislation made clear his disapproval. Dorries, *Constantine the Great*, p. 83, is correct to say that Constantine condemned exposure as a form of murder.

[25]Harris, "Child-Exposure," p. 19: "There was a powerful inhibition in the way of selling a child of citizen parents. That was precisely what could not be allowed to happen to a member of the citizen community. At least some Greeks felt that the selling of children was more abhorrent than exposing them."

[26]Harris, "Child-Exposure," p. 21.

more likely an attempt to enact disincentives to exposing children. If parents know that their children could end up as permanent slaves, they might think twice about setting them out. Constantine's codification of the permission to enslave free-born children was also likely motivated by the same desire to limit child-killing.[27] Better a slave child than a dead child, Constantine seems to have reasoned.

Constantine's legislation on slavery is mixed.[28] Some critics have complained that he did not simply abolish slavery from the beginning. This was hardly a viable social option, given the pervasiveness of slavery and the empire's reliance on slaves. Constantine no more became Abraham Lincoln by virtue of his conversion than did James Madison. More important, there was no consensus among Christian thinkers that Christianity required the abolition of slavery. The apostles instruct slaves to submit to their masters, and Paul even sent the slave Onesimus back to his owner, Philemon. To be sure, the stress on brotherhood among believers transformed the character of slavery at least among Christians. Contrary to common myths, slaves were considered *personae* under Roman law,[29] and slaves often had professional training and managerial responsibilities. Yet the ancient slave system was shot through with Aristotle's conception of the slave as a lesser form of human being, as an "animated tool" and certainly not as a brother.

Postapostolic Christians pressed ahead with the apostolic transformation of slavery. Slavery as a social status was relativized to the "spiritual slavery" to sin, and the stigma of slavery was weakened by the fact that God himself in the person of the Son had taken on the "form of a servant" and came "not to be served but to serve." Slaves were welcomed into the

---

[27]This is often described as a reversal of long-standing Roman law, but W. W. Buckland (*The Roman Law of Slavery: The Condition of the Slave in Private Law from Augustus to Justinian* [Cambridge: Cambridge University Press, 1908], p. 421) points out that Constantine himself claimed that it was permitted by earlier emperors (CTh 5.10.1). According to Buckland, Constantine's "contribution to the matter seems to have been to regulate it by laying down several rules to which such sales must conform."

[28]And, as everywhere, there is controversy about Constantine's interest in and attention to slaves. Jones (*Constantine and the Conversion of Europe*, p. 189) claims that he showed little interest in the problem, while Dorries (*Constantine the Great*, pp. 92-103) argues that his legislation was revolutionary. For details of particular legislation, see Corcoran, *Empire of the Tetrarchs*, pp. 108, 113, 167. See E. J. Jonkers, "De l'influence du Christianisme sur la legislation relative a l'esclavage dans l'antiquité," *Mnemosyne*, 3rd ser. 1 (1933-1934): 265-80.

[29]Buckland, *Roman Law of Slavery*, pp. 3-5.

church, and some rose to positions of leadership. The church thus offered opportunities for upward mobility. "Among us," Lactantius wrote, "there is no slave and we call them all brothers in the spirit and, as to religion, fellow slaves."[30]

Much of Constantine's legislation on slavery reinforced the social system, and slavery, rather than undermining it. He retained restrictions on cohabitation between decurions and slave girls, and in a law of 319 hardened the penalties:

> Although it appears unworthy for men, even though not endowed with any high rank, to descend to sordid marriages [*ad sordida descendere conubia*] with slave women, nevertheless this practice is not prohibited by law; but a legal marriage cannot exist with servile persons, and from a slave union of this kind, slaves are born. We command, therefore, that decurions shall not be led by their lust to take refuge in the bosom of the most powerful houses. For if a decurion should be secretly united with any slave woman belonging to another man and if the overseers and procurators should not be aware of this, We order that the woman shall be cast into the mines through sentence of the judge, and the decurion himself shall be deported to an island. (CTh 12.1.6)

Children of such unions were illegitimate, and any inheritance they received would be confiscated and turned over to legitimate offspring. Persons of higher rank were also discouraged from slave marriages.

> We order that senators or persons of the rank of prefect [*perfectissimus*] or who occupy the office of duumvir or who are decorated with the ornaments of the chief priesthood of Syria or Phoenicia shall be branded with infamy and lose the privileges of the Roman laws if they treat children born to them of a slave, daughter of a slave, freedwoman, daughter of a freedwoman, actress, daughter of an actress, mistress of a tavern, daughter of a tavern keeper, or a low and degraded woman, or the daughter of a panderer or gladiator or a woman who offered herself to public trade, as their legitimate children, either pursuant to their own declaration to that effect or pursuant to the privilege extended by our rescript; and whatever a father shall have given to such children, whether he calls them legitimate or natural, shall be taken from them and shall be turned over to the legitimate offspring, or to his brother, sister, father or mother. (CJ 5.27.1)

---

[30]Lactantius *Divine Institutes* 5.15.3.

Elsewhere, he prohibited slaves from informing against their *domini*, required that damages be paid by anyone who received a fleeing slave without informing the master, and granted, as we saw above, fathers the right to sell their children into slavery.[31]

Yet he also issued laws that enabled slaves to be liberated. Manumission was not at all new, but Constantine opened new avenues for it. Given the long-standing Roman endorsement of freedom, he wrote, the law must provide avenues of freedom for slaves. If, for instance, a man was claimed by another as a slave, the supposed slave was given an opportunity to find a sponsor who would vouch for his free status. Even if he found none, he could renew his claim to freedom at any time later, should he find a sponsor (CTh 4.8.5-6). Constantine passed laws to ameliorate slave conditions. He tried to keep slave families together. Because slaves had a right to a stable home, slave families were not to be split up when a slave was sold, and urban slaves were not to be sold if they were tutors, so that their young pupils would not lose the benefits of their protection.[32] Ancient law, he observed, removes the birthright from women who have children with slaves, without any exceptions made for youth or ignorance. While Constantine "shunned" cohabitation between free women and slaves, he declared that the children of such unions were free, though medial: "free children of slaves and illegitimate children of free persons." They were "freed from the constraints of slavery" while they were "liable to the privileges due to patrons." This law applied whether the woman slept with the slave "ignorantly" or "willingly" (CTh 4.12.3). In a law strikingly reminiscent of Exodus 21:20-21, he ruled that an owner who beat his slave to death with clubs or stones, or killed the slave by hanging, poisoning or throwing him from a height, would be prosecuted as a murderer. If, however, the slave died from normal discipline, the owner was free.[33]

All this legislation can cause us to miss several crucial innovations in Constantine's slavery law. The first, and the lesser of these, was his permission of manumission in the church. This was important in that the church became a place of liberation for slaves, but in essence Constantine

---

[31]For details of these, see Buckland, *Roman Law of Slavery,* pp. 77, 86, 269, 402, 420-22, 606.
[32]CTh 2.25.1; CJ 5.37.22.2-4; Judith Evans Grubbs, *Law and Family in Late Antiquity: The Emperor Constantine's Marriage Legislation* (Oxford: Oxford University Press, 1999), pp. 25-26.
[33]CTh 9.12.1; Grubbs, *Law and Family,* p. 26.

was doing no more than extending a privilege of pagan temples to the Christian church. Far more important was Constantine's endorsement of manumission as an act pleasing to God. In the 321 decree allowing for manumission in the church, he referred to persons who with "pious inten- tion" (*religiosa mente*) want to give freedom to slaves. Manumission before the eyes of a bishop, he stated, had the same legal force as the granting of Roman citizenship, and he added that clerics were allowed to free their own slaves (CTh 4.7.1). Doing something pleasing to God on Sunday was particularly appropriate, and manumission was one of those pleasing acts.

Manumission was endorsed as an act of "piety," and Constantine en- couraged anyone who wished to perform this act to turn to the church to do it. "This is the first time in history that emancipation is praised as godly work and encouraged by an emperor." In fact, Constantine's endorsement of manumission went further than that of most Christian writers of the time. Though not requiring manumission, Constantine did encourage it, and for that there was no "model" in the early church.[34]

WHO RULED AND HOW?

Government is by law, the Romans said, but laws have to be interpreted, enforced and administered by men. This was especially so in the Roman world. Publication of laws was not instant or thorough, and governors were often left to their own resources to determine what was best for their ter- ritory. Patronage and clientage, moreover, were not only the bonds of so- cial life but the sinews of the body politic. A benefactor would grant favors and benefices to clients and thereby win loyalty and support. Politics meant gift-giving, and responding to gifts in a way that would win further ben- efits in the future. Honor was sought by proximity to the emperor, and was conferred by the emperor. Constantine knew how to play this game so well, in fact, that both his friends (Eusebius) and critics (Zosimus) claim that he was overly generous. When he took over the Eastern empire, he came as a Western Augustus to an unknown territory. He needed to make friends, establish connections and secure loyalty if he wanted to stabilize his rule. This he did by funneling a great deal of money and social privi- lege into the East. Constantinople was, among many other things, a mas-

---

[34]Dorries, *Constantine the Great*, pp. 95, 99.

sive gift to the Eastern empire, a gift enhanced by the creation of a senate in the new city.[35] Throughout the empire, the emperor expanded the number of senators, so much so that the traditional "gentry" class of equestrians virtually disappeared, and he formalized the earlier system of imperial "companions," the *comites*.[36] In Palestine, his mother Helena acted as his agent in funding several church buildings.

When Constantine reunited the empire under a single Augustus, he had to re-create or create a new administrative structure.[37] Diocletian had already begun subdividing provinces into smaller units, and Constantine built on his work. The empire was divided into fourteen dioceses, each overseen by a *vicarius*, and the dioceses were bundled together into four larger units—Gaul, Italy, Illyrium and the Oriens—each of which was governed by a praetorian prefect. One of Constantine's innovations was to remove military responsibilities permanently from the prefects, dividing between the bureaucracy and the army in a way that both neutralized potential for coup attempts and gave realistic recognition to the fact that few men are endowed with the abilities of both an accountant and a general.[38]

What kind of men filled these positions? Did Constantine give preference to Christians? Or did he entrust his empire to the most competent Turks he could find? Historians differ on this point,[39] but we have the

---

[35]Christopher Kelly, "Bureaucracy and Government," in *The Cambridge Companion to the Age of Constantine*, ed. Noel Lenski (Cambridge: Cambridge University Press, 2006), pp. 195-97.

[36]A. H. M. Jones, "The Social Background of the Struggle Between Paganism and Christianity," in *The Conflict Between Paganism and Christianity in the Fourth Century*, ed. Arnaldo Momigliano (Oxford: Clarendon, 1963) pp. 26-27; David S. Potter, *The Roman Empire at Bay, AD 180-395*, Routledge History of the Ancient World (London: Routledge, 2004), pp. 387-88.

[37]On Diocletian's and Constantine's administrative reforms generally, see Charles Matson Odahl, *Constantine and the Christian Empire* (London: Routledge, 2004), pp. 229-30; Dorries, *Constantine the Great*, chap. 8; MacMullen, *Constantine*, chap. 10; Jacob Burckhardt, *The Age of Constantine the Great*, trans. Moses Hadas (Berkeley: University of California Press, 1983), pp. 340-41; Timothy D. Barnes, *Constantine and Eusebius* (Cambridge, Mass.: Harvard University Press, 1981), pp. 9-10; Potter, *Roman Empire at Bay*, pp. 367-77; Kelly, "Bureaucracy and Government," pp. 183-204.

[38]Kelly, "Bureaucracy and Government," pp. 183-89; Jones, *Later Roman Empire*, 1:101.

[39]Peter Brown ("Aspects of the Christianization of the Roman Aristocracy," *Journal of Roman Studies* 51 [1961]: 1-11) argues for a "drift into a respectable Christianity" in the two decades following Constantine's death, and Michele Renee Salzman (*The Making of a Christian Aristocracy: Social and Religious Change in the Western Roman Empire* [Cambridge, Mass.: Harvard University Press, 2002]) argues for an even later development, in the 360s. Timothy D. Barnes ("Statistics and the Conversion of the Roman Aristocracy," *Journal of Roman Studies* 85 [1995]: 135-47) vindicates Eusebius, concluding that both Constantine and Constantius "preferred Christians when they appointed men to high office" (p. 144).

testimony of Eusebius that he promoted Christians. Many of the men he promoted were from lower classes: "a considerable number of [Constantine's] new senators, including many who rose to the highest rank, came from lower in the social scale." At least "two peasants . . . rose from the ranks [of the army] to high commands, both of whom assumed high positions in the court." In Rome the senatorial class still included many older families, but the Eastern *honestiores* had been elevated from low origins. Given that these were the classes with the greatest concentration of Christians, it is likely that Constantine was raising Christians to positions of high rank and great responsibility for the empire.[40]

Constantine's appointments to the position of city prefect (*praefectus urbi*) in Rome are a barometer of his strategy in appointments. When he first entered Rome after defeating Maxentius, he retained his rival's *praefectus*, Annius Anullinus, for a month and then replaced him with another member of the old guard, Aradius Rufinus, who had served earlier as *praefectus* and was of an old senatorial family. Constantine's takeover of Rome led to no reprisals against Maxentius's officials, and Constantine's appointments were, to this extent, a pledge of continuity and clemency. Later, though, Constantine's appointments moved in a different, more innovative direction. In 325-26 the *praefectus* was Acilius Severus, a Spanish Christian, and three of the members of the aristocracy who later filled the position were also Christians. At a time when many pagans resided in Rome and occupied positions in the Senate, Constantine appointed Christians to be chief magistrates of the capital.[41] If comparatively few Christians held this position, the fact that *any* did was remarkable.

Though often overlooked, there is direct and obvious evidence of Constantine's preference for Christians in the government of the empire: his favor to the bishops. Bishops formed courts of appeal, distributed relief to the poor and to widows, oversaw large pastoral and administrative staffs in urban parishes, and led public rites of worship in the growing number of great cathedrals throughout the empire. Over the following decades, they used their money to open hospitals, orphanages and hostels.[42] And, of

---

[40]Jones, "Social Background," pp. 28-30; cf. Andreas Alfoldi, *The Conversion of Constantine and Pagan Rome*, trans. Harold Mattingly (Oxford: Clarendon, 1948).
[41]Potter, *Roman Empire at Bay*, pp. 388-89.
[42]Jones, *Later Roman Empire*, 2:901.

course, they were all Christians. By supporting the church and empowering bishops, Constantine created a Christian governing class. Again, it is impossible to know his intentions. Possibly he simply responded to immediate needs: he saw abuses and gaps that needed remedy and sought the remedy nearest to hand. Whatever his intentions, Constantine's largesse to the church prepared the empire for its eventual collapse. Even before the imperial government ended, bishops like Athanasius and Ambrose had become the dominant figures in their cities—not just the dominant religious figures but the dominant figures, full stop, just as abbots soon would become the benevolent *patres familias* in many rural areas. Rome's baptism meant the baptism of the aristocracy, as baptized church members took on imperial authority.

LAW ENFORCEMENT

Murmuring against government is common in every age. That subjects murmur means little, but what they murmur about can be revealing. According to Eusebius, the murmuring in Constantine's time was murmuring about Constantine's laxity. There was "no fear of capital punishment" because of the emperor's uniform inclination to clemency, and as a result no one was deterred from crime. "None of the provincial governors visited offenses with their proper penalties," and as a result the public placed "no small degree of blame on the general administration of the empire."[43] The bishop of Caesarea found in Constantine a political expression of Jesus' exhortation to love enemies. His mind was so full of anxiety to avoid "wanton sacrifice of human life" that he preserved lives of his enemies. He ordered his troops to spare prisoners, reminding them that they shared a "common nature" with opposing soldiers, and he reinforced this rule by promising gold to every Roman soldier who spared a life. "Great numbers even of the barbarians were thus saved, and owed their lives to the emperor's gold."[44]

Eusebius's enthusiasm inevitably leaves us slightly suspicious, and it would be nice to have some outside confirmation of his claims. We have little, and what we do have leaves us unsettled. Far and away the most scandalous exercise of power by Constantine was the execution of his wife

---

[43]Eusebius *Life* 4.31.
[44]Ibid., 2.13.

Fausta and his son Crispus, which occurred shortly after the council of Nicaea and after Constantine's visit to Rome for his *vicennalia* celebration in 326. Eusebius says nothing of this incident, but he must have known about it, since he erased references to Crispus and Fausta from an earlier edition of the *Church History.* Zosimus is the earliest witness, and after him the story became part of the standard account of Constantine. According to Zosimus, Constantine's conversion was tied directly to what the chronicler calls the murder of his wife and son:

> But when he came to Rome, he was filled with pride and arrogance. He resolved to begin his impious actions at home. For he put to death his son Crispus, stiled (as I mentioned) Caesar, on suspicion of debauching his mother-in-law[45] Fausta, without any regard to the ties of nature. And when his own mother Helena expressed much sorrow for this atrocity, lamenting the young man's death with great bitterness, Constantine under pretence of comforting her, applied a remedy worse than the disease. For causing a bath to be heated to an extraordinary degree, he shut up Fausta in it, and a short time after took her out dead.

In the eighth century, the *Passion of Artemius* records a similar story, embellishing it with classical references:

> Constantine did kill his wife Fausta—and rightly so, since she had imitated Phaedra of old, and accused his son Crispus of being in love with her and assaulting her by force, just as Phaedra had accused Theseus' son Hippolytus. And so according to the laws of nature, as a father he punished his son. But later he learnt the truth and killed her as well, exacting the most righteous penalty against her.[46]

A very similar account occurs in the Greek historian Zonaras, who, though writing in the twelfth century, had access to fourth-century sources:

> His [Crispus's] stepmother Fausta was madly in love with him but did not easily get him to go along. She then announced to his father that he [Crispus] loved her and had often attempted to do violence to her. Therefore, Crispus was condemned to death by his father, who believed his wife. But when the emperor later recognized the truth he punished his wife too be-

---

[45]Zosimus is mistaken. Fausta was Crispus's stepmother.
[46]Quoted in David Woods, "On the Death of the Empress Fausta," *Greece and Rome,* 2nd ser. 45 (1998): 71-72.

cause of her licentiousness and the death of his son. Fausta was placed in an overheated bath and there found a violent end of her life.[47]

For obvious reasons, this has been a dark stain on Constantine's record. Voltaire considers the deaths homicides; Burckhardt describes both deaths as "murders" committed by Constantine.[48] Craig Carter points to the incident as evidence that Constantine continued to act like a typical Roman emperor, willing to kill "political rivals" even if the rival was his own son.[49]

The critics may be right, but despite the damning evidence, it is wise to be cautious. Many of the charges go far beyond the evidence that we have. Scholars have doubted whether the stories of sexual dalliance are accurate, and it is not even obvious that the two deaths were related to one another. Even if we assume that their deaths are connected, and even if we assume a sexual relationship between Crispus and Fausta, we cannot be sure what the whole sordid affair means. We can eliminate some possibilities. It is implausible to suggest that Crispus was a political rival. A competent and widely admired young man he was, but if Constantine was fearful of his power, he would not have appointed him Caesar or encouraged his ambitions by giving him a court and command of an army. These facts also undermine the claim, made by some historians, that Crispus was eliminated from the line of potential successors because of his "illegitimacy." It is not clear that he was illegitimate, and even if he were, Constantine's own questionable origins make it unlikely that he would consider illegitimacy a bar to the imperial throne. More fundamentally, if illegitimacy stood in the way, why would Constantine have elevated Crispus to the position of Caesar in the first place? In short, the few facts we know militate against the notion that Constantine was eliminating rivals among his family.

David Woods has suggested a scenario that attempts to sense of all the evidence.[50] He accepts the ancient testimony that Crispus and Fausta had

---

[47]Ibid., p. 72.

[48]Burckhardt, *Age of Constantine*, pp. 283, 339.

[49]Craig Carter, *Rethinking Christ and Culture: A Post-Christendom Perspective* (Grand Rapids: Brazos, 2006), p. 96.

[50]Woods, "On the Death of the Empress." My point is not primarily to endorse Woods's reconstruction. It may be wrong, and scholars who claim that a dynastic struggle lay behind the executions may be closer to the truth. I focus on Woods to show just how little we know about

sex but leaves open the question whether it was rape or consensual. Fausta became pregnant. Constantine could hardly have ignored such a flagrant violation of family and political order. What was his response? Did he execute his son for adultery or for rape? If they were both guilty, the death penalty for adultery was on the books, and Constantine was within his legal rights to condemn them. This case would then be a scandal only if one assumes that the death penalty for adultery is scandalous. Yet there is no other evidence that Constantine applied the death penalty for adultery, and the manner of Crispus's death is unusual. He died by poison on the out-of-the-way island of Pola. Had he been executed, he would have been beheaded rather than poisoned. And the location is unusual too. Shortly before this incident Constantine had exiled a senator because of adultery, and it is possible that Crispus too was exiled. Possibly the exiled Crispus was given the choice that many Romans before had been given, the choice to bury shame in suicide.

Fausta's manner of death is even more unusual. If there is no evidence for poisoning as the punishment for adultery, there is certainly no evidence for death-by-overheated-bath. Ancient medical treatises, however, sometimes recommended hot baths to induce abortion, and Fausta, pregnant by her stepson, may have died in a botched abortion attempt. If Constantine pressured her to have the abortion, he would be free of the charge of murdering his wife but would come under the condemnation of the church as a child-killer, and hence a murderer.

In short, it is possible that Constantine wanted neither Crispus nor Fausta dead, that he sentenced his son to exile and pressured his wife to have an abortion, which, like many ancient abortions, went wrong. Woods's is the construction of the evidence that most fully absolves the emperor,[51] yet even on Woods's reconstruction, Constantine violated strict Christian prohibitions against abortion and enabling abortion. Yet Woods's explanation is not proven, and it is equally possible that in this incident we have the veil drawn back on a sordid domestic political affair, one in which Constantine acted, as when he dispatched Maximian and Licinius, with decisive brutality.

---

the incident and to defuse the frequent charge that Constantine "murdered" his son. He may have, but we simply lack the evidence to make a confident judgment.

[51]The only stronger case is that Constantine is to be commended for applying the law without partiality, even when it meant punishing his own son and wife.

Evangelical Law

The Western legal tradition grew out of the "upheaval" of the Investiture Controversy of the eleventh century,[52] and one of the keys to that revolution was consolidation of a system of canon law. Civil law coexisted with, copied and sometimes competed with canon law. But for the clergy of the time, canon law was superior, and civil law should be changed to conform to the church's standard. The church was the maker of manners:

> Many of the reforms which it promoted command respect even seven and eight centuries later: the introduction of rational trial procedures to replace magical mechanical modes of proof by ordeals of fire and water, by battles of champions, and by ritual oaths; the insistence upon consent as the foundation of marriage and upon wrongful intent as the basis of crime; the development of equity to protect the poor and helpless against the rich and powerful and to enforce relations to trust and confidence.[53]

Canon law was far from perfect, but it set a standard of justice that civil rulers were exhorted to emulate and that founded the Western legal tradition until recently, when the religious foundations of Western law have been severely eroded.

Grafting the evangel on civil law represents, to some theological critics of Constantine, a key instance of the evils of Constantinianism, the wedding of church with power, gospel with civil order. I do not find the evangelization of law[54] at all threatening. Civil law cannot be religiously neutral. It cannot serve Jesus and Jupiter, God and Mammon. It will either love the one and hate the other, or hate the one and love the other. It is a good thing if the law is not organized, as Roman law was, to favor the wealthy and powerful. It is a good thing if the mechanisms and procedures of civil law are modified to make it possible for the injured to find redress and vindication. Indeed, it is an act of neighbor love—love of an enemy, even—for a Christian king to issue an edict opening up episcopal courts to Jews and pagans as well as Christians.

Constantine had no system of canon law to emulate, and as I have ar-

---

[52]Harold Berman, *Law and Revolution: The Formation of the Western Legal Tradition* (Cambridge, Mass.: Harvard University Press, 1983).

[53]Harold Berman, *Faith and Order: The Reconciliation of Law and Religion* (Grand Rapids: Eerdmans, 1993), p. 44.

[54]Thanks to my former student Davey Henreckson for several conversations about this concept.

gued, there is little evidence that he pursued a deliberate program of "Christianization" of Roman law. Yet whatever his intentions or program, if he had any beyond responding to the next appeal, Constantine began the "Christianization" of law. As the later history of Western law indicates, the main contribution of the first Christian emperor was to give the church freedom to be itself, to erect its own legal structures, to organize its own system of conflict resolutions, to carry out its own sanctions. As always, there were costs, a risk and a downside, the risk that the church would simply sacralize the status quo or the will of the emperor. That happened often enough, but not infrequently the opposite happened and the church was able, through example and exhortation, to infuse the evangel into the very structures of civil order, so as to render them more just and compassionate. For planting the seeds of that harvest, we have Constantine to thank.

$$\boxed{11}$$

One God, One Emperor

He was a mighty man who brought to pass whatever he attempted.
He strove for mastery over the entire world.

EUTROPIUS, *BREVIARUM HISTORIAE ROMANAE* 10.4[1]

On March 25, A.D. 101, the emperor Trajan (98-117) set out with four legions on a military expedition against the Dacians, who inhabited a region stretching east from the Pannonian Plains across the Carpathians to the Black Sea.[2] At forty-two, Trajan was at an ideal age for such a campaign, free from both the "recklessness of youth and the sluggishness of old age." Besides that, he took as much "delight in war" as in wine and boys. The Dacians "had good cause to fear him."

During his preparations for battle, someone brought him a large mushroom bearing a Latin inscription written by some of Rome's allies, warning him to turn back. Ignoring the warning, he threw himself into the battle, losing men and killing many Dacians. Bandages gave out, and Trajan tore strips from his own clothing to bind up the wounded. Finally, the Dacian king Decebalus came out, fell to the ground and did obeisance to the Roman emperor, promising to cast aside his arms and befriend Rome. Trajan assumed the title Dacicus and inscribed it on coins; he celebrated

---

[1]Quoted in Hermann Dorries, *Constantine the Great*, trans. Roland Bainton (New York: Harper, 1972), p. 209.

[2]I am following the story as told in Dio Cassius *Roman History* 68.8-14. Additional details from <www.roman-emperors.org/assobd.htm#t-inx> (accessed June 27, 2009).

his triumph in Rome, complete with gladiatorial combats. It seemed a satisfying conclusion.

Decebalus had not given up. Even as many Dacians were submitting to Trajan, Decebalus gathered troops and arms and raised assistance from surrounding nations. He sent some Roman deserters to assassinate Trajan, but they were captured, and they confessed under torture. He invited the Roman commander Longinus to conference, but when he arrived, Decebalus had him arrested and questioned him about Trajan's plans. Longinus frustrated that effort by drinking poison.

Trajan could not let these insults stand. Roman honor was at stake. By 105, he had constructed a massive bridge over the Danube and crossed into Dacian territory. Several detachments from Trajan's army converged on the capital, Sarmizegetuza, destroying fortresses as they went. At the capital, they laid siege. The Dacians resisted, but the Roman war machines were too strong. They blocked the water supply and, after permitting the Dacians to leave, set fire to the city, acclaimed Trajan in the sacred center, and destroyed the fortress. Trajan occupied all the territory of Decebalus, and the latter, seeing he had no chance of winning, fled into the mountains. When the Romans pursued, Decebalus acted like a Roman and committed suicide. Trajan brought his head back to Rome, along with treasures—nearly forty tons of gold and twice as much of silver—discovered in a cave submerged under water that Decebalus had diverted from the Sargetia River. Trajan "drove out or destroyed a large number" of Dacians and resettled the territory with Roman veterans and people from the East.[3]

There was a backstory. Romans believed that "conquest was a good and glorious thing" and considered "desire for a title, a triumph, or a glorious reputation" to be "a perfectly plausible explanation for war."[4] Trajan went on to fight back a Parthian incursion and, energized by success, moved east, incorporating Arabia into the empire in 106, driving the Parthians from Armenia and annexing it, and establishing a province of Mesopotamia. Eventually he reached the Persian Gulf and intended, it appears, to rival Alexander with a march into India.[5]

---

[3]Tenney Frank, *Roman Imperialism* (New York: Macmillan, 1914), p. 355.
[4]Susan P. Mattern, *Rome and the Enemy: Imperial Strategy in the Principate* (Berkeley: University of California Press, 1999), pp. 164, 198-99.
[5]Frank, *Roman Imperialism*, p. 355.

Sheer greed, *ambitio* or lust for the glory of conquest, however, was never sufficient pretext for *just* war. It was not the rationale that appeared in press releases. Dacia had gold and silver mines, but seizing them would not serve as a public reason for war. Trajan's Dacian wars were a response, and Trajan would perhaps have called them a "defensive response." One of Trajan's predecessors, Domitian, had also attempted a war with the Dacians, in reaction to the devastation brought by another Decebalus in an invasion of Roman territory in 84-85. Domitian also aimed to connect the Rhine and the Danube with a chain of fortresses. He did not fare well. The Roman commander, praetorian prefect Cornelius Fuscus, died, and the sacred standard of the Praetorian Guard was captured. In another campaign Domitian came to terms with Decebalus, who allowed the Romans access to his territories in exchange for an annual "gift" from the Romans to the Dacians. After Domitian died, "men made free to call it a tribute."[6]

Domitian had put the best spin he could on the whole affair. He is said to have purchased slaves who were done up to look like captives so that he could celebrate a triumph.[7] But the truce with the Dacians was doubly galling for the Romans. Not only did they have to pay tribute to a barbarian king, but Domitian had done nothing to avenge the death of Fuscus or the humiliating loss of the standard. This was the "threat" that Trajan was subduing, not so much a physical threat to the Danube frontier as a threat to Roman honor.

The Roman Empire did not have a "grand strategy" in the sense that moderns think of it. The Romans lacked the technology in both cartography and communications. There is something to be said for the thesis that Rome's empire was an "unexpected" empire that expanded through a ripple of defensive alliances.[8] Security in the negative sense of safe roads, unpillaged fields, untransgressed borders does not, however, explain Roman imperial behavior. As Augustine knew, what guided foreign policy and imperial expansion was Roman love for honor, *philotimia,* which ex-

---

[6]Frank, *Roman Imperialism*, p. 355; see also Dio Cassius *Roman History* 67.6-10.
[7]Tacitus *Agricola* 39.
[8]This is the thesis of Frank, *Roman Imperialism*, recently popularized, with application to American expansion, by Thomas F. Madden, *Empires of Trust: How Rome Built—and America Is Building—a New World* (New York: Dutton, 2008).

pressed itself in a lust for domination (*libido dominandi*).[9] Romans gained honor and glory by conquest, and by the titles and honors paid to conquerors back home. When a rival treated Rome with mockery, that insult needed to be avenged, with clemency if possible, viciously if necessary. Earlier in Domitian's reign, Nasamones massacred Romans and plundered the camp of Flaccus, but then drank themselves drunk on the spoils. This gave Flaccus the opportunity to "annihilate them, even destroying all the non-combatants." The same Domitian whose hapless Dacian war we have noted was "elated" and boasted to the Senate, "I have forbidden the Nasmones to exist."[10] Terror kept barbarian pride in check; the sacrifice of barbarians and rebels maintained Roman honor.

This was, to the Romans' sense, a defensive posture. Romans reasoned, *If the barbarians get uppity, they might attack. To be safe, we need to make sure they never get uppity. Shock and awe keep them in their place, and any sign of weakness only encourages them.* Roman imperial policy may be described as a pursuit of "security" so long as it is understood that security meant honor.[11] Virgil had written that the Roman Empire existed to subdue pride, *superbia*. That was true, but Romans came to define *superbia* as any opposition to Rome.[12]

Constantinus Imperator

Constantine was immersed in Rome's military culture. He was in the Roman army from his youth to the end of his life, and like nearly every Roman emperor before and most after him, he was ambitious for territory and glory. Like his predecessors, he was willing to use brute force to attain his goals, and he covered his violence with propaganda that makes it impossible to know what actually happened.[13] By the early fourth century, the

---

[9]See especially Mattern, *Rome and the Enemy*, chap. 5. For a discussion of the dynamics of honor in the internal politics of the empire, see J. E. Lendon, *Empire of Honor* (Oxford: Oxford University Press, 2005). These should be balanced and nuanced by the profound meditations of Carlin A. Barton ("Savage Miracles: The Redemption of Lost Honor in Roman Society and the Sacrament of the Gladiator and the Martyr," *Representations* 45 [1994]: 41-71), who emphasizes the "less sanguine and sober strains" in the late republican and early imperial culture, the sense that all of Rome's victories were hollow, and the fascination with heroic death.
[10]Dio Cassius *Roman History* 67.4.6.
[11]Mattern, *Rome and the Enemy*, p. 215.
[12]Ibid., p. 175, notes that *superbia* is "a vice characteristic of people of high status," the "opposite of deference and therefore exactly what one wished to avoid in one's enemies."
[13]I have in mind especially the deaths of Maximian and Licinius, both of whom died after

empire was more defensive than expansive (see below). One index of this stance was the fact that many of Constantine's military victories occurred in wars waged against other Romans, usually relatives.[14] He became the undisputed Western Augustus after putting down a revolt led by his father-in-law Maximian, took Rome by invading Italy while it was under the control of his brother-in-law/uncle-by-marriage Maxentius, and expanded his domains to the east in two wars against another brother-in-law, Licinius. He believed these were wars of liberation, and many of his subjects agreed. Rome greeted him with enthusiasm, and the Christians of the East welcomed him as the church's liberator from the persecution of Licinius. Enthusiastic Eusebius celebrated his victories as gifts of God, and the more sober Augustine attributed his success in war to God's blessing: "In conducting and carrying on wars he was most victorious; in overthrowing tyrants he was most successful."[15] There is no evidence that any bishops criticized Constantine for his conquests and battles with family members, and the evidence that survives suggests that they warmly supported him. Perhaps they knew more than we, and knew that every last one of Constantine's actions was a justifiable act of self-defense. I find that unlikely. Constantine was less brutal than some emperors, but one does not have to be a pacifist to notice unpleasant resemblances between Christian Constantine's career and that of any of a dozen pagan emperors.

Also like many Roman emperors, though more effectively than most, he used the symbols of power to enhance his own imperial reputation and power. From Vespasian and Domitian his father had adopted the name Flavius, a signal of "his own new dynastic pretensions."[16] The original Flavian family was not especially successful, lasting only three generations and ending with the assassination of Domitian in 96. Besides, Domitian had been condemned by Christian writers as a persecutor. Yet Constantine found something to emulate in the Flavians: their contribution to the Ro-

---

Constantine defeated them, and both of whom were charged with conspiring against Constantine. Possibly they really did plot; we can see from other incidents that Maximian was not eager to give up power. But we cannot know for sure, and it is likely that they were executed on Constantine's orders and for the protection of his own power. On Crispus and Fausta, see chapter 10.

[14]A point stressed by Raymond Van Dam, *The Roman Revolution of Constantine* (Cambridge: Cambridge University Press, 2008).

[15]Augustine *City of God* 5.25.

[16]Van Dam, *Roman Revolution*, p. 91.

man cityscape. Domitian had such a reputation for building that people joked he had a Midas touch that turned everything to stone. His most important building was the new Temple of Jupiter Optimus Maximus on the Capitoline Hill, still a landmark by the fourth century.[17] Constantine also tried to channel some of Trajan's success by reusing some of Trajan's Roman monuments. Details of Constantine's triumphal arch were sculpted from Trajan's statues and reliefs, and the colossal statue of himself that he placed in Maxentius's Basilica Nova, of which only an enormous head, a hand and a kneecap remain, "may have originally been a statue of Trajan."[18] He rebuilt Trajan's bridge across the Danube.

Constantine inherited a position as Caesar at his father's death, the Western empire after defeating his brother-in-law Maxentius and the Eastern empire after defeating another brother-in-law, Licinius. He was an imperialist, and apparently aspired to be an imperialist like Trajan, who wanted to be like Alexander.

Yet something had changed. With Constantine, the Roman army and empire, like Roman worship, Roman cityscapes, Roman law and society, were being transformed. Something new was being born. Rome had been baptized and was being desacrificed.

What Does the Emperor Want to Hear?

Late Roman emperors lived in a bubble. Diocletian had introduced all manner of court ceremonial, appropriate to his supposed divine status, and many features of that ceremonial continued after the Tetrarchy collapsed, especially in the florid rhetoric of the panegyrists. Stamped with overconscious artifice, "poetical tricks, avoidance of hiatus or of inelegant words; metrical terminations of sentences or clauses; variation through an apparently limitless vocabulary of periphrasis," panegyrics celebrated the emperor's divine virtues and successes. "One almost imagines . . . that the emperor never had a normal conversation with anybody."[19]

Panegyrists did not tell a story straight, but neither were they necessarily official instruments of court propaganda.[20] Panegyrists thought about

---

[17]Ibid., pp. 94-95.
[18]Ibid., p. 88.
[19]Ramsey MacMullen, *Constantine* (London: Croom Helm, 1987), pp. 14-16.
[20]On the relation of emperor to panegyrist, see C. E. V. Nixon, "Constantinus Oriens Imperator: Propaganda and Panegyric; On Reading Panegyric 7 (307)," *Historia* 42 (1993): 229-46.

how their subjects would receive their praises and told emperors things they thought the emperors wanted to hear. We can wring important historical truths from the panegyrists, so long as we read them upside down and backwards. Panegyrists returned again and again to common themes, and in these themes they laid out a vision of what kind of man the emperor was supposed to be, what kind of man the emperor thought he was. Emperors were to be virtuous men, guided by justice, temperance, courage and prudence. Panegyrists frequently alluded to the imperial *recusatio,* a ritual reluctance to assume power whose precedent had been established by Augustus. Military ability was important, as was readiness to provide for subjects (*providentia*) and cooperate with colleagues (*concordia*). Since Augustus, *pietas* was a leading virtue; an emperor could not expect success without the assistance of the gods.[21] Emperors were also expected to express the imperial strategy of honor.

Constantine's panegyrists no doubt distorted as much as any. A panegyrist told him around 310 in Triers that he was a "most sacred Emperor" to whose "divinity" he offered his address.[22] After his father died, he fought back the tears, the orator said, remembering that "it was not right to mourn any longer a ruler who had been consecrated as a god."[23] Constantine himself had arisen, like every new divinity, from the edge of the earth, as "Mercury from the Nile, the source of which river is unknown, and Liber from the land of the Indians, who are almost privy to the sunrise, have shown themselves to mankind as gods manifest." He had a theory: "Regions next to heaven are more holy than Mediterranean ones," and therefore "it is closer for an Emperor to be sent by the gods from where the land ends."[24]

Godlike conquests were another subject for celebration. Constantine had recently put down the revolt of his father-in-law, Maximian, but the panegyrist focused on Constantine's earlier conquests among the Franks. When the Frankish kings tried to take "the opportunity of your father's absence to violate the peace," Constantine "visited the punishment of their

---

[21]I am drawing on the summary provided by C. E. V. Nixon and Barbara Saylor Rodgers, eds., *In Praise of Later Roman Emperors: The Panegyrici Latini* (Berkeley: University of California Press, 1994), pp. 23-24.

[22]Panegyric 6.1.5, in ibid., p. 218.

[23]Panegyric 6.8.3, in ibid., p. 230.

[24]Panegyric 6.9.4-5, in ibid., p. 232.

rashness" on the "contemptible band of barbarians who tested the very beginnings of your reign with a sudden attack and unexpected brigandage." He imposed the "ultimate penalty," even at the risk of "perpetual hatred of that race and their implacable fury." That was good policy: "clemency is secure insofar as it spares enemies and protects its own interest." Pardon is "more prudent," but "to trample them down in their fury" is "more courageous." That is what Constantine did.

> So that the monstrous power of the barbarians might be broken in every way, and so that the enemy should not merely grieve over the punishment of their kings, you have made in addition, invincible Emperor, a devastating raid on the Bructeri. In this the first aim of your strategy was to attack them when they were off guard by suddenly throwing your army across . . . that this nation, which is accustomed to frustrate warfare by taking refuge in forests and marshes, should lose the opportunity for flight. And so countless numbers were slaughtered, and very many were captured. Whatever herds there were were seized or slaughtered; all the villages were put to the flame; the adults who were captured, whose untrustworthiness made them unfit for military service and whose ferocity for slavery, were given over to the amphitheater for punishment, and their great numbers wore out the raging beasts.[25]

Such an emperor: young, courageous, with flashing eyes and a majesty that "dazzles us at the same time as it invites our gaze." Such an emperor must have been "that great king" Alexander and his hero, Achilles, "the Thessalian hero, whose combination of courage and beauty is celebrated."[26]

Several years later, another panegyrist celebrated Constantine's triumph over the "contemptibly small," "twisted" and slack-limbed Maxentius in similar terms, and drew from this success a warning for barbarians who might consider attacking the empire. Constantine cheerfully "accepts the submission of friendly kings and the very fact of being feared and cultivated by the noblest kings counts the same as praise for victory [*ad laudem victoriae*]," yet barbarians should not think him soft: "he is glad that the fame of his valor [*gloriam virtutis suae gaudet*] is increased as often as it is challenged." Nothing is "lovelier than this triumphal celebration in which

---

[25]Panegyric 6.12.1-3, in ibid., pp. 234-35.
[26]Panegyric 6.17.2, in ibid., p. 243, with n. 79 identifying the references.

he employs the slaughter of enemies for the pleasure of us all, and enlarges the procession of the games out of the survivors of the massacre of the barbarians."[27]

The whole Roman ideology of conquest is there. Swift, godlike Constantine descends to the field seeking praise and fame, whether by clemency or by conquest. Blood and slaughter follow him on campaigns, reducing enemy fury to abject fear. Once Constantine converted, churchmen seem to have played along. Like the panegyrist of 306, Eusebius compared Constantine to Cyrus and Alexander the Great, whose conquests also followed a steady eastward progress. Constantine "began his reign at the time of life at which the Macedonian died, yet doubled the length of his life, and trebled the length of his reign." He started "as far as the Britons, and the nations that dwell in the very bosom of the Western ocean." As he moved through Europe, "he subdued likewise all Scythia, though situated in the remotest North, and divided into numberless diverse and barbarous tribes." His conquests pushed "to the Blemmyans and Ethiopians, on the very confines of the South," and he did not "think the acquisition of the Eastern nations unworthy his care." Though beginning in the far west, his reign was like the sunrise, "diffusing the effulgence of his holy light to the ends of the whole world, even to the most distant Indians, the nations dwelling on the extreme circumference of the inhabited earth." Everywhere, "he received the submission of all the rulers, governors, and satraps of barbarous nations, who cheerfully welcomed and saluted him, sending embassies and presents, and setting the highest value on his acquaintance and friendship; insomuch that they honored him with pictures and statues in their respective countries, and Constantine alone of all emperors was acknowledged and celebrated by all."[28]

---

[27]Panegyric 12.23.2-3, in ibid., p. 329.

[28]Eusebius *Life* 1.8. The poet Publilius Optatianus Porfyrius, known as the "Ovid of the Constantinian Age," thought the same. He described the homage paid by Indians, Arabs, Ethiopians and Armenians to Constantine (Elizabeth Key Fowden, "Constantine and the Peoples of the Eastern Frontier," in *The Cambridge Companion to the Age of Constantine,* ed. Noel Lenski [Cambridge: Cambridge University Press, 2006], pp. 377-98, 389). In the fourteenth of his *Carmena* he, like Eusebius, described Constantine's progress toward the east as the spread of light into the world's darkness:
Iamnunc sub axe placido, beate princeps,
mundo fauente populis, serene, iustis,
numen salubre, tribuens triumpha uictor,
faustis perenne dominans amore saeclis,

Constantine's conception of his own life's work was much the same. "Beginning at the remote Britannic ocean, and the regions where, according to the law of nature, the sun sinks beneath the horizon," he wrote, "I banished and utterly removed every form of evil which prevailed, in the hope that the human race, enlightened through my instrumentality, might be called to a due observance of the holy laws of God, and at the same time our most blessed faith might prosper under the guidance of his almighty hand."[29]

EMPIRE ON DEFENSE

Rhetoric did not match the reality. During the third and fourth centuries, Roman emperors had little time for conquest. Their role was mainly defensive. As we saw in chapter two, the third century witnessed a recurring pattern of internal conflict and external threat. Whenever there was an interregnum, or when two pretenders were vying for power in the empire, the barbarians would seize the chance to invade. As long as Roman armies could concentrate on fighting barbarians, the situation was a decided mismatch in Rome's favor; but when Rome's armies were being deployed against one another, the barbarians had a free hand to invade and pillage. During the third and fourth centuries, the good emperors were the ones who spent their time fighting barbarians rather than other Romans.[30]

When Diocletian wanted to celebrate the achievements of his imperial reign in the prologue to his Price Edict, he pointed to the fact that the empire had been free from barbarian invasions:

We may thank the good fortune of our state, as well as the immortal gods,

---

ibit quietus Oriens, salutis auctor.
Dextra superne domini fauente uotis,
omen regentis placidum subire gaudet;
praestat serena radians uigore uirtus
mundi remota superis uidere sanctis,
numen salubre moderans sub orbe totum,
nutu fauente supero ubique uincens,
solus, beate, dominans per omne saeclum.

[29]Letter to the Provincials of Palestine, quoted in Eusebius *Life* 2.28. Though his movement is from east to west, the roundel on the east side of the arch of Constantine shows Sol rising on his quadriga.

[30]Hugh Elson, "Warfare and the Military," in *The Cambridge Companion to the Age of Constantine*, ed. Noel Lenski (Cambridge: Cambridge University Press, 2006), p. 339; Michael Kulikowski, "Constantine and the Northern Barbarians," in *Cambridge Companion*, p. 358.

on remembering the wars we have waged successfully. The condition of the world has been placed, tranquil, in the lap of the deepest quiet and peace towards good men. For this reason we have labored and spent our effort lavishly. Now both Roman dignity and majesty desire that the public honor be arranged faithfully and fittingly adorned. We, who by supernatural forces' benevolent support have suppressed the raging depredations of the past by slaughtering the very peoples of the barbarian tribes, will secure the quiet we have established with the reinforcements Justice deserves.

It was no little thing when Christians taunted Diocletian about his military failures. Their criticisms challenged "the foundations of his claim to rule."[31]

The turmoil that followed the retirement of Diocletian and Maximian created conditions similar to those of the previous century, but Constantine's rise to sole imperial power again gave the empire internal stability and helped prevent further incursions. Much of Constantine's imperial propaganda supported the image of the emperor as protector of Rome against barbarians. He gave up his family's mythical connection with Hercules and replaced it with a genealogical connection to Claudius, known as Gothicus for his defeat of the Goths during his reign, and linked himself symbolically to Trajan.[32] He claimed to be successful in defending the empire.

Not everyone agreed. In his satirical symposium *Caesares*, Constantine's grand-nephew, the emperor Julian, depicts Constantine boasting of his achievements before an assembly of great conquerors—Alexander, Julius and Octavius, and Trajan. Constantine claims victories over Romans, Germans, Scythians and Asian barbarians. When the host Silenus suggests he has offered "mere gardens of Adonis as exploits," Constantine is confused. Silenus explains that by "gardens of Adonis" he means "those that women plant in pots, in honour of the lover of Aphrodite, by scraping together a little earth for a garden bed. They bloom for a little space and fade forthwith." Julian concluded, "At this Constantinus blushed, for he realised that this was exactly his own performance."[33]

Zosimus too was a critic of Constantine's military and imperial policies.

---

[31]Kulikowski, "Northern Barbarians," p. 358.
[32]Ibid. See also Fowden, "Peoples of the Eastern Frontier," p. 378.
[33]Julian *Caesares*.

Far from protecting the empire against barbarian invasion, Constantine left the empire far more vulnerable than it had been. He "gave the Barbarians free access into the Roman dominions" by reversing Diocletian's policy of garrisoning towns and establishing fortresses along the frontier." Instead Constantine removed "the greater part of the soldiers from those barriers of the frontiers" and sent them to towns farther from the borders. People along the frontier "were exposed to the Barbarians" without defense, and the towns were oppressed "with so great a multitude of soldiers, that many of them were totally forsaken by the inhabitants." In short, "he was the first cause of the affairs of the empire declining to their present miserable state."[34] The anti-Christian bias of Julian and Zosimus distorts their story here. Constantine's reign was marked by comparative peace along the frontier, as well as internally.

Constantine did have one opportunity at the end of his reign to mount a large-scale campaign. Persia had long been the eastern nemesis of the Roman Empire. In 260, the Roman emperor Valerian was defeated and captured by the Persian ruler Shapur I. Galerius recovered some of Rome's dignity with a devastating victory over Shapur's son Narseh in 297, but the memory of Valerian's flayed skin, which was dyed and hung in a Persian temple after his death, continued to haunt the Roman consciousness.[35] Gripped by the anxiety of influence, Constantine was again playing Trajan, contemplating an eastern campaign that would surpass his predecessor's.[36]

Constantine had contemplated an invasion of Persia since 325. Around that time, he minted a medallion depicting him as Jupiter with an orb and phoenix, a symbol of eastern revival. The medallion also depicted Dionysus, a deity associated with Galerius and thus evoking the memory of that emperor's earlier triumph in Persia. According to Elizabeth Fowden, "Dionysus, the mythical conqueror of India, combined with the Phoenix looked forward not simply to the defense of Rome's eastern frontier but to the expansion toward the world's eastern reaches."[37]

---

[34]Zosimus *New History* 2.

[35]For an excellent brief summary of the pre-Constantinian relations with Persia, see Fowden, "Peoples of the Eastern Frontier," p. 382-84.

[36]Timothy D. Barnes, "Constantine and the Christians of Persia," *Journal of Roman Studies* 75 (1985): 135-36, analyzes an early-fourth-century text known as the *Itinerarium Alexandri* that links Alexander and Trajan and hints that Constantine's son Constantius was getting ready to invade Persia. The text, Barnes argues, illustrates "the hopes which Constantine aroused."

[37]Fowden, "Peoples of the Eastern Frontier," p. 390-91; see also Barnes, "Constantine and the

Only in 336 did he follow through on those plans. When he learned "of an insurrection of some barbarians in the East," the emperor "observed that the conquest of this enemy was still in store for him, and resolved on an expedition against the Persians. Accordingly he proceeded at once to put his forces in motion." Winning the bishops' approval was an essential part of the preparation, since "he judged it right to take [some] with him as companions, and as needful coadjutors in the service of God." For their part, the bishops cheerfully "declared their willingness to follow in his train, disclaiming any desire to leave him, and engaging to battle with and for him by supplication to God on his behalf. Full of joy at this answer to his request, he unfolded to them his projected line of march." To provide a place for their ministry, "he caused a tent of great splendor, representing in shape the figure of a church, to be prepared for his own use in the approaching war. In this he intended to unite with the bishops in offering prayers to the God from whom all victory proceeds."[38]

Constantine's death at Nicomedia in 337 cut short what might have been his most important campaign. Shapur wasted no time in taking advantage. He devastated Mesopotamia and then besieged Nisibis for two months before the city surrendered. The only descendant of Constantine who attempted to revive the effort was Julian, and he died from a hemorrhage caused by a spear wound after being pushed back from the walls of Ctesiphon. In 363, Shapur II forced major concessions from Julian's successor Jovian. Territories returned to their pre-Galerian borders, as Rome ceded five regions and fifteen forts to the Persians and agreed not to assist the Armenian king Arsak.[39]

GOD AND EMPEROR

Constantine's abortive Persian conquest looks like another Roman adventure driven by sacrificial frenzy for honor, vengeance and a desire to keep enemies in their subordinate place. Yet there are hints that between 306 and the 330s something had changed. Sometime before, Constantine had written a "tactful, allusive, and indirect"[40] letter in his own hand to

---

Christians," pp. 126-36; Garth Fowden, "The Last Days of Constantine: Oppositional Version and Their Influence," *Journal of Roman Studies* 84 (1994): 146-53.
[38]Eusebius *Life* 4.56.
[39]Fowden, "Peoples of the Eastern Frontier," p. 393.
[40]Barnes, "Constantine and the Christians," p. 131.

Shapur.[41] Addressing the Persian king as a "brother," he summarized the
"most holy religion" that had given him "deeper acquaintance with the
most holy God." Finding common ground with nonsacrificial Persian Zo-
roastrian practice, Constantine emphasized that the "God I invoke with
bended knees" is horrified by "the blood of sacrifices" and recoils from
"their foul and detestable odors." The sacrifice he craves is "purity of mind
and an undefiled spirit" that manifests itself in "works of moderation and
gentleness." "He loves the meek," Constantine continued, "and hates the
turbulent spirit. . . . While the arrogant and haughty are utterly overthrown, he requites the humble and forgiving with deserved rewards."

The purpose of the letter was to advise Shapur about how to deal with
the sizable Christian community in his own realm. Constantine was an
eyewitness of "the end of those who lately harassed the worshipers of God
by their impious edicts," and he warned Shapur not to follow their example. Everything is "best and safest" when men follow God's laws and recognize that God is at work through the church, endeavoring to "gather all
men to himself." He expressed his joy at hearing that Persia was full of
Christians, and he closed the letter with a prayer that "you and they may
enjoy abundant prosperity, and that your blessings and theirs may be in
equal measure," so that "you will experience the mercy and favor of that
God who is the Lord and Father of all."

Constantine's letter has been called a "veiled warning"[42] and has been
interpreted as a provocation, a threat and a sign of his belief that as Roman
emperor he had responsibility for all Christians. Constantine's Persian
policies certainly backfired. He initiated his final campaign when a delegation from Armenia visited Constantinople in 336 to ask him for assistance against a Persian coup. Since the conversion of the Armenian king
Trdat (Tiridates) in 314, Armenia had been officially Christian, more explicitly so than was the Roman Empire under Constantine. In the 330s,
Persians under Shapur II had invaded, captured and blinded the Armenian king Tirhan, and placed Shapur's brother Narseh on the Armenian
throne. Constantine responded swiftly. He designated his nephew Han-
nibalianus as "king of kings" and gave him authority over Armenia and

---

[41]Eusebius *Life* 4.9-13, along with notes in Eusebius, *Life of Constantine*, trans. Averil Cameron
and Stuart G. Hall (Oxford: Clarendon, 1999), pp. 313-15.
[42]Barnes, "Constantine and the Christians," p. 132.

Pontus.[43] Like his letter, his preparations for war with Persia were intended, among other things, to defend a Christian people. When Constantine died before the campaign could be launched, Shapur, apparently suspicious that the Christians of Persia were allied with Rome, initiated a violent persecution. Persian Christians, in response, kept themselves aloof from the dominant orthodoxy of the West.[44]

Yet I cannot agree that the letter to Shapur was intended as a provocation. Constantine warned Shapur, but he warned him of divine judgment, not that he would personally take vengeance if Shapur were to attack Christians. In the closing section Constantine issued an altar call, inviting Shapur to protect Christians and to join him in worship of the high God, the God of the Christians. Hermann Dorries summarizes the message of the letter as an invitation to share in the blessing of Christianization: "what the true faith had done for the Roman Empire," Constantine urged, "it could do also for the Persian." It was an unprecedented diplomatic move— a Roman emperor who "attributed his success to heavenly assistance . . . invited his only formidable enemy to share in this aid." More broadly, the letter reveals how far Constantine had moved from tetrarchic political theology. For Diocletian "religion and nation meant the same thing," but for Constantine there was a potential unity, even between East and West, even between Persia and Rome, that transcended boundaries and national interests.[45] Dorries says that Constantine wrote to Shapur like a modern politician disclosing to his rival the secret of the atom bomb.[46]

Constantine's letter to Shapur was not an isolated anomaly. Panegyrists told emperors what they thought emperors wanted to hear. It signaled a "Constantinian shift" (though not the one Yoder identifies) when the panegyrist Nazarius refused to tell the emperor in 317 he was a god, referred instead to "God the ruler of things [who] regards us from on high" and made other clumsy references to a God he did not know.[47] Nazarius still reviewed Constantine's conquests of Italy and ran through a quick list of

---

[43]Fowden, "Peoples of the Eastern Frontier," pp. 391-92.

[44]Barnes, "Constantine and the Christians," p. 136.

[45]Dorries (*Constantine the Great*, pp. 128-29) gets the tone right in describing it as "evangelistic" and an offer of "brotherhood."

[46]Hermann Dorries, *Constantine and Religious Liberty*, trans. Roland Bainton (New Haven, Conn.: Yale University Press, 1960).

[47]Panegyric 6.7.3, in *In Praise of Later Roman Emperors*, ed. and trans. Nixon and Rodgers, p. 351. Nazarius refers to God as *summa illa maiestas* (16.1) and *benigna maiestas* (19.2).

Frankish peoples subdued by the emperor—"Bructeri, Chamavi, Cher-
usci, Lancionae, Alamanni, Tubantes."[48] But these conquests were placed
in a different, uncertain, theology of empire.

We know that something more than a shift, something closer to a revolution, has occurred when Eusebius, at Constantine's *tricennalia*, delivered
a panegyric that explicitly reminded the emperor that he was only a *man*.
Half of Eusebius's oration was theology, and the portion that addressed
the emperor subordinated him, in a fashion that recalls Hellenistic theories of kingship, to the One God whose rule he mimicked. Constantine
derived not only his authority but all his imperial virtues from God. If he
was wise, good and just, it was by participation, because he had "fellowship with perfect Wisdom, Goodness, and Righteousness."[49] Eusebius
commended Constantine for offering God no sacrifice, "no blood and
gore," no smoke to "propitiate the infernal deities," but rather the sacrifice
of a pure mind, of imitation of "Divine philanthropy" in "imperial acts."
Above all, he offered himself: "wholly devoted to him, he dedicates himself as a noble offering, a first-fruit of that world, the government of which
is entrusted to his charge."[50] Eusebius celebrated victories since "the Almighty Sovereign . . . has made him victorious over every enemy that disturbed his peace,"[51] but the virtues he celebrated were not traditional military virtues but contempt for "earthly sovereignty" over "a petty and
fleeting dominion," disdain for "his vesture, embroidered with gold and
flowers," self-restraint in food and wine, chastity.[52] Gone were the celebrations of cruelty and terror, the endorsement of fame and pride, the sacrificial apparatus of the Roman imperial honor system. Yoder claims that
under the Constantinian system Christian rulers were expected to act like
non-Christian rulers, accepting the "natural" limits of their vocation.[53]
But Eusebius—the Constantinian theologian par excellence—did just
what Yoder said nobody did, and went a step further. Yoder makes the
broad, rather surprising claim that under the Constantinian system Caesar

---

[48]Panegyric 4.18.1, in ibid., p. 363.
[49]*Oration* 5.
[50]Ibid., 2.
[51]Ibid., 3.
[52]Ibid., 5.
[53]John Howard Yoder, *The Priestly Kingdom: Social Ethics as Gospel* (Notre Dame, Ind.: Univer-
    sity of Notre Dame Press, 1984), pp. 82-83, 145.

can never be asked to live like a Christian because the gospel contains no ethics for officials.[54] But Eusebius did expect Constantine to act like a Christian, and it was not unheard of for rulers in the subsequent "Constantinian" centuries to live like monks.

Eusebius maintained the same vision of empire and emperor in the *Vita Constantini*. He mentioned Constantine's conquests in passing, stressing, with suitable biblical echoes, Constantine's *pietas* and Moses-like meekness as barbarians are brought beneath his feet.[55] He defeated Licinius, but Eusebius said nothing about tactics and little about the battle—that we have to get from Zosimus. Instead, he recorded the prayer that Constantine's soldiers said before the battle.[56] Constantine prohibited images of himself in temples, spurned sacrifices offered to him, and went to battle wearing a cross on his shield behind a standard that is an explicitly Christian symbol.[57] A flash of the old ideology comes through when Eusebius recounted how Constantine attacked the Scythians because he could no longer bear the "indignity" of paying them tribute, and then had the cheek to combine this very Roman motivation with a reference to Constantine's "confidence in the Savior's aid."[58] Even this, however, is on the far side of a chasm from standard imperial theology, according to which the emperor *was* the *soter* rather than reliant on One.[59]

History's Core

Thomas Heilke characterizes Eusebius's imperial theology as an expression of Constantinianism, the subservience of Christianity to the empire. Prior to Constantine, Heilke says, the ruler was "an agent with a specific role that is in accordance with good social order." In the Eusebian/Lactantian ideology of Christian empire, by contrast, the ruler becomes a "representative of cosmic order" such that "earthly rule imitates the heavenly." In

[54]John Howard Yoder, *Christian Attitudes to War, Peace and Revolution*, ed. Theodore J. Koontz and Andy Alexis-Baker (Grand Rapids: Brazos, 2009), p. 58. This is true in the trivial sense that the gospel contains no "mirror for magistrates."

[55]Eusebius *Life* 1.46; see comments in Eusebius, *Life*, ed. and trans. Cameron and Hall, p. 222.

[56]Eusebius *Life* 2.12; 4.19-20.

[57]Ibid., 4.16, 21.

[58]Ibid., 4.5-7; see Cameron and Hall's edition, pp. 311-13, for the background.

[59]See also ibid., 2.28, where Constantine tells the people of Palestine that he "banished and utterly removed every form of evil." This sounds like hubris, but he claims to be nothing more than God's instrument who, by "the aid of divine power," recalls all nations to "the holy laws of God."

fact, Eusebius was normally doing precisely the reverse of what Heilke claims: his "Oration" and *Life* do not make the church subservient to the empire, nor do they accommodate Christian faith to the sacrificial honor system of the empire, but rather they fit the emperor and his empire into a cosmic Christian framework. As Heilke himself says, summing up Eric Voegelin's analysis of Christendom, "Secular rulership, as it begins to emerge in the panegyrics of Eusebius and Lactantius, becomes an explicitly Christian function, so that by the ninth century, the 'royal function' has been integrated 'into the order of the charismata.'"[60]

Did Eusebius become a "Constantinian" by identifying the emperor as the "primary bearer of meaning in history"?[61] It might seem so, but the fact that he took the unprecedented step of writing a history of the *church* suggests otherwise. Earlier chroniclers wrote about battles, kings, warriors, but the backbone of Eusebius's history was a chronological list of bishops.[62] Even when he wrote about Constantine, he emphasized his piety rather than his prowess. History writing had been baptized.

Prudentius (348-c. 413) gave poetic expression to a similar theology of empire. Rome's story was not the master narrative of history. Instead history was structured by biblical episodes of creation, fall, redemption, judgment. Yet Rome, like every other people, had its place within that narrative. Pagan Rome functioned typologically, as "all kings, prophets, judges,

---

[60]Thomas Heilke, "Yoder's Idea of Constantinianism: An Analytical Framework Toward Conversation," in *A Mind Patient and Untamed: Assessing John Howard Yoder's Contributions to Theology, Ethics and Peacemaking,* ed. Ben C. Ollenburger and Gayle Gerber Koontz (Telford, Penn.: Cascadia, 2004), pp. 89-125. According to Yoder, the early Christians believed that "creation" and its institutions, including the state, were subordinate to the order of redemption, but after Constantine this was reversed—Christian life became a matter of submitting to the standards internal to created institutions. Heilke's criticism reverses Yoder's standard criticism; his complaint is that post-Constantine Christian writers subordinated the order of creation to the order of redemption.

[61]This, once again, is one of Yoder's formulations of the "heresy of Constantinianism." He says that for the Bible "the meaning of history had been carried by the people of God as people, as community" (*Priestly Kingdom*, p. 138). While true in a sense, this concept neglects the central role of representation in Scripture; the history of the Davidic kingship is the history of the people because the Davidic king personally embodies Yahweh's son, Israel (cf. Exodus 4:23; Peter J. Leithart, *A Son to Me: An Exposition of 1 and 2 Samuel* [Moscow, Ida.: Canon, 2003]). Besides, while Scripture includes accounts of patriarchs and Moabite widows, it also includes 1-2 Kings and 1-2 Chronicles, telling the story of the monarchy twice! There is no 1-2 Peasants.

[62]Robert L. Wilken, *The Myth of Christian Beginnings* (Notre Dame, Ind.: University of Notre Dame Press, 1970), pp. 57-59.

and rulers / . . . did not cease to depict the form of the cross."[63] Rulers
provided various goods for their subjects, and so Christians offered prayers
for the emperor "so that his battle-array may be favorable, and / that when
his enemies are subdued he as leader may govern with his laws a peaceful
world."[64] Alone among fourth-century writers, Prudentius went so far as
to suggest that Christ rather than Romulus was the true founder of Rome
(*auctor horum moenium*). Christians therefore rightly inherit what their
Lord founded. Overarching this endorsement of a Christian empire is
Prudentius's insistence that the conversion of the soul is the key to Christian politics and to the renewal of Rome after Constantine. Peace, he
writes, is the true sacrifice: "Whoever would worship God / properly with
the whole burnt offerings, let him above all offer peace. / No sacrifice is
sweeter to Christ; this gift alone pleases him with a pure / aroma when he
turns his face toward the holy altar."[65]

Augustine and Eusebius held the same views at least on this point: The
virtues that make an emperor worthy of the title "the Great" are not love
of honor, prowess in battle or bloodthirsty ruthlessness. Rather,

> we say that they are happy if they rule justly; if they are not lifted up amid
> the praises of those who pay them sublime honors, and the obsequiousness
> of those who salute them with an excessive humility, but remember that
> they are men; if they make their power the handmaid of His majesty by
> using it for the greatest possible extension of His worship; if they fear, love
> and worship God; if more than their own they love that kingdom in which
> they are not afraid to have partners; if they are slow to punish, ready to
> pardon; if they apply that punishment as necessary to government and de-
> fense of the republic, and not in order to gratify their own enmity; if they
> grant pardon, not that iniquity may go unpunished, but with the hope that
> the transgressor may amend his ways; if they compensate with the lenity of
> mercy and the liberality of benevolence for whatever severity they may be
> compelled to decree; if their luxury is as much restrained as it might have
> been unrestrained; if they prefer to govern depraved desires rather than any
> nation whatever; and if they do all these things, not through ardent desire
> of empty glory, but through love of eternal felicity, not neglecting to offer

---

[63]Quoted in Marc Mastrangelo, *The Roman Self in Late Antiquity: Prudentius and the Poetics of the Soul* (Baltimore: Johns Hopkins University Press, 2008), p. 56.
[64]Quoted in ibid., p. 54.
[65]Ibid., p. 116.

to the true God, who is their God, for their sins, the sacrifices of humility, contrition, and prayer.[66]

Rather than fitting the church into a grand narrative of Roman *imperium,* Eusebius was trying to find a place for the empire in the Christian story. It may all be exaggerated, or worse, Eusebius may have been nothing more than a court toady, worming himself into the emperor's favor. I think not. Even if he is, panegyrists tell emperors what they want to hear, and we can be sure that if Constantine was not the kind of man Eusebius said he was, at least we may conclude that the emperor Eusebius described was the emperor Constantine *aspired* to be. Even if we do not trust a word Eusebius said about Constantine, he delivered to the emperor a dramatically novel vision of imperial character and conduct.

FALL OF THE CHURCH?

Still, it was an empire, and there's the rub.[67] If it is empire, no matter how Christian the emperor might be, it is not good.

So, at least, is the widespread opinion among Christian thinkers. Yoder and other theological critics of Constantine have three main criticisms of Constantine and Constantinianism with regard to his imperialism. First and foremost, Constantinianism simply *is* the identification of nation or empire with the purposes of God. By misidentifying the location of God's action in history—which Christianity assigns to the church, but Constan-

---

[66]Augustine *City of God* 5.24.

[67]Thousands of books have been published on empire, many in recent years. Theologians and biblical scholars have entered the fray. See, for example, Wes Avram, ed., *Anxious About Empire: Theological Essays on the New Global Realities* (Grand Rapids: Brazos, 2004); Richard A. Horsley, ed., *Paul and Empire: Religion and Power in Roman Imperial Society* (Harrisburg, Penn.: Trinity Press International, 1997), *Jesus and Empire: The Kingdom of God and the New World Disorder* (Minneapolis: Fortress, 2003), and *In the Shadow of Empire: Reclaiming the Bible as a History of Faithful Resistance* (Louisville, Ky.: Westminster John Knox, 2008); Bruce Ellis Benson and Peter Goodwin Heltzel, eds., *Evangelicals and Empire: Christian Alternatives to the Political Status Quo* (Grand Rapids: Brazos, 2008); John Dominic Crossan, *God and Empire: Jesus Against Rome, Then and Now* (San Francisco: Harper, 2007). In the wider debate, the works of Noam Chomsky have a large place; see also various works by Chalmers Johnson and Andrew Bacevich. Yale Ferguson, "Along the Imperial Continuum: Varieties of Empire," paper presented at the annual meeting of the American Political Science Association, 2007, available at <www.allacademic.com/one/www/research/index.php?click_key=1&PHPSESSI D=56cb1a454165afe64be71e12aef6296a>, and Alexander Motyl, "Is Everything Empire? Is Empire Everything?" *Comparative Politics* 39 (2006), are representative of the debate within academic political science.

tinianism assigns to the prince, the empire or the nation—Constantinians operate on the premise "that one nation or people or government can represent God's cause in opposition to other peoples who, being evil, need to be brought into submission."[68] This is ecclesiological and eschatological "heresy"—ecclesiological because the church gets absorbed into some worldly system, eschatological because the eschatological community, the church, gets absorbed into the realm of this world (empire) and because the eschatological order is dragged forward into the present age. As a result of the collapse of the church's independent identity and the mergence of *Romanitas* with *Christianitas,* the mission of the church was, after Constantine, profoundly distorted.

The fall into Constantinianism, second, represents a shift from an earlier anti-imperial stance.[69] Earlier, most Christians would have agreed with the sharp antithesis drawn by Tertullian: "One soul cannot be indebted to two, God and Caesar."[70] Origen, Tertullian and Cyprian all believed the empire to be "diabolical."[71] Yet during the second and third centuries something was changing. Christians were becoming comfortable with the Roman world, a comfort evidenced by the apologists who cared about the unbelieving world, its culture and its patterns of thought and language. There are signs of "creeping empire loyalty."[72] After Constantine, this loyalty stopped creeping and began to gallop as Christians found it quite easy to serve God and Caesar both, even—and this is the third of Yoder's criticisms—when Caesar told Christians to kill. Yoder argues that early Christians were uniformly opposed to Christians in military service. During the second and third centuries, Christians entered the Roman military and slowly acclimated to using violence. It was wrong, it was apostasy, but there was a "growing tolerance of apostasy," and so even though "nobody approved" their presence in the army, they were "not excommunicated."[73] Constantine opened the floodgates and thus has come

---

[68]John Howard Yoder, *The Original Revolution: Essays on Christian Pacifism* (Scottdale, Penn.: Herald, 1971, 2003), p. 68.

[69]Yoder wrote his books before the current obsession with empire, and he rarely deals with the subject directly.

[70]Tertullian *On Idolatry* 19. The Latin reads "non potest una anima duobus deberi, deo et Caesari."

[71]Yoder, *Christian Attitudes,* p. 49.

[72]Ibid., pp. 49-51.

[73]Ibid., pp. 53-54.

to symbolize, for Yoder and his followers, the transition from the church of the martyrs, ready to be killed rather than kill, to the church of the Crusaders, ready to smash in Arab skulls with a cry of *Iesu Dominus*.

As in the previous chapters, my interest here is historical rather than theological.[74] I realize that this does not get to the heart of Yoder's thought. Still, asking the historical questions is important since Yoder's theology is so deeply bound up with an account of Christian history. If he got Christian history wrong, that sets a question mark over his theology.

Taking Yoder's criticisms in reverse order, the following chapters probe a series of questions: First, in the next chapter, *Was* the early church in fact uniformly opposed to Christians serving in the Roman army? Was there a shift in Christian attitudes toward war and violence with Constantine's ascent to the throne? If so, what sort of shift was it, and what drove the shift? Then, in chapter thirteen: did the earliest Christians oppose the Roman Empire, and was there a dramatic change during the second to fourth centuries? Finally, also in chapter thirteen: did the Roman Christians so identify the church with the empire that they ignored or despised the barbarians who encircled it?

At every point Yoder can point to evidence to support his claims, and at times he provides a provocative new framework for addressing a question. As I demonstrate in the following chapters, however, his claims are, as historical claims, sometimes questionable, sometimes oversimplified to the point of being misleading, sometimes one-sided, sometimes simply wrong.

---

[74]I examine some of these theological and ethical concerns in the final chapter, though even there it will be impossible for me to deal fully with Yoder's concerns, especially the issue of pacifism.

12

Pacifist Church?

Concerning those who lay down their weapons in peacetime
it is resolved that they be excluded from fellowship.

CANONS OF THE COUNCIL OF ARLES, 314

The Christian faith burst into the world as a message of peace.[1] At Jesus' birth, angels descended singing, "Peace on earth among men of God's favor." Jesus the Prince of Peace preached an anti-Zealot message of reconciliation and renunciation of vengeance. "Turn the other cheek" replaced, in the eyes of some interpreters of Jesus' teaching, the Torah's "an eye for an eye" as the rule for Christians. While Paul acknowledged that the civil authorities were established by God and that they provided some goods, the relation of Christians to the state was, it is argued, mainly a relation of antagonism and enmity.

The early fathers emphasized that the gospel brought peace wherever it took hold. Justin pointed the Jew Trypho to the fact that humans "who were filled with war, and mutual slaughter, and every wickedness, have each through the whole earth changed our warlike weapons—our swords into ploughshares, and our spears into implements of tillage." In place of warfare, "we cultivate piety, righteousness, philanthropy, faith, and hope,

---

[1]Though Yoder asserts more than he can prove on the historical question, his careful and probing ethical treatments of the subject are very challenging for just war thinkers. See especially John Howard Yoder, *When War Is Unjust: Being Honest in Just-War Thinking* (1996; reprint, Eugene, Ore.: Wipf and Stock, 2001).

which we have from the Father Himself through Him who was crucified."[2] He returned to the theme in his first *Apology*, noting the radiating effects of piety from Jerusalem to the ends of the earth. "From Jerusalem there went out into the world, men, twelve in number," he wrote, and by the power of God these illiterates "proclaimed to every race of men that they were sent by Christ to teach to all the word of God." "As a result, we who formerly used to murder one another do not only now refrain from making war upon our enemies, but also, that we may not lie nor deceive our examiners, willingly die confessing Christ." He compared the commitment of martyrs to that of loyal soldiers and sons: "If the soldiers enrolled by you, and who have taken the military oath, prefer their allegiance to their own life, and parents, and country, and all kindred, though you can offer them nothing incorruptible, it were verily ridiculous if we, who earnestly long for incorruption, should not endure all things, in order to obtain what we desire from Him who is able to grant it."[3]

Christians, of course, were exhorted to love their enemies, and that meant cheerful submission to political powers. Yet early Christians, Yoder alleges, would never have considered exercising that power themselves, and they explicitly and absolutely refused to share in the violence of the state. According to Yoder, this is not capitulation to the powers but instead a revolutionary "free subordination" that undoes the knots of power. Nor is this an apolitical stance. Submission to the authorities for the sake of Jesus, the King of all creation, is a radical political stance, one that challenges the claims of power just as thoroughly as any movement of violent revolution.

Yoder claims that the church "fell" from this gospel of peace into endorsement of violence and war, and this is an important, though, Yoder says, not the most fundamental, dimension of the Constantinian apostasy.[4] Yoder

---

[2]Justin *Dialogue with Trypho* 110.

[3]Justin *First Apology* 39.

[4]Yoder argues in many places that the basic problem of Constantinianism is its ecclesiology and eschatology. Yet pacifism looms very large in his analysis of church history, and hence of Constantinianism. Without pacifist assumptions, much of Yoder's edifice crumbles. Yoder describes Constantinianism as, in part, the belief that "the Roman emperor and their God were allies" (John Howard Yoder, *The War of the Lamb: The Ethics of Nonviolence and Peacemaking*, ed. Glen Stassen et. al. [Grand Rapids: Brazos, 2009], p. 45). But how can Yoder know that this is *not* the case? The apparent presumption that it is impossible for a political ruler to be an "ally" of God rests on his pacifist ethic. Perhaps it is best to say that the church's supposedly shifting views on war and peace are, for Yoder, the leading *symptom* of the church's apostasy.

does not insist on the term *pacifist* as a description of the early church views, suggesting that much of the debate over early church pacifism indulges in "semantic quibble[s]." Rather, he claims that "Christians rejected Caesar's wars," which he describes as "a fact that no historians deny." The debate, he indicates, is only "about just why they did so."[5]

Yoder has in mind historical work such as that of John Helgeland, who concludes that "there is practically no evidence from the Fathers which would support the argument that the early church denied enlistment on the ground that killing and war were opposed to the Christian ethic." Having defined pacifism in that specific fashion, he adds that "the pacifist argument is an artificial construct" that arranges patristic fragments "in a way no Father ever could have done." After his exhaustive survey, Helgeland finds "no unequivocal statement to support" pacifism, and "certainly not one of any length such as a paragraph."[6] Yoder's point is that narrowing the definition of pacifism misses the larger picture. Early Christians, he argues, may not have had a worked-out pacifist ethic, but we can still speak in global terms of the "primitive Christian rejection of Caesar's wars."[7] My use of *pacifist* throughout this chapter acknowledges Yoder's proviso. I am using it in a loose sense not to denote a specific rationale for Christian opposition to war and violence but in reference to the simple fact of Christian opposition to violence and war. No matter what his reasons, a church father who condemns all Christian participation in war, or violent service to the state, is "pacifist."

The usefulness of Yoder's formulation—"rejection of Caesar's wars"—is questionable. For starters, it is ambiguous. Does "rejection of Caesar's wars" mean that Christians refused to fight or that they refused to support Caesar's wars in any way? Is a Christian who prays for the *success* of Caesar's wars, yet refuses to fight himself, "rejecting Caesar's wars"? And who is Caesar? Does "Caesar" stand in for any political ruler? For pagan political rulers? As we shall see below, this is a central question in assessing the early church view of war. If early Christians opposed wars because they were "Caesar's," what would happen if they become convinced (rightly or

---

[5]Ibid., p. 204, n. 10.
[6]John Helgeland, "Christians and the Roman Army from Marcus Aurelius to Constantine," *ANRW* 2.23.1 (1979): 764-65.
[7]Yoder, *War of the Lamb*, p. 45.

wrongly) that the wars were no longer Caesar's but Christ's? Would they still reject them? Or does Yoder consider *all* wars to be "Caesar's wars" and thus illegitimate for Christians? Yoder wants to subordinate the question of why to what he claims is the universally held view that Christians rejected Caesar's wars, but the why question cannot be put aside so swiftly. To make his historical case for a "Constantinian shift," Yoder has to prove not only that Christians "rejected Caesar's wars" but that they would have rejected wars regardless of whose they were.

Yoder knows that the change he describes did not happen all at once in the early fourth century, but that admission does not get him off the historical hook. Debating about the timing does not get at the issue. It does not matter *when* the shift happened, but if there was a shift at all, it had to happen *sometime*. This is crucial if Yoder is going to present a coherent account of the "Constantinian heresy." He argues that the early church was uniformly, or almost uniformly, pacifist and that Christians who served in the military would have been excommunicated. Then he argues that the evidence for Christians in the army in the mid-second century represents an accommodation to worldliness, a sign of drift and ultimately apostasy. Finally, he claims that Constantine consolidated and institutionalized this drift into a centuries-long apostasy. If the first premise is false, however, and the church was not uniformly pacifist, then the other stages of the argument collapse.

To assess the evidence of a shift, we have to examine befores and afters. What did Christians think and say about military service before "Constantinianism" took hold, and what, if anything, did they say differently after? More specifically, did the earliest Christians who wrote on the subject take a "pacifist" position, and if so, what were their reasons? On the other hand, did Christians after Constantine become bloodthirsty warmongers? Or do we find as much commitment to the Sermon on the Mount among "Constantinian" theologians as we find among pre-Constantinian theologians?[8] Equally important, what did Christians *do* with regard to the Roman army prior to Constantine? Af-

---

[8]Again, assumptions about pacifism shape the answer. If one takes the Sermon on the Mount as a pacifist manifesto, then of course Ambrose and Augustine and others who formulated Christian "just war" theory abandoned the Sermon on the Mount. But if the Sermon on the Mount does not entail pacifism, the assessment of post-Constantinian theologians will be very different.

ter all, however vigorously intellectuals like Origen and Tertullian opposed service in the army, and whatever their reasons, it is entirely possible that they represented a small, articulate minority that has come to be considered spokesmen only because they had the wherewithal to speak. What did the countless, nameless and forgotten local pastors think? How did they treat the converted soldiers who dropped in wanting to share the Eucharist with them? We have little evidence one way or another, but the sparseness of the evidence is crucial. How can we conclude anything about "what all Christians thought and did" when we are relying on tiny fragments of extant evidence?[9]

My argument does not bear the same burden as Yoder's. Yoder is correct only if he can prove a high degree of early Christian consensus in favor of pacifism. My argument, fortunately, does not have to leap such a high bar. If I can demonstrate that the evidence shows that the pre-Constantinian church uniformly acknowledged the legitimacy of Christian participation in the military, then of course I have shown that there was not a shift of the sort that Yoder claims. There may still have been a shift, as one would expect with a professing Christian running the empire and the army, but it would not be the fundamental change that Yoder claims. But I do not *have* to prove that the early church uniformly acknowledged the legitimacy of war and violence to make my case. I have to prove only diversity or ambiguity. If the church was not united on these issues prior to the "Constantinian shift," then it is possible that the church after Constantine took up one thread of earlier teaching, the thread that seemed most relevant to its changed political circumstances. Again, this would be a shift, but it would have been an internal shift of emphasis as the church applied Christ's teaching with a new set of responsibilities, rather than a fall from grace. That is not only possible but, I will argue, precisely what happened.[10]

Yoder's argument depends on drama, the drama of a fall from a primitive pacific paradise. To prove that a shift happened, Yoder has to find a starting point—a first act when Christians were exclusively or predominantly anti-

---

[9]James Jordan regularly makes this point in many different contexts.

[10]See the summary of research in David G. Hunter, "A Decade of Research on Early Christian Military Service," *Religious Studies Review* 18, no. 2 (1992): 87-94. On page 93 he concludes that the recent research has shown that "the efforts of Christians to justify participation in warfare for a 'just' cause . . . stand in fundamental continuity with at least one strand of pre-Constantinian tradition."

military pacifists—and then show that at some later time they no longer were pacifists. Can he do that? The answer is, unequivocally, no.

BEFORE CONSTANTINE

Christians are called to manifest and pursue the peace of Christ, and for some early Christian writers this quite directly implied that public life and particularly martial life was off limits. Athenagoras said that Christians never "strike back, do not go to law when robbed; they give to them that ask of them and love their neighbors as themselves."[11] Tertullian (ca. 160-ca. 220) did not remain consistent over his career. As we will see in the next chapter, early in his career he articulated a theory of empire that anticipated Eusebius, yet even in the pre-Montanist *Apology* he argued that Christians have put to death "all ardour in the pursuit of glory and honour" and thus "have no pressing inducement to take part in your public meetings." In fact, nothing is "more entirely foreign to us than affairs of state" (*nec ulla magis res aliena, quam publica*).[12] Origen admitted that public coercion and violence provide goods but found in this no endorsement of political power as such. A criminal might be condemned to "public works useful to the community" while in fact "he himself was engaged in an abominable task, in which no one possessed of moderate understanding would wish to be engaged." Wicked rulers too "contribute to the good of the whole, while in themselves they will be among the vile," but that is no argument for joining them.[13]

Participation of Christians in the Roman military, however, is more difficult to judge. The New Testament includes accounts of converted centurions (Matthew 8:1-13; perhaps Matthew 27:54 and Mark 15:39; Acts 10–11) and soldiers who sought baptism from John (Luke 3:14). It was part of Jesus' anti-Zealot program to minister to representatives of the Roman establishment, including tax collectors and soldiers. After the New Testament, we have no evidence whatever prior to 170-180.[14] The total absence

---

[11]Quoted in Roland Bainton, *Christian Attitudes Toward War and Peace: A Historical Survey and Critical Re-evaluation* (Nashville: Abingdon, 1960), p. 72.

[12]Tertullian *Apology* 38.

[13]Origen *Contra Celsum* 4.70.

[14]John Howard Yoder (*For the Nations: Essays Public and Evangelical* [Grand Rapids: Eerdmans, 1997], p. 70, n. 46) admits that "Christians did in some way participate in the Roman army" and accurately adds that "we know about it only from the words of those who thought they should not, and there is no way to know how many there were, or what their roles were." Yet

of evidence is important. Between the New Testament, where we have explicit evidence of Christians in the Roman military, and the latter part of the second century, we hear *nothing* about Christian soldiers. We could bridge this gap of silence by saying that after the events chronicled in the book of Acts no soldiers converted and no Christians entered the military; or we could bridge the gap by assuming that the pattern we find in the Gospels and Acts continued until new evidence emerges. One option receives as much support from the nonevidence as the other. I happen to think that one way of bridging the gap is more plausible than the other, but the *only* thing we can conclude with certainty is that we do not know whether the church of the first two centuries was pacifist in practice. Because we do not know about the practice of the church, we cannot really know about its convictions. The few writers whose works are preserved from the early centuries speak against Christian participation, but do their convictions match the view of the majority of Christians? What were local pastors saying? We simply cannot know.

After the mid-second century, there is a good deal of evidence for Christians in the army. From Celsus's charge that Christians would leave the emperor and empire defenseless we can infer that he knew of no Christians in the Roman military.[15] But by the latter decades of the century, we know for sure. When Marcus Aurelius was fighting Germans and Sarmatians in the late second century, the army ran out of water. Christian soldiers "kneeled on the ground" to pray, and soon "lightning drove the enemy to flight and destruction, but a shower refreshed the army of those who had called on God."[16] A handful of pre-Constantinian tomb inscrip-

---

somehow (as he adds in the same sentence) he knows that those who participated were not motivated by "any responsible theocratic visions of taking charge of history, or controlling the destiny of the empire." Rather, they participated—"in peacetime" only—because "the work was easy and the rewards generous," and they did not take time with "much moral analysis." That latter point may well be true, but Yoder's comments are sheer speculation. See also Yoder, *Christian Attitudes to War, Peace and Revolution*, p. 47.

[15]Bainton, *Christian Attitudes Toward War and Peace*, p. 68. For more on Christians in the Roman army, see Arthur Darby Nock, "The Roman Army and the Roman Religious Year," *Harvard Theological Review* 45, no. 4 (1952): 223-29.

[16]Eusebius *Church History* 5.5.1-2; see Bainton, *Christian Attitudes Toward War and Peace*, p. 157. Interestingly, Tertullian also knows of this story. This is likely the same event recounted in chapter 2, though Dio tells the story without reference to Christians. Whether or not the incident happened is somewhat immaterial. Helgeland notes that "there must have been enough Christians enlisting" to make the Christian use of the story plausible ("Christians and the Roman Army from Marcus Aurelius," p. 796).

tions for Christian soldiers survive, which not only show that there were Christians in the Roman army but "prove that the Christian communities where these men were buried did not prohibit the recording of the military profession upon their tombs."[17] Regional variations were important. Opposition to military service was most prevalent in the safe "interior of the *Pax Romana* and [was] less prevalent in the frontier provinces menaced by the barbarians." The exception to this generalization was Rome, where the church was more accommodating to military service than elsewhere. The Hellenistic East, with its base in Alexandria, was the most rigidly opposed to military service.[18]

Tertullian provides direct and indirect evidence of Christian participation in the army by the early third century. His treatise on the military crown was inspired by an account of a military martyrdom.[19] And in his early *Apology*, in response to the charge that Christians hold themselves aloof from the rest of humanity, Tertullian argued that Christians, though "but of yesterday," are still everywhere: "cities, islands, fortresses, towns, market-places, the very camp, tribes, companies, palace, senate, forum." Immediately he added, "For what wars should we not be fit, not eager, even with unequal forces, we who so willingly yield ourselves to the sword, if in our religion it were not counted better to be slain than to slay?" But the previous statement indicates that not all Christians avoided military service. Tertullian's Latin is "urbes, insulae, castella, municipia, conciliabula, castra ipsa, tribus, decurias, palatium, senatum, forum," and two of these terms—*castella* and *castra*—refer to military bases or fortresses.[20] Tertullian added the emphatic *ipsa* to *castra*; "even in military camps" captures the sense and suggests that the charge about Christian unsociability focused on their unwillingness to fight for the emperor.[21] The fact that Tertullian used this as part of a defense of Christianity indicates that he did not object, at that stage of his career, to some level of participation in the army.

The sheer intensity of some of Tertullian's later opposition to military

---

[17]Bainton, *Christian Attitudes Toward War and Peace*, p. 68.

[18]Ibid., pp. 69-70.

[19]Ibid., p. 152.

[20]Stephen Gero, "*Miles Gloriosus*: Christians and Military Service according to Tertullian," *Church History* 39 (1970): 292, calls these "technical military terms."

[21]Tertullian *Apology* 37.

service indicates that he was dealing with real Christians who were really entering military service. "To begin with," he wrote in his treatise on the military corona, "I think we must first inquire whether warfare is proper at all for Christians." His answer was no, but the negative answer had to be argued. That some Christians had been willing to take the *sacramentum* is evident from his impassioned, "Do we believe it lawful for a human oath to be superadded to one divine, for a man to come under promise to another master after Christ, and to abjure father, mother, and all nearest kinsfolk, whom even the law has commanded us to honor and love next to God Himself?" If Christians are forbidden to take suits to court, "shall the son of peace take part in the battle?" If Christians are not to avenge their own wrongs, "shall he apply the chain, and the prison, and the torture, and the punishment?" How can a Christian guard temples, protect demons in the process, carry a flag or obey orders from the emperor? "Shall he be disturbed in death by the trumpet of the trumpeter, who expects to be aroused by the angel's trump? And shall the Christian be burned according to camp rule, when he was not permitted to burn incense to an idol, when to him Christ remitted the punishment of fire?" According to Tertullian, "many other offences there are involved in the performances of camp offices," but this should be sufficient to keep Christians far away.[22] What is the point of all this rhetorical fervor unless some Christians were answering yes? Far from providing evidence for a universally pacifist church, Tertullian's antimilitary writings demonstrate "a divergence in Christian opinion and practice" by his time.[23]

Tertullian was reacting to the way many Christians responded to significant changes in the reputation and work of the Roman military. During the imperial reigns of Septimius Severus and Caracalla, power was shifting from the Senate to the military. Severus's deathbed advice to his sons, Geta and Caracalla, was probably legendary, but it captures the shifting balance of power: "Agree, enrich the soldiers and you can despise everybody else." Military settlements were established throughout the empire, soldiers at the frontier were given land of their own, and many of the soldiers settled down to a life of local service rather than campaigning. Marriage rules for soldiers were made more regular, and "families were

---

[22]Tertullian *De corona militis* 11.
[23]Hunter, "Decade of Research," p. 93.

allowed to live within the camp precincts."[24] As the empire became militarized, the military became civilianized. With military life becoming more settled, it became an increasingly attractive life for Christians, a development that alarmed Tertullian. This, Stephen Gero has argued, accounts for the striking shift in his writings on the army. When fewer Christians were in the military, Tertullian happily used their participation to score apologetic points; when Christians began clamoring to enter the army, he sternly warned about the evils of military service.

By the early fourth century Christian participation in the army was widespread, though participation in the army did not entail unquestioning obedience. Some of the Christians in the Roman military became martyrs. St. Sebastian is one of the best-known icons in Western art. Mantegna gave us a sculpted classical figure, arms and feet tied to a column in the ruins of a temple, looking mournfully to heaven as arrows protrude from his torso and legs. Carlo Saraceni's seventeenth-century depiction is softer, more clinical, as the figure reclines like an eroticized pietà with a single arrow that has penetrated near his groin. George de la Tour depicts a later part of the story, when the dead martyr is discovered to be alive by St. Irene. In all paintings the pincushion saint is nearly naked, clothed only in a loincloth, a sign both of his identification with Christ and of his renunciation of his military calling.[25]

St. Sebastian was one of many military martyrs of the early church, a victim, according to the thirteen-century Golden Legend, of Diocletian's purge.[26] Soon after his Christian friends Marcellianus and Marcus were killed, "S. Sebastian was accused to the emperor that he was Christian." Diocletian was furious: "I have always loved thee well," he protested, "and have made thee master of my palace; how then hast thou been Christian privily against my health, and in despite of our gods?" Sebastian insisted that he worshiped Jesus "for thy health and for the state of Rome," but Diocletian was not mollified. He had Sebastian tied to a stake and ordered archers to shoot at him "till he was as full of arrows as an urchin is full of pricks." He was left for dead, but Irene found him and nursed him back to

---

[24]This entire paragraph is indebted to Gero, *"Miles Gloriosus,"* esp. pp. 289-91. The summary of the "domestication" of the military is on p. 290.

[25]Saraceni's painting has the discarded armor and weaponry next to the dying saint.

[26]The text is available online at <www.fordham.edu/halsall/basis/goldenlegend/Golden Legend-Volume2.htm#Sebastian>.

health. Ignoring friendly advice to flee, Sebastian stood in a place where he knew Diocletian would find him. When Diocletian recognized him, he took him to prison, where he was beat to death with stones and thrown "into a great privy." Much of this is legendary, but the core story—that Sebastian was a martyred soldier in Diocletian's army—is given in the fourth century by Ambrose.

Outside the empire, Christians were willing to use coercive violence. During the persecution of Daia, the Christians of Armenia mounted armed opposition and defeated the persecuting Roman emperor. When the "tyrant" tried to force them to sacrifice, the Armenians, being Christian and "zealous in their piety toward the Deity," turned from allies into enemies of Rome. Daia "was defeated in the war with the Armenians, and the rest of the inhabitants of the cities under him were terribly afflicted with famine and pestilence, so that one measure of wheat was sold for twenty-five hundred Attic drachms."[27] The Syrians of Edessa, led by their Christian king Abgar IX, converted in the early third century, a full century prior to Constantine, and it is unlikely "that the ruler of a frontier province would have embraced the faith if by so doing he deprived himself of military resources."[28]

POLICE FORCE?

Yoder acknowledges that Christians entered the Roman army in the second and third centuries but sees this as a sign of creeping pre-Constantine Constantinianism, the church's slide into accommodation and apostasy. Earlier Christian participation in the military is defensible because it did not involve war but only "police" responsibilities. Commenting on Paul's statement that the rulers "do not bear the sword in vain," he argues that the sword in view is "the symbol of judicial authority" rather than of capi-

---

[27]Eusebius *Church History* 9.8.2-4.

[28]Bainton, *Christian Attitudes Toward War and Peace*, p. 70. Bainton summarizes the evidence up to Constantine: "Until the decade A.D. 170-80 we are devoid of evidence; from then on the references to Christian soldiers increase. The numbers cannot be computed. The greatest objection to military service appears to have been in the Hellenistic East. The Christians in northern Africa were divided. The Roman church in the late second and early third centuries did not forbid epitaphs recording the military profession. The eastern frontier reveals the most extensive Christian participation in warfare, though concurrently we find there a protest against it among groups tending to ascetic and monastic ideals" (pp. 71-72). On Edessa, see also L. W. Barnard, "The Origins and Emergence of the Church in Edessa During the First Two Centuries A.D.," *Vigiliae Christianae* 22, no. 3 (1968).

tal punishment or warfare. It was "but a long dagger," more a "symbol of authority" than a cop's pistol or a broadsword. He admits that Roman government was neither "mild" nor merely symbolic, but he insists that the police force represented by the sword is structurally different from military force: "In the police function, the violence or threat thereof is applied only to the offending party," and police action is subject to review by superiors. War is different: in battle, force is never truly discriminate, and there is no authority to review actions or enforce rules.[29]

Yoder's distinction does not hold. It is true, as Ramsay MacMullen once wittily put it, that many Roman soldiers spent a lifetime in the military without striking out in anger, except in the tavern. Yet this limit on opportunities for violence had little to do with a distinction between military and police. Rome had no "police" force distinct from the military,[30] and, more important, this distinction does what Yoder wants it to do only if he is right in assuming that "police duties were peaceful" and "military duties were violent." In reality, "the opposite may have been more true," since "life within the empire could hold a candle to the violence on its borders." *Frumentarii* were "police" soldiers charged with collecting tariffs on grain imports, but they "arrested Christians, beat up the bakers of Antioch and extorted money during famine," in addition to being "detested political spies." *Vigiles* were the police and firemen of the city of Rome, "but in the year 270 they broke the siege of Autun and plundered the city."[31] No church father, at least, ever made the distinction between police work and warfare as a way of justifying Christian military service: "there is no recorded statement of any Christian theologian, or anyone else for that matter, permitting Christians to become policemen but not soldiers."[32]

Focusing exclusively on Christian participation in the Roman military, further, misses an important dimension of early Christian attitudes toward violence. Neither in the ancient world nor in the modern was vio-

---

[29]John Howard Yoder, *The Politics of Jesus* (Grand Rapids: Eerdmans, 1972), pp. 206-7.

[30]Oliver O'Donovan, *The Desire of Nations: Rediscovering the Roots of Political Theology* (Cambridge: Cambridge University Press, 1996), p. 152.

[31]John Helgeland, "Christians and the Roman Army, A.D. 173-337," *Church History* 43, no. 2 (1974): 162. Bainton (*Christian Attitudes Toward War and Peace*, p. 79) acknowledges that Christians served in this detachment of the Roman military.

[32]Helgeland, "Christians and the Roman Army from Marcus Aurelius," pp. 793-94.

lence confined to the authorized violence of the police or military. Christians resorted to violence against one another, and against pagans, with surprising regularity. Athanasius was acquitted of the charge of murder, but he never quite denied charges of using lower-level forms of intimidation and roughing-up. Militant Donatists attacked Catholics in North Africa, and Catholics returned the favor. Bishops and other clergy often egged on the mobs. In the East, militant monks tore down pagan altars and put an end to sacrifice. "The monks commit many crimes," Theodosius lamented.[33]

To be sure, these incidents all occur after Constantine, and Yoder could perhaps cite them as more evidence of the evil effects of Constantinianism. But none of these acts of violence were encouraged by the empire, and none of them depended on the presence of a Christian emperor. My point is certainly not to endorse monastic vigilantism, which was often appalling. Nor is the point simply that ancient Christians—like medieval and modern ones—often failed to exhibit the peaceableness of Jesus. The point is this: without any help from Constantine or other emperors, Christians, including "pious" monks and bishops, acted violently and justified violence, and this suggests that the image of an early church universally and uncompromisingly committed to peace is an illusion.

REASONS FOR RENUNCIATION

Above I noted Yoder's effort to detach the question of Christian military service from the question of why. "No historians deny" that the primitive church "rejected Caesar's wars," he argues, though they differ in their account of the reasons for that rejection. But I have shown that the evidence is more ambiguous than Yoder claims, and I have also suggested that the why question cannot be detached from the factual question. If Christians renounced military service because of Jesus' command to love enemies, then presumably they, like Yoder, would have renounced military service no matter who the commander-in-chief happened to be. If, however,

---

[33]On Christian violence in the post-Constantinian period, see Michael Gaddis, *There Is No Crime for Those Who Have Christ: Religious Violence in the Christian Roman Empire* (Berkeley: University of California Press, 2005); the quotation from Theodosius is on p. 208. K. A. Harl ("Sacrifice and Pagan Belief in Fifth- and Sixth-Century Byzantium," *Past and Present* 128 [1990], p. 21) mentions the destruction of shrines in the East as a key element in the decline of paganism.

Christians renounced military service because it involved idolatry or because particular military actions were unjust, then they might reconsider if a Josiah were to come along to pull down the images and altars. As we might expect, the arguments against military service varied.

Some appealed directly to the example and teaching of Jesus. Tertullian tried to rebut Christian uses of the Old Testament in defense of war by pointing to the normative character of the Gospels. Yes, he admitted, "Moses carried a rod, and Aaron wore a buckle, and John [the Baptist] is girt with leather and Joshua the son of Nun leads a line of march; and the People warred." This, however, gives no support to Christian involvement in war: "How will a Christian man war nay, how will he serve even in peace, without a sword, which the Lord has taken away? For albeit soldiers had come unto John, and had received the formula of their rule; albeit, likewise, a centurion had believed; still the Lord afterward, in disarming Peter, ungirded the sword-belt of[34] every soldier. No dress is lawful among us, if assigned to any unlawful action."[35] Cyprian similarly acknowledged that iron might be used to make implements of war, but the fact that it can be used for such purposes no more proves that this is its purpose than the existence of a voice and music proves that they should be used for lewd songs.[36]

Origen's arguments, however, were often linked with conceptions of pollution. He appealed to the pagan practice of exempting priests from military service, arguing that Christians are priests and thus fight in prayer and worship rather than with the sword. "Do not those who are priests at certain shrines, and those who attend on certain gods, as you account them," he asked Celsus, "keep their hands free from blood, that they may with hands unstained and free from human blood offer the appointed sacrifices to your gods; and even when war is upon you, you never enlist the priests in the army?" Given this, "how much more so, that while others are engaged in battle, these too should engage as the priests and ministers of God, keeping their hands pure." Christians wrestle "in prayers to God on behalf of those who are fighting in a righteous cause, and for the king who reigns righteously, that whatever is opposed to those who act righteously

---

[34]Thanks to my colleague Tim Griffith for his help in translating Tertullian's "omnem postea militem, in Petro exarmando, discinxit."

[35]Tertullian *On Idolatry* 19.

[36]Tertullian *On the Dress of Virgins* 11.

may be destroyed!" But more important, "we by our prayers vanquish all demons who stir up war, and lead to the violation of oaths, and disturb the peace." Thus, Christians "are much more helpful to the kings than those who go into the field to fight for them. . . . None fight better for the king than we do. We do not indeed fight under him, although he require it; but we fight on his behalf, forming a special army—an army of piety—by offering our prayers to God."[37]

This passage damages Yoder's thesis in several ways. Origen, often cited as a key proponent of early Christian pacifism, here *supports* rather than "rejects" Caesar's wars. To be sure, he limits the assistance that Christians provide to prayer, and even then to prayers on behalf of "those who are fighting in a righteous cause." Yet this implies that *some* of Caesar's wars are "righteous" and that some "Caesars" might be classified among kings "who reign righteously." And this, further, implies the larger conviction that there is such a thing as a righteous cause for war. The force of the passage is pacifist, of course, and that should not be missed. But Origen's promise that Christians provide prayerful support for just wars ought not be missed either.

Tertullian's most vigorous and extensive arguments concerned idolatry. That was not a tangential issue for Roman soldiers. Religion was central to the military life:

> The army was a religious world in its own right, but one integrated with the state cult of Rome. . . . The army religion was highly liturgical, and it was prescribed for all army installations of at least cohort strength; certainly every legion observed all the specified rites. Probably the creation of this religious system went all the way back to the religious policies of Augustus who took old military festivals and incorporated them into this new framework. . . . The worship of Mithra, Christ, and many various local deities did not interfere with the discipline of the army . . . and as long as they were conducted outside the walls of the camp, military authorities paid little attention to them; probably most officers personally were involved in at least one of them.[38]

That tolerance began to weaken in the early second century, during the rule of Caracalla. As I discussed in chapter two, Caracalla promulgated

---

[37]Origen *Contra Celsum* 8.73.
[38]Helgeland, "Christians and the Roman Army from Marcus Aurelius," p. 817.

the "Antonine Constitution" (212), which granted citizenship to all the residents of the empire and had the effect of turning the empire into a single civic order, replacing the earlier crazy-quilt of local laws and customs. As we saw, that constitution was the basis for Decius's demand that all Roman citizens offer sacrifice to demonstrate their loyalty to the empire. That too is the context for the earliest empire-wide persecutions, the brutal imperial response to the Christian refusal to carry out the required sacrifice. Not only the empire but also the military was consolidated. Soldiers were still allowed to believe whatever they liked and even privately celebrate their personal cults, but they would continue in the army only if they were willing to offer sacrifice to the virtue of the emperor. Otherwise the empire itself would be endangered, as hungry and unhappy gods would take their unhappy vengeance on Rome.[39]

This is the setting for the military martyrdoms, and also the setting for Tertullian's treatises against military idolatry. His main argument against Christians in military service—not, to be sure, his only one—was that they would be required to participate in pagan rites. He argued that the military oath, the *sacramentum,* was incompatible with the Christian's commitment to Jesus, and he insisted that military standards, considered sacred by the Roman troops, were demonic instruments.[40] His later treatise *De corona militis* is the sole surviving treatise on Christian participation in the military, and its focus was overwhelmingly on the idolatry involved in wearing the military crown, rather than on the issue of bloodshed.[41] His antithetical "You cannot serve God and the Emperor" occurs in a discussion of military service.[42]

For Tertullian, this danger was not confined to military service. He attacked Christian participation in art, literature, and nonviolent civil service and even argued that signing contracts involved idolatry.[43] What other Christians were viewing as an opportunity—the domestication of the military and the expansion of citizenship—Tertullian recognized as a dangerous temptation to compromise, and he recommended a fairly wholesale

---

[39]In addition to my summary in chapter 2, see Elizabeth DePalma Digeser, *The Making of a Christian Empire: Lactantius and Rome* (Ithaca, N.Y.: Cornell University Press, 2000).
[40]Helgeland, "Christians and the Roman Army, A.D. 173-337," p. 151.
[41]Ibid., p. 152.
[42]Tertullian *On Idolatry* 19.
[43]Ibid. 23.

Christian withdrawal from a civilization infused with idolatry.[44]

This sort of argument is not absolute. What happens when civil magistracy no longer demands sacrifice to false gods, or contracts may be signed without commitment to idolatry, or artisans start sculpting scenes from the Gospels instead of from pagan mythology? What happens when the emperor expunges sacrifice from the army and changes the standard to a Christian cross? May Christians then rejoin the world, assume political responsibilities, even fight in just wars?

Many Christians said yes, and none illustrates this point so well as Lactantius. In the *Divine Institutes* he condemned all coercion, violence and bloodshed, more absolutely and thoroughly than any other early Christian writer.[45] "With regard to this precept of God," he wrote, "there ought to be no exception at all; but that it is always unlawful to put to death a man, whom God willed to be a sacred animal." Lactantius condemned the indiscriminate killing of the arena: "I ask now whether they can be just and pious men, who, when they see men placed under the stroke of death, and entreating mercy, not only suffer them to be put to death, but also demand it, and give cruel and inhuman votes for their death, not being satiated with wounds nor contented with bloodshed." Once they are "wounded and prostrate," they are "attacked again" so that "no one may delude them by a pretended death." Crowds become "angry with the combatants, unless one of the two is quickly slain; and as though they thirsted for human blood, they hate delays." "It is not therefore befitting that those who strive to keep to the path of justice should be companions and sharers in this public homicide," since "when God forbids us to kill, He not only prohibits us from open violence, which is not even allowed by the public laws, but He warns us against the commission of those things which are esteemed lawful among men." He made a broader demand as well: "it will be neither lawful for a just man to engage in warfare, since his warfare is justice itself, nor to accuse any one of a capital charge, because it makes no difference whether you put a man to death by word, or rather by the sword, since it is the act

---

[44]Gero (*"Miles Gloriosus,"* p. 298) puts it vividly, if prejudicially: "The church in North Africa could not sell her soul, so to speak, to Constantine; she had already sold it much earlier, to Septimius Severus and to Caracalla."

[45]This is the opinion of James J. Megivern, "Early Christianity and Military Service," *Perspectives on Religious Studies* 12, no. 3 (1985): 181.

of putting to death itself which is prohibited."[46] If there is a patristic poster boy of pacifism, Lactantius is it.

The complication is that Lactantius later added a dedication to this very treatise, offering it to Constantine, whom he knew to be a soldier. The dedication praised Constantine as the "greatest of emperors" because he had "cast aside error" and determined "to acknowledge and honor the majesty of the one true God." Constantine "brought back justice, which had been overturned and blotted out," and "expiated the horrible crimes of other rulers," and Lactantius reminded him that the Father, a "very strict judge toward the wicked," would avenge persecutors in other parts of the world.[47] He commended courage when "fighting for your country," and he celebrated the victory of Constantine at Milvian Bridge in the same tone as Eusebius: "With great rejoicing, let us celebrate the triumph of God; let us extol the victory of the Lord; day and night let us pour out our prayers in rejoicing; let us pray that he establish forever the peace that has been granted to his people after ten years."[48]

Perhaps Lactantius was a power-hungry sycophant, ready to abandon pacifist convictions to trim his teaching when fresh political winds started blowing. Perhaps he was simply frightened of the strongman on the throne, whose claim to follow Jesus was less than wholly believable. If so, he was not alone in these sentiments, for there was, quite strikingly, *no* controversy over war and pacifism at the time of Constantine's conversion.[49] The evidence we have of a controversy on these issues is from Tertullian, during Yoder's "proto-Constantinian" period. But even there the controversy did not engulf the church. We have only Tertullian on the one side and unnamed opponents, including Christians actually in the military, on the other. In any case, if the early church was uniformly pacifist, and pacifist by conviction, then the overnight adjustment to Constantine's conversion was a fall indeed, a breathtaking lapse of nerve. We might even call it a

---

[46]Lactantius *Divine Institutes* 6.20.15-16.

[47]The passage is quoted in Louis J. Swift, *The Early Fathers on War and Military Service,* Message of the Fathers of the Church, 19 (Wilmingon, Del.: Michael Glazier, 1983), pp. 67-68. See also Gregory M. Reichberg, *The Ethics of War,* ed. Henrik Sye and Endre Begby (Oxford: Wiley-Blackwell, 2006), p. 66. Perhaps revealingly, Yoder (*Christian Attitudes,* pp. 54-55) quotes the "pacifist" passage but not the dedication.

[48]Lactantius *Death* 52. The passage about courage in found in his *Epitome,* quoted in Swift, *Early Fathers on War and Military Service,* p. 65.

[49]Helgeland, "Christians and the Roman Army from Marcus Aurelius," pp. 815-16.

breathtaking lapse of attention. Did none of these convinced pacifists even notice what was happening? It would seem not.

As we have seen, though, there is a more likely explanation: the church was *never* united in an absolute opposition to Christian participation in war; the opposition that existed was in some measure circumstantial, based on the fact that the Roman army demanded sharing in religious liturgies that Christians refused; and once military service could be pursued without participating in idolatry, many Christians found military service a legitimate life for a Christian disciple. As for Lactantius, either he did not see any contradiction between the dedication and the treatise, or he modified his views in the light of the new circumstances that Constantine inaugurated. Even if he shifted his views, we cannot trace the sources of Lactantius's apparent shift in detail, though we can be sure he was neither a coward nor a relativist.

CHRISTIANS IN THE "CONSTANTINIAN" ARMY
The "afters" support this account of the "befores."

Constantine did not purge the military or his administration of pagans, and it is always important to remember the massive continuity of personnel between the Tetrarchy and Constantine. Some of the soldiers who enforced decrees against the Donatists, or who hurried Arius (and then Athanasius) off to exile, might well have participated in the persecution. Yet with a Christian on the imperial throne, promoting other Christians to high administrative positions, certain avenues of service—in the army and the civil service—opened for Christians as they had not before. Christians had been in these positions before, but they had had to ignore, side-step or accommodate to the religious demands of imperial service. Constantine removed the requirement of sacrifice for civil service, so even Christians who were zealously antipagan could enter the service.

Bishops acknowledged the change by giving permission to Christians to join the army and to serve in Constantine's government. But the permission came with other instructions. The council of Arles in 314 did not, as Constantine hoped, solve the Donatist problem, but it issued several canons that indicate how the bishops were addressing the new political situation. As at earlier councils, the bishops strictly forbade Christians to participate in certain entertainments:

4. Concerning charioteers who are among the faithful, it is resolved that as long as they continue to drive in chariot races they be excluded from fellowship.

5. Concerning actors, it is also resolved that as long as they continue to carry on that occupation they be excluded from fellowship.

The canon on civil officials instructed them to be transferred in good order from one church to another in the case of transfer of office, so that the local bishop could give oversight:

7. Concerning officials who are among the faithful who take up government office, thus it is resolved that, when they be transferred, they receive letters of reference from their churches, so that, therefore, in whatever places they serve, care be administered them by the bishop of that place, and when they begin to act against the church's discipline, that only then they be excluded from fellowship.

8. Similarly also concerning those who wish to pursue a public career.

An earlier canon (56) from the Council of Elvira had declared that "magistrates are not to enter the church during the year in which they serve as duumvir,"[50] presumably because the magistrate would be forced to participate in pagan rites. Since civil officials no longer had to sacrifice, the bishops now permitted Christians to remain in the church and participate in its fellowship, with the proviso that they were to conduct their public business under the oversight of a local bishop. One might see this as accommodation to the empire, but it is explicitly an assertion of ecclesiastical authority over civil officials, even in their civil capacity.[51]

The council also issued an unusual decree concerning Christians in military service: "Concerning those who lay down their weapons in peacetime it is resolved that they be excluded from fellowship." Various interpretations have been offered. Perhaps Christians had been tempted to desert during the persecutions, but now that Christianity had been legalized they were to retain their arms. But the canon seems to be splitting the difference more finely. Soldiers, the canon instructed, had to retain their

---

[50]On Elvira and its canons, see H. A. Drake, *Constantine and the Bishops: The Politics of Intolerance* (Baltimore: Johns Hopkins University Press, 2000), pp. 223-25. Duumvir normally refers to an alliance of two magistrates.
[51]Arles VII, in Migne, *PL,* 84; Elvira LVI, in Migne, *PL,* 84.

arms in peacetime, but, Hermann Dorries suggests, "he is not forbidden to do so in time of war."[52] We cannot "look upon the decision at Arles as mere conformity to the will of the emperor." Instead of simply repudiating its principles, the church was attempting to make room for conscientious objectors while acknowledging the new political realities: "military service was not rejected per se and yet was not unconditionally endorsed."[53] The date is important here. Arles took place only two years after Constantine's victory over Maxentius, but already the church was adjusting its pastoral counsel to meet the new situation. The fact that this took place without any apparent controversy is a sign that the church was already prepared for the eventuality.

Martin of Tours apparently operated by the principle articulated in the Arles canon. Converted while serving in the Roman military in a campaign in Gaul in 336, he remained in the Roman army until the day before a battle. When his turn came to receive the donative, he said, "Hitherto I have served you as a soldier: allow me now to become a soldier to God: let the man who is to serve you receive your donative: I am the soldier of Christ: it is not lawful for me to fight." His commander charged that Martin had withdrawn "from fear of the battle" rather than "from any religious feeling." Martin, however, offered to stand at the front of the battle without shield or helmet, protected only by the cross. He was arrested overnight, and plans were made to make good on his offer the next day. Before that could happen, the enemy sought peace and Martin was released.[54]

Ambiguity continued to mark the church's relation with the military after the church was thoroughly integrated into public life. Late in the fourth century, Basil claimed that the church had not condemned killing in war as murder and that it did not in his time exercise discipline against active soldiers: "Homicide in war is not reckoned by our Father as homicide; I presume from their wish to make concession to men fighting on behalf of chastity and true religion." Yet Basil also advised that it may be well to

---

[52]Hermann Dorries, *Constantine the Great,* trans. Roland Bainton (New York: Harper Torchbooks, 1972), p. 112.

[53]Ibid., p. 113; Dorries's interpretation of the canon is endorsed by Bainton, *Christian Attitudes Toward War and Peace,* p. 81. Yoder, *Christian Attitudes to War, Peace and Revolution,* ed. Theodore J. Koontz and Andy Alexis-Baker (Grand Rapids: Brazos, 2009), pp. 50-51, claims that this "sword" is not a fighting sword but a "ceremonial" sword that symbolizes "administrative status."

[54]Sulpicious Severus *Vita Martini* 4.

counsel that those "whose hands are not clean only abstain from communion for three years."[55] With Athanasius, ambiguity yielded to endorsement of military virtues and the military life: "Whereas killing is otherwise forbidden, in war it is legitimate and even praiseworthy to kill enemies. He who distinguishes himself in this receives great honor."[56] Eventually things turned full circle, and *pagans* were excluded from the army.

JUST WARRIORS

Even so, the church did not become a hotbed of militaristic mania. The very writers who formulated the Christian version of "just war" theory continued, in fact, to emphasize some of the main points, and use the same passages, that the early fathers had. Ambrose defended violence not only on the part of civil officials in war and punishment but even in some private circumstances, when one acted—as Moses did—to defend the innocent against the oppressor.[57] At the same time, Ambrose renounced self-defense and claimed that even the "thought of warlike matters seems to be foreign to the duty of our office," the office of priests. It is not the priest's business to "look to arms, but rather to the forces of peace."[58] He famously faced down the emperor Theodosius, forbidding him to receive the Eucharist with the blood of innocents on his hands. It is inaccurate to say that he is simply giving a Christian gloss to the just war tradition of Roman political thinkers. Even in Ambrose, "pacifist arguments retained much of their old vigor, and the dilemma of Christian violence and love remained to a considerable extent unresolved."[59]

Ambrose did not penetrate the problem with anything like the depth of Augustine. Like Ambrose, Augustine is often accused of adopting a thinly Christianized version of the Roman defense of war, but that does little justice to the profundity of his wrestling with questions of war and peace. Against the Manichaean Faustus, Augustine argued that the Old Testament retains its authority and gives sanction to war and even to religious

---

[55]Basil *Epistle* 188, 13.

[56]Athanasius, quoted in Dorries, *Constantine the Great,* p. 114.

[57]That characterization of Moses' "murder" of the Egyptian comes from the first martyr, Stephen (Acts 7:24). On Ambrose, see Louis J. Swift, "St. Ambrose on Violence and War," *Transactions and Proceedings of the American Philological Association* 101 (1970).

[58]Ambrose *De officiis* 1.35, quoted in Swift, "St. Ambrose on Violence and War," p. 537.

[59]Swift, "St. Ambrose on Violence and War," p. 538.

coercion. As he grew older he became less sanguine about politics, more cynical about the uses of violence. While he continued to defend the necessity of war and violent coercion, in the *City of God* he did it in the context of a radical subversion of Christian national and ethnic loyalties.[60]

Even where he defended the use of violence and coercion, he consciously defended it from within a Christian framework, with Jesus' demand for love of enemies always at the forefront of his mind. Turning the other cheek

> does not forbid punishment which serves as corrective. In fact, that kind of punishment is a form of mercy. . . . The only person suitable for inflicting punishment is the man whose love has driven out that normal hatred which rages in us when we have a desire for revenge. We do not have to fear, for instance, that parents seem to hate their young son if he has done wrong, and they box his ears to prevent a recurrence. . . . This example is the best illustration of the fact that one can love and punish a son all at the same time.[61]

Augustine appealed to the same analogy to draw a conclusion about war. When "the earthly city observes Christian principles," then it wages war "with the benevolent purpose that better provision might be made for the defeated to live harmoniously together in justice and godliness." Freedom is not the ultimate good, and restraining freedom can be a good when the freedom is being use to do evil. If possible, "wars would be waged as an act of mercy by good men so that by controlling unbridled passions they could stamp out those vices that ought to be removed or suppressed by any responsible government."[62]

Augustine was no jingoist, and he knew that warfare was most often perverted with pride, greed, lust for domination. He knew that the wars waged for just causes were few and far between. For Augustine, war had to

---

[60]This is the argument of R. A. Markus, "St. Augustine's Views of the 'Just War,'" in *The Church and War*, ed. W. J. Shiels (Oxford: Blackwell, 1983), as summarized in Hunter, "Decade of Research," p. 89. The relativization of political loyalties is a major theme of Markus's *Saeculum* and will be taken up in the following chapter.

[61]Augustine, "On the Lord's Sermon," quoted in Swift, *Early Fathers on War and Military Service*, pp. 124-25.

[62]Augustine Letter 138, quoted in Swift, *Early Fathers on War and Military Service*, p. 122. Stressing this point is one of the important achievements of Daniel Bell, *Just War as Christian Discipleship: Recentering the Tradition in the Church rather than the State* (Grand Rapids: Brazos, 2009).

be waged, when it was waged, for the sake of peace. Peace, not war, was still the Christian vision of the world subdued by the gospel.

CONCLUSION

Yoder claims that the church slid or fell into Constantinianism from an earlier renunciation of violence and war. In fact, things are more messy and complicated, and therefore Yoder is wrong. Where Yoder needs an unambiguous consensus in the earlier church, the evidence is instead small, divided and ambiguous. Where Yoder needs a uniform pro-Constantinian consensus after the fourth century, the evidence continues to be divided and ambiguous. There *was* certainly a shift. After Constantine, when the Roman emperors began to look to the church for ethical guidance, the church began to be more overt in making the discriminating decisions that characterize the "just war" tradition. But the shift is more plausibly a result of a change in the church's political position than a result of a fundamental theological modification. Some Christians after Constantine maintained the pacifist views expressed by some of the earlier fathers, and even the theologians most responsible for the development of mainstream Christian views on war and violence were hardly warmongers. In short, the story of the church and war is ambiguity before Constantine, ambiguity after, ambiguity right to the present. Constantine is in this respect a far lesser figure than Yoder wants to make him.

So far the argument about war and peace. What about early Christian views of empire, and later views of the empire and Christian mission? That is the subject of the next chapter.

13

Christian Empire,
Christian Mission

[Christians give the emperor] such reverential homage as is lawful for us
and good for him; regarding him as the human being next to God who
from God has received all his power, and is less than God alone.

TERTULLIAN, *AD SCAPULUM*

Though he labeled what he opposed "Constantinian," John Howard Yoder knew that it did not begin with Constantine. Christians in the second and third centuries were already, he says, in the grip of a proto-"Constantinianism," and this had an effect on their beliefs and practices about war, empire, the world, the church and its future. Still, Yoder's thesis relies on a historical narrative. He needs to demonstrate that there was a time of pacifism from which the church declined. As I have argued, he cannot do that.[1]

Yoder cannot prove that the church "fell" from an anti- into a pro-imperial stance either. As with Yoder's claims about pacifism, it is essential for him to establish an *ante quo* in order to prove a "shift." Yoder must show

---

[1]Yoder claims that "there is wide recognition that the Christians of the first two centuries were pacifist, or at least that their most articulate teachers of whom we have record were" (John Howard Yoder, *For the Nations: Essays Public and Evangelical* [Grand Rapids: Eerdmans, 1997], p. 68). The second formulation is the more accurate, but it nullifies the opening assertion. We have record of only a tiny handful of the articulate leaders; if the only evidence we have comes from a small number of "articulate leaders" whose writings have, providentially, survived, then we simply have no way to know that "Christians of the first two centuries were pacifist."

that there was a time when the church was uniformly anti-imperial and that the church fell from that holy consensus. He cannot prove that Christians were united in opposition to the empire any more than he can demonstrate that all early Christians were pacifists. In fact, there is even less evidence for the sort of shift in attitudes toward the empire that Yoder describes than there is for a shift in ideas about war and peace.

PAX ROMANA

The New Testament does not, in my view, help Yoder. Jesus was condemned by a time-serving Roman governor, and his claims to be King and Lord frontally challenged imperial claims. Yet he did not urge his followers to throw off the shackles of empire; He ate with tax collectors and invited one to join his band of intimates. In Acts, Luke repeatedly shows us Roman officials intervening to protect Christians from mobs, usually mobs of Jews. Paul used his Roman citizenship to advance his ministry, and Roman roads and Roman ships as he traveled. He spoke respectfully to Roman authorities and urged the Christians at Rome to submit even to hostile governing authorities because of the "good" they provided. Revelation 13 indicates that the bestial empire has turned demonic, but that is only one side of the New Testament's complex portrait of the Roman empire.

After the New Testament, nearly every writer who commented on the subject expressed the views summed up nicely by Tertullian. Writing about military service, Tertullian, in his charmingly antithetical way, asked whether Christians could serve God and the emperor. He thought not, but he and other writers were glad that *somebody* was serving the emperor, because they believed the empire guaranteed stability.

Tertullian knew the evils of empire. Rome did not grow powerful through its *pietas,* as Rome's apologists liked to claim. On the contrary, "all kingship or empire is sought in war and extended by victory." War destroys cities; cities enclose sanctuaries and priests and the stuff of the gods. War is sacrilege, and "the sacrileges of the Romans are exactly as many as their trophies; their triumphs over gods as many as over races; their spoils in war as many as the statues still left of captured gods." *Impietas,* not *pietas,* was the secret of Rome's success.[2] Yet Tertullian also wrote that "a Christian is

---

[2]Tertullian *Apology* 25; here I am using the translation found in Mark A. Burrows, "Christians in the Roman Forum: Tertullian and the Apologetic Use of History," *Vigiliae Christianae* 42,

enemy to none, least of all to the Emperor of Rome," whom he knew to be "appointed by his God" and whom therefore he was bound to "love and honor." Tertullian was committed to desiring the "well-being" of both the emperor and "of the empire over which he reigns so long as the world shall stand— for so long as that shall Rome continue."

Anticipating Eusebius, he insisted that Christians rendered "such reverential homage as is lawful for us and good for him; regarding him as the human being next to God who from God has received all his power, and is less than God alone." Christians, Tertullian argued, were even perfectly willing to offer sacrifice on behalf of the emperor, though it had to be a Christian sacrifice: "We therefore sacrifice for the emperor's safety, but to our God and his, and after the manner God has enjoined, in simple prayer." Pagan sacrifices are useless, the "food of devils." Christians appeal to God, praying "for the imperial well-being, as those who seek it at the hands of Him who is able to bestow it."[3] The Latin of the relevant line is "Itaque et sacrificamus pro salute imperatoris sed Deo nostro et ipsius: sed quomodo præcepit Deus, prece pura." Tertullian cleverly makes use of the language of the imperial cult, which required sacrifice for the health of the emperor (*sacrificium pro salute imperatoris*).[4] Christians do just what the imperial cult demands, though in their own way.[5]

Tertullian drew on "the Greek apologists of the previous generation, such as Melito of Sardis," in developing his ideas of empire. Following their lead, he "regarded the empire as a God-ordained institution, whose end would portend the chaos accompanying the last times, and that its ruler should be honoured and obeyed." In short, "his quarrel was not with the empire as such but against its administrators who made unlawful de-

---

no. 3 (1988): 223. Thanks to David Rankin for the reference. Tertullian probably draws this from Minucius Felix: "quidquid Romani tenent colunt possident audaciae praeda est: templa omnia de manubiis, id est re ruinis urbium, de spoliis deorum, de caedibus sacerdotum" (quoted in R. P. C. Hanson, "The Christian Attitude to Pagan Religions up to the Time of Constantine the Great," *ANRW* 23 [1980]: 932).

[3]Tertullian *Ad scapulum* 2.

[4]As one proconsul told a group of condemned Christians, *Et nos religiosi sumus et simplex est religio nostra, et iuramus per genium domini nostri imperatoris et pro salute eius supplicamus.*

[5]John Howard Yoder, *Christian Attitudes to War, Peace and Revelation,* ed. Theodore J. Koontz and Andy Alexis-Baker (Grand Rapids: Brazos, 2009), p. 50, mentions that Origen claims to be more helpful to Caesar with his prayers than with his sword, but Yoder sees it as a sign of growing identification with the world. He does not mention that Tertullian says virtually the same thing.

mands on its Christian inhabitants." His attacks on "the 'bad emperors,'
Nero and Domitian, who persecuted the Church, were no harsher than
Tacitus' or Dio's. In his assertion that Rome did not gain her empire by
justitia, he was following criticisms that had been made by Cicero (e.g., *De
Republica* v. 2). Where he went further than the Stoic critics was his addition of *irreligiositas* to Rome's other failings. Only when it turned from
Jupiter to Christ would Rome deserve to become eternal." Far from being
a critic of empire as such, Tertullian upheld the ideal of "a Christian empire," and until that arrived he remained "a loyal servant to the emperors
whom he recognized as protectors of all their subjects, including the
Christians."[6]

In his apologetic works, Tertullian focused incessantly on the question
of origins, arguing against defenders of classical culture that Judaism was
older, and hence more reliable, than Greek philosophy or Roman law.
Seeds come before trees, and Jewish law is the seed from which Roman
law grew. Christians are the heir to Judaism, separated from the parent,
and the church therefore is the carrier of this ancient wisdom into the
Greco-Roman world. Christianity, in short, is not simply compatible with
Roman citizenship and involvement in Roman life; it is the foundation of
Romanitas, and Christians are truer to Rome's original heritage than are
polytheist pagans. Christianity is new as yesterday yet as old as creation;
nova et vetera, and hence "we alone are innocent." Pagan Romans, not
Christians, despise their tradition.[7]

Origen agreed. When Celsus charged that Christians would leave the
emperor alone against the barbarians, Origen protested,

> We help the emperor in his extremities by our prayers and intercessions more
> effectively than do the soldiers. Just as the priests must keep their hands un-
> sullied for sacrifice, so also must the Christians, who are all priests and ser-
> vants of God, keep their hands unstained by blood that they may be able to
> pray for the Emperor and the army in just cause. In this way we overcome the
> real disturbers of the peace, the demons. Thus we fight for the Emperor more
> than the others, though we do not fight with him, nor at his command. We
> constitute an army of piety by our intercession with the Deity.

---

[6]W. H. C. Frend, review of *Tertullian und das Romische Reich,* by Richard Klein, *Classical Review,* n.s. 20, no. 1 (1970): 47.
[7]This summarizes the argument of Burrows, "Christians in the Roman Forum."

Origen was opposed to Christian involvement in war, but Christian misgivings about bloodshed did not translate into opposition to the imperial order. Origen "linked the Church to the Roman peace," arguing that "in the days of Jesus justice came forth and fullness of peace. God prepared the place for his teaching and arranged that the Roman Empire should rule the whole world." Since Christianity was disseminated under conditions of relative peace, "Christians had a responsibility . . . to maintain this peace. If they could not contribute to the support of the empire against external assault, they were all the more obliged to strengthen it from within."[8]

Most of the works of Melito of Sardis (died ca. 180) have been lost, particularly the apology in which he addressed the emperor Marcus Aurelius concerning what he claimed were recent efforts to suppress Christianity.[9] Eusebius preserved a portion of that apology, in which Melito made it clear that he considered Christianity a boon to the empire:

> For our philosophy formerly flourished among the Barbarians; but having sprung up among the nations under your rule, during the great reign of your ancestor Augustus, it became to your empire especially a blessing of auspicious omen. For from that time the power of the Romans has grown in greatness and splendor. To this power you have succeeded, as the desired possessor, and such shall you continue with your son, if you guard the philosophy which grew up with the empire and which came into existence with Augustus; that philosophy which your ancestors also honored along with the other religions.[10]

Melito thought that Christianity helped the empire flourish; he offered as proof the fact that "there has no evil happened since Augustus' reign, but that, on the contrary, all things have been splendid and glorious, in accordance with the prayers of all."[11]

These expressions of qualified appreciation for the goods that the Roman empire provided the church may be evidence of "creeping empire loyalty," but it is important to put them in context. As noted in an earlier

---

[8]Hermann Dorries, *Constantine the Great,* trans. Roland Bainton (New York: Harper Torchbooks, 1972).

[9]For a brief sketch of the background to this complaint, see W. H. C. Frend, review of *Il Christianesimo e Roma*, by Marta Sordi, *Classical Review*, n.s. 17, no. 2 (1967): 196.

[10]Melito of Sardis, quoted in Eusebius *Church History* 4.26.

[11]Ibid.

chapter, Persia's defeat of Valerian in 258 began nearly a half-century of toleration during which the church grew rapidly and Christians, naturally enough, began to think that the empire was not so bad. That was naive, but it is understandable, and it helps to explain Christian attitudes toward the state. Christians had one less danger to worry about, one very large item: emperors were no longer killing them.

Be that as it may, the main point is that Yoder's thesis of a "fall" fails. From the New Testament through the first three centuries, Christians acknowledged the goods provided by the empire as well as its idolatries and evils. What happened after the emperor saw his cross and began building churches?

AUGUSTINE, CONSTANTINIAN?
By Yoder's account, Constantinian Christians identified the "church and world in the mutual approval and support exchanged by Constantine and the bishops." This merging came to its classic expression between 313 and the early fifth century, and Yoder uses as his symbolic reference points the Edict of Milan and the completion of Augustine's *City of God*. Yoder sees this history as a straight line, Eusebius and Augustine as equally "Constantinian" theologians. In fact, this is true only in the sense that both wrote during or after Constantine and both wrote in a baptized empire. In purpose and substance, however, Augustine wrote the *City of God* precisely to rebut "Eusebian Rome-theology."[12]

Yoder's scattered comments on Augustine are among the worst moments in his writing.[13] Occasionally he hits on something true, such as his

---

[12]R. A. Markus, *Saeculum: History and Society in the Theology of Augustine* (Cambridge: Cambridge University Press, 1970), p. 53. Charles Mayo Collier, "A Nonviolent Augustinianism? History and Politics in the Theologies of St. Augustine and John Howard Yoder" (Ph.D. diss., Duke University, 2008), p. 91, calls this Augustine's "disavowal of Constantine," but that is overstated. Augustine, rather, *relativized* Constantine. He plays only a small role in *City of God,* and his conversion does not, for Augustine, mark a new epoch. Robert L. Wilken, *John Chrysostom and the Jews: Rhetoric and Reality in the Late 4th Century* (Eugene, Ore.: Wipf and Stock, 1983), p. 129, writes that in the time of John Chrysostom, Eusebian euphoria had been replaced by "the memory of orthodox bishops languishing in exile, of an emperor offering sacrifices in cities throughout the east [Julian], of laws prohibiting Christians from teaching literature in the schools, of resourceful and aggressive Arian leaders attacking the Nicene decrees."

[13]Collier ("Nonviolent Augustinianism") agrees, referring to Yoder's "historically inaccurate criticisms" accompanied by occasional expressions of "condescending gratitude." At least Augustine gets some gratitude; Constantine gets none.

claim that Augustine was "Neoplatonic" in philosophical orientation, but usually his comments are glaringly wrong, not merely in niggling details but in the big picture. Augustine, he says, identified the "Roman church" with the "millennium," which, Yoder thinks, is not surprising since he took the "Constantinian church as a matter of course." As a result, in Augustine eschatology evaporates because "the conquest of the world by the church," the goal of human history, "had been reached." Yoder concedes that Augustine did not "underestimate the reality of sin," but he thinks the bishop "seriously overestimated the adequacy of the available institutional and sacramental means for overcoming it."[14] There is a kernel of truth in one of Yoder's statements: According to Augustine, John used the image of a thousand years as a symbol "for the whole duration of this world."[15] But even that accurate comment is undermined by Yoder's blatant misreading of its significance. Though the church age and the millennium are identified, Augustine surely did not see this period as a time of uninterrupted progress. It was the time of wheat and tares, the *saeculum*, the time between. Augustine did not think that he had reached the end of history. Anyone who thinks eschatology is missing from Augustine has not read him with much sympathy.

Yoder's summaries of Augustine's views on the church-world relation are worse, nothing short of bizarre. He claims that Augustine offers "a consensus kind of moral thought," a moral thought based on "what everybody thinks." He goes on: Augustine's ethics "does not radically ask, do you get that from the Bible? Can you get that from revelation? It does not ask, can you get that from Plato? It just asks, does that make sense to all of us? Is it part of our cultural agreement?" This does not count as a fair summary of Augustine by any standard. More obviously wrong is Yoder's claim that "Augustine's thought merges New Testament reconciliation language with classical peace language and Roman order language, as if they were all the same thing. Rome, nature, and providence are all seen as essentially the same. Religion celebrates the unity of everything and the way things are."[16] "Merging" the New Testament language of peace with "Roman order" is precisely

---

[14]John Howard Yoder, *The Original Revolution: Essays on Christian Pacifism* (Scottdale, Penn.: Herald, 1971, 2003), p. 66.
[15]Augustine *City of God* 20.7.
[16]Yoder, *Christian Attitudes*, 60-65.

what Augustine is *not* doing. His entire, very long, book aimed to distinguish the *tranquilitas ordinis* of the temporal city from the genuine *shalom* of the kingdom. To suggest that Augustine "celebrates" the way things are is equally baffling. Even an inattentive and hostile reader should notice that Augustine did have a word or two to say about the deep distortions of desire and order caused by sin. John Milbank is right to say that Augustine is involved in a profound deconstruction of *Romanitas,* picking at the knot of Roman virtue until it is shown to be *libido dominandi.* Yoder's Augustine is so far from the real Augustine that it is difficult to find a response beyond pointing to a copy of *City of God* with the exhortation *Tolle lege.*

Facing a Vandal invasion of Romanized north Africa and responding to the fall of Rome to Alaric in 410, Augustine wanted to assure his readers that the city of God persists even beyond Rome. For Augustine, Constantine was not the hinge of the ages, and "the christianization of the Roman Empire is as accidental to the history of salvation as it is reversible."[17] Though his analysis was far more searching, Augustine assessed the empire in the same dual manner as Tertullian. On the one hand, the empire, like all things, comes from God and by his providence does limited good. It was not enough to prove that Rome did not fall because of Christians' abandonment of the gods; Augustine had to give some account of Rome's success. "I must," he wrote at the end of book one of *City of God,* "show what social well-being the true God, in whose hand are all kingdoms, vouchsafed to grant to them that their empire might increase."[18] At the same time, the empire grew because of its brutality and found that its anxiety and discord only increased as it grew. After Rome conquered Carthage, "concord was weakened, and destroyed by fierce and bloody seditions," and this was followed by civil war, massacres, bloodshed, lawless plundering, cruelties committed by one citizen against the other. "The lust of rule" brought no contentment, but "after it had taken possession of the more powerful few, subdued under its yoke the rest, worn and wearied."[19]

Given that Augustine was the dominant theologian of the medieval West, it is hard to take seriously Yoder's claim that "Constantinian" merger remained the paradigm of church-world relations through a millennium

---

[17]Markus, *Saeculum,* 54.
[18]Augustine *City of God* 1.36.
[19]Ibid., 1.30.

and beyond. Prior to Constantine, Christians saw the empire as a providential setting for the life of Jesus and the spread of the gospel; during Constantine's life, Eusebius viewed the Christian empire as a fulfillment of prophecy and a renewed golden age that might last until the end of time. By the end of the fourth century, Eusebian optimism had cooled, and the difference between the empire and the city of God had become all too evident. If "Constantinian" is taken to mean a "merger" of church and empire in which Christians identify some nation or empire or ruler with the movement of God in history, there was a brief, ambiguous "Constantinian moment" in the early fourth century, and there have been many tragic "Constantinian moments" since.

There was no permanent, epochal "Constantinian shift."

WHOSE MISSION?

Perhaps we can grant that Christians after the fourth century did not kowtow to power, but according to Constantine's critics his conversion fundamentally altered Christianity's mission. According to Thomas Heilke, "The church under Constantine is 'imperialized,' and made 'subservient' to the interests of the empire."[20] Heilke relies on Yoder to suggest that the church's mission was nullified by Constantinianism. After Chalcedon "relegated Nestorianism to Persia and Monophysitism to Abyssinia, thus identifying the concepts of 'heretic' and 'barbarian,' the church effectively turned over the expansion of Christianity for a millennium to the heterodox."[21] Insofar as the Constantinian church had a mission at all, it was identified with the mission of imperial expansion.[22] In the centuries after Constantine, Yoder claims, most mission work was carried out not by orthodox "Roman Christians" but by heretics.[23]

---

[20]Thomas Heilke, "Yoder's Idea of Constantinianism: An Analytical Framework Toward Conversion," in *A Mind Patient and Untamed: Assessing John Howard Yoder's Contributions to Theology, Ethics and Peacemaking* (Telford, Penn.: Cascadia, 2004), p. 96.

[21]Heilke is quoting from John Howard Yoder, *The Royal Priesthood: Essays Ecclesiological and Ecumenical,* ed. Michael G. Cartwright (Grand Rapids: Eerdmans, 1994), p. 259. Elsewhere Yoder claims that Constantinian Christianity identified the mission of the church with the expansion of the empire, regarded those outside the empire as a "challenge" and simply "wrote off" the world outside the Roman empire (*The Priestly Kingdom: Social Ethics as Gospel* [Notre Dame, Ind.: University of Notre Dame Press, 1984], pp. 137, 143).

[22]Heilke, "Yoder's Idea."

[23]Yoder (*Body Politics: Five Practices of the Christian Community Before the Watching World* [Scottdale, Penn.: Herald, 2001], p. 32) also claims that there were "no more outsiders to

Constantine himself had a deep sense of historical destiny, and as a result his foreign policy was guided in part by the desire to extend the church's reach. He envisioned a universal empire united in confession of the Nicene Creed, an empire that would have a symbolic center in the Church on Golgotha in Jerusalem and that would stretch to India and Ethiopia and someday include even Persia. But Constantine did not necessarily regard annexation into the Roman empire as an essential element of that vision. He seems instead to have envisioned a Christian commonwealth. Perhaps the empire would have remained dominant, but in Constantine's cosmopolitan mind it would not have been coextensive with "Christ's dominion."

Though he probably did not impose Christianity on conquered Goths, his triumphs among the Goths assisted the spread of Christianity. After his victory in 332, Bishop Ulfila was consecrated and sent as a missionary in Gothic territory.[24] Churches were also established in the "Mountain Arena," the Arab territories that served as a buffer between the empire and Persia. Eusebius mentions Arab Christian communities, and there was an Arab bishop at the council of Nicaea. Further east in Iberia (Georgia) there were Christians, and to the south Ethiopia (Aksum) also became Christian under Ezana.[25] As already noted, Armenia became officially Christian shortly after Constantine defeated Maxentius. By the time he died, Constantine had left behind a "universal Christian commonwealth embracing Armenians, Iberians, Arabs, and Aksumites" that continued to take form under his Byzantine successors.[26] This was *not*, it should be noted, an extension of Roman governance; it is rather that Roman imperial order had been reshaped, to some degree, by the demands of Christian mission.

What of the church's mission activity? In the immediate aftermath of

---

convert" after the fifth century because the world had been declared already Christian "by imperial edict."

[24]Elizabeth Key Fowden, "Constantine and the Peoples of the Eastern Frontier," in *The Cambridge Companion to the Age of Constantine*, ed. Noel Lenski (Cambridge: Cambridge University Press, 2006), pp. 361-62; E. A. Thompson, "Christianity and the Northern Barbarians," in *The Conflict Between Paganism and Christianity in the Fourth Century*, ed. Arnaldo Momigliano (Oxford: Clarendon, 1963), p. 63, claims that the Ulfila's mission was to be bishop to "Roman prisoners or their descendants" who lived in Gothia.

[25]Fowden, "Constantine and the Peoples," pp. 385-86; A. H. M. Jones, *Constantine and the Conversion of Europe* (Toronto: University of Toronto Press, 1978), pp. 170-72.

[26]Fowden, "Constantine and the Peoples," p. 392.

Constantine's conversion and reign, there is some truth to Yoder's and Heilke's arguments. There is little evidence of orthodox mission into barbarian territories. Even when Roman Christians found themselves captured and confined outside the empire, the church was slow to send pastoral assistance. Christianity was planted among the barbarians, but it was carried by captives and traders, or through barbarians who served in Constantine's Roman army, rather than through missionaries.[27] Meanwhile, Arians did score some successes, converting a number of Germanic tribes prior to the collapse of the Western empire.

Yet this needs to be qualified in two ways. Barbarians did convert, but they converted not because missionaries were sent to them but because they migrated into the empire. Late in the fourth century, a Christian visited the Marcomanni north of the Danube and spoke animatedly to Queen Fritigil about the great bishop Ambrose of Milan. The queen converted and wrote to Ambrose asking for more instruction in her faith. Ambrose wrote her a catechism of sorts and also urged the queen to prevail on her husband the king to make peace with the empire. She did, and the entire tribe migrated and settled in a Roman province as *federates*.[28] That is one qualification: barbarians converted, readily and thoroughly, *when* they crossed into the empire. Moving from "the wilds of *barbaria* into the social relationships of *Romania* brought about a marked and comparatively sudden transformation in their religion."[29] The other qualification is this: heretics—the great missionaries of Yoder and Heilke's narrative—typically converted barbarians in precisely the same way. Visigoths "converted to Arianism when settled as Federates in Moesia between 382 and 395," and the Burgundians likewise "converted when settled as Federates in Germania Prima between 412 and 436." In 476, small Christian communities were scattered throughout northern and eastern Europe, but "none of the great Germanic peoples living outside the frontier was Christian."[30] A Constantinian "merger" of faith and empire seems to have been a most effective evangelistic method

---

[27]Conversion through these "normal" channels was in all likelihood also common in the earlier history of the church. Yoder's thesis appears to assume a Billy Graham–style crusade or a Hudson Taylor model of missions. For a stimulating, though admittedly speculative, account of the spread of early Christianity, see Rodney Stark, *The Rise of Christianity* (San Francisco: Harper, 1997).

[28]Thompson, "Christianity and the Northern Barbarians," pp. 60, 66.

[29]Ibid., p. 78.

[30]Ibid., p. 72.

during the fourth and fifth centuries.

Yoder and Heilke, however, spread their net wider. Heretics were the great missionaries "for a *millennium*." A millennium is a long time. Add a millennium to the year of Constantine's death, and we come to 1337. In 1337 the Hundred Years' War was getting under way, and a decade later the Black Death would ravage Europe. The church had experienced the East-West schism, the Western church had endured the investiture struggle and the Aristotelian revival, English barons had forced the Magna Carta on the hapless King John, and Thomas Aquinas had lived and died. *All that time*, Yoder asserts, the orthodox so closely identified themselves with the Roman Empire that they did nothing in the way of missions.

This is false, and betrays either dishonesty or a quite breathtaking ignorance of medieval history. By 1337 Patrick had begotten a crusading army of Irish monks that begat Columba that begat Columbanus that begat missionary monasteries throughout Europe; Pope Gregory had sent Augustine to evangelize the Britons (who turned out to already have been evangelized); Boniface had wowed the Saxons by cutting down a holy tree; the Franks had established a formally Christian empire; sent by the caesaropapists in Byzantium, Cyril and Methodius had evangelized the Slavs; in Kiev, St. Vladimir had chosen Byzantine rather than Catholic Christianity for the Rus; to the far north, the peoples of Scandinavia turned to Christianity in droves just before the turn of the first millennium. Missionaries of course bore the gospel in a cultural form, but in many cases they were careful to impose as little of that cultural form on their converts as prudent.[31] That Cyril and Methodius did not identify Byzantine culture with Christianity is evident from the fact that they did not force Greek on the Slavs but invented an alphabet so they could give them Christianity and the Bible in their own language.[32] Yoder would remind us that this was a "Constantinian" mission effort; nearly everywhere missionaries evangelized kings, who changed their tribal religion en masse, becoming "New Constantines."[33] True enough; still it belies Yoder's astonishing charge that the church gave up on missions for a millennium.

---

[31]See the discriminating letters of Gregory to Augustine.

[32]On all this, see now Richard Fletcher, *The Barbarian Conversion: From Paganism to Christianity* (New York: Henry Holt, 1997).

[33]The term is Fletcher's.

UNINTENDED CONSEQUENCES

In chapter ten I examined some of the consequences of Constantine's legislation and policies, suggesting that whatever his intentions, his reign had a revolutionary impact on the empire, an impact that, if it did not quite rise to the level of thorough "Christianization," began that process and prepared the way for it to continue. Similar observations may be made about Constantine's imperial agenda. He no doubt wished to maintain the borders of the empire, keep the barbarians at bay, invade Persia, extend the empire, protect and enrich the church. Perhaps he believed that it would all last forever.

Whatever Constantine's intentions, however, the empire's devotion to the church was one of the causes for its eventual decline. Geza Alfoldy concludes his *Social History of Rome* with the suggestive observation that

> the role of Christianity in the collapse of the Roman system of power resulted from the fact that it was taken over by the Germans and carried on. Throughout previous Roman history, the value system of Roman society had been the *mos maiorum*, which set up an insurmountable barrier between Romans and non-Romans. But Christian Romans were linked to the Christian barbarians by their common religion and morality: in the words of Orosius, a Christian Roman was *"inter Romanos Romanus, inter Christianos Christianus, inter homines homo"* [among Romans a Roman, among Christians a Christian, among men a man] . . . : for such men Christian barbarians were not longer *hostes* [enemies] but *fraters* [brothers]. . . . From Orosius' standpoint even Alaric's capture of Rome in AD 410 did not seem a really bad thing for, after all, the Western Goths were also Christians. For Salvian, the Germans embodied the Christian virtues very much more than the Romans. Orosius had a vision that Romans and Germans should live together in a Christian Romania.[34]

Arnaldo Momigliano likewise points out that the church had ways of dealing with the barbarian threat that were not available to pagans: "The educated pagan was by definition afraid of barbarians. There was no bridge between the aristocratic ideals of a pagan and the primitive violence of the German invader." At best, a few barbarians might be educated and become Roman, but "the ordinary barbarian as such was nothing more than a night-

---

[34]Geza Alfoldy, *The Social History of Rome*, trans. David Braund and Frank Pollock (Baltimore: Johns Hopkins University Press, 1988).

mare to educated pagans." Christians, on the other hand, "could convert the barbarians and make them members of the Church. They had discovered a bridge between barbarism and civilization." In the East, though, the church supported the Byzantine emperors in their persistent struggle against the barbarians, and there "the defence of the empire could be presented as the defence of the Church." Thus, "in the West the Church gradually replaced the dying State in dealing with the barbarians," while in the East "the Church realized that the Roman state was much more vital and supported it in its fight against the barbarians." On both sides of Europe, ordinary people needed leaders and largely found them in their bishops. More, Roman civilization had no way of accommodating barbarians. There was no basis for a common civilization. After converting to Christianity, though, the "Germans were, at least to a certain extent, Romanized and made capable of living together with the citizens of the Roman empire."[35]

In short, the conversion of the empire did not bond empire and church inseparably together. It had, as we would expect and Yoder would want, the opposite effect. It *loosened* the bonds that many Romans felt to the empire, even as it *strengthened* their bonds to another city, another kingdom, one that spilled far over the limits of the empire. Baptized Rome found that it could join with baptized *barbaria,* since Jesus had broken down the dividing wall.

Constantine's conversion subverted the empire in another way as well. As we have seen, Constantine saw the unity of the church as essential to the unity and health of the empire. He normally described that in terms of maintaining the favor of God, but his religious policies make it clear that he also wished to unify the empire theologically and ecclesiastically. When the bishops at Nicaea had determined the relationship of the Son to the Father, that became the creed of the churches of the Roman empire. Arius was exiled and kept at arm's length until he could come up with a convincing confession of Nicaea. This creedally based empire had one great advantage for Constantine: it gave Rome a universal cultural and religious mission that it had never had, and made it a rival of the more ideologically focused Persian empire.

---

[35]Arnaldo Momigliano, "Christianity and the Decline of the Roman Empire," in *The Conflict Between Paganism and Christianity in the Fourth Century,* ed. Arnaldo Momigliano (Oxford: Clarendon, 1963).

Assume the worst: Constantine was a cynical hypocrite, using the church as a means to achieve his own imperial ambitions. Suppose that he did not believe a word of the Nicene Creed but only hoped to force the whole world into a mold more Roman than Christian. Assume the worst, yet his program was doomed to crash, precisely on the shoals of heresy. Once the empire was a creedal empire, heresy could not be seen as a tolerable difference of opinion; it was subversive, an attack on the vitals of the imperial body, and had to be expelled. Inevitably, then, the empire founded on a monotheistic creed fractured and eventually yielded to a commonwealth of Christian peoples, the Byzantine "empire."[36]

It was not long after Constantine, as Alasdair MacIntyre points out, that people of goodwill decided that maintaining justice, peace and civilized life did not require the maintenance of the Roman empire. Some left for monasteries, while others continued in the empire but not of it. Whatever Constantinian moment there had been was over, ironically assisted by Constantine himself, who not only failed to prevent the empire's inevitable collapse but probably helped to hasten it.

JEREMIAN ECCLESIOLOGY

In both the last chapter and this one, I have argued that to sustain his thesis of a "Constantinian shift," Yoder must discover a moment in the church's history in which the church was universally opposed to violence and war, universally hostile to empire and universally committed to a particular interpretation of Jesus' injunctions in the Sermon on the Mount. I have argued too that Yoder never did find such a starting point, and that he did not because he cannot, and he cannot because no such moment ever existed.

Yoder would respond by saying that the fixed starting point—the height from which the church fell—lies in the teaching and example of Jesus, as seen in the context of the "Jeremian" paradigm of the Jewish diaspora. Historians and exegetes have, he says, missed the point by quibbling "about this or that legalistic reading of a few words of Jesus" while "ignoring both the sociological and theological contexts within which first-century believers sustained their view of history under God." According to this "Jew-

---

[36]This is the argument of Garth Fowden, *Empire to Commonwealth: Consequences of Monotheism in Late Antiquity* (Princeton, N.J.: Princeton University Press, 1993).

ish quietism," God is in charge, not humans, and accordingly the faithful renounce Maccabean or Zealot efforts to "take charge" of history through nationalism or violence. Jesus drew on and deepened that tradition.[37]

For Yoder, the Jeremian model of Jewish life and identity does more than simply provide a way of making sense of Jesus' teaching in the Gospels. It provides a model for the church in its relation to worldly powers.[38] Jeremiah ranks with Constantine as symbol and legend, a marker of an epochal shift in the life of the people of God. Yoder's Jeremiah instructed the people to settle into the *galuth*, exile, not as a temporary "hiatus" before a new kingship and temple were established, nor simply as a punishment for their sins. Jews were to "seek the salvation of the culture" of Babylon by accepting their dispersion as a call to mission. They were to retain their separate identity by adherence to a peripatetic moral and liturgical life— they defined themselves by a "text which can be copied and read anywhere," centered their worship on "reading and singing the texts," established places of worship without priesthoods wherever ten households gathered, maintained their international unity by "intervisitation, by intermarriage, by commerce, and by rabbinic consultation," found the "ground floor of identity" in "the common life, the walk, halakah," and confounded kings and emperors "with the superior wisdom and power of the one authentic God."[39] There was no "Jewish emperor," and they were not to hope for one; their leaders might be in king's palaces, but it would be as "intermediaries" between "the community and the Gentiles."[40]

Jeremiah's vision for Israel in exile was neither an effort to "Hebraize" Babylon (they were not asked "to teach the Babylonians Hebrew") nor a retreat from cultural engagement. Jews served "the entire ancient Near Eastern world as expert translators, scribes, diplomats, sages, merchants, astronomers." They were to turn their status as resident aliens to "cultural advantage" because they refused to expend themselves or their resources "fighting over civil sovereignty."[41] Far from being a place of resignation and lament, "Babylon itself very soon became the cultural

---

[37]Yoder, *For the Nations*, pp. 66-69.
[38]Ibid., p. 66.
[39]Ibid., pp. 58-59.
[40]Ibid., p. 59.
[41]Ibid., p. 71.

center of world Jewry."[42] Dispersion became the permanent setting for Jews, and this is the cultural and political program that the church inherited from Judaism.

Yoder's vision of Christian engagement with the powers that be is invigorating, and is just right in many respects. As a historical thesis, it accurately describes the experience of the church in the first three centuries. In the end, however, it is unconvincing. It fails mainly because it badly truncates the biblical story on which it relies. Yoder makes only a passing reference to the hope for return found in Isaiah, but more important, he does not even read Jeremiah to the end. Jeremiah repeatedly holds out the hope for a renewed Davidic dynasty (23:5; 30:9; 33:15-17) in a community that has been restored to the land (30:1; 31:8, 16-17, 27-28). If exile was supposed to be permanent and normative, should Daniel have given up praying for release (Daniel 9)? Yoder sees the scattering at the original Babel as a similar call to mission, insisting that "the 'confusion of tongues' is not a punishment or a tragedy but the gift of new beginnings, liberation from a blind alley," and that the diversity that resulted was God's "original divine intent."[43] He is entirely correct that the diversity of Babel presented no problem to the "polyglot Jews," just as multiculturalism should be no problem for Christians. But if Babelist diversity is the original divine intent, what was the Spirit up to when he began to reverse Babel's scattering with the language miracle of Pentecost?[44]

Yoder dismisses the "standard account" that "sees the course of history moving back from Babylon to Jerusalem" and argues that if we take Jeremiah seriously both Ezra and Nehemiah "need to be seen as inappropriate deviations from the Jeremiah line, since each reconstituted a cult and a polity as a branch of the pagan imperial government."[45] That is a highly

---

[42]Ibid., p. 57.

[43]Ibid., pp. 63-64. He makes the odd claim, though, that "the one thing that never would have occurred to the Jews in Babylon was to try to bridge the distance between their language world and that of their hosts by a foundationalist mental or linguistic move" and that they "did not look for or seek to construct common ground" (p. 73). But that sounds very much like Philo's life work. Philo in fact went beyond foundationalism, allegorizing biblical stories to turn them into parables of Greek virtue, and it is hard to see how Hellenistic Judaism (which is a reality, whatever qualifications need to be made) fits into Yoder's picture.

[44]Yoder (ibid., p. 75) is aware of the issue but says only that "a fair reading of the account of Luke in Acts 2 will be compatible" with his reading of Genesis.

[45]Ibid., p. 74. He characterizes Ezra as a book full of "politicking for imperial authorization to rebuild the temple" and says that Ezra's title of "scribe" meant "secretary for Jewish affairs" to

prejudicial reading of Ezra-Nehemiah, but it is true that they reestablished a Jewish community in the land with imperial money and support. The author of Ezra-Nehemiah, however, does not breathe a critical word against his heroes. Nor is the author of Ezra-Nehemiah alone in endorsing the project. Isaiah goes so far as to designate the temple-building Persian emperor Cyrus as Yahweh's "Christ" and "shepherd" (Isaiah 44:28; 45:1). What Yoder calls the "standard account" is the *canonical* account, which does not dismiss Ezra and Nehemiah as agents of a pagan empire but rather sees them as fulfillment of prophecies, *Jeremiah's* prophecies not least.

It is not clear, further, how Yoder distinguishes between the "deviations" of Ezra and Nehemiah on the one hand from what he sees as the faithful witness of Joseph, Daniel, Esther and others on the other. Such heroes "found themselves involuntarily at the heart of the idolatrous empire" and "ran the risk of faithfulness" by "civil disobedience" that could have cost them their lives. God saved them, and as a result "the pagan tyrant was converted to the recognition of the one true God."[46] All true, and Yoder is also ready to endorse Joseph's management of famine relief and Daniel's assistance to Darius as contributions "to secular well-being which is far more than mere minority survival." These efforts fulfill the Jeremian injunction to "seek the salvation of the culture to which God has sent you."[47] But surely Daniel and Joseph both did their share of "politicking" and, even more than Ezra and Nehemiah, were dependent on the imperial treasury. If an anti-imperial Jew were looking for a minion of the emperor, it would probably be Daniel. Babylon, it is true, did not get a Jewish emperor, but it got (at least) four Jewish administrators (Daniel 2:46-49), and Persia got more than one (Daniel 6:1-3; Esther 10:3). By what measure does Yoder distinguish Daniel's fulfillment of the Jeremian vision from Ezra's deviation? Why do they not represent two different, equally legitimate, responses to empire? Whatever the measure, it is not the measure of the text itself, which celebrates the achievements of both.[48]

---

the Persian emperor: "It was a title for a cabinet role in the pagan empire" (p. 74, n. 57).

[46]Ibid., p. 57.

[47]Ibid., p. 76, n. 60.

[48]More deeply and broadly, Yoder's account of exile-without-return raises the question of vindication, which I will address in the next chapter.

The examples of Joseph, Daniel, Esther, Ezra and Nehemiah take us back where we started, to Constantine. I wrote above that Yoder's vision of Jewish mission in exile is invigorating, and I meant that. It is the key vision that should guide the twenty-first-century Christian response to empire in a world after Christendom. It is what Christians should be busy doing. But it does not address the question that Constantine's career raises: what does the church do if the emperor sees a vision and wants to help Christians start building a temple back in Jerusalem? Yoder does not think that is "an available option."[49] St. Sebastian may have thought the same as he was shot full of arrows and then pelted with stones, but as Yoder himself would be the first to admit, God tends to surprise us with *un*available options. That's what makes him God.

If we are going to do justice to Constantine, we cannot sidestep certain questions: Should fourth-century Christians, like the Jews, have rejoiced in the king's confession of the God of heaven? They did. Should they, like Daniel and Joseph and Mordecai, have served in the imperial administration? They did. Should they, like Ezra and Nehemiah, have gratefully accepted the king's largesse, which helped them build magnificent places of worship? They did. Should they, like Joseph and Daniel, have witnessed to the truth even in the face of enticements, threats and imperial fury? The best of them did. Should they, like Daniel, have acknowledged that God, not the emperor, controlled history and that God's people, not Babylon or Rome, was the secret center of the world? Nearly all of them did. Should they have recognized that the church has its own power and does not need to be bound to the sword to carry on its mission? Most of them did.

By what measure does Yoder characterize "legends" about the conversion of pagan Pharaoh and pagan Nebuchadnezzar as fulfillments of the Jeremian mission to "seek the salvation of the city," while dismissing the imperial church of Constantine as apostate and heretical? There is, I think, an answer to that question, but it will have to wait until the final chapter.

THE PURPLE AND THE WHITE

Then there was the time when Constantine came down with leprosy.

---

[49]Yoder, *For the Nations*, p. 107. He adds that the "time is past when it could be attempted with any hope of success." But when, one wants to ask, did success become the criterion of Christian action?

He had already conquered the empire west to east when the "blighting leprosy possessed the whole flesh of [his] body." Doctors from every end of the empire tried to help and failed. Priests then came from Rome with a solution. It is going to take blood, they said: lots of blood, the blood of infants. When it "ran warm I could be cleansed by washing in it." Constantine collected thousand of infants, but then "perceiving the tears of their mothers," he suddenly "felt an immediate abhorrence of the crime," which had apparently not occurred to him before. He had pity and returned sons to their mothers, along with compensatory gifts.

Still he was a leper. Then one night he saw in a dream Peter and Paul, who commended him for putting "an end to the atrocities" and showing "abhorrence of shedding innocent blood," and promised in return that the emperor would be healed. Bishop Silvester of Rome had fled from the city because of Constantine's persecutions and was hiding out in mountain caves with the rest of the Roman clergy. Silvester will help, the apostles said: "he will show you the bathing-pool of piety, and when you have immersed yourself in this for a third time, this leprous condition will leave you." In return for restored health, Constantine would have to give up "all idolatrous superstition, and adore and worship the true and living God."

So Constantine summoned "the universal pope" Silvester, told him of the dream, and was able to identify Peter and Paul from portraits in Silvester's possession. The emperor prepared himself with "vigils, fasting, tears also and prayers," renounced "Satan's mummery" and all idols, and confessed the living God in the words of the Nicene Creed. Finally the day of his baptism came:

> The font was blessed, and there the water of salvation purified me with a triple immersion. And when I had been placed in the bosom of the font, I saw with my own eyes a hand from heaven touching me. And rising from it clean, I apprehended that I had been cleansed from the whole blight of leprosy. And once I had been raised from the holy font, and had put on white clothes, he applied to me the sealing of the sevenfold Holy Spirit with the oil of the blessed chrism, and smeared the banner of the Holy Cross on my forehead.

From that day on, "my body had been cured of the blight of leprosy," and Constantine renounced all the demonic gods of the nations and worshiped only "the Trinity in unity and unity in Trinity." He helped build a church for the pope with his own hands, handed over Rome, Italy and the entire empire to Silvester and his successors (the grant known as the "Donation of Constantine"), and took on "the office of a squire" to the papacy.[50]

This anachronistic account from a medieval bestseller does *not* give the facts about Constantine's baptism and tells us a great deal more about the time it was written than about Constantine. Still, it has some interest for our investigation. The writer depicts the transition from pre- to post-Constantinian Rome in several ways: it marks the end of sacrifice, particularly human sacrifice, and persecution; it involves the devotion of the emperor and the empire to the church (and the pope in particular); it marks this transition with baptism. The *Acts of the Blessed Silvester* gives us a medieval perspective on the baptism of Rome under Constantine, a baptism that brought the end of sacrifice. That is a perspective I have implicitly endorsed throughout this book and will explain more fully in the final chapter.

Eusebius's account gives us the real story. In the midst of preparations for a war with Persia, building projects and general imperial administration, Constantine began to feel "some light bodily indisposition." According to Eusebius, his first desire was to visit hot baths and to spend time in prayer at the Church of the Martyrs in Constantinople, but he soon became convinced that he was dying. He did not want to die until he had purified his soul from "whatever errors he had committed as a mortal man" in baptism, and decided to travel to Palestine to be baptized, like Jesus, in the Jordan. He got only as far as Nicomedia before he was unable to go farther. Bishop Eusebius of Nicomedia came to his bedside with other bishops and listened as Constantine expressed his desire to "obtain the salvation of God" through "that seal which confers immortality . . . the seal of salvation." The bishops "performed the sacred ceremonies in the usual manner" and, having given him instructions, "made him a partaker of the mystic ordinance." By this, Constantine became "the first of all sovereigns who was regenerated and perfected in a church dedicated to the martyrs of Christ." Gladdened and "filled with heavenly light," Constantine put aside the purple that had lain on his shoulders since his father's

---

[50]*Acts of the Blessed Silvester* 6-10, 16-17; in *Constantine and Christendom*, trans. Mark Edwards (Liverpool: Liverpool University Press, 2003), pp. 99-104, 112-13. For discussion of the various accounts of Constantine's baptism, see Garth Fowden, "The Last Days of Constantine: Oppositional Versions and Their Influence," *Journal of Roman Studies* 94 (1994): 153-68.

death thirty years before and "arrayed himself in shining imperial vestments, brilliant as the light, and reclined on a couch of the purest white." He refused to take up the purple again.[51]

Caesar Flavius Valerius Aurelius Constantinus Augustus died during the Pentecost season, A.D. 337, having, at long last, been received into the bosom of the church.

Eusebius's account is revealing for our purposes, particularly in the contrast that Eusebius draws between Constantine the emperor and Constantine the baptized Christian. Baptism was the moment of his "regeneration and perfection," the moment when the emperor was received into the people of God. Constantine had the same view. Not only did he discard the imperial purple when he took on the baptismal white, but in his final speech to Eusebius and the other bishops he expressed his wish that, should his life continue, he would be "associate[d] with the people of God, and unite with them in prayer as a member of his church" and devote himself to "such a course of life as befits his service."[52] This comes in the closing chapters of a biography that has described Constantine's vision before the battle with Maxentius, his support for the church and suppression of paganism, his Christian legislation, his devotion to prayer and study, his victories in wars often presented as holy wars, his missionary zeal. At the end of all this, Eusebius quoted Constantine saying that *in the future* he would devote himself to the service of the God whose salvation was sealed to him in his baptism. As Eusebius recounted the story, Constantine seemed to believe there was a basic incompatibility between being an emperor and being a Christian, between court and church, warfare and prayer, the purple and the white.

It would be an ironic conclusion: Constantine, the first anti-Constantinian. Constantine the Yoderian.

---

[51]Eusebius *Life* 4.61-64.
[52]Ibid., 4.62.

14

Rome Baptized

God is not the ruler of the city of the impious,
because it disobeys his commandment that
sacrifice be offered to himself alone.

AUGUSTINE, *CITY OF GOD*

Constantine was a soldier, and a great one. He rarely lost a skirmish and never lost a war. He was not an ignorant grunt. Educated in Diocletian's court, he retained an interest in theology, philosophy, and literature throughout his life, his dabbling that of a competent amateur. A man of high moral standards, of which he was somewhat vain, sometimes a bit of a prig, he expected everyone else to live up to his expectations. He liked to see the big picture and could be impatient with details. He had a strong sense of justice, and when aroused by what he believed unjust, he could be imperious, brutal, hectoring. He was aggressive and ambitious but was a strategist with the self-restraint to wait out an opponent. When the situation called for it, he knew how to politick, compromise and build consensus. He had a sense of symbol and ceremony, knew the right gesture. He enjoyed the kitschy gaudiness of the court and its adornments; the flowered robe rested easily on his shoulders, he liked his jeweled slippers, and he did not think a golden throne too much. But he also knew that he should treat it with disdain, and that disdain was sincere too. He was an imperial performer who liked performing but knew he was assuming a role. He was formal and cold, keeping a safe distance even from those who knew him best. He could be witty in conversation. When the Novatian bishop Acesius opined that someone who sinned mortally after baptism should be barred from the sacrament, Constantine cracked, "Place a ladder, Acesius, and climb alone to heaven."[1] His religion went to the edge of superstition; he was a dreamer and visionary and never quite gave up the expectation that examining a liver or the stars might yield a clue about the future. He believed that the Christian God guaranteed the success of his wars and that God had called him to support the church, expand Christianity in the Roman world and extend the faith beyond.

Constantine grew up in a family that respected Christianity and may have included Christians, but he did not personally identify with Christianity until after 312, when Christians provided a Christian reading of a stunning sun halo he had seen two years before and interpreted his dream on the night before a battle as a dream of Christ. From that time on, Constantine used his imperial power to protect and support the Christian church. He was a sincere if somewhat simple believer. He knew some portions of the Old Testament and perhaps the basic outline of biblical history, and he could summarize the story of the Gospels. For Constantine, God was a providential Judge who supports the righteous and destroys the wicked, and he believed that the church had to be unified if it was going to offer pleasing worship to God.

Constantine ended the persecution of Christians in the Western empire and restored property to the Western churches several years before he defeated Maxentius at Rome. In 313 that policy was extended, because of the agreement between Constantine and Licinius at Milan, to the Eastern empire. When he took the Eastern empire in 324, Constantine adopted a religious policy that, with some limits, tolerated pagans and Jews while giving obvious favor to the church. He destroyed some temples, plundered more, decreed that sacrifice should end, and reiterated and slightly intensified legal limits on Jewish proselytism. He did not adopt a policy of forced conversion, did not punish pagans for being pagans or Jews for being Jews. Pagans remained at his court and were given weighty responsibilities in the empire. His rhetoric against both pagans and Jews was forceful, some-

---

[1]Preserved by Socrates; quoted in H. A. Drake, *Constantine and the Bishops: The Politics of Intolerance* (Baltimore: Johns Hopkins University Press, 2000), p. 269.

times vicious, and this, along with the legal restrictions, created an atmosphere that discouraged but did not destroy paganism. He Christianized public space in Rome, funded the restoration of sacred sites in Palestine, and founded Constantinople.

Constantine expended an enormous amount of treasure on churches; it was used both on buildings and, with the emperor's explicit encouragement, on establishing ministries of mercy to the poor, sick and widows. When disputes arose in the church, Constantine believed it was his right and duty as Roman emperor to guide the warring factions toward a resolution. His first instinct was to pacify and negotiate, working toward *concordia*, but he found that many of the bishops did not share his passion for unity. He called councils of bishops and provided venues, funding and transport. He attended some of the councils and contributed to discussions but did not chair any council or determine the outcome. Once the bishops had arrived at a decision, Constantine accepted it as a divine word and backed up conciliar decisions with legal sanctions, mainly exile for those found guilty of heresy. Though he preferred bishops who were team players, he admired the uncompromising holy passion of Athanasius. Councils could be rancorous, and during Constantine's lifetime council fought with council. The emperor meddled in church affairs when he did not see the bishops coming to a decent and timely resolution. He eventually took up the Donatist controversy directly, and he met with Arius and tried to force Alexander and Athanasius to restore the heretic to the Alexandrian church. Many of the bishops quietly went along or were too distant from the center of activity to know or care. Some bishops, especially Athanasius, stood up to Constantine when they believed the truth was at stake.

Constantine did not try explicitly to Christianize the legal system, Roman society or Roman government. He appointed Christians to leading positions in his administration, and many men, often Christians, rose from lower ranks of society to positions of power. One law made explicit reference to Christian principles (the image of God in man), and some were inspired by Christianity. The most important of these were exemptions from taxes and other public obligations for clergy and the emperor's legislation against sacrifice, but his laws closing the gladiatorial shows and condemning exposure of children also drew on Christian teaching. Constantine's laws were both conservative and innovative—conservative in maintaining or hardening legally sanctioned social divisions, innovative in the ways he provided for the weaker and poorer citizens of the empire. Like pagan emperors before him, Constantine addressed the obstacles that excluded the poor and poorly connected to justice, but unlike his predecessors he found part of the solution in allowing appeals to episcopal courts.

Constantine's laws were more often Christian in effect than in intent. Outlawing gladiatorial shows struck down one of the main institutions for the propagation of Roman values, culture and power and was more transformative than Constantine could have known. His support for the church made the church financially dependent on the empire to a large extent, but it also had the effect of enriching and empowering the bishops, who eventually provided a counterweight to imperial power. Whatever his intentions, over the long run Constantine's support of the church strengthened the church's status as an alternative society and polity within the Roman Empire. Already during Constantine's lifetime, and even more during the reigns of his sons, church leaders became more aggressively confrontational toward the empire, fighting to protect the church's independence from imperial intrusions.

Constantine spent his life in the Roman military. He fought with Diocletian, and with his father, and when he became emperor he continued to fight, sometimes against barbarians threatening from the frontier, sometimes against other Romans, who were usually members of his extended family. By the time his life ended, he was (indirectly in every case, so far as we know) responsible for the deaths of his father-in-law Maximian, his brother-in-law Maxentius, another brother-in-law Licinius along with his son, his wife Fausta and his son Crispus, and a few other relatives. Some or all of these executions may have been just acts of punishing rivals and rebels. Some or all of them may have been acts of a paranoid emperor eager to maintain his hard-won power. We know too little to be sure. On the other hand, he never engaged in a purge. Maxentius's supporters were not slaughtered in Rome when Constantine took the capital; Licinius's son died with his father, and Constantine ordered the execution of one of Licinius's chief supporters, but no other members of Licinius's family or court were executed. Constantine believed his military expeditions were divinely commissioned, and he attributed his victories to God. During his long reign, the empire was comparatively peaceful.

How did the church fare under Constantine? It is important to recall where our story began, with Diocletian's edict of persecution and the sacrificial slaughter of Christians. Toleration edicts had already been decreed in East and West before Constantine became the sole emperor, but he secured the church's freedom and made it permanent. Externally, the church flourished during the early fourth century. It had new, magnificent buildings and the prestige and power that partly arose from Constantine's conversion and his support for their mission. Church membership became legal, and attractive, and for reasons good (devotion to Jesus) and bad (tax exemptions, prestige) men sought church leadership. Constantine had considerable influence on the church but did not dominate it, dictate the election of bishops or make final decisions about doctrine. Councils met without his approval, and bishops were elected locally. He did not have "absolute authority" over the church, and there is no evidence that he wanted to get it. With power, money and prestige came the temptation to accommodate, a problem that nearly every church father after Constantine addressed repeatedly and explicitly. Christian missions did not cease after the fourth century. Barbarians who migrated into Constantine's empire frequently converted, and some missionaries crossed the frontier to shepherd Roman citizens living outside the empire or, in some cases, to evangelize barbarians. The conversion of many Romans bored holes in the fixed boundary between Roman and barbarian, and eventually dissolved the distinction entirely. Constantine's conversion was a crucial prelude to the decline of the empire and the rise of medieval Christendom's cultural cocktail of *Romanitas, Germanitas* and *Christianitas.*

That, I think, is a fair historical portrait of the man, his career, his times and his effect on the church. In my judgment, it is a history that John Howard Yoder and other theological and historical critics get wrong on many particulars and in the general outline. Yoder cannot know as much as he claims about the pacifist consensus of the early church, badly misreads major figures like Eusebius and especially Augustine, oversimplifies the history of "mainstream Christianity" to the point of caricature, and tries to convince us that the orthodox church handed missionary activity to heretics for a millennium after Constantine. His rhetoric of anti-Constantinianism discourages Christians from a serious and sympathetic engagement with more than a millennium of Christian theological, and political theological, reflection. Using Yoder's definition of "Constantinian," I think it is more accurate to describe the early fourth century as a "Constantinian moment" than as an epoch-making "Constantinian shift"; further, the worst abuses that Yoder identifies arose after Constantine, sometimes long after. As I argue below, I think there *was* a "Constantinian shift," but it is one that Yoder quite misses.

This book, however, is not intended to be a Big Book of Quibbles. That would be too easy and also would set me up as a target for similar treatment, as readers (if any there be) sift through this book and (inevitably) discover my own historical errors, big and small. My main interest in this project has been theological. Theology and history, as Yoder is the first to remind us, are not ultimately divisible. My historical portrait has implied a political theology. But it is time to make that political theology more overt, to explain where I think Yoder goes wrong and to offer an alternative account of the theological meaning of Constantine.

ANTI-CONSTANTINIANISM

Anti-Constantinianism has a long history. Early on, most of the opposition came from pagans like Julian and Zosimus, and in the modern era Enlightenment and post-Enlightenment thinkers like Voltaire, Gibbon and Burckhardt assaulted the first Christian emperor as a usurper, a murderer, a tyrant whose only redeeming quality was his impatience with theological dispute. That pagans and rationalists would dislike Constantine is unsurprising, but there has also been a strong anti-Constantinian tradition within the church that is more interesting because it is more unexpected.

Francis of Assisi already traced the corruption and degeneration of the church to the Constantinian period, and in the fourteenth century "proto-Reformers" like John Wycliffe and Jan Hus took up the theme. Often medieval critics of the Constantinian settlement focused their attacks on the Donation of Constantine, mentioned at the end of the previous chapter, Constantine's legendary gift of Rome, Italy and episcopal supremacy to the bishop of Rome. Anti-Constantinianism was thus entwined with antipapalism, leading Wycliffe, for instance, to repudiate "the entire papal system on the grounds of having been founded by Constantine and not

Christ."[2] Papal supporters like Bernard of Clairvaux also condemned the Donation, because it corrupted the church with a grant of worldly power and property.[3] Dante's allegorical vision of church history at the end of *Purgatorio* gave this view its classic poetic expression, as the golden wings of the Roman eagle drop into and damage the chariot of the church, just before the fox of heresy slips in.

Radical Reformation attacks on the Constantinian church made the same linkage with papal power. Radical Reformers aimed, they said, to reach back beyond the Constantinian corruption to a primitive church that was spiritually alive, simple, nonsacramental. For Melchior Hoffmann, the church of Constantine corresponded to the church of Pergamon in the book of Revelation, a church "where divine truth became polluted by human wisdom and moral compromise was generally accepted." This was the period when "the pope and antichrist were very pleased to accept the same power, authority and strength of worldly rule."[4] Pietist Lutheran Gottfried Arnold (1666-1714) reinterpreted the whole of church history along anti-Constantinian lines, brandishing an early "pure church" as a measuring rod to show how far the mainstream church fell into "the poisonous embrace of Constantine." In Arnold's story, the true church "had been preserved over the centuries, not by powerful prelates and conciliar decrees, but by the despised dissenters, sometimes labeled as the heretics of the age."[5] During the nineteenth century Ludwig Keller developed a similar account of the church's history, tracing a persistent *altevangelische Brüdergemeinden* from the apostles through the Waldensians to the Reformation Anabaptists, a paradigm that, in turn, inspired the work of Ernst Troeltsch.[6]

From at least the seventeenth century, criticism of Constantine has taken the form of a critique of "caesaro-papism." In early usage, as in the work of the Protestant jurist Iustus Henning Bohmer, the term referred equally to systems in which popes take worldly power and to systems in

---

[2]Daniel H. Williams, "Constantine, Nicaea and the 'Fall' of the Church," in *Christian Origins: Theology, Rhetoric and Community*, ed. Lewis Ayres and S. Gareth Jones (London: Routledge, 1998), p. 119.
[3]Ibid.
[4]Ibid., p. 120; the second quotation is from Hoffmann.
[5]Ibid., p. 123.
[6]Ibid.

which laymen assume the responsibilities of bishops. Eventually "only the second caught on," and the term was used less as an analytic concept than as a Western club specially designed to beat Byzantine Christianity. Johann Christian Hesse made caesaro-papism the hinge of his account of Western political Christianity: "Constantine was now the villain of the piece; he had opted for Christianity for political reasons and had made religion serve what he perceived as his own interests." Taking up this tradition, Jacob Burckhardt found analogies between Byzantine and Islamic political order, and thereby discarded Byzantium as "un-European."[7]

Much of this critique, especially in the modern period, is fairly easy to dispose of. Burckhardt's hostility to what he thought of as caesaro-papism is based on the conviction that religion and power can never mix; politics is the arena of amoral combat, religion of contemplation, prayer, soft pieties. The charge of caesaro-papism deconstructs into an unlikely alliance of "Roman [Catholic] fundamentalism" and Protestant pietism, and relies on "the radical distinction between the spiritual and the temporal, which was intended to separate religion from politics" and has the ironic consequence of endorsing clerical power and reproaching "the founder of the Christian empire . . . for having lacked an ideal of laicity."[8] In short, critiques of Constantinianism, especially in the modern period, have lacked an ecclesiology and have operated with what John Milbank describes as the "liberal Protestant metanarrative," according to which the church gradually sheds its external political encrustations and is revealed as what in essence it always has been, something "purely religious." On those premises, the critique of Constantinianism is preloaded; no matter how faithfully the church gives cultural form to its gospel, it is abandoning the "spiritual" message of Jesus.

For all its celebration of the martyrs, furthermore, Christian anti-Constantinianism does little justice to the martyrs' hopes. Martyrs endured flame and sword because in that anguish they shared in the sufferings of Christ. But they also knew that the sufferings of Christ were not perpetual. Jesus suffered, died, was buried and then rose again, vindicated by his Father over against all the condemnations of the world and the devil. Mar-

---

[7]This entire paragraph is indebted to Gilbert Dagron, *Emperor and Priest: The Imperial Office in Byzantium,* trans. Jean Birrell (Cambridge: Cambridge University Press, 2003), pp. 282-86.
[8]Ibid., pp. 294-95.

tyrs went to their deaths expecting vindication, and expecting that vindication not only in heaven and at the last day but on earth and in time. That is what Lactantius's treatise on the death of persecutors is all about. "Behold," he writes to one Donatus, "all the adversaries are destroyed, and tranquillity having been re-established throughout the Roman empire, the late oppressed Church arises again, and the temple of God, overthrown by the hands of the wicked, is built with more glory than before." Just like Jesus.

The political reversal accomplished by Constantine is testimony to God's mercy:

> For God has raised up princes to rescind the impious and sanguinary edicts of the tyrants and provide for the welfare of mankind; so that now the cloud of past times is dispelled, and peace and serenity gladden all hearts. And after the furious whirlwind and black tempest, the heavens are now become calm, and the wished-for light has shone forth; and now God, the hearer of prayer, by His divine aid has lifted His prostrate and afflicted servants from the ground, has brought to an end the united devices of the wicked, and wiped off the tears from the faces of those who mourned. They who insulted over the Divinity, lie low; they who cast down the holy temple, are fallen with more tremendous ruin; and the tormentors of just men have poured out their guilty souls amidst plagues inflicted by heaven, and amidst deserved tortures. For God delayed to punish them, that, by great and marvelous examples, He might teach posterity that He alone is God, and that with fit vengeance He executes judgment on the proud, the impious, and the persecutors.[9]

God's vengeance against his persecutors comforts the mourners, vindicates the dead, and, more important, vindicates God himself, teaching that "He alone is God."

This form of anti-Constantinianism is theologically erroneous and historically hopeless. Fortunately, that is, by and large, *not* Yoder's brand of anti-Constantinianism.

YODER'S ANTI-CONSTANTINIANISM

Yoder's opposition to Constantine suffers from the same oversight as ear-

---

[9]Lactantius *Death* 1.

lier forms of anti-Constantinianism with regard to martyrs.[10] He longs for the hardy faithfulness of the martyr church but does not recognize that the martyrs were motivated by something very different from anti-Constantinianism. They died, one might almost say, in hope that the Lord would raise up an emperor very like Constantine, through whom the Lord would show that their blood had not seeped silent into the earth.

Yet Yoder's anti-Constantinianism is more challenging precisely because he does not sacrifice ecclesiology but highlights it. His is an ecclesiological and eschatological critique of Constantinianism. As noted a number of times before, Yoder does not identify "Constantinianism" with the achievements or policies of Constantine or any of his successors. Constantinianism is a set of mental, spiritual, and institutional habits that get into the blood of careless Christians. Yoder's is in part a historical thesis; he does believe that "Constantinianism" took its first form in the period between the mid-second century and the fifth, or, more narrowly, between the "Edict" of Milan and the *City of God*. Yet he discerns forms of Constantinianism in pre-Christian Judaism and even charges that ethnically restricted Anabaptist groups might become "Constantinian."

Constantinianism is not dependent on Constantine. What exactly is it? In his most systematic account, Yoder begins with the obvious: After Constantine, Christianity was no longer a minority religion, beleaguered and persecuted, but instead became the favored religion of the empire, in time the majority religion, eventually the established religion. This created a crisis of Christian identity and forced a shift in the meaning of *Christian*.

---

[10]On Constantiniasm in Yoder's writings, see John Howard Yoder, *The Priestly Kingdom: Social Ethics as Gospel* (Notre Dame, Ind.: University of Notre Dame Press, 1984), and *The Royal Priesthood: Essays Ecclesiological and Ecumenical*, ed. Michael G. Cartwright (Grand Rapids: Eerdmans, 1994). For secondary literature, see Thomas Heilke, "Yoder's Idea of Constantinianism: An Analytical Framework Toward Conversation," in *A Mind Patient and Untamed: Assessing John Howard Yoder's Contributions to Theology, Ethics and Peacemaking*, ed. Ben C. Ollenburger and Gayle Koontz (Telford, Penn.: Cascadia, 2004), pp. 89-125; Craig A. Carter, *The Politics of the Cross: The Theology and Social Ethics of John Howard Yoder* (Grand Rapids: Brazos, 2001), and *Rethinking Christ and Culture: A Post-Christendom Perspective* (Grand Rapids: Brazos, 2006); J. Alexander Sider, "'To See History Doxologically': History and Holiness in John Howard Yoder's Ecclesiology" (Ph.D. diss., Duke University, 2004); "Constantinianism Before and After Nicaea: Issues in Reconstitutionist Historiography," in *A Mind Patient and Untamed*, ed. Ollenburger and Koontz; Gerald W. Schlabach. "Deuteronomic or Constantinian: What Is the Most Basic Problem for Christian Social Ethics?" in *The Wisdom of the Cross: Essays in Honor of John Howard Yoder*, ed. Stanley Hauerwas et al. (Eugene, Ore.: Wipf and Stock, 2005), pp. 449-71.

Prior to Constantine, it took some chutzpah to be a Christian; after, it took chutzpah not to be one. In short, "after Constantine the church was everybody."[11]

What interests Yoder here is the fact that this new social status brought with it a new ecclesiology. Prior to Constantine, the church could be identified concretely, visibly, by the lifestyle and practices of the Christian community, particularly the Christian renunciation of violence. If someone was baptized, gathered for Eucharist on Sunday and refused to pick up a sword or retaliate against enemies, he or she was a Christian. After Constantine, the visible markers of baptism, the Lord's Supper and church membership no longer identified the community of sincere believers, since everyone was in the church. A baptized person could be a rank pagan at heart, baptized only to secure a promotion in the provincial administration or to qualify for service in the army; or he could be a sincere, peaceable disciple of Jesus. Baptism told you nothing.

As a result, some new mark of Christian identity had to be found, and it could not be an external mark. It had to be an internal mark, the invisible mark of faith, or of regeneration or of some other spiritual reality. Because of Constantine, Christians developed a "doctrine of the invisibility of the true church" and the distinction between an inner ring of true (elect, believing) Christians, which remains a tiny minority within the visible community, and the vast majority of baptized tagalongs. Augustine's formulation of the idea of an *ecclesia invisibilis* is the dogmatic systematization of the identity crisis that followed Constantine's conversion and promotion of Christianity.[12] Among other things, this is politically problematic. An invisible church has no distinctive way of life that can critique, call, challenge or model an alternative to the wider society. Constantinianism is a historical irony: just when the church believes it has reached the pinnacle of influence and power, its political and social witness gets neutered.

A double church brings a double ethic. Because *Christian* changes meaning to include everyone, the church redefines discipleship on two levels. Not everyone is expected to obey the Sermon on the Mount, only the special and spiritual believers, monks and ascetics. Everyone else pretty

---

[11]Yoder, *Priestly Kingdom*, 136.
[12]Ibid.

much goes about business as usual.[13] In the world, Christians no longer operate by the example and teachings of Jesus but by an ethic of "vocation" that depends on a theory of natural law or "creation ordinances." There is a natural, created order to the family, for example. Being a father does not mean I bear the cross and imitate Jesus in my family. It means rather that I live by natural standards internal to the institution as created. This problem becomes especially acute, for Yoder, for Christians in politics. For someone of a Constantinian mindset, the state, with its violence and war, is a natural institution with its own rules of operation. When Christians assume office in that institution, they are "called" to function according to the demands of that calling. They punish others and fight wars, just like their pagan counterparts, and ignore Jesus' commands to do otherwise (Yoder thinks). A public-private dualism also results. What Christians would not, could not do in personal life (shoot an enemy) they can do if they have a public vocation in the natural institution of the state.

Along with this new ecclesiology come a new eschatology and a new view of providence. For Yoder, eschatology is central to the problem of Constantianism. Constantinianism is, he says in various places, an eschatological heresy. In the early church, eschatology focused on Christ's victory over the world, and especially over the powers and principalities that structure the world. In *The Politics of Jesus,* Yoder explains that the powers are good and necessary for human life, yet fallen. Because they are fallen, these structures (political and social institutions, traditions, mammon, power, etc.) are, or can be, demonic. God does overrule and orchestrate the powers so that they promote human flourishing. Tyranny is better than chaos, and tradition better than aimless innovation. But the powers are largely inimical to human existence. Jesus, however, has triumphed over the powers, and the very existence of the church is a declaration that the powers are not-gods whose authority is limited. In the church, and in the church only, is a people that refuses to bow the knee to the idols. The church's refusal to conform to fashion, to traditionalism, to violence is a continuous evangelical announcement: The gods are dethroned. By his triumph, Jesus liberates Christians. This liberation is not complete, but it has begun, and it is a sign of the inbreaking of the eschatological kingdom

---

[13]Ibid., pp. 137, 139.

and an announcement that the powers are doomed. The church's efforts are poured into resisting the seductions of the powers.[14]

Constantinianism changes this. Principalities and powers, though they are not subdued and do not acknowledge Jesus, "could not escape from His hidden control or from the promise of His ultimate victory." Jesus denied them free rein, using even their evil designs for his purposes. This hidden control suddenly became visible in Constantine: "after Constantine, one had to believe without seeing that there was a community of believers, within the larger nominally Christian mass, but one knew for a fact that God was in control of history." Why is this a problem? Mainly, Yoder says, because this paradigm identifies the providence of God, the purposes of God, with the good of the empire or, later, the nation. Mission is thus redefined: "beyond the limits of empire it had become identical with the expansion of Rome's sway." [15] The empire becomes identified with Christianity, but there is no deep conversion or change. Constantinianism misidentifies the locus of meaning in history, displacing it from the church to the empire or nation, and thus misreads history itself. Ethically, this leads to a universalizability principle. The church no longer asks, Is this what Jesus demands? but rather, because it has identified itself with power, Can you ask this behavior of everyone?

Constantinian Christianity succumbs to the original temptation of Satan, to seize godlikeness and try to wrest control of history from God. Because providence is now visible in the emperor, or the nation, or the class, directing that institution gives leverage for moving history in the direction we want it to go. Because Constantinian Christianity wants to direct history, it wants to know what works. In place of obedience to Jesus' counterintuitive commands, the church lives by the standard of efficiency: Will this action have the result I'm looking for? Will it give me control over the direction of history? Anti-Constantinian faith is, by contrast, a joyful "not being in charge," manifest in a politics of patience. Anti-Constantinian Christians obey Jesus, come what may.

More subtly and perhaps long-lastingly, Constantinianism brings a new metaphysics and a new epistemology. The metaphysics is dualistic. Augustinian Neoplatonism is the intellectual form, but the success of his meta-

---

[14]John Howard Yoder, *The Politics of Jesus* (Grand Rapids: Eerdmans, 1972), chap. 8.
[15]Yoder, *Priestly Kingdom*, pp. 136-37.

physics is its "usefulness" in legitimizing "the new social arrangement and resolve the problems it raised. The church we see is not the believing community; the visible/invisible duality names, and thereby justifies, the tension. The dominant ethic is different from the New Testament in content (Lordship is glorified rather than servanthood) as in source (reason and the 'orders of creation' are normative, rather than the particularity of Jesus' and the apostles' guidance)."[16]

The epistemological consequences go in the opposite direction. Constantinianism is the first form of a Western universalism that comes to secular expression in the Enlightenment. If you do not have to rule or convince everyone, you can root your epistemological and ethical claims on your own local, tribal traditions. Once Christians rule non-Christians, decisions have to be justified on a universal base that makes sense to unbelievers. The result is what Chris Huebner calls a "methodological Constantinianism" similar to what recent thinkers have dubbed "foundationalism." This is characterized by "appeals to the universal, natural law, common sense, a system, or a set of universally acknowledged axioms," and its goal is to "justify the social order as it exists."[17]

As noted above, *Constantinianism* does not refer to a particular church-state settlement. During the course of Western history, the relation of the church to the world has undergone several transformations. "Neo-Constantinianism" is the small-potatoes Constantinianism of identifying the meaning of history with the fortunes of an individual nation-state, or a class, or a future people, rather than with the fortunes of a universal empire. Disestablished churches can be as Constantinian as established ones, insofar as the church considers its duty to be supporting the "good

---

[16]Ibid., p. 141.

[17]Carter, *Politics of the Cross,* p. 172. Carter summarizes Yoder's eschatological critique of Constantinianism under eight points: (1) the emperor takes the place of Christ, and people submit to his demands regardless of Jesus' commands to the contrary; (2) instead of a dual already/not yet eschatology, Constantinianism says that the eschaton has arrived in the person of the ruler; (3) Constantinianism either denies that the powers are fallen or adjusts to the powers, cooperates and compromises with them, and calls it "realism"; (4) the kingdom is identified with the empire or nation, with a human institution or construction; (5) the church becomes part of culture and an aspect of society; (6) as a result, the church is no longer the sign of the kingdom to the world but instead conforms to the world; (7) the meaning of history is carried by the powerful and not by the weak, suffering church; and (8) the state becomes the bearer of God's purposes in history, instead of simply an institution providing order for the church to carry out its mission.

guys," that is, us Americans or us South Africans. With each new phase of Constantinianism, something is lost. Fourth-century Constantinianism welded the church onto an empire, and medieval Christians retained some sense that the church had an independent base of power and a catholic reach that went beyond Europe. After the Reformation, each new phase of Constantinianism has set its sights more narrowly and has progressively lost a sense of catholicity. In each manifestation the Constantinian church misconstrues the locus of meaning in history, shifting it from the church to some other institution.

Charles Mayo Collier has emphasized that Yoder's entire theological program is animated by a "Christological historicism."[18] Yoder's deepest complaint against Constantinianism is a christological one, the pretense that one can go beyond the unsurpassable Christ. There can be nothing new after Christ, because Christ brings in the end of the ages, the fullness of the times. We may ask, *which* Christ is unsurpassable? Or, better, at which stage of Christ's work does he become unsurpassable? For Yoder, the answer is that the crucified Christ, Christ in his suffering, defeat and weakness, is the unsurpassable Christ. If one says that Christ is now resurrected and vindicated, exalted to the throne at the Father's right hand, Yoder would reply that this exaltation is the exaltation of the *crucified* Lord; the Lamb, the *slain* Lamb, sits on the throne. Jesus never reverses his kenotic act, because kenosis is the very form of his lordship. At times Yoder claims that what is unsurpassable is not only Jesus himself but the "community he creates."[19] My question is the same, *which* community? Clearly, for Collier and Yoder, the community that is foundational is the community that remains in the way of Jesus, that renounces the sword and embraces the cross.[20]

---

[18]Charles Mayo Collier, "A Nonviolent Augustinianism? History and Politics in the Theologies of St. Augustine and John Howard Yoder" (Ph.D. diss., Duke University, 2008).

[19]Quoted in ibid., pp. 157-58.

[20]Though Collier tells me that "nothing could be further from the truth," both of those answers leave me suspicious that time has been forgotten. What Yoder identifies as Constantinianism is clearly a historical entity, shifting and changing; it is a protean heresy. But the "community that Jesus creates," the faithful community, is still in the apostolic age. Its contours never change; its minority status never changes; its relation to the world never changes, even though the world is clearly changing; the demands on it never change, no matter what cultural setting it finds itself in. Yoder seems to say this quite clearly toward the end of *The Politics of Jesus:* "What medieval Christendom . . . has in common with post-Enlightenment progressivism is precisely *the assumption that history has moved us past the time of primitive Christianity, and*

Yoder's critique is powerful because it offers a comparatively simple paradigm that proliferates new insights and seems to explain a great deal about the history of the church and the West. It is powerful too because it exposes the bonds between foundational theological grids (nature-grace, for instance), conceptions of church-state relations, theological method and the social location of the church. It is also powerful because so much of what Yoder attacks is so familiar, and so wrong. And it is powerful because it gives blunt names—heresy and apostasy—to habits of thought and Christian practice that can and have become instinctive.

Where he fails, however, is in showing that this heresy actually deserves the name *Constantinian,* and therefore that this heresy has characterized the mainstream church for the better part of its history. Yoder is trying to wed two things that do not go together: a capitulation of the church to the world on the one hand, and an Anabaptist narrative of the Constantinian "fall of the church" on the other.[21] I agree with a great deal of Yoder's critique of "Constantinianism"—I abhor nature-grace schemes, I repudiate any effort to get to some deeper foundation for Christian life and practice than Jesus and his Word (though I differ with Yoder about what that Word teaches us), I renounce epistemological dualism with all its pomp and show, and so on. But these renunciations do not compel me to believe that the "church" "fell" in the fourth, or the sixth, or the sixteenth, or the twentieth century.[22] I do not believe that this is true, and it

---

therefore out from under the relevance of the apostolic witness" about the meaning of history (quoted in ibid., p. 140, n. 160; emphasis added). Surely the apostolic witness is of highest relevance, but just as surely, "history has moved us past the time of primitive Christianity." Yoder appears to freeze time in the first century; the church of the apostolic and immediate postapostolic age—the church of which we can find virtually no historical record—is the unsurpassable church just as Jesus on the cross is the unsurpassable Jesus.

[21]Or, I should say, they go together only on Anabapist/pacifist grounds. From that angle, the church *must* fall as soon as it permits its members to bear arms without protest or sanction. If the pacifist position cannot be sustained, however, then the two elements of Yoder's thesis are separable. I address the pacifist issue, all too briefly, below. Yoder uses the language of "fall" in *Priestly Kingdom,* p. 209, n. 1; *The Jewish-Christian Schism Revisited,* ed. Michael G. Cartwright and Peter Ochs (Grand Rapids: Eerdmans, 2003), throughout; *Royal Priesthood,* p. 58; and many other places.

[22]Wedded together, the two cannot help but imply that the mainstream church has been "apostate" for nearly seventeen hundred years. In John Howard Yoder, *For the Nations: Essays Public and Evangelical* (Grand Rapids: Eerdmans, 1997), pp. 70-71, he claims that Western thinkers have been in the grip of "univocality" from Eusebius to Hegel. That is a long time to be in the grip of anything. Such sweeping historical claims should rouse nearly everyone's internal skeptic.

seems true only if one accepts Yoder's account of the early church, which I have argued is erroneous.

I want to break asunder what Yoder has put together. Of the two partners, I want to focus on the "fall of the church." Can we send that packing? Yes, and I believe Yoder has provided much of the evidence to justify the divorce.

THE CONSTANTINIANISM OF ANTI-CONSTANTINIANISM

Yoder assumes his inherited Anabaptist narrative of the fall of the church, and this shapes his treatment not only of the fourth century but of the whole of church history. But this narrative is, ironically, a "Constantinian" construct (using the term in Yoder's sense). That is true in two main senses.

First, methodologically: J. Alexander Sider has argued that Yoder's account of the patristic period relies on historical work that is "not very good" and badly outdated.[23] That is a flaw, but not an uncommon one. More seriously, Yoder makes no effort to penetrate the biases and politics that animate the historical work he uses. Again, not an uncommon flaw, but for Yoder it is a serious oversight, given his insistence that historical work is always done from a particular location for a particular purpose. He knows quite well that he is socially located, and he knows that his location is politically charged. Yet he naively accepts other historians' accounts as if they were not. Of course they are. Burckhardt's attack on Constantine is bound up with Protestant-Catholic polemics and opposition to the *Reichskirche* of Kaiser Wilhelm II.[24] Scholarship on Eusebius has been distorted by scholars who think they find echoes in Eusebius of the German church's endorsement of the Third Reich,[25] and Yoder's own training in postwar Europe moved him in similar directions.[26] Some of Constantine's and Eusebius's fiercest critics seem to have conflated Constantine with modern tyrannies and totalitarianisms.

---

[23]Sider, "To See History Doxologically," p. 136.

[24]Ibid., p. 145; Timothy D. Barnes, "Constantine, Athanasius and the Christian Church," in *Constantine: History, Historiography and Legend*, ed. Samuel Lieu and Dominic Montserrat (London: Routledge, 1998), p. 9.

[25]Michael J. Hollerich, "Religion and Politics in the Writings of Eusebius: Reassessing the First 'Court Theologian,'" *Church History* 59, no. 3 (1990): 3.

[26]Sider, "To See History Doxologically," p. 157.

In Yoder's work, "Constantinianism" functions not as a detailed historical hypothesis but in a "legendary" or mythical fashion, as a "narrative trope," or even in a "transcendental" way.[27] All historians work with types and tropes and fill historical figures and movements with conceptual significance that goes beyond anything the historical figures themselves could have known or done. I have offered my own story line for the period, and it does not include everything; certain events contextualize other events, and I have developed the threads of the story that I think are most revealing and representative. Plus, I have written the history of Constantine with polemical intention, in order to redress an imbalanced popular portrait of the first Christian emperor. I could have told the story of Constantine with the death of Crispus at the center, and the results would have been very different.

The problem is not types and tropes but the fact that Yoder's use of the "Constantinian" trope and the historical scholarship on which it is based are "monologic."[28] He knows that history is always full of mess and misjudgment, and that all historical work is full of difficulty and equivocation—is this source reliable? what is his or her agenda? who has been silenced? what has been left out? Yoder knows that there are always multiple voices. He is quite good in bringing out suppressed voices. But not with Constantinianism; Constantinianism changes and morphs, but in its basic outlines remains a monolith. Why so?

But his methodological problem is actually more serious: Yoder charges that any effort to mold history into smooth contours betrays a "Constantinian" effort at conceptual mastery, a heretical attempt to "seize godlikeness" by taking control of history and historical narrative, a Constantinian epistemology and method. That, however, is precisely what *he* has done. Further, he insists that history is done well only when the historian makes the imaginative effort to get into the "psychic skin" of his or her subjects in order to capture the openness of the choices before them. Historical actors

---

[27]"Legend" is Yoder's own term; he also uses "larger than life" to describe both the Constantinian and the Jeremian shift (Yoder, *For the Nations,* p. 8; quoted in Sider, "To See History Doxologically," p. 144). "Narrative trope" and "transcendental" are from Sider, "To See History Doxologically," pp. 165-67. By the latter term, he emphasizes that Constantinianism "prescribes the form of knowledge that would constitute and govern empirico-historical investigation" and thus sets the "criteria by which we know what counts as history" (p. 165).

[28]The term is Sider's, "To See History Doxologically," p. 153.

do not know ahead of time how it will all turn out, and we ought not project our knowledge of the outcome back on the actors. This again would be a Constantinian move, a "closure" imposed on a history that for the participants is still very open.[29] Yoder knows that the world is a complicated place, and he claims to honor the passage of time and the liquid configurations of social and political life. When it comes to the fourth century, though, he seems to forget everything he has warned us about. He does not attempt to get into the skin of the participants but keeps them very much at arm's length. He does not allow the story to remain open. Yoder's "Constantinianism" is plausible only because he follows what he condemns as a "Constantinian" methodology.

Again, why? I believe Yoder has worked with a "prior narrative" of the church's fall. He *starts* with a closed narrative, the one he inherited from sixteenth-century Anabaptists. Everything else remains open, everything else discussable; that narrative remains fixed and foundational.

Second, substantively: what deepens the irony is that the specific myth Yoder depends on is itself—in both the literal sense and in Yoder's sense—a Constantinian myth. Literally: it was *Eusebius* who first taught Christians to think that the past was pristine, and the Eusebian story line was part of the post-Constantinian effort to stave off mediocrity and compromise.[30] It was a way of saying, "Look how far we have fallen! Get back to the fathers!" I have raised questions throughout this book about the accuracy of Yoder's portrayal of the church between the apostles and the sec-

---

[29]Yoder, *Jewish-Christian Schism*, p. 44; for a thorough and illuminating discussion of these themes in Yoder, see Sider, "To See History Doxologically," chap. 3. As a heuristic device, imagining along with historical actors that "it could have been otherwise" is an essential tool of research, but as Arthur Danto says, historical narrative always involves reading earlier events in the light of later, episodes in the light of the denouement. In addition to the reasons below, I believe Yoder's basic use of "Constantinianism" is a significant violation of his claim that history should be treated as "open," since Constantine clearly did not intend Constantinianism as Yoder means it; further, Yoder reads much of subsequent church history as a series of variations on the Constantinian settlement and arguably reads back later concerns into the fourth century, again violating his principle of "open" history. See Peter J. Leithart, *Deep Exegesis: The Mystery of Reading Scripture* (Waco, Tex.: Baylor University Press, 2009), chap. 2, for detailed discussion of the hermeneutical import of this point.

[30]Robert L. Wilken, *The Myth of Christian Beginnings* (Notre Dame, Ind.: University of Notre Dame Press, 1970), chap. 3, points out that Eusebius focused on purity of doctrine rather than purity of practice or witness. That is a major difference from Yoder. See also R. A. Markus, *The End of Ancient Christianity* (Cambridge: Cambridge University Press, 1990), which speaks of the church's effort after Constantine to create identity boundaries.

ond century, and have argued that, at best, Yoder claims to know more about that period than any of the evidence allows, and, at worst, his portrayal is a misreading of what little evidence there is. I am left, like Nigel Wright, wondering whether the church Yoder wants has ever existed.[31] Actually, I do not wonder; I am convinced that it never did, at least in the first three centuries.[32] But the crucial point is more subtle. Yoder claims to be able to lead Christians out of the Egypt of Constantinian captivity, but he remains in that captivity himself. Yoder might well embrace this irony; he may recognize the irony that the conditions of possibility of his own opposition arise from the thing opposed. But for him to make his anti-Constantinian case, he *has* to be able to get outside those conditions. He has to be able to break the distorting lenses of Constantinianism and see the early church with the naked eye. He often writes as if he has done that, but in fact he is still looking through the same lenses—to repeat, the same *Eusebian* lenses—though perhaps he has turned them upside down.

In Yoder's sense, too, the myth of the fall of the church is a Constantinian myth. One of the crucial errors of Constantinianism, Yoder argues, is the misplacement of God's action in history. For Scripture, that action centers on the community of the church, but for the Constantinian it centers on rulers, wars, powerful figures, "real" powers to which the church must attach itself to get things done. Has Yoder done that when he identifies the crucial shift of all church history as a "Constantinian shift"? Yoder cleverly minimizes the role of Constantine as a man and emphasizes that the crucial shift was the church's own "apostasy." Yet he explains much of church history in reference to the great "epochal" change by using the name of the emperor. At least rhetorically, Yoder makes an odd move here, and one that raises questions about the coherence of his rhetoric with his

---

[31]Nigel Goring Wright, *Disavowing Constantine: Mission, Church and the Social Order in the Theologies of John Howard Yoder and Jürgen Moltmann*, Paternoster Theological Monographs (2000; reprint, Eugene, Ore.: Wipf and Stock, 2006), p. 61. Collier, "Nonviolent Augustinianism," pp. 71-72, makes the point that through the introduction of Constantinianism the tradition became divided, so that there is no easy appeal to tradition. A "Trojan horse" entered the church and unleashed wily Ulysses on an unsuspecting city. What is intriguing about Collier's point is that he claims that the Trojan horse entered the "tradition's consensus" concerning Jesus, violence and the powers. So there *was* an undivided tradition prior to Constantine! My point is that this is just as simplistic as later appeals to a post-Constantinian tradition.

[32]Perhaps one could find "Yoderian" local communities in the first three centuries. That would qualify, but not undermine, my point. Unless the church as a whole was Yoderian, the myth of a Constantinian fall will not work.

substance: Does his anti-Constantinian rhetoric undermine his protest against misidentifying the meaning of history? Who is putting too much weight on princes—Yoder, who wrote constantly about Constantine, or Augustine, who dispatches Constantine in a brief chapter in *City of God* so that he can rush ahead to relate the history of God's city?

To put the question the other way round: Why does Yoder not identify the heresy as "Eusebian"? That would be more accurate, though, as I have argued, not entirely fair to the maligned bishop of Caesarea. "Eusebian," though, is too specific; Eusebius's views were too obviously eccentric, too quickly corrected (by Augustine especially). Eusebius is too obscure. One cannot construct grand schemes of history on the foundation of Eusebius. Ultimately, I again suspect that Yoder employs the rhetoric he does because he is reading church history through the framework provided by Anabaptist protest since the sixteenth century.

In sum: Yoder's narrative of the church's fall comes under his own judgment as "Constantinian." We should abandon it, if for nothing else than for Yoderian reasons.

THE GOOD MIDDLE AGES

His narrative of the "fall of the church" fails for a second major reason, again one internal to Yoder's own work. Though at times Yoder seems to claim that, apart from a few pockets of radical faithfulness, the church has been in a state of "apostasy" since the fourth century,[33] he generously acknowledges in several places that the medieval synthesis was superior at least to later nationalist Protestantism. He warns that "the risk of caricature is great" when discussing the Middle Ages and observes that "significant elements of the otherness [of the church] in structure as in piety" remained during those centuries. The church's consciousness of being distinct from the world was "more than vestigial," manifested in "the higher level of morality asked of the clergy, the international character of the hierarchy, the visibility of the hierarchy in opposition to the princes, the gradual moral education of the barbarians into monogamy and legality, foreign missions, apocalypticism and mysticism," which "preserved an awareness, however distorted and polluted, of the strangeness of God's

---

[33]Yoder, *Priestly Kingdom*, p. 144.

people in a rebellious world."[34] The medieval church's "hierarchy had a power base and a self-definition" that, importantly, gave the church enough distance to criticize rulers, call them to repentance, demand justice and place limits like "the rules of chivalry, the Peace of God" on the lusts and ambitions of princes.[35] Over the centuries, the scope of the church's "chaplaincy" steadily reduced, and as a result the church's commitment to catholicity steadily evaporated.[36] Throughout the Middle Ages, however, the original conviction that the church is the center of history remained "half alive."[37] In the atrophied Constantinianism of American civil religion, by contrast, the nation is so closely identified with God's purposes that the church is reduced to being a cheerleader for the world's last superpower.

It is, again, *rhetorically* odd that Yoder insists on describing what he opposes as "Constantinian" when it comes to its most developed form after the Reformation. The oddity is especially startling in one passage where he moves from an observation about the "depth of the great reversal" that began in the second to fourth centuries to an assessment of the Renaissance and Reformation, thus leaving the whole of the Middle Ages hidden in the white space between two successive sentences. In part, he moves from the fourth to the sixteenth century because he is trying to show that the Constantinian consciousness remains in place "even as the situations which brought it forth no longer obtain."[38] But that does not smooth out the bump or fill in the abyss of a millennium. In this passage he gives *no* examples of the Constantinian consciousness during the time when the "situations which brought it forth" *did* obtain. That is, from this section of Yoder's writing we have specific evidence of "Constantinianism" only after the circumstances that created it have disappeared. His relative endorsement of the medieval period makes it clear that he thinks the church in the Middle Ages fought off the worst effects of Constantinianism. One would think, though, that if the Constantinian consciousness is correlated to a particular social and political situation, namely, one in which Christians are in power and try to control history, then the Middle Ages would display a significant degree of corruption. Can he account for the "good" Middle Ages?

---

[34]Yoder, *Royal Priesthood*, p. 58.
[35]Yoder, *Priestly Kingdom*, p. 144.
[36]Ibid., pp. 143-44.
[37]Yoder, *Royal Priesthood*, p. 60.
[38]Yoder, *Priestly Kingdom*, p. 141.

Yoder might say that Constantinianism was slowly seeping into European Christianity throughout the medieval period and finally burst out in its more virulent forms when the Catholic Church fractured. That solution runs up against a basic historical objection. Despite the efforts of the Reformers to purify the *corpus Christianorum*, Reformation "Constantinianism" was not a development of the medieval system but a destruction of it. Nationalist Protestantism begins to rise, further, in the period when Lorenzo Valla was exposing the Donation of Constantine as a fraud, when Anabaptists were attacking Constantine as the betrayer of Christ, when even some Lutherans found something to hate in Constantine. Overt anti-Constantinianism begins to rise at the same time that Yoder says Constantinianism is entering its new modern phase.

It is to his credit that Yoder acknowledges the achievements of the Middle Ages. Earlier Anabaptists rarely did but dismissed the whole period as corruption and apostasy. But Yoder has a problem: his thesis of the "fall of the church" cannot account for the period that immediately followed the shift itself. His historical paradigm breaks apart on the shoals of the medieval period.[39]

Yoder's assault on "Constantinianism" is not merely about the theological meaning of the first Christian empire. Since he insists on wedding his prophetic critique of compromise and confusion with an Anabaptist "fall of the church" narrative, however, it is *partly* about the theological meaning of Constantine and his age. Since his thesis fails both historically and, as measured against his own account, methodologically, an alternative account is needed. That account must accomplish several things. To pass muster as a historical thesis, it must at least take seriously the major (if not exactly epochal) shift that took place when Constantine converted, it must be able to explain how the good Middle Ages arose from the rubble of a Christian empire, and it must provide an accurate account of what Constantine actually did. For my purposes, it will be serendipitous if it also provides some modest defense of Constantine's role in Western history. Below, I can only give the barest schematic outline of this alternative.

---

[39]The tension is more pronounced in Stanley Hauerwas, who combines anti-Constantinianism, which depends on a fourth-century "fall," with antimodernity, which is typically allied with nostalgia for medieval premodernity.

Rome Baptized

When Yoder uses the word *baptism* in connection with Roman, Germanic or any other culture, he uses it derisively. The church "merely baptized" this or that cultural norm, institution, value.[40] How, on Yoder's terms, could a culture or nation ever be baptized in anything but a superficial, and hence hypocritical, sense? By contrast, I mean the word seriously, though metaphorically. Not everyone in Rome was baptized in 312 or 324; Constantine himself was not baptized until he was on his deathbed. By using *baptized* to describe what happened, I want to capture, first, the fact that *something* happened, some border was crossed; second, that this something made the Roman Empire "Christian" in some important respects; and, third, that this something was, like every baptism, only a beginning. It was, like every baptism, an infant baptism.

Let me begin where Yoder does, with eschatology. According to Galatians 4, when the Father sent his Son and Spirit into the world, they came to deliver the Jews ("we," v. 3) from childhood, which Paul characterizes as a state of slavery under the "elementary things of the world" (*stoicheia tou kosmou*). Identifying those "elementary principles" is difficult. Within the context of Galatians 4, bondage to the *stoicheia* is tied somehow to slavery to the "not-gods" (Galatians 4:8), and this and other considerations have led some to conclude that the *stoicheia* are identical with the powers and principalities that Paul elsewhere says governed human beings in their minority.[41] That may be; Israel too was governed by angels (cf. Galatians 3:19). But the similarity of Galatians 4:3 to Galatians 3:23 is more suggestive.[42] Bondage under the *stoicheia* correlates to being under the custody of the schoolmaster Torah, and this linkage in Galatians seems to fit another New Testament use of *stoicheia*, Hebrews 6:1-2. Bondage under the *stoicheia*, I submit, refers to the life of Israel under the dietary, sacrificial and purity regulations imposed by Torah. That is the bondage from which Jews are delivered in the great exodus led by the Son and the Spirit-pillar; that is the highly regulated childhood that Israel outgrew in the fullness of time.

---

[40]For a small sampling, see Yoder, *Royal Priesthood*, pp. 56, 57, 58, 246.

[41]On powers and principalities, see G. B. Caird, *Principalities and Powers: A Study in Pauline Theology* (1956; reprint, Eugene, Ore.: Wipf and Stock, 2003); Yoder, *Politics of Jesus*; Hendrik Berkhof, *Christ and the Powers*, trans. John H. Yoder (Scottdale, Penn.: Herald, 1977).

[42]More so because, as I think, these sections of Paul's letter correlate in a chiastic structure that covers chapters 3-4.

Paul is not talking only about Jews, however. "We" were in bondage until the One who came born under the Torah; but "you" (vv. 6, 8) who did not know God have also been liberated by receiving the Son and Spirit. Paul radically flattens out the difference between Jew and Gentile. Unlike in Romans, here he does not say that all are under "sin" but rather that all are in bondage to the *stoicheia*. For Gentiles as much as Jews, this bondage meant adherence to animal sacrifice, the keeping of days, the avoidance of contamination.[43]

Yoder insists, rightly, that the victory over the powers was won on A.D. 29/30, not in 312.[44] Incarnation and Pentecost are Paul's coordinates in Galatians 4. Yet though Jesus defeated the powers on the cross and liberated "us" and "you" from the *stoicheia* through the Spirit, *something* happens when that victory is proclaimed and accepted by people who are still in their childhood. Church history is not an empty parenthesis between the cross and the eschaton. The proclamation of repentance to all nations is part of the promised fulfillment, part of the evangel itself (Luke 24). Jesus won on the cross and in the resurrection, but the reality of that victory breaks through when the Spirit comes in the preaching of the gospel and the response of faith (e.g., Acts 2 and 10–11). The victory over the powers and the liberation from the *stoicheia* happened once for all in the first century, but Constantine learned of it in the fourth. For him as an individual, liberation from the *stoicheia* did not happen until three centuries after the cross. That was when the news of Jesus' triumph came to him, and when it came to him, he was swept up in it.

What happens when one is liberated from bondage to the *stoicheia?* If I am right about the *stoicheia* themselves, freedom from their bondage would mean liberation from structures organized by distinctions of holy-profane and clean-unclean, from worries about unclean foods, from distinctions between impure Gentiles and pure Jews, from the fear of contagion. Above

---

[43]On impurity in Greek religion, see Robert Parker, *Miasma: Pollution and Purification in Early Greek Religion* (Oxford: Clarendon, 1996); on sacrifice in the Greek world, see Maria-Zoe Petroupoulou, *Animal Sacrifice in Ancient Greek Religion, Judaism and Christianity, 100 BC to AD 200* (Oxford: Oxford University Press, 2008) and Marcel Detienne and Jean-Pierre Vernant, *The Cuisine of Sacrifice Among the Greeks* (Chicago: University of Chicago Press, 1998); on Roman sacrifice see George Heyman, *The Power of Sacrifice: Roman and Christian Discourses in Conflict* (Washington, D.C.: Catholic University of America Press, 2007), and John Scheid, *Quand faire, c'est croire: Les rites sacrificiels des Romains* (Aubier, 2005).
[44]Yoder, *Royal Priesthood*, p. 64.

all, liberation from the *stoicheia* will be evident in the end of sacrifice. The great sign of Constantine's personal deliverance from *stoicheia* was his abandonment of childish things, that is, his renunciation of sacrifice.

City of Sacrifice

According to R. A. Markus[45] and others, Augustine offered an "eschatological" defense of the secular, and especially of secular politics. By insisting that the perfected city is the city of the future and that the perfect peace is the peace of the kingdom, Augustine relativized the proximate peace and justice of the earthly city. Earthly republics were no longer of ultimate concern and could no longer demand ultimate sacrifice. That may have something to it as a theoretical model, and I will return to Augustine in a moment. But I am more interested in how that Augustinian insight works out in the cultural and political world that Constantine bequeathed to the West.

What Constantine established was surely *not* secular polity, if *secular* is used in the modern sense of an autonomous sphere of social life, impervious to God's action, free from religious guidance, vigorously protected from divine interventions of any and all sorts. His policies did not secularize Rome in that sense. He adopted religious policies, favored the church and gave the church a significant role in the "secular" life of the empire. Bishops dispensed justice, mediated disputes, built hospitals and hostels, fed the hungry. On modern (at least modern American) grounds, Constantine regularly disdained the boundary between sacred and secular.

When he died, Constantine did not leave behind a "secular" Roman political order, but he did leave behind something other than he inherited. He left behind a political order that had been "desacrificed." The end of sacrifice announced by the gospel was effected in the actual history of Rome, during the reign of Constantine Augustus. Just as that was the moment of his personal liberation from the *stoicheia*, so it was the deliverance of Rome from its childhood.

This is the "baptism" that I refer to, a moment in history, or a period of history, when a people, nation or empire receives the gospel of the victory of Jesus and is blown by the Spirit from the world of sacrifice, purity,

---

[45]R.A. Markus, *Saeculum: History and Society in the Theology of Augustine* (Cambridge: Cambridge University Press, 1970).

temples, and sacred space and is transferred into a new religio-socio-political world. It is a baptism out of the world of the *stoicheia*, which, at least for Gentiles, involved the worship of "not-gods," into a world without sacrifice, a world after the end of sacrifice.[46] Before the fourth century, the world had already seen such a baptism: "it was the destruction of the Temple of Jerusalem . . . that activated the slow—overly slow—transformation of religion to which we owe, among other things, European culture." With the fall of the temple, the Jews "offered the example of a society that had succeeded in conserving its ethnic and religious identity, even after the destruction of the only temple where daily sacrifices could be offered." Such a "sudden disappearance of sacrifices in a community represents a deep transformation of the very structures of its religious life."[47] The waves from that baptism in Jerusalem eventually reached the Roman Empire. After the fourth century, many other civilizations were baptized in the same way, until by the high Middle Ages the European continent was baptized to the four points of the compass. Baptisms have continued since and will continue until the nations are made disciples. That, after all, is Jesus' commission to his church (Matthew 28:18-20).

Constantine began to eliminate sacrifice from Roman life, and this was no mean achievement. Roman sacrifice was at the center of Roman civilization. It was the chief religious act by which Romans communicated and communed with the gods, keeping the gods happy so Romans could be happy. Sacrifice disclosed the secrets of the future, as the *haruspex* read the entrails of a slaughtered animal. Sacrifice was essential to Roman politics. Senatorial decisions were sealed with sacrifice, and so too imperial decrees. Soldiers sacrificed to the gods to win their favor before they went to

---

[46]The phrase "end of sacrifice" comes from the brilliantly suggestive Guy G. Stroumsa, *The End of Sacrifice: Religious Transformations in Late Antiquity*, trans. Susan Emanuel (Chicago: University of Chicago Press, 2009). Among other things, Stroumsa gives Judaism a central role in the "religious transformation of late antiquity" that the book traces, specifically arguing that the fall of the temple made Judaism the first nonsacrificial religion in history. As Christians inherited that nonsacrificial Judaism, they transformed the meaning of religion. Origen and Celsus were speaking past one another; they were not merely talking about two religions, two species within a genus, but two genera. I have two reservations about Stroumsa: first, his claim that Christians were innovative in tying religion to truth may be overstated (see Clifford Ando, *The Matter of the Gods: Religion and the Roman Empire* [Berkeley: University of California Press, 2008]); second, he minimizes the continuing role of ritual, and specifically sacrifice, in the Christian church.

[47]Stroumsa, *End of Sacrifice*, pp. 62-63.

slaughtering enemies in battle in order to restore the offended honor of the Roman *imperium*. It was not only good politics; it was also cathartic. Roman citizens, at least during times of persecution, were required to manifest their submission and devotion to gods, to the emperor and to Rome by acts of sacrifice. By sacrificing for or to the emperor, they acknowledged him as Lord, Savior, Deliverer, even, at times, as God. Christians refused because they knew there was another King, another world Emperor, who filled that role, and Romans tried to suppress this Christian rebellion by sacrificing Christians. Sacrifice was essential to Roman society, as *humiliores* were devoted to the comfort of *honestiores*. Sacrificial slaughter in the arena was one of the empire's chief entertainments.[48]

Through Constantine, Rome was baptized, and sacrifice in all these senses either came to an end or began to. Constantine stopped the slaughter of Christians. He refused to sacrifice at the Capitol during his triumph in 312. He ended sacrifice for officers of his empire, thus opening imperial administration to Christians, and eventually outlawed sacrifice entirely. He closed a few temples where sacrifices were being offered, though he permitted various forms of divination to continue. He stopped the gladiatorial combats and gave legal support to *humiliores* who wanted access to the judicial system so that they would not be chewed up by the system. Torture continued, and despite Constantine's decree, sacrifice persisted throughout the empire. Constantine himself fought imperial wars, but his savagery was not celebrated as the honor-wars of previous emperors had been. With Constantine, the Roman Empire became officially a desacrificial polity. If he did not entirely expunge sacrifice, Constantine displaced sacrifice from the center of Roman life, pushed it to the margins and into dark corners. Constantine's reign marked the beginning of the end of sacrifice. He took away the smoky food of the not-gods (Galatians 4:8), and the demons began to atrophy.

To this extent, Constantine's polity has remained in place until the present. A desacrificed civilization has become so commonplace that we think it is the natural order of things. We are horrified when we hear that some bizarre Wiccan cult has performed a sacrifice in a wood nearby; we sense that this portends ghoulish assaults on our ordered world. If a session

---

[48]See Heyman, *Power of Sacrifice*; Scheid, *Quand faire*.

of the Senate or Supreme Court opened with sacrifice, talk radio would be abuzz for months and we might have marches in the streets. Historically speaking, though, *we* are the aberrations. For millennia every empire, every city, every nation and tribe was organized around sacrifice. Every polity has been a sacrificial polity. We are not, and we have Constantine to thank for that.

THERE WILL BE BLOOD

That is only one side of the story, however; because *there will be blood.* Every ancient city was a sacrificial center, ever since Cain slaughtered his brother before setting up the walls of Enoch, the city named for his son. Rome, in mythology if not in fact, was built over the blood of Remus, the blood of Dido and Turnus, the blood of the many thousands trampled beneath the lusty domination of Rome. Negatively, Constantine created and left a desacrificed city. Positively, he recognized and welcomed the church into his realm, to the center of the Roman Empire. There was blood there too, but it was the blood of Jesus that announced the end of bloodshed. The church too was a sacrificial city, the true city of sacrifice, the city of final sacrifice, which in its Eucharistic liturgy of sacrifice announced the end of animal sacrifice and the initiation of a new sacrificial order.

Even before we reflect on this theologically, we should make some effort to grasp the earth-quaking significance of Constantine's decision. Every city is sacrificial, but Constantine eliminated sacrifice in his own city and welcomed a *different* sacrificial city into Rome. For a fourth-century Roman, eliminating sacrifice from the city was as much as to say, "My city is no longer a city." For a fourth-century Roman, acknowledging the church's bloodless sacrifice as *the* sacrifice was as much as to say, "The *church* is the true city here." When Constantine began to end sacrifice, he began to end Rome as he knew it, for he initiated the end of Rome's sacrificial lifeblood and established that Rome's life now depended on its adherence to another civic center, the church.

For Augustine, the Eucharist not only announces the end of sacrifice but also ritually embodies a sacrificial movement that encompasses the entire life of the church. The church is a priesthood not only at the table on the Lord's Day but in its life together. Sacrifice, Augustine said, is any work by which we seek to adhere to God in holy society with him.[49] What God above all desires is mercy, and so the highest sacrifice is the work of compassion done in order to adhere to God. When a group lives out this sacrifice, it is not only continuously joined to the society of the transcendently sociable triune God but also united together in that union with God. The whole city becomes a *universale sacrificium* through Christ, the priest who offers himself, and offers us in him:

> Since, therefore, true sacrifices are works of mercy to ourselves or others, done with a reference to God, and since works of mercy have no other object than the relief of distress or the conferring of happiness, and since there is no happiness apart from that good of which it is said, It is good for me to be very near to God, it follows that the whole redeemed city, that is to say, the congregation or community of the saints, is offered to God as our sacrifice through the great High Priest, who offered Himself to God in His passion for us, that we might be members of this glorious head, according to the form of a servant.[50]

Christ's is the founding sacrifice of the new city, the eschatological city. But that sacrifice is perpetuated by the body in mutual love and service. *Hoc est sacrificium Christianorum: multi unum corpus in Christo*—this is the sacrifice of Christians, we who are many are one body in Christ.[51]

By virtue of this sacrifice, the church does justice.[52] The just city, Augustine famously argued, is the city that does justice to all, above all to God. Only the city that renders God his due, which is the true sacrifice of the one body united in peace and love, only *that* city is truly just. When the Roman world passed through its "baptism" from bondage to the *stoicheia*, Constantine eliminated sacrifices to the gods in the earthly city and thereby renounced any claim that the Roman city was a just city. A city without justice, Augustine insisted, is no city at all, so by eliminating sacrifice Constantine was admitting that Rome had become decivilized.

---

[49]Augustine *City of God* 10.4-6. "Proinde verum sacrificium est omne opus, quo agitur, ut sancta societate inhaereamus Deo, relatum scilicet ad illum finem boni, quo veraciter beati esse possimus."

[50]Ibid., 10.6.

[51]Ibid.

[52]See Robert Dodaro, *Christ and the Just Society in the Thought of Augustine* (Cambridge: Cambridge University Press, 2004).

At the same time, Constantine welcomed into his city another city, a truly just city, a city of the final sacrifice that ends sacrifice. He may have believed he was erecting a new civic cult, a new and more effective priestly college, a patriotic religious institution that would secure the *pax Dei* for Rome as the earlier cults guaranteed the *pax deorum*. If that is what he expected, he was wrong, because the church is not a cult but a polis. And despite its very real peccability and fallibility, it is *Christ's* city, his body, and therefore a city that cannot finally be co-opted. This or that communion of the church may become a synagogue of Satan; the Spirit may leave a church with a screech of *Ichabod*. But if the Spirit leaves one house desolate, he finds another.

The church did not "fall" in the fourth century. It is more resilient than that. The church, instead, was recognized and honored, precisely as the true city. By eliminating the civic sacrifice that founded Rome and protecting and promoting the Eucharistic *civitas*, Constantine was, in effect if not in intent, acknowledging the church's superiority as a community of justice and peace. He was acknowledging, whether he recognized it fully or not, that the church was the model that he and all other emperors should strive to imitate.

This is the "Christianization" achieved by Constantine, Rome baptized. This was the eschatological establishment, not of secular civilization, but of the desacrificial civilization.

Model City

Once the ecclesial city is welcomed, acknowledged, honored by the earthly city, it is time for it to get to work. That is the story of the medieval world, as Christian civilization grew from the seed of Constantine's desacrificialization (and consequent decivilization) of Rome and his acknowledgment of the church and its King. As the medieval Christians saw it, the ecclesial city is called to serve, advise, judge, lead, set an example for the earthly city, so that the earthly city can begin to bear some resemblance, in a proximate desacrificial fashion, to the just city. Constantine welcomed the church, and he and his successors had to accept the consequence: they would be taught the politics of Jesus. Rome was baptized out from under the *stoicheia* into a world beyond sacrifice, and after baptizing the church begins to "teach all that Jesus has commanded" (Matthew 28:18-20).

As noted above, unlike earlier modern forms of anti-Constantinianism, Yoder's critique is not premised on a dichotomy of power and religion, or politics and religion. Yoder says the opposite. The dualism he prefers is church-world, rather than church-state or religion-politics,[53] and that is because the church is a polity, the only true polity, because it is the only polity that does justice in worshiping God. Precisely *because* it is already political, it is a betrayal for the church to attach itself to and find its identity in an existing worldly power structure. Precisely *because* the church is always a political power in itself, it does not need to find the stockpile of worldly weapons before it carries out its mission. On all this Yoder is correct.

He is also correct in refusing the nature-grace dichotomy[54] on which so much traditional political theology has been based. That has often been the undergirding structure for just war responses to pacifism: coercion has no place in the church because the church is an institution of grace, but the state, being a *natural* institution, operates with other weapons. Nature-grace can find expression in a moral man–immoral society dualism: "do good to those who abuse you" and "give to those who ask" are principles of personal, not political, ethics, but in public life there are no constraints on how much we may terrorize terrorists to keep them far from our borders. Or it can take the form of a sacred-secular dichotomy, in which the secular is considered a sphere impervious to, and resolutely protected against, intrusions of sacred or spiritual life.

Yoder rejects all of these options and insists instead that Jesus taught a social ethic. The church is a polity, and thus any ethical or political system that minimizes or marginalizes Jesus and his teaching hardly counts as Christian.[55] Here again I think Yoder is correct. If there is going to be a Christian politics, it is going to have to be an evangelical Christian politics, one that places Jesus, his cross and his resurrection at the center. It will not do to dismiss the Sermon on the Mount with a wave of the hand ("that's for personal life, not political life"). If a Christian political theol-

---

[53]Thanks to Charlie Collier for highlighting the point.

[54]To my knowledge, he never states the issue in precisely these terms.

[55]This is not to say that Jesus' teachings should be isolated from the rest of Scripture. I believe that Scripture as a whole is the standard for Christian ethics and politics. But Jesus' example and teaching occupy the center of that ethics. He comes to "fulfill," not destroy, the Law and Prophets, to bring the law to its fullest expression. To follow Jesus is to do what the Law always aimed at.

ogy cannot justify war, coercive punishment and judgment evangelically, it cannot justify them convincingly.

It may seem, then, that Yoder has finally won the day. Perhaps he lost the historical argument but wins the theological one. If Jesus and the Sermon on the Mount are central to Christian political theology, does that not mean Yoder is correct that the only Christian politics is the politics of the church? Does that not mean that Christian politics must be nonviolent, noncoercive, nonresistant, pacifist? Does that mean that Constantine did in fact betray Jesus when he welcomed the church and set down his sacrificial knife but refused to sheath his sword?

The answer to those questions, I believe, is no. What I can say in this brief space is inadequate, but I must say something.

TEACHING HANDS TO FIGHT

I do not find Yoder's claims that Jesus was a pacifist convincing, but I do agree with his insistence that questions about war and peace be answered not by blinkered examination of specific texts but by attention to the full sweep of biblical history. What is the Bible about?

That question can be answered in a variety of ways, but one important answer to the question is this: the Bible is from beginning to end a story of war.[56] Yahweh, the Creator and the God of Israel, is a "man of war" (Exodus 15:3), who threatens to make war against Amalek until that notoriously vicious nation is destroyed (Exodus 17:16). He sends Joshua into Canaan to conquer the land, and his Angel, the second person of the Trinity, is the captain of a host who leads Israel in conquest (Joshua 5:13-15). Yahweh has his own armor (Isaiah 59), in which he arms himself for battle.

From the beginning, this Creator made men to participate in and prosecute his wars. His goal in history is to train hands to fight. Adam was formed and placed in Eden's garden with instructions to perform a priestly service that was also quasi-military. He was to "dress and guard" the garden (Genesis 2:15). He was to keep intruders from the garden of God and, eventually, from his bride, Eve. When the serpent tempted Eve, Adam had his first opportunity to carry out his duty as garden watchman. He was "with her" (Genesis 3:8), but instead of crushing the head of the ser-

---

[56]I am picking up one threat from James Jordan's triple summary of the story arcs of biblical narrative: Scripture is about maturation, about redemptive history and about holy war.

pent, he stood watching and doing nothing. Adam's fall was a renunciation of war, a capitulation to the enemy, a failure to defend his bride and to
take up the war of Yahweh.

Eye for eye, tooth for tooth: so goes the pattern of biblical justice. Adam
refused to carry out his role as guardian of the garden, and so he was dismissed from his post. He did not want to guard, so he got what he wanted.
This pattern is also evident in the symbolism of the tree of knowledge. In
Scripture, "knowledge of good and evil" refers to the judicial discernment
and authority of a king (see 1 Kings 3:9). Adam was formed as a king-in-
training, and combat with the serpent was his first test. Had he passed the
test, he would presumably have been given the fruit of the tree of knowledge and ascended to share in the rule of his heavenly Father, the human
king beside the High King. Eye for eye again: because Adam refused to act
as a king, he was cut off from the royal tree. In place of Adam, Yahweh set
cherubim at the gate of the garden, armed with flaming swords (Genesis
3:24). Yahweh removed the sword, as it were, from Adam's hand and gave
it to angels.

That was never intended as a permanent arrangement. When he confronted Adam and Eve in the garden, Yahweh promised that he would
send another human, a "last man" to overcome the sin of the first man,
who would do what Adam refused to do, "crush the serpent's head" while
suffering a bruise upon his heel (Genesis 3:15). This is famed as the first
messianic prophecy of Scripture, but its content is too often ignored: it is a
promise of a warrior-savior, a conqueror. That is nearly the last vision of
Jesus we see in Scripture as well, the rider on a white horse who "judges
and wages war" in righteousness, who is armed with a "sharp sword" that
comes from his mouth, who "smites the nations" and rules them with a rod
of iron, whose eyes are flames of fire (Revelation 19:11-18).

The first covenant, the covenant with angels, was a childhood covenant.
Swords are sharp, and fire burns, and so long as human beings were in
their minority, the Lord restricted access to dangerous implements.[57] Yet
even in childhood, some men, and some women, were given authority by
the Lord to wield the sword and to play with fire. Priests were vested with
armor (Exodus 28), given swords and fire to slaughter animals to offer to

---

[57]I owe this to my colleague Toby Sumpter. Please note: this is a charming way to put it, but it is
   not merely charming. It is a profound theological point.

God. They were new Adams in the new garden of the temple. Outside the temple in the land, Yahweh chose men and women to carry out coercive, deadly acts of justice—Moses, Phinehas, Joshua, Jael, Samson, David and so on. Yoder thinks he can close debate when he says that the God of Israel was incarnate in the form of Abraham and not of Constantine.[58] That does not close the debate at all: Abraham too bore a sword, at the head of a small army of 318 fighting men (Genesis 14).[59] The issue also looks very different if we substitute David for Constantine in Yoder's formula; do we really want to polarize Jesus and the king whose dynasty he revives and perpetuates?

With the coming of the conquering Seed of the Woman, the sword and fire of angels are given back to a man, to Jesus. In union with her husband and head, the church is a warrior bride, called to carry out his wars in and with him. Yahweh's armor is distributed to us (compare Isaiah 59 and Ephesians 6). We are priests and kings by his blood, anointed for priestly and royal service by baptism, baptized into armor, baptized for battle. In fact, we receive weapons even more powerful than the weapons of a Samson or a David. We have the Spirit of the risen and exalted Jesus, the Last Adam who has eaten from the tree of knowledge, and our weapons are not fleshly but Spiritual, powerful for demolishing fortresses and destroying speculations raised up against the knowledge of God (2 Corinthians 10:3-6). Our armor is righteousness, truth, faith, salvation, the Word of God and the gospel of peace.

To this point, if they can get past the militant rhetoric I have adopted (which is simply the biblical rhetoric), pacifists might well agree with much of what I have said. After all, I have sketched a history that involves a transition from the iron sword and fire that Joshua used to slaughter Canaanites and burn Jericho to the sword and fire of the Spirit and the Word that Jesus uses to overwhelm his enemies and, as often as not, to remake them into allies. For several reasons, however, mine is not a pacifist narrative. First, unless one follows an almost Marcionite contrast of Old and New, the Old Testament remains normative for Christians. Though it is

---

[58]John Howard Yoder, *The Original Revolution: Essays on Christian Pacifism* (1971; reprint, Scottdale, Penn.: Herald, 2003), p. 119.

[59]One of my favorite paintings in the Hermitage is a ceiling fresco of armored Abraham, taking off his helmet to receive bread and wine from Melchizedek. Abraham the warrior was at the table.

normative in a new covenant context, it is impossible to escape the fact that Yahweh carried out his wars through an Israel armed with swords, spears and smooth stones. That is part of our story, preserved "for our instruction." Second, the New Testament does not endorse anything like a Marcionite view of Old Testament wars. To the writer of Hebrews, Old Testament heroes were models of faith not only in their endurance of persecution but also in being "mighty in war" and putting "armies to flight" (Hebrews 11:34). Nor were the earliest Christians pacifists. Stephen—Christlike, full of the Spirit, the first martyr—thought that Moses' killing the Egyptian was an act of just vengeance to protect the oppressed, the beginning of the liberation of Israel from captivity (Acts 7:23-24), and the Jews did not stone him for saying *that*.[60]

Third, Yoder makes the important point that even in the Old Testament Israel relied on Yahweh to fight for it. That is true, but the story I have sketched is one of increasing responsibility on the part of human beings. When we were children, Yahweh our Father intervened to save us from bullies. Now that we have reached maturity in Jesus, we share more fully in those wars. This is precisely why we are allowed to use spiritual weapons: through his death and resurrection, Jesus has made us capable of putting these most powerful of weapons to right uses. The point is that the story of Scripture is not a story of increasing passivity but of increasing participation in the activity of the ever-active God. We are being raised as kings to fight alongside our elder Brother in service to our Father. Finally, we might make an argument from greater to lesser: if the Lord lets Christians wield the most powerful of spiritual weapons, does he not expect us to be able to handle lesser weapons? If he has handed us a broadsword, does he not assume we know how to use a penknife?

I am painting with a broad brush, and it seems I have left a blank at the center of the panorama: What of Jesus? Does he not teach us to turn the other cheek? Does he not tell Peter to put his sword back in his sheath?

---

[60]This is distinct from the question whether a purely noncoercive ethic is possible or desirable. If I intercept a child who is about to step in front of oncoming traffic, I exercise coercion, but the coercion is, on almost any account, an act of love, not of violence. The vagueness of "violence" is a significant problem here. Milbank argues that evil is violence, violence evil, but insists, rightly in my view, that not all coercive action is violence. I command my children to clean up and I spank them if they defy me. That, I believe, is a coercive right that I as a parent can exercise over my children. It is not an act of violence or child abuse.

Does he not go to the cross, like a lamb to slaughter, and just in this way win his great victory? Are we not supposed to follow him? Doesn't any attempt to "contexualize" Jesus, even if the context is the rest of the Bible, amount to displacing him from the center of our politics? If we are to embody the politics of Jesus, does that not mean renunciation of the sword and embrace of the cross?

This is surely the most powerful pacifist line of argument. One might answer by questioning the specific applicability of certain texts. Is "turn the other cheek" a rebuke of self-defense or the defense of others? Is Jesus' instruction to Peter the law for all Christians in all places and times? Is there something unique about Jesus' death that demands his unresisting passivity? More globally, are pacifists not short-circuiting, and relieving too quickly, the apparent tensions on the surface of the text?

Though I believe those questions are legitimate and detailed exegesis is essential, that kind of questioning can seem like another avenue to avoid the hard teachings of Jesus. Augustine's handling of these questions encourages us in the right direction. He does not silence the teaching of Jesus by burying it under Old Testament narratives of battle, but neither does he detach Jesus and his teaching from their canonical setting. Instead, he attempts to take the whole of Scripture into account and to infuse everything with the light that comes uniquely through the Word made flesh. Augustine, as we have seen, was skeptical about the capacity of civil rulers to achieve justice and conscious of the limits of war. Yet he understood that war was at times the only or the best way to achieve the Christian aim of peace. "One does not pursue peace in order to wage war; he wages war to achieve peace," and even in the conduct of war, the warrior and commander aim to defeat enemies so that "you can bring them the benefits of peace."[61]

All That Jesus Commands

If we reject pacifism, do we still have a politics of Jesus? We do. Yoder rightly stresses that Jesus embodied a politics and is, in his teaching and

---

[61]Augustine, Letter 189, quoted in Louis J. Swift, *The Early Fathers on War and Military Service*, Message of the Fathers of the Church 19 (Wilmington, Del.: Michael Glazier, 1983), pp. 114-15.

example, the ground for Christian social ethics.[62] Strangely, he also says that post-Constantinian Christians had to reach for Cicero to come up with an ethic for officials and rulers, since Jesus offered little guidance on the subject (not expecting his followers ever to be in charge). Yoder's pacifism blinds him and keeps him from seeing that the whole of Jesus' teaching and activity is abundantly instructive to rulers. Welcomed into the city of man, the Eucharistic city models and teaches rulers to rule like Jesus.

- "Turn the other cheek" gives instruction not about self-defense but about honor and shame. To slap someone on the right cheek, you have to slap back-handed, and a back-handed slap expresses contempt, not threat.[63] Is this relevant to political ethics? Of course. The Roman Empire was built on a system of honor, insult and retaliation. Before Rome, Thucydides knew that wars arose from "fear, honor, and interest." Remove retaliation and defense of honor from international politics, and a fair number of the world's wars would have been prevented. There would have been a lot of slapping but not nearly so much shooting.

- The Eucharistic city would teach rulers to agree with their adversaries quickly, to defuse domestic and international disputes before they explode.

- What if rulers were instructed not to look at a woman lustfully? That would also prevent some wars, keep presidents busy with papers and things at their desks, protect state secrets, save money and divisive scandals. The church would insist that rulers be faithful to their wives and not put them away for expediency or a page girl (or boy).

- The church would insist on honesty and truth telling, urging rulers to speak the truth even when it is painful.

- The church would insist that a ruler not do alms or pray or fast or do any other good things to be seen by others, especially by others with cameras—a rule that would revolutionize modern politics.

---

[62]Yoder, *Politics of Jesus*.
[63]David E. Garland, *Reading Matthew: A Literary and Theological Commentary on the First Gospel* (Macon, Ga.: Smyth and Helwys, 1999).

- Rulers would be instructed to love enemies and do good to all. Obama would be seeking the best for the Republican Party, Ms. Anonymous Republican would be doing her best to serve the president. A ruler would have to stand firm against the antics of tyrants, not out of hatred but out of love, to prevent the tyrant from doing great evil to himself and others. If the tyrant attacked, the ruler would have to defend his people out of love for them *and* out of love for his enemy.[64] Punishments would be acts of love for the victims, the public and the punished, just as a father disciplines his son in love. The church would insist that the ruler not use his legitimate powers of force for unjust ends, on pain of excommunication.

- The church would urge rulers not to lose sleep over budget shortfalls or stock market declines, and exhort them instead to store up treasure in heaven by acts of mercy and justice.

- The church would urge rulers to beware their own blind spots and re-move logs from their eyes so they can see rightly in order to judge.

- The church would remind a ruler that she will face a Judge who will inquire what she had done for the homeless, the weak, the sick, the imprisoned, the hungry.

- At the extreme, a ruler might place himself on a cross, sacrifice his political future and his reputation, for the sake of righteousness. In cer-tain kinds of polities, he would be the first soldier, the first to fly against the enemy, because being the leader means you get to die first.[65] In great extremity, he might follow Jeremiah's example and submit to con-quest, defeat, deportation—endure a national crucifixion to preserve a people for future rebirth.

The church would have these, and many more things, to teach the rul-ers in their desacrificial political order. The ruler would get an earful of the politics of Jesus.

---

[64]This does *not* revert to a Kantian intentionalist ethic. Intentions so inhere in actions that a different intention changes the action itself. I spank my child out of love, and that can be a legitimate exercise of coercive force; a molester might perform exactly the same bodily move-ment in order to excite his perverted sexual tastes. The distinction between these is not that the "same" act is done with different intentions; different acts are being done, which is why we have two different words—*discipline* and *abuse*.

[65]Thanks to my colleague Toby Sumpter for this memorable phrase.

THERE WILL BE BLOOD, AGAIN

The alternative story I have been telling has gotten us from the gospel, through Constantine, into the Middle Ages. It can provide a practical Christian politics that is recognizably a politics of Jesus. Can it get us to modernity? What happens to sacrifice and the city in the modern age?

Modern politics is the renunciation of both poles of the Constantinian settlement. Modern politics is apostasy from the fourth-century baptism.

Modern states, first, do not welcome the church, as true city, into their midst. They are happy to welcome the church if it agrees to moderate its claims, if it agrees to reduce itself to religion, or private piety, or aesthetical liturgy, or mystical piety. Modern states are happy to be Diocletian, supporting the priesthoods as a department of the empire. The modern state will not, however, welcome a competitor. It will not kiss the Son as the King of a different city, and it will not honor the Queen unless she is a floozy.[66] All modern states, totalitarian and democratic, renounce the Constantinian system; that is what makes them modern states. There are differences, and important ones. Totalitarian states attack the sacrificial city of the church, seeking to turn it into Diocletian's sacrifice of Christians. Democratic states more or less peacefully marginalize the church, and the Christians of democratic states too often cheer them on. For all their differences, totalitarian and democratic systems are secretly united in their anti-Constantinianism.

Second, because the modern state refuses to welcome the church as city, as model city, as teacher and judge, the modern state reasserts its status as the restored sacrificial state. This means that there must be blood. Medieval life was rough and brutish in plenty of ways and had its share of blood. But believing that the Eucharistic blood of Jesus founded the true city provided a brake on bloodshed. Bishops imposed the peace and truce of God, and monks and others continuously modeled Christ before kings. Modern states have no brakes. Modern nations thus get resacralized because they are resacrificialized,[67] they demand the "ultimate sacrifice" (*pro patria mori*), they expel citizens of the wrong color or nationality or reli-

---

[66]William T. Cavanaugh, "A Fire Strong Enough to Consume the House: The Wars of Religion and the Rise of the State," *Modern Theology* 11, no. 4 (1995); *Torture and Eucharist* (Oxford: Blackwell, 1998).

[67]See Michael Burleigh, *Earthly Powers: Religion and Politics in Europe from the French Revolution to the Great War* (London. Burleigh, 2005), and *Sacred Causes* (New York: Harper, 2007).

gion. In modernity, the "Constantinianism" that Yoder deplores becomes a horrific reality, as the church has too often wedded itself to power.

This is the origin of nihilistic politics. Nihilistic modern politics is not the product of Scotism or nominalism or any other system of ideas. Nihilistic politics is the product of the history of Western politics, from Constantine's desacrificialization of Western politics back to modernity's resacrificialization. Nihilistic politics arises when the modern state reassumes the role of sacrificer but then realizes there are no more gods to receive the sacrifice—no more gods but itself. And there can be no more goats and bulls, since animal sacrifice is cruel and inhumane. Yet there is blood, more blood than ever, more blood than any ancient tyranny would have thought possible, and *all of it human*. To put it back into the biblical framework developed above: modern nations have in certain respects returned to the *stoicheia*, apostatized from the new order beyond sacrifice. Alternately, we might say that modern nations are post-Christian; they benefit from the new covenant privilege of handling the sword and the fire but refuse to listen to Jesus when he tells them how to avoid cutting or burning themselves.

Conclusion

In the end it all comes round to baptism, specifically to infant baptism. Rome was baptized in the fourth century. Eusebian hopes notwithstanding, it was not instantly transformed into the kingdom of heaven. It did not immediately become the city of God on earth. Baptism never does that. It is not meant to. Baptism sets a new trajectory, initiates a new beginning, but every beginning is the beginning of something. Through Constantine, Rome was baptized into a world without animal sacrifice and officially recognized the true sacrificial city, the one community that *does* offer a foretaste of the final kingdom. Christian Rome was in its infancy, but that was hardly surprising. All baptisms are infant baptisms.

Yoder is famed for his patience, but in dismissing Constantine and the world he left behind, his patience failed. For Yoder, Rome was not radically Christian, Rome's adherence to the faith was infantile, and because of that, he reasons, it was not Christian at all but apostate. He failed, as Augustine said against Pelagius, to give due weight to "the interim, the interval between the remission of sins which takes place in baptism, and the permanently established sinless state in the kingdom that is to come, this middle time [*tempus hoc medium*] of prayer, while [we] must pray, 'Forgive us our sins.'" He failed to acknowledge that all—Constantine, Rome, ourselves—stand in medial time, and yet are no less Christian for that.[68]

What can we expect in this middle time? Not much, Yoder thinks. He says that the project of Christianizing the state is doomed. The time when that could happen has long ago passed away. If he is right, we are facing nothing short of apocalypse. I believe that here too Yoder is wrong, and that we can escape apocalypse. But this can only happen on certain conditions: only through reevangelization, only through the revival of a *purified* Constantinianism, only by the formation of a Christically centered politics, only through fresh public confession that Jesus' city is the model city, his blood the only expiating blood, his sacrifice the sacrifice that ends sacrifice. An apocalypse can be averted only if modern civilization, like Rome, humbles itself and is willing to come forward to be baptized.

---

[68]Augustine *De gestis Pelagii* 12.28; quoted in Markus, *Saeculum,* p. 54.

Bibliography

Ancient Sources

I have relied a great deal in this study on secondary literature. Much of the primary literature I have examined is available on the Web, and unless otherwise noted I have used these translations. Unless otherwise noted below, I have used the translations of patristic sources available at <www.newadvent.org>. There is also a wonderful collection of documents regarding the Nicene debates, Constantine's legislation and letters, and much else at <www.fourthcentury.com>. The Theodosian Code is available only in Latin on the Web, at <http://ancientrome.ru/ius/library/codex/theod/liber16.htm>, and an English translation of the Justinian Code can be found at <http://uwacadweb.uwyo.edu/blume&justinian>. Constantine's letters and many of his coin issues can be found at <www.constantinethegreatcoins.com>. I also made use of the incomplete Web editions of the Migne *Patrologia Latina* (*PL*) and *Patrologia Graeca* (*PG*), both available at <www.documentacatholicaomnia.eu>. A nineteenth-century translation of Zosimus's *New History* is available at <www.tertullian.org/fathers/zosimus01_book1.htm>.

In the footnotes I have usually cited ancient sources with an abbreviated title, unless the title is only a word or two long. In the list below, if the full title is longer, I supply it in parentheses.

Athanasius. *Defense* (*Defense of the Nicene Definition*).
———. *On the Synods.*

Augustine. *City of God.*

Basil. *Epistles.*

Cicero. *De domo* (*De domo sua*). Trans. N. H. Watts. Loeb Classical Library 158. Cambridge, Mass.: Harvard University Press, 1923.

CJ (Codex Justianus).

CTh (Codex Theodosianus).

Cyprian. *Ad Donatum.*

Dio Cassius. *Roman History.* Trans. Earnest Cary. Available at <http://Penelope.uchicago/edu/Thayer/e/roman/texts/cassius_dio/home.html>.

Dionysius of Halicarnassus. *Roman Antiquities.* Trans. Earnest Cary. Available at <http://penelope.uchicago.edu/Thayer/E/Roman/Texts/dionysius_of_halicarnassus/home.html>.

Eusebius. *Church History* (*The History of the Church from Christ to Constantine*).

———. *Life* (*Life of Constantine*). Trans. Averil Cameron and Stuart G. Hall. Oxford: Clarendon, 1999.

———. *Oration* (*Oration in Praise of Constantine*).

Eutropius. *Breviarium* (*Abridgement of Roman History*). Trans. John Selby Watson. Available at <www.forumromanum.org/literature/eutropius>.

Herodian. *Roman Histories.* Trans. Edward C. Echols. Available at <www.tertullian.org/fathers>.

Historia Augusta. Selections available at <http://penelope.uchicago.edu/Thayer/E/Roman/Texts/historia_augusta/home.html>.

Julian. *Caesares.* Trans. W. C. Wright. Available at <www.attalus.org/translate/caesars.html>.

Justin. *Dialogue with Trypho.*

———. *First Apology.*

Lactantius. *Death* (*Of the Manner in Which the Persecutors Died*).

———. *Divine Institutes.*

Livy. *From the Foundation of the City.* Available at <www.thelatinlibrary.com/liv.html>.

Optatus. *Against the Donatists.* Trans. and ed. Mark Edwards. Liverpool: Liverpool University Press, 1998.

Origen. *Contra Celsum.*

Ovid. *Ars amatoria*. Trans. J. Lewis May. Available at <www.sacred-texts
.com/cla/ovid>.

Rufinus. *Church History*. Trans. Eusebius, with additional material to 395.

Seneca. *Epistles*. Trans. Richard M. Gumere. Available at <www.stoics.
com/books.html#SENECAEP1>.

———. *On Providence*. Trans. William Bell Langsdorf. Available at
<http://www45.homepage.villanova.edu/thomas.w.smith/Documents/
Seneca,%20On%20Providence.doc>.

Socrates. *Ecclesiastical History*.

Sozomen. *Ecclesiastical History*.

Sulpicius Severus. *Vita Martini*.

Tacitus. *Agricola*.

Tertullian. *Ad scapulum*.

———. *Apology*.

———. *De corona militis*.

———. *De spectaculis*.

———. *On Idolatry*.

———. *On the Dress of Virgins*.

Theodoret. *Ecclesiastical History*.

Zosimus. *New History*. English translation available at <www.tertullian
.org/fathers/zosimus01_book1.htm>.

SECONDARY WORKS

Alfoldi, Andreas. *The Conversion of Constantine and Pagan Rome*. Trans.
Harold Mattingly. Oxford: Clarendon, 1948.

———. "The Helmet of Constantine with the Christian Monogram."
Journal of Roman Studies 22, no. 1 (1932).

———. "On the Foundation of Constantinople: A Few Notes." *Journal of
Roman Studies* 37, nos. 1-2 (1947).

Alfoldy, Geza. *The Social History of Rome*. Trans. David Braund and Frank
Pollock. Baltimore: Johns Hopkins University Press, 1988.

Ando, Clifford. Review of *Law and Empire in Late Antiquity*, by Jill Harries,
and *Laying Down the Law*, by John Matthews. *Phoenix* 56, nos. 1/2
(2002): 198-203.

———. *The Matter of the Gods: Religion and the Roman Empire*. Berkeley:
University of California Press, 2008.

Armstrong, Gregory T. "Constantine's Churches: Symbol and Structure." *Journal of the Society of Architectural Historians* 33, no. 1 (1974).

———. "Imperial Church Building and Church-State Relations, A.D. 313-363." *Church History* 36, no. 1 (1967).

Avram, Wes, ed. *Anxious About Empire: Theological Essays on the New Global Realities.* Grand Rapids: Brazos, 2004.

Ayres, Lewis. *Nicaea and Its Legacy: An Approach to Fourth-Century Trinitarian Theology.* Oxford: Oxford University Press, 2006.

Ayres, Lewis, and S. Gareth Jones, eds. *Christian Origins: Theology, Rhetoric and Community.* London: Routledge, 1998.

Bacevich, Andrew. *American Empire: The Realities and Consequences of U.S. Diplomacy.* Cambridge, Mass.: Harvard University Press, 2004.

———. *The Limits of Power: The End of American Exceptionalism.* New York: Holt Paperbacks, 2009.

Bainton, Roland. *Christian Attitudes Toward War and Peace: A Historical Survey and Critical Re-evaluation.* Nashville: Abingdon, 1960.

Ball, Warwick. *Rome in the East: The Transformation of an Empire.* London: Routledge, 2000.

Barnard, L. W. "The Origins and Emergence of the Church in Edessa During the First Two Centuries A.D." *Vigiliae Christianae* 22, no. 3 (1968).

Barnes, Timothy D. *Athanasius and Constantius: Theology and Politics in the Constantinian Empire.* Cambridge: Harvard University Press, 1983.

———. "Constantine After Seventeen Hundred Years: *The Cambridge Companion*, the New York Exhibition and a Recent Biography." *International Journal of the Classical Tradition* 14 (2008).

———. "Constantine and the Christians of Persia." *Journal of Roman Studies* 75 (1985).

———. *Constantine and Eusebius.* Cambridge, Mass.: Harvard University Press, 1981.

———. "Constantine, Athanasius and the Christian Church." In *Constantine: History, Historiography and Legend*, ed. Samuel Lieu and Dominic Montserrat. London: Routledge, 1998.

———. "Constantine's Prohibition of Pagan Sacrifice." *American Journal of Philology* 105 (1985).

————. "The Emperor Constantine's Good Friday Sermon." *Journal of Theological Studies* 27 (1976).

————. "Hilary of Poitiers on His Exile." *Vigiliae Christianae* 46, no. 2 (1992).

————. "Monotheists All?" *Phoenix* 55, nos. 1/2 (2001).

————. "Publilius Optatianus Porfyrius." *American Journal of Philology* 96, no. 2 (1975).

————. "Sossianus Hierocles and the Antecedents of the 'Great Persecution.'" *Harvard Studies in Classical Philology* 80 (1976).

————. "Statistics and the Conversion of the Roman Aristocracy." *Journal of Roman Studies* 85 (1985).

Barton, Carlin A. "Savage Miracles: The Redemption of Lost Honor in Roman Society and the Sacrament of the Gladiator and the Martyr." *Representations* 45 (1994).

————. "The Scandal of the Arena." *Representations* 27 (1989).

————. *The Sorrows of the Ancient Romans: The Gladiator and the Monster.* Princeton, N.J.: Princeton University Press, 1993.

Bartsch, Shadi. *The Mirror of the Self: Sexuality, Self-Knowledge and the Gaze in the Early Roman Empire.* Chicago: University of Chicago Press, 2006.

Baynes, Norman H. *Constantine the Great and the Christian Church.* Raleigh Lecture on History. London: Humphrey Milford, 1929.

Beard, Mary. *The Roman Triumph.* Cambridge, Mass.: Belknap/Harvard University Press, 2007.

Beard, Mary, John North and Simon Price. *Religions of Rome*, vol. 1, *A History.* Cambridge: University of Cambridge Press, 1998.

Becker, Adam H., and Annette Yoshiko Reed, eds. *The Ways That Never Parted: Jews and Christians in Late Antiquity and the Early Middle Ages.* Minneapolis: Fortress, 2007.

Bell, Daniel. *Just War as Christian Discipleship: Recentering the Tradition in the Church rather than the State.* Grand Rapids: Brazos, 2009.

Benson, Bruce Ellis, and Peter Goodwin Heltzel, eds. *Evangelicals and Empire: Christian Alternatives to the Political Status Quo.* Grand Rapids: Brazos, 2008.

Berkhof, Hendrik. *Christ and the Powers.* Trans. John H. Yoder. Scottdale, Penn.: Herald, 1977.

Berman, Harold. *Faith and Order: The Reconciliation of Law and Religion*. Grand Rapids: Eerdmans, 1993.

———. *Law and Revolution: The Formation of the Western Legal Tradition*. Cambridge, Mass.: Harvard University Press, 1983.

Bleckmann, Bruno. "Ein Kaiser als Prediger: Zur Datierung der Konstantinischen 'Rede an die Versammlung der Heiligen.'" *Hermes* 125, no. 2 (1997).

Bowersock, G. W. *Martyrdom and Rome*. Cambridge: Cambridge University Press, 1995.

Boyarin, Daniel. "Judaism as a Free Church: Footnotes to John Howard Yoder's *The Jewish-Christian Schism Revisited*." *Crosscurrents*, Winter 2007.

Bradbury, Scott. "Constantine and the Problem of Anti-pagan Legislation in the Fourth Century." *Classical Philology* 89, no. 2 (1994).

———. "Julian's Pagan Revival and the Decline of Blood Sacrifice." *Phoenix* 49, no. 4 (1995).

Bradshaw, Paul. *The Search for the Origins of Christian Worship*. 2nd ed. Oxford: Oxford University Press, 2002.

Brenneman, Laura L. "Further Footnotes on Paul, Yoder and Boyarin." *Crosscurrents*, Winter 2007.

Brown, Dan. *The Da Vinci Code*. New York: Doubleday, 2003.

Brown, Peter. "Aspects of the Christianization of the Roman Aristocracy." *Journal of Roman Studies* 51 (1961).

———. *Augustine of Hippo: A Biography*. New ed. Berkeley: University of California Press, 2000.

———. *Authority and the Sacred: Aspects of the Christianisation of the Roman World*. Cambridge: Cambridge University Press, 1997.

———. *Power and Persuasion in Late Antiquity: Toward a Christian Empire*. Madison: University of Wisconsin Press, 1992.

———. *Society and the Holy in Late Antiquity*. London: Faber and Faber, 1982.

Brunt, P. A. Review of *Social Status and Legal Privilege in the Roman Empire*, by Peter Garnsey. *Journal of Roman Studies* 62 (1972).

Bruun, Christer. "The Thick Neck of the Emperor Constantine: Slimy Snails and 'Quellenforschung.'" *Historia* 44, no. 4 (1995).

Bruun, Patrick. "The Christian Signs on the Coins of Constantine." *Arctos*, n.s. 3 (1962).

————. "The Disappearance of Sol from the Coins of Constantine." *Arctos*, n.s. 2 (1958).

————. "Portrait of a Conspirator: Constantine's Break with the Tetrarchy." *Arctos*, n.s. 10 (1976).

Buckland, W. W. *The Roman Law of Slavery: The Condition of the Slave in Private Law from Augustus to Justinian.* Cambridge: Cambridge University Press, 1908.

Buell, Denise Kimber. "Rethinking the Relevance of Race for Early Christian Self-Definition." *Harvard Theological Review* 94, no. 4 (2001).

Burckhardt, Jacob. *The Age of Constantine the Great.* Trans. Moses Hadas. Berkeley: University of California Press, 1983.

Burleigh, Michael. *Earthly Powers: Religion and Politics in Europe from the French Revolution to the Great War.* London: Harper, 2005.

————. *Sacred Causes.* New York: Harper, 2007.

Burrows, Mark A. "Christians in the Roman Forum: Tertullian and the Apologetic Use of History." *Vigiliae Christianae* 42, no. 3 (1988).

Cadbury, Henry J. "The Basis of Early Christian Antimilitarism." *Journal of Biblical Literature* 37, nos. 1/2 (1918).

Cagniart, Pierre. "The Philosopher and the Gladiator." *Classical World* 93, no. 6 (2000).

Caird, G. B. *Principalities and Powers: A Study in Pauline Theology.* 1956. Reprint, Eugene, Ore.: Wipf and Stock, 2003.

Cambi, Nenad. "Tetrarchic Practice in Name Giving." In *Diokletian und die Tetrarchie: Aspekte einer Zeintenwende*, ed. Alexander Demandt, Andreas Goltz and Henrich Schlange-Schoningen. Berlin: Walter de Gruyter, 2004.

Cameron, Averil. *The Later Roman Empire.* Cambridge: Harvard University Press, 1993.

Carroll, James. *Constantine's Sword: The Church and the Jews.* Boston: Houghton Mifflin, 2001.

Carter, Craig A. *The Politics of the Cross: The Theology and Social Ethics of John Howard Yoder.* Grand Rapids: Brazos, 2001.

————. *Rethinking Christ and Culture: A Post-Christendom Perspective.* Grand Rapids: Brazos, 2006.

Casenove, John Gibson. *St. Hilary of Poitier and St. Martin of Tours.* The Fathers for English Readers. London: SPCK, 1883.

Cavanaugh, William T. "A Fire Strong Enough to Consume the House: The Wars of Religion and the Rise of the State." *Modern Theology* 11, no. 4 (1995).

———. *Torture and Eucharist*. Oxford: Blackwell, 1998.

Chadwick, Henry. *The Early Church*. The Pelican History of the Church 1. New York: Penguin, 1967.

Cohen, Eliot A. "History and the Hyperpower." *Foreign Affairs* 83, no. 4 (2004).

Coleman, Christopher Bush. *Constantine the Great and Christianity*. Columbia Studies in History, Economics and Public Law 146. New York: Columbia University Press, 1914.

Coleman, K. M. "Fatal Charades: Roman Executions Staged as Mythological Enactments." *Journal of Roman Studies* 80 (1990).

Coles, Romand. "The Wild Patience of John Howard Yoder: 'Outsiders' and the 'Otherness of the Church.'" *Modern Theology* 18, no. 3 (2002).

Collier, Charles Mayo. "A Nonviolent Augustinianism? History and Politics in the Theologies of St. Augustine and John Howard Yoder." Ph.D. diss., Duke University, 2008.

Corcoran, Simon. "Before Constantine." In *The Cambridge Companion to the Age of Constantine*, ed. Noel Lenski. Cambridge: Cambridge University Press, 2006.

———. *The Empire of the Tetrarchs: Imperial Pronouncements and Government, AD 284-324*. Rev. ed. Oxford Classical Monographs. Oxford: Oxford University Press, 2000.

Crook, John A. "Ivs Romanvm Doli Revm." Review of *Social Status and Legal Privilege in the Roman Empire*, by Peter Garnsey. *Classical Review* 22, no. 2 (1972).

Crossan, John Dominic. *God and Empire: Jesus Against Rome, Then and Now*. San Francisco: Harper, 2007.

Curran, John. "Constantine and the Ancient Cults of Rome: The Legal Evidence." *Greece and Rome*, 2nd s., 43, no. 1 (1996).

Dagron, Gilbert. *Emperor and Priest: The Imperial Office in Byzantium*. Trans. Jean Birrell. Cambridge: Cambridge University Press, 2003.

———. *Naissance d'une capitale: Constantinople et ses institutions de 330 a 451*. 2nd ed. Paris: Presses universitaires de France, 1984.

Davies, P. S. "The Origin and Purpose of the Persecution of A.D. 303." *Journal of Theological Studies* 40, no. 1 (1989).

Demandt, Alexander, Andreas Goltz and Heinrich Schlange-Schoningen, eds. *Diokletian und die Tetrarchie: Aspekte einer Zeintenwende.* Berlin: Walter de Gruyter, 2004.

Depeyrot, Georges. "Economy and Society." In *The Cambridge Companion to the Age of Constantine*, ed. Noel Lenski. Cambridge: Cambridge University Press, 2006.

De Ste. Croix, G. E. M. "Aspects of the 'Great' Persecution." *Harvard Theological Review* 47, no. 2 (1954).

———. "Why Were the Early Christians Persecuted?" *Past and Present* 26 (1963).

Detienne, Marcel, and Jean-Pierre Vernant. *The Cuisine of Sacrifice Among the Greeks.* Chicago: University of Chicago Press, 1998.

Digeser, Elizabeth DePalma. *The Making of a Christian Empire: Lactantius and Rome.* Ithaca, N.Y.: Cornell University Press, 2000.

Dodaro, Robert. *Christ and the Just Society in the Thought of Augustine.* Cambridge: Cambridge University Press, 2004.

Dodds, E. R. *Pagan and Christian in an Age of Anxiety: Some Aspects of Religious Experience from Marcus Aurelius to Constantine.* New York: W. W. Norton, 1965.

Dorries, Hermann. *Constantine and Religious Liberty.* Trans. Roland Bainton. New Haven, Conn.: Yale University Press, 1960.

———. *Constantine the Great.* Trans. Roland Bainton. New York: Harper Torchbooks, 1972.

Drake, H. A. "Constantine and Consensus." *Church History* 64, no. 1 (1995).

———. *Constantine and the Bishops: The Politics of Intolerance.* Baltimore: Johns Hopkins University Press, 2000.

———. "The Impact of Constantine on Christianity." In *The Cambridge Companion to the Age of Constantine*, ed. Noel Lenski. Cambridge: Cambridge University Press, 2006.

———. "Suggestions of Date in Constantine's 'Oration to the Saints.'" *American Journal of Philology* 106, no. 3 (1985).

———. "What Eusebius Knew: The Genesis of the 'Vita Constantini.'" *Classical Philology* 83, no. 1 (1988).

Dungan, David L. *Constantine's Bible: Politics and the Making of the New Testament*. Minneapolis: Fortress, 2007.

Dupoint, Florence. *L'acteur-roi: Le théâtre dans le Rome antique*. Paris: Societe d'édition, 1985.

———. *Daily Life in Ancient Rome*. Trans. Christopher Woodall. Oxford: Blackwell, 1993.

Dvornik, Francis. "Emperors, Popes and General Councils." *Dumbarton Oaks Papers* 6 (1951).

Edwards, Catherine. *Death in Ancient Rome*. New Haven, Conn.: Yale University Press, 2007.

Edwards, M. J. "The Arian Heresy and the Oration to the Saints." *Vigiliae Christianae* 49, no. 4 (1995).

Edwards, Mark, trans. *Constantine and Christendom*. Liverpool: Liverpool University Press, 2003.

Elliott, T. G. *The Christianity of Constantine the Great*. Scranton, Penn.: University of Scranton Press, 1996.

Elsner, Jas'. "From the Culture of *Spolia* to the Cult of Relics: The Arch of Constantine and the Genesis of Late Antique Forms." *Papers of the British School at Rome* 68 (2000).

———. "The Itinerarium Burdigalense: Politics and Salvation in the Geography of Constantine's Empire." *Journal of Roman Studies* 90 (2000).

———. "Perspectives in Art." In *The Cambridge Companion to the Age of Constantine*, ed. Noel Lenski. Cambridge: Cambridge University Press, 2006.

Elson, Hugh. "Warfare and the Military." In *The Cambridge Companion to the Age of Constantine*, ed. Noel Lenski. Cambridge: Cambridge University Press, 2006.

Ferguson, Yale H. "Along the Imperial Continuum: Varieties of Empire." Paper presented at American Political Science Association annual meeting, 2007. Available at <www.allacademic.com//meta/p_mla_apa_research_citation/2/1/0/1/1/pages210119/p210119-1.php>.

———. "Illusions of Superpower." *Asian Journal of Political Science* 11, no. 2 (2003).

Fletcher, Richard. *The Barbarian Conversion: From Paganism to Christianity*. New York: Henry Holt, 1997.

Fowden, Elizabeth Key. "Constantine and the Peoples of the Eastern Frontier." In *The Cambridge Companion to the Age of Constantine*, ed. Noel Lenski. Cambridge: Cambridge University Press, 2006.

Fowden, Garth. "Constantine's Porphyry Column: The Earliest Literary Allusion." *Journal of Roman Studies* 81 (1991).

———. *Empire to Commonwealth: Consequences of Monotheism in Late Antiquity.* Princeton, N.J.: Princeton University Press, 1993.

———. "The Last Days of Constantine: Oppositional Versions and Their Influence." *Journal of Roman Studies* 84 (1994).

Frank, Tenney. *Roman Imperialism.* New York: Macmillan, 1914.

Fredricksen, Paula. *Augustine and the Jews: A Christian Defense of Jews and Judaism.* New York: Doubleday, 2008.

Freeman, Charles. *A.D. 381: Heretics, Pagans and the Dawn of the Monotheistic State.* Woodstock, N.Y.: Overlook, 2009.

———. *The Closing of the Western Mind: The Rise of Faith and the Fall of Reason.* New York: Vintage, 2002.

Frend, W. H. C. "The Failure of Persecutions in the Roman Empire." *Past and Present* 16 (1959).

———. Review of *Il Christianesimo e Roma*, by Marta Sordi. *Classical Review*, n.s. 17, no. 2 (1967).

———. Review of *Tertullian und das Romische Reich*, by Richard Klein. *Classical Review*, n.s. 20, no. 1 (1970).

———. *The Rise of Christianity.* Philadelphia: Fortress, 1984.

Friesen, Duane K. "Normative Factors in Troeltsch's Typology of Religious Association." *Journal of Religious Ethics* 3, no. 2 (1975).

Futrell, Alison. *Blood in the Arena: The Spectacle of Roman Power.* Austin: University of Texas Press, 1997.

Gaddis, Michael. *There Is No Crime for Those Who Have Christ: Religious Violence in the Christian Roman Empire.* Berkeley: University of California Press, 2005.

Garland, David E. *Reading Matthew: A Literary and Theological Commentary on the First Gospel.* Macon, Ga.: Smyth and Helwys, 1999.

Garnsey, Peter. "Legal Privilege in the Roman Empire." *Past and Present* 41 (1968).

Gaudemet, Jean. *Formation du droit canonique et gouvernement de l'Église de l'antiquité à l'âge classique.* Strasbourg: Presses universitaires, 2007.

Gero, Stephen. *"Miles Gloriosus*: Christians and Military Service According to Tertullian." *Church History* 39 (1970).

Gibbon, Edward. *The Decline and Fall of the Roman Empire.* 3 vols. New York: Modern Library, 1982.

Goffart, Walter. "Rome, Constantinople and the Barbarians." *American Historical Review* 86, no. 2 (1981).

Grubbs, Judith Evans. *Law and Family in Late Antiquity: The Emperor Constantine's Marriage Legislation.* Oxford: Oxford University Press, 1999.

Gunderson, Erik. "The Ideology of the Arena." *Classical Antiquity* 15, no. 1 (1996).

Hall, Linda Jones. "Cicero's *instinctu divino* and Constantine's *instinctu divinitatis*: The Evidence of the Arch of Constantine for the Senatorial View of the 'Vision' of Constantine." *Journal of Early Christian Studies* 6, no. 4 (1998).

Hanson, R. P. C. "The Christian Attitude to Pagan Religions up to the Time of Constantine the Great." *ANRW* 23 (1980).

———. *The Search for the Christian Doctrine of God: The Arian Controversy, 318-381.* Grand Rapids: Baker Academic, 2005.

Harink, Douglas. *Paul Among the Postliberals: Pauline Theology Beyond Christendom and Modernity.* Grand Rapids: Brazos, 2003.

Harl, K. A. "Sacrifice and Pagan Belief in Fifth- and Sixth-Century Byzantium." *Past and Present* 128 (1990).

Harris, W. V. "Child-Exposure in the Roman Empire." *Journal of Roman Studies* 84 (1994).

Hauerwas, Stanley, and Chris K. Huebner. "History, Theory and Anabaptism: A Conversation on Theology After John Howard Yoder." In *The Wisdom of the Cross*, ed. Stanley Hauerwas et al. Grand Rapids: Eerdmans, 1999.

Hauerwas, Stanley, Chris K. Huebner, Harry J. Huebner, and Mark Thiessen Nation, eds. *The Wisdom of the Cross: Essays in Honor of John Howard Yoder.* Grand Rapids: Eerdmans, 1999.

Helgeland, John. "Christians and the Roman Army, A.D. 173-337." *Church History* 43, no. 2 (1974).

———. "Christians and the Roman Army from Marcus Aurelius to Constantine." *ANRW* 2.23.1 (1979).

————. "Roman Army Religion." *ANRW* 2.16.2 (1978).

Heilke, Thomas. "Yoder's Idea of Constantinianism: An Analytical Framework Toward Conversation." In *A Mind Patient and Untamed: Assessing John Howard Yoder's Contributions to Theology, Ethics and Peacemaking,* ed. Ben C. Ollenburger and Gayle Koontz. Telford, Penn.: Cascadia, 2004.

Heyman, George. *The Power of Sacrifice: Roman and Christian Discourses in Conflict.* Washington, D.C.: Catholic University of America Press, 2007.

Hollerich, Michael J. "Religion and Politics in the Writings of Eusebius: Reassessing the First 'Court Theologian.'" *Church History* 59, no. 3 (1990).

Holloway, R. Ross. *Constantine and Rome.* New Haven, Conn.: Yale University Press, 2004.

Holscher, Tonio. *The Language of Images in Roman Art.* Translated by Anthony Snodgrass and Annemarie Kunzl-Snodgrass. Cambridge: Cambridge University Press, 2004.

Holt, Elizabeth Gilmore, ed. *A Documentary History of Art,* vol. 1, *The Middle Ages and the Renaissance.* Princeton, N.J.: Princeton University Press, 1981.

Horsley, Richard A., ed. *In the Shadow of Empire: Reclaiming the Bible as a History of Faithful Resistance.* Louisville, Ky.: Westminster John Knox, 2008.

————. *Jesus and Empire: The Kingdom of God and the New World Disorder.* Minneapolis: Fortress, 2003.

————, ed. *Paul and Empire: Religion and Power in Roman Imperial Society.* Harrisburg, Penn.: Trinity Press International, 1997.

Huebner, Chris K. *A Precarious Peace: Yoderian Explorations on Theology, Knowledge and Identity.* Scottdale, Penn.: Herald, 2006.

————. "Unhandling History: Anti-theory, Ethics and the Practice of Witness." Ph.D. diss., Duke University, 2002.

Humphries, Mark. "From Usurper to Emperor: The Politics of Legitimation in the Age of Constantine." *Journal of Late Antiquity* 1, no. 1 (2008).

Hunt, E. D. "Constantine and Jerusalem." *Journal of Ecclesiastical History* 48, no. 3 (1997).

Hunter, David G. "A Decade of Research on Early Christians and Military Service." *Religious Studies Review* 18, no. 2 (1992).

Johnson, Mark J. "Architecture of Empire." In *The Cambridge Companion to the Age of Constantine*, ed. Noel Lenski. Cambridge: Cambridge University Press, 2006.

Jones, A. H. M. *Constantine and the Conversion of Europe*. Toronto: University of Toronto Press, 1978.

———. *The Later Roman Empire, 284-602: A Social, Economic and Administrative Survey*. 2 vols. Baltimore: Johns Hopkins University Press, 1964.

———. "The Social Background of the Struggle Between Paganism and Christianity." In *The Conflict Between Paganism and Christianity in the Fourth Century*, ed. Arnaldo Momigliano. Oxford: Clarendon, 1963.

Jones, Mark Wilson. "Genesis and Mimesis: The Design of the Arch of Constantine in Rome." *Journal of the Society of Architectural Historians* 59, no. 1 (2000).

Jonkers, E. J. "De l'influence du Christianisme sur la législation relative à l'esclavage dans l'antiquité." *Mnemosyne*, 3rd ser. 1 (1933-34).

Kelly, Christopher. "Bureaucracy and Government." In *The Cambridge Companion to the Age of Constantine*, ed. Noel Lenski. Cambridge: Cambridge University Press, 2006.

Kerr, Nathan R. *Christ, History and Apocalyptic: The Politics of Christian Mission*. Theopolitical Visions. Eugene, Ore.: Wipf and Stock, 2009.

———. "Transcendence and Apocalyptic: A Reply to Barber." *Political Theology* 10, no. 1 (2009).

Kilde, Jeanne Halgren. *Sacred Power, Sacred Space: An Introduction to Christian Architecture and Worship*. Oxford: Oxford University Press, 2008.

Kinney, Dale. "Roman Architectural Spolia." *Proceedings of the American Philosophical Society* 145, no. 2 (2001).

———. "'SPOLIA. DAMNATIO' and 'RENOVATIO MEMORIAE.'" *Memoirs of the American Academy in Rome* 42 (1997).

Knipfing, John R. "The Libelli of the Decian Persecution." *Harvard Theological Review* 16, no. 4 (1923).

Kousoulas, D. G. *The Life and Times of Constantine the Great: The First Christian Emperor*. 2nd ed. Author, 2007.

Krautheimer, Richard. "The Constantinian Basilica." *Dumbarton Oaks Papers* 21 (1967).

─────. *Early Christian and Byzantine Architecture.* 3rd ed. Pelican History of Art. New York: Penguin, 1979.

Kroeker, P. Travis. "Is a Messianic Political Ethic Possible? Recent Work By and About John Howard Yoder." *Journal of Religious Ethics* 233, no. 1 (2005).

Kuefler, Mathew. *The Manly Eunuch: Masculinity, Gender Ambiguity and Christian Ideology in Late Antiquity.* Chicago: University of Chicago Press, 2001.

Kulikowski, Michael. "Constantine and the Northern Barbarians." In *The Cambridge Companion to the Age of Constantine*, ed. Noel Lenski. Cambridge: Cambridge University Press, 2006.

Lamirande, Emilien. "La signification de 'christianus' dans le théologie de saint Augustin et la tradition ancienne." 1963. Available at <documents.irevues.inist.fr/bitstream/2042/766/1/63_IX_3_4_03.pdf>.

Leach, Edmund. "Melchisedech and the Emperor: Icons of Subversion and Orthodoxy." *Proceedings of the Royal Anthropological Institute of Great Britain and Ireland*, 1972.

Leadbetter, Bill. "The Illegitimacy of Constantine and the Birth of the Tetrarchy." In *Constantine: History, Historiography and Legend*, ed. Samuel Lieu and Dominic Montserrat. London: Routledge, 1998.

Lee, A. D. "Decoding Late Roman Law." *Journal of Roman Studies* 92 (2002).

Leithart, Peter J. *Deep Exegesis: The Mystery of Reading Scripture.* Waco, Tex.: Baylor University Press, 2009.

─────. *A Son to Me: An Exposition of 1 and 2 Samuel.* Moscow, Ida.: Canon, 2003.

Lendon, J. E. *Empire of Honor.* Oxford: Oxford University Press, 2005.

Lenski, Noel, ed. *The Cambridge Companion to the Age of Constantine.* Cambridge: Cambridge University Press, 2006.

Liebeschuetz, J. H. W. G. *Continuity and Change in Roman Religion.* Oxford: Oxford University Press, 1979.

Lieu, Samuel N. C., and Dominic Montserrat, eds. *Constantine: History, Historiography and Legend.* London: Routledge, 1998.

─────, eds. *From Constantine to Julian: Pagan and Byzantine Views—A Source History.* London: Routledge, 1996.

Linder, Amnon. Review of *Claudian Policymaking and the Early Imperial*

Repression of Judaism at Rome by H. Dixon Slingerland. *Jewish Quarterly Review* 91, nos. 1/2 (2000).

Locke, John. *Political Essays*. Ed. Mark Goldie. Cambridge Texts in the History of Political Thought. Cambridge: University of Cambridge Press, 1997.

Lundestad, Geir. "Empire by Invitation? The United States and Western Europe, 1945- 1952." *Journal of Peace Research* 23, no. 3 (1986).

MacMullen, Ramsay. *Constantine*. London: Croom Helm, 1987.

———. "Cultural and Political Changes in the 4th and 5th Centuries." *Historia* 52, no. 4 (2003).

———. *Roman Social Relations, 50 B.C. to A.D. 284*. New Haven, Conn.: Yale University Press, 1974.

———. "What Difference Did Christianity Make?" *Historia* 35, no. 3 (1986).

Madden, Thomas F. *Empires of Trust: How Rome Built—and American Is Building—a New World*. New York: Dutton, 2008.

Marcus, Joel. "Crucifixion as Parodic Exaltation." *Journal of Biblical Literature* 125, no. 1 (1996).

Markus, R. A. *The End of Ancient Christianity*. Cambridge: Cambridge University Press, 1990.

———. *Saeculum: History and Society in the Theology of Augustine*. Cambridge: Cambridge University Press, 1970.

Mastrangelo, Marc. *The Roman Self in Late Antiquity: Prudentius and the Poetics of the Soul*. Baltimore: Johns Hopkins University Press, 2008.

Mathews, Thomas F. *The Clash of Gods: A Reinterpretation of Early Christian Art*. Rev. and exp. ed. Princeton, N.J.: Princeton University Press, 1999.

Mattern, Susan P. *Rome and the Enemy: Imperial Strategy in the Principate*. Berkeley: University of California Press, 1999.

Megivern, James J. "Early Christianity and Military Service." *Perspectives in Religious Studies* 12, no. 3 (1985).

Milbank, John. *Being Reconciled: Ontology and Pardon*. London: Routledge., 2003.

Millar, Fergus. *The Emperor in the Roman World*. 2nd ed. London: Duckworth, 1992.

———. "Emperors, Frontiers and Foreign Relations, 31 B.C. to A.D. 378." *Britannia* 13 (1982).

Mitchell, Stephen. "The Cities of Asia Minor in the Age of Constantine." In *Constantine: History, Historiography and Legend*, ed. Samuel Lieu and Dominic Montserrat. London: Routledge, 1998.

———. *A History of the Later Roman Empire, AD 284-641*. Blackwell History of the Ancient World. London: Blackwell, 2007.

———. "Maximinus and the Christians in A.D. 312: A New Latin Inscription." *Journal of Roman Studies* 78 (1988).

Momigliano, Arnaldo. "Christianity and the Decline of the Roman Empire." In *The Conflict Between Paganism and Christianity in the Fourth Century*, ed. Arnaldo Momigliano. Oxford: Clarendon, 1963.

———, ed. *The Conflict Between Paganism and Christianity in the Fourth Century*. Oxford: Clarendon, 1963.

Motyl, Alexander. "Is Everything Empire? Is Empire Everything?" *Comparative Politics* 39 (2006).

Muller, H. *Christians and Pagans from Constantine to Augustine*, pt. 1, *The Religious Policies of the Roman Emperors*. Pretoria: Union Booksellers, 1946.

Murray, Alexander. "Peter Brown and the Shadow of Constantine." *Journal of Roman Studies* 73 (1983).

Neufeld, Justin. "Just War Theory, the Authorization of the State and the Hermeneutics of Peoplehood: How John Howard Yoder Can Save Oliver O'Donovan from Himself." *International Journal of Systematic Theology* 8, no. 6 (2006).

Neusner, Jacob. *Judaism and Christianity in the Age of Constantine: History, Messiah, Israel and the Initial Confrontation*. Chicago: University of Chicago Press, 1987.

Nibley, Hugh. "Christian Envy of the Temple," pts. 1-2. *Jewish Quarterly Review*, n.s. 50, nos. 2-3 (1959).

Nicholson, Oliver. "Constantine's Vision of the Cross." *Vigiliae Christianae* 54, no. 3 (2000).

———. "The 'Pagan Churches' of Maximinus Daia and Julian the Apostate." *Journal of Ecclesiastical History* 45, no. 1 (1994).

Nixon, C. E. V. "Constantinus Oriens Imperator, Propaganda and Panegyric: On Reading Panegyric 7 (307)." *Historia* 42, no. 2 (1993).

Nixon, C. E. V., and Barbara Saylor Rodgers, eds. and trans. *In Praise of Later Roman Emperors: The Panegyrici Latini*. Berkeley: University of California Press, 1994.

Nock, Arthur Darby. "The Roman Army and the Roman Religious Year."
    Harvard Theological Review 45, no. 4 (1952).

Odahl, Charles Matson. *Constantine and the Christian Empire.* London:
    Routledge, 2004.

———. "God and Constantine: Divine Sanction for Imperial Rule in the
    First Christian Emperor's Early Letters and Art." *Catholic Historical
    Review* 81, no. 3 (1995).

O'Donovan, Oliver. *The Desire of Nations: Rediscovering the Roots of Politi-
    cal Theology.* Cambridge: Cambridge University Press, 1996.

Ollenburger, Ben C., and Gayle Gerber Koontz, eds. *A Mind Patient and
    Untamed: Assessing John Howard Yoder's Contributions to Theology, Ethics
    and Peacemaking.* Telford, Penn.: Cascadia, 2004.

Parker, Robert. *Miasma: Pollution and Purification in Early Greek Religion.*
    Oxford: Clarendon, 1996.

Paschoud, Francois. "Zosime 2,29 et la version paienne de la conversion de
    Constantin." *Historia* 20, nos. 2/3 (1971).

Petroupoulou, Maria-Zoe. *Animal Sacrifice in Ancient Greek Religion, Juda-
    ism and Christianity, 100 BC to AD 200.* Oxford: Oxford University Press,
    2008.

Pohlsander, Hans A. "Crispus: Brilliant Career and Tragic End." *Zeitschrift
    fur Alte Geschichte* 33, no. 1 (1984).

Pollock, Frederick. *Essays in Jurisprudence and Ethics.* London: Macmillan,
    1882.

Potter, David S. "Martyrdom as Spectacle." In *Theater and Society in the
    Classical World*, ed. Ruth Scodel. Ann Arbor: University of Michigan
    Press, 1993.

———. *Prophets and Emperors: Human and Divine Authority from Augus-
    tine to Theodosius.* Cambridge, Mass.: Harvard University Press, 1994.

——— *The Roman Empire at Bay, AD 180-395.* Routledge History of the
    Ancient World. London: Routledge, 2004.

———. "Roman Religion." In *Life, Death and Entertainment in the Roman
    Empire*, ed. David S. Potter and D. J. Mattingly. Ann Arbor: University
    of Michigan Press, 1999.

Potter, David S., and D. J. Mattingly, eds. *Life, Death and Entertainment
    in the Roman Empire.* Ann Arbor: University of Michigan Press, 1999.

Price, S. R. F. *Rituals and Power: The Roman Imperial Cult in Asia Minor.*

Cambridge: Cambridge University Press, 1984.

Radin, Max. "The Exposure of Infants in Roman Law and Practice." *Classical Journal* 20, no. 6 (1925).

Ramage, Nancy H., and Andew Ramage. *Roman Art.* 5th ed. Upper Saddle River, N.J.: Pearson / Prentice Hall, 2009.

Rawson, Beryl, ed. *Marriage, Divorce and Children in Ancient Rome.* Oxford: Oxford University Press, 1996.

Reichberg, Gregory M., Henrik Syse, and Endre Begby, eds. *The Ethics of War.* Oxford: Wiley-Blackwell, 2006.

Reno, R. R. "Stanley Hauerwas." In *The Blackwell Companion to Political Theology,* ed. Peter Scott and William T. Cavanaugh. Oxford: Blackwell, 2004.

Rives, J. B. "The Decree of Decius and the Religion of Empire." *Journal of Roman Studies* 89 (1999).

Roldanus, Johannes. *The Church in the Age of Constantine: The Theological Challenges.* London: Ashgate, 2006.

Rubenstein, Richard L. *The Cunning of History: The Holocaust and the American Future.* New York: Harper, 1975.

Rupke, Jorg. *Religion of the Romans.* Trans. Richard Gordon. Cambridge, U.K.: Polity, 2007.

Rushdoony, Rousas John. *The Foundations of Social Order: Studies in the Creeds and Councils of the Early Church.* Fairfax, Va.: Thoburn, 1978.

Salzman, Michele Renee. "The Evidence for the Conversion of the Roman Empire to Christianity in Book 16 of the 'Theodosian Code.'" *Historia* 42, no. 3 (1993).

———. *The Making of a Christian Aristocracy: Social and Religious Change in the Western Roman Empire.* Cambridge, Mass.: Harvard University Press, 2002.

Scheid, John. *Quand faire, c'est croire: Les rites sacrificiels des Romains.* Paris: Aubier, 2005.

Schlabach, Gerald W. "Deuteronomic or Constantinian: What Is the Most Basic Problem for Christian Social Ethics?" In *The Wisdom of the Cross: Essays in Honor of John Howard Yoder,* ed. Stanley Hauerwas et al. Eugene, Ore.: Wipf and Stock, 2005.

Scodel, Ruth, ed. *Theater and Society in the Classical World.* Ann Arbor: University of Michigan Press, 1993.

Scott, Peter, and William T. Cavanaugh, eds. *The Blackwell Companion to Political Theology*. Oxford: Blackwell, 2004.

Seznec, Jean. *The Survival of the Pagan Gods*. Princeton, N.J.: Princeton University Press, 1995.

Sider, J. Alexander. "Constantinianism Before and After Nicaea: Issues in Reconstitutionist Historiography." In *A Mind Patient and Untamed: Assessing John Howard Yoder's Contributions to Theology, Ethics and Peacemaking*, ed. Ben C. Ollenburger and Gayle Koontz. Telford, Penn.: Cascadia, 2004.

———. "'To See History Doxologically': History and Holiness in John Howard Yoder's Ecclesiology." Ph.D. diss., Duke University, 2004.

Simon, Marcel. *Verus Israel: A Study of the Relations Between Christians and Jews in the Roman Empire, AD 135-425*. Trans. H. McKeating. London: Littman Library of Jewish Civilization, 1996.

Skarsaune, Oskar. *In the Shadow of the Temple: Jewish Influences on Early Christianity*. Downers Grove, Ill.: InterVarsity Press, 2002.

Smith, R. R. R. "The Public Image of Licinius I: Portrait Sculpture and Imperial Ideology in the Fourth Century." *Journal of Roman Studies* 87 (1997).

Stark, Rodney. *The Rise of Christianity*. San Francisco: Harper, 1997.

Stauffer, Ethelbert. *Christ and the Caesars: Historical Sketches*. Trans. K. and R. Gregor Smith. Philadelphia: Westminster Press, 1955.

Straub, Johannes A. "Constantine as KOINOS EPISKOPOS: Tradition and Innovation in the Representation of the Christian Emperor's Majesty." *Dumbarton Oaks Papers* 21 (1967).

———. "Konstantins Verzicht auf den Gang zum Kapitol." *Historia* 4, nos. 2/3 (1955).

Stroumsa, Guy G. *The End of Sacrifice: Religious Transformations in Late Antiquity*. Trans. Susan Emanuel. Chicago: University of Chicago Press, 2009.

Swift, Louis J. "Augustine on War and Killing: Another View." *Harvard Theological Review* 66 (1973).

———. *The Early Fathers on War and Military Service*. Message of the Fathers of the Church 19. Wilmington, Del.: Michael Glazier, 1983.

———. "St. Ambrose on Violence and War." *Transactions and Proceedings of the American Philological Association* 101 (1970).

Talbert, Richard J. A. Review of *Corruption and the Decline of Rome* by Ramsay MacMullen. *Phoenix* 45, no. 1 (1991).

Thielman, Frank S. "Another Look at the Eschatology of Eusebius of Caesarea." *Vigiliae Christianae* 41, no. 3 (1987).

Thompson, E. A. "Christianity and the Northern Barbarians." In *The Conflict Between Paganism and Christianity in the Fourth Century*, ed. Arnaldo Momigliano. Oxford: Clarendon, 1963.

Tomlin, Roger. "Christianity and the Late Roman Army." In *Constantine: History, Historigraophy and Legend*, ed. Samuel Lieu and Dominic Montserrat. London: Routledge, 1998.

Treggiari, Susan. "Divorce Roman Style: How Easy and How Frequent Was It?" In *Marriage, Divorce and Children in* Ancient Rome, ed. Beryl Rawson. Oxford: Oxford University Press, 1996.

Trocmé, Andrew. *Jesus and the Nonviolent Revolution*. Maryknoll, N.Y.: Orbis, 2003.

Troeltsch, Ernst. *The Social Teaching of the Christian Churches*. Trans. Olive Wyon. 2 vols. New York: Harper Torchbooks, 1960.

True, David. "Embracing Hauerwas? A Niebuhrian Takes a Closer Look." *Political Theology* 8, no. 2 (2007).

Turchetti, Mario. "Religious Concord and Political Toleration in Sixteenth- and Seventeenth-Century France." *Sixteenth Century Journal* 22, no. 1 (1991).

Ullmann, Walter. "The Constitutional Significance of Constantine the Great's Settlement." *Journal of Ecclesiastical History* 27 (1976).

Van Dam, Raymond. *The Roman Revolution of Constantine*. Cambridge: Cambridge University Press, 2008.

Veyne, Paul. *Bread and Circuses: Historical Sociology and Political Pluralism*. Trans. Brian Pearce. New York: Penguin, 1960.

———. "Clientele et corruption au service de l'État: La venalité des offices dans le Bas-Empire romain." *Annales* 36, no. 3 (1981).

Voltaire. *Philosophical Dictionary, Volume 1*. Translated by John G. Gorton. Available at Google Books.

———. *On Toleration*. Available at <http://classicliberal.tripod.com/voltaire/toleration.html>, accessed June 10, 2009.

Wallace-Hadrill, Andrew. "*Civilis princeps*: Between Citizen and King." *Journal of Roman Studies* 72 (1982).

Wardman, Alan. *Religion and Statecraft Among the Romans*. Baltimore: Johns Hopkins University Press, 1982.

———. "Usurpers and Internal Conflicts in the 4th Century A.D." *Historia* 33, no. 2 (1984).

Watson, Alan. *The Law of the Ancient Romans*. Dallas: Southern Methodist University Press, 1970.

———. *The Spirit of Roman Law*. Athens: University of Georgia Press, 1995.

Weaver, Alain Epp. "After Politics: John Howard Yoder, Body Politics and the Witnessing Church." *Review of Politics* 61, no. 4 (1999).

Weaver, J. Denny. "A Footnote on Jesus." *Crosscurrents*, Winter 2007.

Weiss, Peter. "The Vision of Constantine." Trans. A. R. Birley. *Journal of Roman Archaeology* 16 (2003).

Wiedemann, Thomas. *Emperors and Gladiators*. London: Routledge, 1992.

Wilken, Robert L. *John Chrysostom and the Jews: Rhetoric and Reality in the Late 4th Century*. Eugene, Ore.: Wipf and Stock, 1983.

———. *The Land Called Holy: Palestine in Christian History and Thought*. New Haven, Conn.: Yale University Press, 1992.

———. *The Myth of Christian Beginnings*. Notre Dame, Ind.: University of Notre Dame Press, 1970.

Williams, Daniel H. "Constantine, Nicaea and the 'Fall' of the Church." In *Christian Origins: Theology, Rhetoric and Community*, ed. Lewis Ayres and S. Gareth Jones. London: Routledge, 1998.

Williams, George Huntston. "Christology and Church-State Relations in the Fourth Century," pts. 1-2. *Church History* 20, nos. 3-4 (1951).

Williams, Rowan. *Arius: Heresy and Tradition*. Rev. ed. Grand Rapids: Eerdmans, 2001.

Willis, Geoffrey Grimshaw. *Saint Augustine and the Donatist Controversy*. 1950. Reprint, Eugene, Ore.: Wipf and Stock, 2005.

Wilson, Anna. "Biographical Models: The Constantinian Period and Beyond." In *Constantine: History, Historiography and Legend*, ed. Samuel Lieu and Dominic Montserrat. London: Routledge, 1998.

Wirszubski, Chaim. *"Libertas" as a Political Idea at Rome During the Late Republic and Early Principate*. Cambridge: Cambridge University Press, 1950.

Wolterstorff, Nicholas. "Fallen Powers." Lecture presented at Consultation on Good Power: Divine and Human, Yale Center on Faith and Culture, October 5-6, 2007.

Woods, David. "On the Death of the Empress Fausta." *Greece and Rome*, 2nd ser. 45, no. 1 (1998).

Wright, David H. "The True Face of Constantine the Great." *Dumbarton Oaks Papers* 41 (1987).

Wright, Nigel Goring. *Disavowing Constantine: Mission, Church and the Social Order in the Theologies of John Howard Yoder and Jürgen Moltmann.* Paternoster Theological Monographs. 2000. Reprint, Eugene, Ore.: Wipf and Stock, 2006.

Yoder, John Howard. *Body Politics: Five Practices of the Christian Community Before the Watching World.* Scottsdale, Penn.: Herald, 2001.

————. *Christian Attitudes to War, Peace and Revolution.* Ed. Theodore J. Koontz and Andy Alexis-Baker. Grand Rapids, Mich.: Brazos, 2009.

————. *For the Nations: Essays Public and Evangelical.* Grand Rapids: Eerdmans, 1997.

————. *The Jewish-Christian Schism Revisited.* Ed. Michael G. Cartwright and Peter Ochs. Grand Rapids: Eerdmans, 2003.

————. *Nevertheless: Varieties of Religious Pacifism.* Scottdale, Penn.: Herald, 1992.

————. "On Not Being Ashamed of the Gospel: Particularity, Pluralism and Validation." *Faith and Philosophy* 9, no. 3 (1992).

————. *The Original Revolution: Essays on Christian Pacifism.* 1971. Reprint, Scottdale, Penn.: Herald, 2003.

————. *The Politics of Jesus.* Grand Rapids: Eerdmans, 1972.

————. *Preface to Theology: Christology and Theological Method.* Grand Rapids: Brazos, 2002.

————. *The Priestly Kingdom: Social Ethics as Gospel.* Notre Dame, Ind.: University of Notre Dame Press, 1984.

————. *The Royal Priesthood: Essays Ecclesiological and Ecumenical.* Ed. Michael G. Cartwright. Grand Rapids: Eerdmans, 1994.

————. *The War of the Lamb: The Ethics of Nonviolence and Peacemaking.* Ed. Glen Stassen et al. Grand Rapids: Brazos, 2009.

————. *When War Is Unjust: Being Honest in Just-War Thinking.* 1996. Reprint, Eugene, Ore.: Wipf and Stock, 2001.

Zanker, Paul. *The Power of Images in the Age of Augustus*. Trans. Alan Sha-
    piro. Ann Arbor: University of Michigan Press, 1990.
Zerubavel, Eviatar. *The Seven Day Circle: The History and Meaning of the
    Week*. New York: Free Press, 1985.

Author Index

Subject Index